Diuersi instrumenti

pignatta   butiglia   mortaro   crinello

pignatta grande   Cucumo   schiumarelo da cucina   gratta cassio

bolsoneto per far oua   cuchiari da menestrar

cazzolo conil manico sburiato   cazzolo cò il manico sburiato   foratoro colmanico

lecarda   ghiottela   piastrella

[Tavola X]

THE CLASSIC ITALIAN COOKBOOK

THE CLASSIC ITALIAN COOKBOOK

The Art of Italian Cooking

and the Italian Art of Eating

*

Marcella Hazan

DRAWINGS BY

George Koizumi

Adapted by Anna Del Conte

M

ISBN 0 333 27259 5

*This revised and metricated edition
first published 1980 by*
MACMILLAN LONDON LIMITED
*4 Little Essex Street London WC2R 3LF
and Basingstoke
Associated Companies in Delhi, Dublin,
Hong Kong, Johannesburg, Lagos, Melbourne,
New York, Singapore and Tokyo*

The Classic Italian Cookbook was first published in 1973 by
Harper's Magazine Press, New York, and reissued by Alfred
A. Knopf, Inc., New York, and by W. H. Allen Ltd, London,
in 1976. The present edition has been completely revised and
metricated for European readers.

Printed in Great Britain by
BUTLER AND TANNER LIMITED
Frome and London

To Victor, my husband,
con tutto il mio amore e profonda tenerezza.
Without his confidence I would not have started this work,
without his support I would soon have abandoned it,
without his hand next to mine
I could not have given it its final form and expression.
His name really belongs on the title page.

Contents

Illustrations

The endpaper illustrations are taken from a treatise on cooking by Bartolomeo Scappi, chef to Pope Pius V, *Opere di Messire Bartolomeo Scappi, Cuoco Secreto di Papa Pio Quinto, divisa in sei libri*, first edition 1570.

Acknowledgements

It is impossible for cooks ever to give a full account of their debts. Our skills, our tastes, our discoveries, all rest upon the compressed layers of experience of family, friends, chance acquaintances, other cooks, and the long ranks of the generations that have preceded us.

I regret that time and an ungrateful memory have blurred the identity of some of my benefactors. Among them are a deft and patient woman in the vegetable market at the foot of the Quirinale hill, turning from her work to give me the best artichoke-trimming demonstration I have ever seen, and a perfect recipe for making artichokes *alla romana*. The fishermen of my home town of Cesenatico, making their dinner on the cobblestone quay after unloading and selling their catch, grilling their fish to absolute perfection. The maids of my youth, working in my father's and my uncle's houses, from whose superb, natural skills I was learning how to cook, unawares, as I discovered many years later.

Fortunately, not all my creditors need to remain anonymous. First, and most important among them, are my family. My father's mother, Nonna Polini, whose hand-made pasta remains the paragon to which I must compare every other. My father, Fin, who was skilled and true in everything he put his hand to. My mother, Maria Leonelli, who is still the best cook in the family, my aunt Licia Conconi, who taught me how to make *polenta*, and my cousin Armando Sabbadini. I am grateful too to my mother-in-law, Julia Hazan, through whom I discovered a remarkable new world of cooking.

I should also like to express my debt to Ada Boni, whose *Talismano della Felicità* was indeed a happy talisman in the early period of my marriage, when I first faced alone the mysteries of the kitchen and the expectations of a food-loving husband.

I am further indebted for recipes and assistance to 'Zia' Ines Anzuoni; Maria Bartoli; Evio Battellani, creator of the Scrigno di Venere and master of Al Cantunzein, Bologna's temple of pasta; Stella Donati, of Star food products; Claudia Fioravanti; Marchese Giuseppe Gavotti, chancellor of the Accademia Italiana della Cucina, sage and witty gentleman of Italian gastronomy; Lorenza Magnani; Roberto Moglia; Pietro Molesini, owner-chef of Al Caminetto, Padriciano (Trieste); Silvano Renna of L'Osteriaccia at Cusercoli; Bruna Saglio; Valeria and Margherita Simili of Bologna's great bakery; and Bruno Tasselli, of the Pappagallo, Bologna.

To Lucia Parini, for her irreplaceable and skilful assistance, I owe special thanks.

I am also particularly grateful to Grace Chu, from whom I learned about teaching cooking; to my students, whose experiences have contributed so much to this book; and to Craig Claiborne, whose warm interest has been chiefly responsible for my cooking having come to public notice.

As for the making of the book, my gratitude for ever goes to my editor and publisher, Peter Mollman, for his generous and never-flagging support, to Jane Mollman for her saintly patience and her sensitive, informed reading of the manuscript, and to George Koizumi, for the liveliest and clearest illustrations with which a cookbook author has ever had her recipes illuminated.

*   *   *

This book was originally written for American readers, and used American measurements and terminology. The original ingredients were in some cases unobtainable in the United States because pork products may not be imported and so locally available imitations or substitutes were suggested instead. For this new edition, the recipes have been converted back to metric measurements and their imperial equivalents and the terminology to that familiar to British and Commonwealth readers. I am most grateful to Anna del Conte who has painstakingly undertaken this task.

The coming of the E.E.C., the spread of foreign communities in our large towns and an upsurge in interest in, and enthusiasm for, food has meant that far more of the ingredients necessary for Italian cooking are readily available. For the best quality, though, you must still go to Italy, or at least insist on ingredients – for instance tinned tomatoes and pork products – imported from Italy.

Preface

Nothing significant exists under Italy's sun that is not touched by art. Its food is twice blessed because it is the product of two arts, the art of cooking and the art of eating. While each nourishes the other, they are in no way identical accomplishments. The art of cooking produces the dishes, but it is the art of eating that transforms them into a meal.

Through the art of eating, an Italian meal becomes a precisely orchestrated event, where the products of the season, the traditions of place, the intuitions of the cook, and the knowledgeable joy of the participants are combined into one of the most satisfying experiences of which our senses are capable.

I hope that these pages will reward those looking for new dishes with which to please themselves and their friends. But I have tried to put something more here. In my classes I attempt to demonstrate not only how to make dishes but how to make meals. I hope that this book can be used to that same end, and that it will help its readers discover some of the happiness and beauty of the total Italian food experience.

M. H.

New York City
December, 1972

Bologna
June, 1979

INTRODUCTION

Italian Cooking:
Where does it come from?

THE first useful thing to know about Italian cooking is that, as such, it actually does not exist. 'Italian cooking' is an expression of convenience rarely used by Italians. The cooking of Italy is really the cooking of its regions, regions that until 1861 were separate, independent and usually hostile states. They submitted to different rulers, they were protected by sovereign armies and navies, and they developed their own cultural traditions and, of course, their own special and distinct approaches to food.

The unique features of each region and of the individual towns and cities within it can still easily be observed when one travels through Italy today. These are living differences that appear in the physical cast of the people, in their temperament, in their spoken language, and, most clearly, in their cooking.

The cooking of Venice, for example, is so distant from that of Naples, although they are both Italian cities specialising in seafood, that not a single authentic dish from the one is to be found on the other's table. There are unbridgeable differences between Bologna and Florence, each the capital of its own region, yet only sixty miles apart. There are also subtle but substantial distinctions to be made between the cooking of Bologna and of other cities in its region, such as Cesena, fifty-two miles away, Parma, fifty-six miles, or Modena, just twenty-three miles to the north.

It is not only from the inconstant contours of political geography that cooking in Italy has taken its many forms. Even more significant has been the forceful shaping it has received from the two dominant elements of the Italian landscape – the mountains and the sea.

Italy is a peninsula shaped like a full-length boot that has stepped into the Mediterranean and Adriatic seas up to its thigh. There it is fastened to the rest of Europe by the uninterrupted chain of the Alps. At the base of the Alps spreads Italy's only extensive plain, which reaches from Venice on the Adriatic coast westward through Lombardy and into Piedmont. This is the dairy zone of Italy, and the best-irrigated land. The cooking fat is butter, almost exclusively, and rice or maize or sweet-corn (polenta) are the staples. In Turin and Milan, factory-made pasta was virtually unknown until thousands of workers from the south came north to find jobs.

The northern plain gives out just before touching the Mediterranean shore, where it reaches the foothills of the other great mountain chain of Italy, the Apennines. This chain extends from north to south for the whole length of the country like the massive, protruding spine of some immense beast. It is composed of gentle, softly rounded hills sloping toward the seas on the eastern and western flanks and, in the central crest, of tall, forbidding stone peaks. Huddled within the links of this chain are countless valleys, isolated from each other until modern times like so many Shangri-Las, giving birth to men, cultures and cooking styles profoundly different in character.

To a certain extent, the Apennine range helps determine that variety of climates which has also favoured diversity in cooking. Turin, the capital of Piedmont, standing in the open plain at the foot of the Alps, has winters more severe than Copenhagen. The Ligurian coast, just a few miles to the west, nestles against the Apennines, which intercept the cold Alpine winds and allow the soft Mediterranean breezes to create that mild, pleasant climate which has made the Riviera famous. Here flowers abound, the olive begins to flourish, and the fragrance of fresh herbs invades nearly every dish.

On the eastern side of the same Apennines that hug the Riviera coast lies the richest gastronomic region in Italy, Emilia-Romagna. Its capital, Bologna, is probably the only city in all Italy whose name is instantly associated in the Italian mind not with monuments, not with artists, not with heroes, but with food.

Emilia-Romagna is almost evenly divided between mountainous land and flat, with the Apennines at its back and at its feet the last remaining corner of the northern plain rolling out to the Adriatic. This Emilian plain is extraordinarily fertile land enriched by the alluvial deposits of the countless Apennine torrents that have run through it toward the sea. It leads all Italy in the production of wheat, which perhaps explains why here it is almost heresy to sit down to a meal that does not include a dish of home-made pasta. The vegetables of Emilia-Romagna may well be the tastiest in the world, surpassing even the quality of French produce. The fruit from its perfumed orchards is so remarkable in flavour that local consumers must compete with foreign markets for it. Italy's best hams and sausages are made here and also some of its richest dairy products, among which is the greatest Italian cheese, Parmesan.

In Emilia-Romagna the sea has been as bountiful as the land. The Adriatic, perhaps because it contains less salt than the Mediterranean, perhaps because it is constantly purified by fresh waters from Alpine streams, produces fish famous in all Italy for its fine delicate flesh. When a restaurant in any part of Italy offers fish from the Adriatic it makes sure its patrons know it. Since the quality of the fish is so fine it requires little enhancement in the kitchen, and Adriatic fish cookery has become the essence of masterful simplicity. Nowhere else, except perhaps in Japan, is fish fried or grilled so simply and well.

In crossing Emilia-Romagna's southern border into Tuscany every aspect of cooking seems to have turned over and, like an embossed coin, landed on its reverse side. Tuscany's whole approach to the preparation of food is in such sharp contrast to that of Bologna that their differences seem to sum up two main and contrary manifestations of Italian character.

Out of the abundance of the Bolognese kitchen comes cooking that is exuberant, prodigal with precious ingredients, and wholly baroque in its restless exploration of every agreeable combination of texture and flavour. The Florentine, careful and calculating, is a man who knows the measure of all things, and his cooking is an austerely composed play upon essential and unadorned themes.

Bologna will sauté veal in butter, stuff it with the finest mountain ham, coat it with aged Parmesan, simmer it in sauce, and smother it with the costliest truffles. Florence takes a T-bone steak of noble size and grills it quickly over a blazing fire, adding nothing but the aroma of freshly ground pepper and olive oil. Both are triumphs.

From Tuscany down, the Apennines and their foothills in their southward march spread nearly from coast to coast so that the rest of Italy is almost entirely mountainous. As a result, two major changes take place in cooking. First, as it is cheaper and simpler on a hillside to cultivate a grove of olive trees than to raise a herd of dairy cows, olive oil supplants butter as the dominant cooking fat. Second, as we get farther away from the rich wheat fields of Emilia-Romagna, soft, home-made egg and flour pasta gives way to the more economical, mass-produced, eggless hard pasta, the staple of the south.

From Naples southwards the climate becomes considerably warmer. A harsher sun bakes the land, inflames the temper of the inhabitants, and ignites their sauces. At the toe-tip of the peninsula and in the heart of Sicily there is little rainfall, and most of that only in the winter months. The lands are parched by harsh, burning winds and the temperatures are sometimes higher than in southern Florida and Texas. The food is as extreme as the climate. The colours of the vegetables are intense and violent, the pastas are so pungent that they often need no topping of cheese, and the desserts are of the most overpowering richness.

There is no need here and certainly there is no room to examine in greater detail all the richly varied forms that history and geography have pressed upon the cooking of Italy. What is important is to be aware that these differences exist and that behind the screen of the too-familiar term 'Italian cooking' lies concealed, waiting to be discovered, a multitude of riches.

The Italian Art of Eating

Not everyone in Italy may know how to cook, but nearly everyone knows how to eat. Eating in Italy is one more manifestation of the Italian's age-old gift of making art out of life.

The Italian art of eating is sustained by a life measured in nature's rhythms, a life that falls in with the slow turning of the seasons, a life in which, until very recently, produce and fish reached the table not many hours after having been taken from the soil or the sea.

It is an art that has also been abetted by the custom of shutting down the whole country at midday for two hours or more. Fathers come home from work and children from school, and there is sufficient time for the whole family to celebrate, not just the most important meal, but more likely also the most important event of the day.

There probably has been no influence, not even religion, so effective in creating a rich family life, in maintaining a civilised link between the generations, as this daily sharing of a common joy. Eating in Italy is essentially a family art, practised for and by the family. The finest accomplishments of the home cook are not reserved like the good silver and china for special occasions or for impressing guests, but are offered daily for the pleasure and happiness of the family group.

The best cooking in Italy is not, as in France, to be found in restaurants, but in the home. One of the reasons that Italian restaurants outside Italy are often so poor is that they do not have Italian home cooking with which to compete. The finest restaurants in Italy are not those glittering establishments known to every traveller, but the very small, family-run *trattorie* of ten or twelve tables that offer home cooking only slightly revised by commercial adaptations. Here the menus are unnecessary, sometimes non-existent, and almost always illegible. Patrons know exactly what they want, and in ordering a meal they are evoking patterns established countless times at home.

Italian food may be a midnight spaghetti snack after the theatre, a pizza and a glass of wine, a cool salad on a sultry summer noon. But an Italian *meal* is something else entirely; it is a many-layered experience far richer and more complete than this.

Out of the potentially infinite combinations of first and second courses, of vegetable dishes, of sauces and seasonings, an Italian meal, whether it is set out at home for the entire family or consumed in solitary communion in a restaurant, emerges as a complex composition free of discordant notes. Its elements may vary according to the season and the unique desires of the moment, but their relationships are governed by a harmonious and nearly invariable arrangement.

There is no main course to an Italian meal. With some very rare exceptions, such as *ossobuco* with *risotto*, the concept of a single dominant course is entirely foreign to the Italian way of eating. There are, at a minimum, two principal courses, which are never, never brought to the table at the same time.

The first course may be pasta either in broth or with sauce, or it can be a risotto or a soup. *Minestra*, which is the Italian for 'soup', is also used to mean the first course whether it is a soup or not. This is because, to the Italian mind, the first proper course, even when it has been preceded by antipasti (hors d'œuvres) and even when it is sauced pasta or *risotto*, is still a soup in the sense that it is served in a deep dish and that it always precedes and never accompanies the meat, poultry or fish course.

After there has been sufficient time to relish and consume the first course, to salute its passing with some wine, and to regroup the taste buds for the next encounter, the second course comes to the table. The choice of the second course is usually a development of the theme established by the first. The reverse may also be true, when the first course is chosen in anticipation of what the second will be. If the second course is going to be beef braised in wine, you will not preface it with spaghetti in clam sauce or with a dish of *lasagne* heavily laced with meat. You might prefer a *risotto* with asparagus, with zucchini (courgettes), or with plain Parmesan cheese. Or a dish of green *gnocchi*. Or a light potato soup. If you are going to start with *tagliatelle alla bolognese* (home-made noodles with meat sauce), you might want to give your palate some relief by following with a simple roast of veal or chicken. On the other hand, you would not choose a second course so bland, such as steamed fish, that it could not stand up to the impact of the first.

The second course is often attended by one or two vegetable dishes, which may sometimes develop into a full course of their own. The special pleasures of the Italian table are never keener or more apparent than in this moment when the vegetables appear. In Italian menus the word for a vegetable dish is *contorno*, which can be translated literally as 'contour'. This reveals exactly what role vegetables play, because it is the choice of vegetables that defines the meal, that gives it shape, that encircles it with the flavours, textures and colours of the season.

The sober winter taste, the austere whites and grey-greens of artichokes, cardoons, celery, cauliflower; the sweetness and the tender hues of spring in the first asparagus, the earliest peas, baby carrots, young broad beans; the voluptuous gifts of summer: the luscious aubergine, the glossy green pepper, the sun-reddened tomato, the succulent zucchini; the sharp and scented taste of autumn in leeks, fennel, fresh spinach, red cabbage; these do more than quiet our hunger. Through their presence the act of eating becomes a way of sharing our life with nature. And this is precisely what is at the heart of the Italian art of eating.

An Italian meal is a story told from nature, taking its rhythms, its humours, its bounty and turning them into episodes for the senses. As nature is not a one-act play, so an Italian meal cannot rest on a single dish. It is instead a lively sequence of events, alternating the crisp with the soft and yielding, the pungent with the bland, the variable with the staple, the elaborate with the simple.

It takes a theme such as 'fish', states it very gently in a simple antipasto of tender, boiled young squid delicately seasoned with olive oil, parsley and lemon, contrasts it with a rich and creamy shrimp risotto, and restates it with a superbly grilled bass that sums up every pure and natural quality with which fish has been endowed. All this subsides in a sharp salad of seasonal greens and closes on the sweet, liquid note of fresh sliced fruit in wine.

This book has been organised in the same sequence as an Italian meal: first courses first, second courses second, vegetable dishes. Antipasti lead the procession, salads and dessert close it. Recipes for one course carry suggestions on how to choose a course to follow or precede it. The most suitable vegetable accompaniment is suggested with the second course. Through this constant reminder of those patterns which form the Italian way of eating, I hope the reader will discover that there is something more significant to an Italian meal than a single overpowering dish oozing sauce and melted cheese.

In the relationships of its varied parts an Italian meal develops something very close to the essence of civilised life itself. No dish overwhelms another, either in quantity or flavour, each leaves room for new appeals to the eye and palate, each fresh sensation of taste, colour, and texture interlaces a lingering recollection of the last.

Of course, no one expects that the Italian way of eating can be wholly absorbed into everyday life elsewhere. Even in Italy it is succumbing to the onrushing uniformity of an industrial society. In Blake's phrase, man's brain is making the world unlivable for man's spirit. Yet it is possible even from the tumultuous centre of the busiest city life to summon up the life-enhancing magic of the Italian art of eating. What it requires is generosity. You must give liberally of time, of patience, of the best raw materials. What it returns is worth all you have to give.

INGREDIENTS

The character of a cuisine is determined more by basic approach than by ingredients. Ingredients come and go, depending on popular taste and the changing patterns of commerce. It is a picture that emerges more clearly as one steps away from it. It is hard to imagine Italian cooking, and that of Naples in particular, without tomatoes. And Venetians would die of shock if they were deprived of *polenta*. But tomatoes and maize are both fairly recent newcomers to the two venerable cuisines. In the recipes in this book I have introduced shallots, which, although they are an ancient Mediterranean commodity, are not generally available in Italy. Yet they adapt themselves with perfect grace to Italian cooking, and in many instances are preferable to onions.

This is not said to encourage indifference to a precise choice of ingredients but rather to discourage an exaggerated dependence on them. A heavy hand with the garlic or the tomato sauce does not make Italian cooking. There is no question that there are certain components without which it would be impossible to reproduce the taste of Italian cooking as we know it today. Fortunately, these are all available outside Italy in some form. In the following list, some of the most important ones are briefly considered.

Alloro
BAYLEAVES

Bayleaves go very nicely with roasts of meat and chicken. Adding them to the fire when grilling fish over charcoal is also a nice touch. Buy them whole from Greek or Italian grocers and store them in a tightly closed glass jar in a cool cupboard. And, if you have a garden or patio, the bay (*Laurus nobilis*) is both a handsome and, in most places, easy-to-grow plant.

Brodo
BROTH

Broth is almost as necessary to Italian cooking as stock is to French cooking, although Italian broth is much thinner and less concentrated in flavour than stock. All you need for broth is a few vegetables, some beef, veal, and chicken bones, and, ideally, some good scraps of meat and chicken. If you are making *ossobuco* (page 216) ask the butcher to saw the bony ends off the shins, and save them for a broth. Do the same when boning a breast of chicken. If you are not ready to cook these scraps immediately, store them in the freezer and make your broth when you have a nice assortment of bones and meat trimmings. A broth keeps indefinitely in the refrigerator if you boil it for

15 minutes every 3 or 4 days. Or you may freeze it for longer periods. You should always have some on hand. Stock cubes can be used as a short cut, and when only small quantities are required for a recipe, but *never* when broth is an important ingredient in its own right.

HOME-MADE MEAT BROTH

Makes about 1½ litres (2½ pints) of
*   broth*

Salt
1 carrot, peeled
1 small onion, peeled
1 stick celery
¼ sweet green pepper

1 tinned or 1 very ripe fresh Italian
        tomato
1 small potato, peeled
1 kg (2lb) assorted bones and meat
        scraps

Put all the ingredients in a stockpot or tall saucepan and cover with cold water by 50 mm (2 inches). Set the cover askew and bring to the boil. When boiling, regulate the heat so that the liquid cooks at the barest simmer. From time to time, but especially during the first few minutes, skim off the scum that rises to the surface. Cook for 2 to 3 hours, without ever letting the liquid come to a steady boil. Strain the broth into an ovenproof glass or porcelain container and allow to cool uncovered. When cool, store, uncovered, in the refrigerator. When the fat on the surface has hardened, remove it.

If you have not used it up after 4 days, bring the broth to the boil for 10 minutes, allow it to cool, and refrigerate again. If in the meantime you have accumulated other good scraps of meat and bones, add them to the broth, add more vegetables (all but the tomato), add enough water to cover by about 50 mm (2 inches), and repeat the whole cooking process. In this manner you will never be without good home-made broth. It also freezes well. Prepare the broth up to the point where you have removed the fat. Pour the clear broth into ice-cube trays, freeze, then divide up the cubes into small plastic bags. Seal the bags tightly, and return to the freezer compartment until needed.

Note   Do not use lamb or pork bones unless you need a particularly strong-tasting broth.

Luganega Sausage

Luganega sausage comes in long continuous coils and is obtainable from Italian delicatessens. A high-meat-content mild sausage can be substituted for it.

Mortadella

Mortadella is Bologna's most famous pork product, and many Italians consider it the finest sausage in Italy. A well-made *mortadella* is very smooth in texture and possesses a subtle and delicate tastiness. It consists of various cuts of pork finely ground, boiled and larded. It is delicious in a sandwich, excellent in a plate of mixed cold meats and necessary to the cooking of many Bolognese dishes. *Mortadella* is the largest of sausages, in Bologna often reaching a girth of 450 mm (18 inches) or more. 'Export' or non-Italian varieties are less than half that size. Unfortunately, non-Italian mortadella is, at best, an only partially satisfactory imitation of the original product.

Funghi secchi
DRIED WILD MUSHROOMS

In the autumn and spring one of the most thrilling sights in Italian markets is that of mountains of orange, cream-coloured, and nut-brown wild mushrooms fresh from the woods. Ah, the haunting aroma of giant mushroom caps, sautéed with oil, garlic and parsley! The same varieties grow elsewhere in Europe, but are nowhere as revered as in Italy. The most favoured kind – *porcini* (*Boletus edulis*) – can even be found in Central London, but, like all wild food, should be treated with extreme caution. Buy a good book or consult an expert. And when in any doubt, *don't* take risks.

While we may not be able to obtain fresh wild mushrooms, their woody fragrance has been captured in dried porcini. Drying deprives the mushroom of its succulence but compensates for this by concentrating its flavour. Dried mushrooms can no longer be used as a vegetable, but they are a marvellous seasoning for sauces, *risotto*, meat and chicken. They are available in Italian groceries, and sometimes at supermarkets. When buying them, look for large, creamy-brown sections. Avoid the dark brown, crumbly kind. Choice funghi are expensive, but a little goes a long way. If stored in a tightly closed metal box, they will keep indefinitely.

The water in which dried mushrooms are reconstituted is full of flavour and should never be discarded, though it should be filtered to remove grit. Wherever dried mushrooms are called for, the recipe will indicate how the water is to be used.

Olio d'oliva
OLIVE OIL

In the centre and south of Italy, in the islands, and along both coasts, olive oil is the fundamental cooking fat. Unlike peanut (arachide) oil or other vegetable oils, olive oil has a decided taste, which should not be used indiscriminately. The recipes in this book reflect the current trend in Italian cooking by using olive oil only where its presence is essential. In those circumstances where its flavour would be obtrusive and unnecessary to the harmony of a dish it has been supplanted by vegetable oil, of which the best varieties are arachide and sunflower-seed. However, where raw oil is required, as in salads, the use of anything but olive oil is inconceivable.

Most olive oil packed for export has been so highly refined that it has only the faintest suggestion of olives. This is true of nearly all the widely distributed brands. A recipe calling for olive oil will not be entirely successful with such thin, impalpable oil. Good olive oil should have both the colour and taste of the green olive, and that is what you should look for.

After you open a tin, decant the oil into a large glass bottle or ceramic jug and leave it uncorked. It will keep indefinitely.

Pancetta

Pancetta is exactly the same cut of pork as bacon, except that it is not smoked. Instead, it is cured in salt and spices. It comes tightly rolled up in a salami shape, and it is sliced to order. The convenient way to buy it is to get 100 to 200 g ($\frac{1}{4}$ to $\frac{1}{2}$ pound) in thin slices and an equal amount in a single slice. For some recipes you will use the slices just as they are, while for others you will cut the larger piece into cubes or strips. *Pancetta* keeps for up to three weeks in the refrigerator, if carefully sealed in plastic film.

When it is of good quality, *pancetta* can be eaten as it is, like prosciutto (Parma ham) or any other cold meat. In Italian cooking it is used as a flavouring agent in sauces, pasta fillings, vegetables and roasts. When used next to veal it bastes it as it cooks, and keeps it from drying.

There are no exact substitutes for *pancetta*, but if it is not obtainable you can replace it with dry-cured salt pork or green bacon or, at a pinch, with prosciutto or unsmoked ham. As far as I know, *pancetta* is available only in Italian delicatessens.

Parmigiano-Reggiano
PARMESAN CHEESE

This precious cheese, which is an inseparable part of much Italian cooking, is produced by just five small provinces in the old Duchy of Parma, now absorbed into Emilia. It is made only during the mild months of the year, from spring to autumn, when the cows can amble out and feed upon the richest pasture in Italy. It is aged for at least two years, but good food shops in Italy carry Parmesan that is three or four years old, and even older.

Parmesan is straw yellow in colour and has a mellow, rounded, slightly salty taste. It is the finest cheese for cooking because it melts without running and without disintegrating into a rubbery tangle. It has no peer, of course, for grating over pasta, and when it is freshly cut it deserves to be eaten as it is, accompanied by the best red wine you can afford.

When buying Parmesan cheese, ask to look at it and taste it before it is cut for you. If it is whitish and dry, and leaves a bitter aftertaste, do not buy it or, if you must, buy as little as you can get away with. If it is pale yellow, slightly moist on the tongue, and pleasantly salty, invest in a good-sized piece. A 1·5-kg or 3-lb piece of properly wrapped Parmesan will keep for a few weeks in the refrigerator.

How to Store Parmesan

To maintain the freshness of Parmesan cheese you must prevent its moisture from escaping. As soon as you get it home, wrap the cheese in a double or triple thickness of aluminium foil. Make sure the foil is not torn at any point and that it is tightly sealed. Keep it on the bottom shelf of the refrigerator.

Parmesan is usually sold with some of its crust. When cutting off a piece, always cut it with part of the crust attached, because the cheese left next to the crust tends to dry faster. Do not discard the crust. Wrap it and store it like the cheese and save it to use in soups. Do not grate much more cheese than you need. Grated cheese does not keep.

After you have had the cheese a while, you may notice that it has become drier and whiter. If this happens, moisten a piece of muslin and twist it until it is no more than damp. Wrap it around the cheese, then wrap and seal with aluminium foil. Refrigerate overnight. The following day remove the muslin and rewrap with just aluminium foil.

The recipes in this book call for freshly grated Parmesan cheese. Do not under any circumstances use ready-grated cheese sold in jars. Even if this commercially grated cheese were of good quality, which it is not, it would have lost all its flavour long before getting to the market. It is of no interest whatever to Italian cooking.

Prezzemolo
PARSLEY

All Italian, Cypriot and Middle Eastern shops sell Italian or 'Continental' parsley. It has a larger, less curly leaf than ordinary parsley, and a better developed, yet less pungent fragrance. The stem is milder than the leaf, and can sometimes be substituted for the leaves for a more toned-down flavour. For Italian cooking you really should use this kind of parsley, but if it is not available do not let it worry you. The curly variety is quite satisfactory.

Pomodori
TOMATOES

The perfect, round, tasteless tomatoes grown for the British market are a grave disappointment in Italian cooking. Home-grown tomatoes are best, or for salads search out the large, irregular ones in ethnic shops. *Marmande* is the best variety to buy or grow. For sauces, use plum tomatoes or tinned Italian tomatoes (see page 79).

Pepe
PEPPER

Ready-ground pepper is one of those modern conveniences that keep giving progress a bad name. Why it exists I do not know. It is certainly no more work to twist a pepper mill than to brandish a shaker, but there is an enormous difference in the result. The aroma of pepper is short-lived. All that you get with ready-ground pepper is some of its pungency.

Black pepper is the whole fruit of the pepper plant. White pepper is simply black pepper stripped of its shell. White pepper is stronger, but black pepper is used more frequently in Italian cooking because it is more aromatic. Unless you are addicted to pepper, do not buy a large amount at one time. Its flavour is perishable.

Riso
RICE

Italian rice is thicker and shorter than American or long-grain rice. It takes a little longer to cook, but it has more 'tooth' and body. It is ideal for *risotto* because the grains adhere creamily to each other without surrendering their individual firmness. It is also excellent for all Italian soups.

'Arborio' is the generic name of the most commonly exported variety of Italian rice. It is available under more than one brand name and can be obtained not only from Italian groceries but also from the food halls of major department stores and from large urban supermarkets.

Ricotta

Ricotta is a soft, bland, white milk product made from whey, that watery part of the milk which separates from the curd when this is made into cheese. Much use of it is made in Emilia, where it is put into delicate fillings for pasta. Also famous are the ricotta cheese-cakes of the south. Fresh, true ricotta can be obtained at a few Italian delicatessens. It is extremely perishable, and even under refrigeration it should be used within 24 to 48 hours. A passable substitute is the more long-lived whole-milk ricotta available at some supermarkets.

Perhaps because they are so similar in appearance, some authors suggest that ricotta and cottage cheese are interchangeable. This is a most grievous error. Cottage cheese is completely un-Italian in taste, and should not be contemplated as a replacement for ricotta. If you cannot obtain ricotta locally, you can make your own in the following manner:

Boil 1 litre (1¾ pints) of milk (which may be pasteurised but should not be either skimmed or long-life) in a pan over low heat with one teaspoon of salt and four teaspoons of lemon juice. Bring to the boil and simmer gently for 15 minutes, then place the resulting curds in a muslin or cheesecloth bag and hang up to drain for two or three hours.

Pecorino romano
ROMANO CHEESE

Romano is Italy's oldest cheese, whose beginnings probably coincide with those of Rome. It is a hard grating cheese made from sheep's milk, hence also called *pecorino*, by which name it is more usually known in Italy and in Britain. It is very much sharper than Parmesan and, when grated, breaks down into smaller, more powdery granules. It is not to be considered a tastier alternative to Parmesan. The aggressiveness of Romano enhances such spicy dishes as *Bucatini all' Amatriciana* (page 89), but it would be out of character and strike a jarring note in Tuscan soups, delicate Bolognese pastas, or the *risotti* of the north.

Rosmarino
ROSEMARY

This herb is so frequently used to flavour roasted meat or chicken that in Italy the fragrance of rosemary in the house almost invariably means that there is a roast in progress in the kitchen. It is an easy herb to grow in a window box and is as common a wild plant in southern Europe as it is a common garden plant in northern Europe. Lacking a fresh supply, you can use dried whole leaves, but avoid the powder.

Salvia
SAGE

The grey-green furry leaves of the sage plant are an excellent flavouring for meat and chicken and have a particular affinity with veal cooked in white wine. If you can grow your own sage or buy it fresh, it is preferable to the dried variety. But dried whole sage leaves can be quite satisfactory. Buy them in branches from Italian or Greek grocers. They will keep almost indefinitely when stored in a tightly closed glass jar or a plastic bag in a cool cupboard. Do not buy powdered sage – it is perfectly useless.

Semolino
SEMOLINA

Semolino is the coarse-grained particles of durum wheat, the same wheat from which spaghetti and other commercial pasta is made. Imported Italian *semolino* can be ordered from Italian groceries, and if you are fond of *gnocchi* you would be well advised to buy a substantial quantity that you can keep on hand. Italian *semolino* has more body and colour than other varieties and it gives markedly superior results. Do not confuse *semolino* with quick-cooking breakfast farina.

Maggiorana e origano
SWEET MARJORAM AND OREGANO

Marjoram and oregano are closely related plants. Marjoram is considerably milder than oregano, and is used on occasion in northern and central cooking, in soups and braised meats. Oregano is virtually never used outside southern cooking, where it appears frequently in tomato sauces, and sometimes with fish or salads.

Acqua
WATER

Water is the phantom ingredient in much Italian cooking. One of my students once protested, 'When you add water, you add nothing!' But that is precisely why we use it. Italian cooking is the art of giving expression to the undisguised flavours of its ingredients. In many circumstances, an over-indulgence in stock, wine or other flavoured liquids would tinge the complexion of a dish with an artificial glow. That is why some recipes will direct that if the quantity of broth used is not sufficient, you should continue cooking with water, as needed. We sometimes use water for deglazing, because it lasts just long enough to help scrape loose the cooking residue stuck to the pan, and then evaporates without a trace. Whenever broth or wine has a part in developing the flavour of a dish, it is in the recipe. Otherwise use water.

La batteria di cucina
SOME NOTES ON KITCHEN EQUIPMENT

This is not a full-scale discussion of kitchen equipment, a subject that has been handled very competently in many other cookbooks. It is principally a list of those tools that are particularly necessary to Italian cooking and are sometimes missing from otherwise well-furnished kitchens.

I tegami
POTS AND PANS

The traditional pan of Italian peasant kitchens is made of earthenware. It is unsurpassed for cooking beans and all vegetables, to which aluminium sometimes imparts a harsh, metallic taste. Earthenware is excellent also for stews, fricassees and slow-simmered sauces. The drawback to earthenware, apart from its fragility, is that it is porous and absorbs some of the cooking fat. If used frequently, it need not cause any concern. If unused for long intervals, however, the fat may turn rancid and give off a disagreeable odour.

The best all-purpose cooking ware is heavy, enamelled cast-iron. It transmits and retains heat magnificently, is suited to all foods, is both oven-safe and flameproof, and you can usually serve directly from it at the table. It is also very easy to clean. Have several sizes and shapes available. Little pans are perfect for making a small amount of sauce. Oval casseroles with lids are all but indispensable for long, narrow roasts. Low, open baking pans are what you need for gratinéing vegetables. Two rectangular pans, 60 to 80 mm ($2\frac{1}{2}$ to 3 inches) high, in different lengths and widths, can be used for *lasagne*.

Absolutely necessary for Italian cooking is a series of heavy frying pans. You should have at least three – small, medium and large. They should have very solid, thick bottoms, to help prevent scorching. There are some aluminium alloys that give you thickness without excessive weight. It is also useful to have at least one heavy cast-iron frying pan, excellent for all high-temperature frying and for pan grilling steaks.

For cooking pasta, you need a pot that will comfortably contain at least 4 litres (7 pints) of water plus the pasta.

An asparagus cooker makes it considerably simpler to cook asparagus perfectly, and it is useful for other purposes, such as making broth. If you do not have one, you can use a fish kettle, which is indispensable for poaching fish whole. Do not use the fish kettle for high-temperature cooking if it is made of thin-gauge metal.

Per tagliare
CUTTING TOOLS

In addition to the usual assortment of knives (which should include, incidentally, two or three well-sharpened paring knives), you need one with a large, flat, well-balanced blade for cutting pasta (like the one shown in the illustration opposite). A Chinese cleaver is perfect.

A sharp, efficient peeler, because, for Italian dishes, vegetables and fruit frequently require peeling.

A straight pastry wheel for cutting *tortelloni* and other pasta, and a fluted wheel for *pappardelle* noodles.

A *mezzaluna* (half-moon) for effortless chopping of vegetables.

Food Processors

Since I wrote the first edition of this book, a range of powerful top-loading electric food processors has come on the market and after some initial doubts I now use them for many purposes. For instance, I use the processor to knead bread and pizza dough and sweet pastry. It is invaluable for chopping fatty substances such as *pancetta*, lard and prosciutto, which are tricky to do by hand. It makes far better *pesto* than the blender, it handles all the ingredients for pasta stuffings, and it chops up everything you need for a meat sauce. It does a neater job of chopping parsley than a knife. It will shred a head of cabbage in no time. For smaller quantities of vegetables, I prefer slicing or chopping by hand. However, there are two things for which I never use the processor: one is chopping onions – it forces out too much liquid, and instead of sautéeing, the onions steam in their own moisture; the other is kneading dough for pasta. Some things are still done better by hand.

Aggeggi vari
ODDS AND ENDS

A steak beater for flattening *scaloppine* and cutlets.

One or more large hardwood chopping boards.

Several wooden spoons with handles of varying lengths.

A large ladle for soups, and a small one for degreasing sauces.

A long-handled fork for turning frying food without getting too close to the pan.

A slotted spatula and a slotted spoon for retrieving food from cooking fat.

A deep slotted spoon for retrieving *gnocchi* and other pasta. Chinese shops have lovely ones made of bamboo and wire.

*Pasta-cutting tools: knife and fluted pastry
wheel and mezzaluna for all-purpose
chopping.*

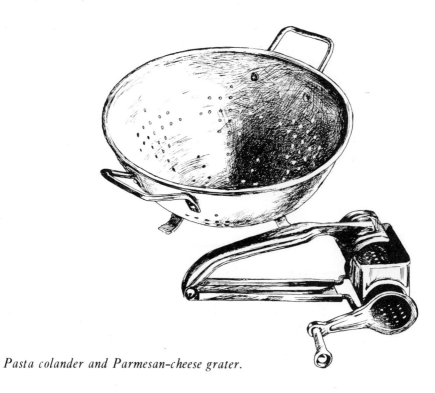

Pasta colander and Parmesan-cheese grater.

A large pasta colander with handles which you can stand in the sink when
  draining pasta.
A three-footed ring which will fit into any pan and convert it into the bottom
  half of a double boiler or a bain-marie.
A food mill – mouli-légumes – with three different discs.
Wire whisks in different sizes.
A rotary grater for Parmesan cheese.
A four-sided grater for vegetables, mozzarella, nutmeg and so on.
An Italian rolling-pin for pasta (see page 95).
A pepper mill.
Italian coffee-pots in two-, four- and six-cup sizes.

Recipes

SAUCES

Le Salse

THIS is the briefest chapter in the book because, except for pasta dishes, sauces are used infrequently in Italian cooking. Most fish, meat and poultry courses stand or fall on their own merits, with no more sauce to enhance their appeal than can be gleaned from loosening the residue or thickening the cooking juices they leave in the pan. Unlike classic French cuisine, Italian cooking has no basic central sauces, branching off and spreading their network throughout the repertoire.

The most important Italian sauces are those used for pasta. In Italian, however, they are not even called *salsa* (the Italian for sauce). The correct term is *sugo*, for which there is no accurate English equivalent. There is an infinite number of them, but for an Italian cook, they do not have an independent existence of their own; they are a natural offshoot of the dish in which they appear. For this reason, and to help steer the reader away from unsuccessful combinations, pasta and its sauces are dealt with together in the chapter on first courses. Here you will find just four recipes: mayonnaise, béchamel, green sauce and red sauce.

There is no need to discuss the uses of mayonnaise, which go well beyond the boundaries of any cuisine. In Italy it is used with many cold dishes, especially cold poached fish. It is indispensable in the preparation of the tuna sauce that is part of one of the most splendid of all cold meat dishes, *vitello tonnato* (page 233).

Béchamel, despite its name, is a thoroughly Italian sauce. It is a key element in many pasta and vegetable dishes. The technique for béchamel given here produces a particularly fine, silken white sauce that you might want to use even for non-Italian recipes.

The green sauce and the red sauce are traditionally served with *bollito misto* (page 273), but they are very nice, too, with simple pan-grilled steaks or veal cutlets. The green sauce is also excellent with fish, such as a fine cold, poached sea bass.

Maionese

MAYONNAISE

I cannot imagine anyone with a serious interest in food using anything but home-made mayonnaise. Once you have had a little practice, it becomes one of the easiest and quickest sauces you can make. You can even prepare it two or three days ahead of time, storing it in the refrigerator in a small bowl tightly sealed with plastic film. Let it return to room temperature before using it. Mayonnaise can make or break any recipe of which it is a part. The commercial variety is so sugary and watery that it is beneath discussion.

You can make mayonnaise with olive oil or vegetable oil. It is lighter and more delicate with vegetable oil, but with fish, olive oil is best. Use a pale yellow-green olive oil, such as the oil from Lucca or the Riviera. The deeper-green variety from the south of Italy or from Spain gives mayonnaise a somewhat bitter taste.

A most important point to remember when making mayonnaise is to have all the ingredients at room temperature. The bowl in which the eggs will be beaten and the blades of the beater should also be warmed up by dipping them in hot water and drying them quickly.

Makes approximately 300 ml ($\frac{1}{2}$ pint)

2 egg yolks
Salt
250 to 300 ml (scant to generous $\frac{1}{2}$
      pint) olive oil **or** vegetable oil
      (see note below)

2 tablespoons lemon juice,
      approximately

1 In a round-bottomed bowl, and, if possible, using an electric beater set at medium speed, beat the egg yolks together with a good pinch of salt until the yolks are very pale yellow and the consistency of thick cream. (Until you acquire more confidence in making mayonnaise, you might want to use the low setting on the beater.)

2 Add oil, drop by drop, while beating constantly. Stop pouring oil every few seconds, while you continue beating, until you see that all the oil you have added has been absorbed by the egg yolks and there is none floating free. Continue dribbling in oil and beating until the sauce has become quite thick. Add a teaspoon or less of lemon juice and continue beating. This will thin out the sauce a little. Add more oil, at a slightly faster pace than before, stopping from time to time while you continue beating to allow the egg yolks to absorb the oil completely. When the sauce becomes too thick add more

lemon juice, until you have added the full 2 tablespoons. When you have finished adding all the oil, the mayonnaise is done.

3 Taste for salt, which it will certainly need, and lemon. If the sauce is to be used for fish you will want it a bit on the sharp side. Mix in any addition of salt or lemon with the beater.

REMEMBER:
— all ingredients must be at room temperature.
— the egg yolks must be beaten until they are pale yellow and creamy before adding oil.
— the oil must be added drop by drop until the sauce thickens.
And finally, *note*: Do not exceed 150 ml ($\frac{1}{4}$ pint) of oil per egg yolk. If you have no experience with making mayonnaise do not use more than *8 tablespoons of oil per egg yolk* the first few times.

Salsa balsamella
BÉCHAMEL SAUCE

Long before the French christened it 'béchamel', a sauce of flour and milk cooked in butter, called *balsamella*, was a part of the cooking of Romagna. It is essential to many of its pastas and vegetables, and such an unquestionably native dish as *lasagne* could not exist without it.

Balsamella is possibly the simplest and most quickly made of sauces. The only problem it poses is the formation of lumps. If you add the milk as directed, a little bit at a time, off the heat, beating the sauce constantly with a wooden spoon, you should have absolutely no difficulty in producing a perfectly smooth *balsamella* every time.

Makes 300 ml ($\frac{1}{2}$ pint) medium-thick
       sauce

450 ml ($\frac{3}{4}$ pint) milk   50 g ($1\frac{3}{4}$ oz) plain flour
60 g (2 oz) butter   Salt

1 In a small pan, heat the milk until it comes to the very edge of the boil.

2 While you are heating the milk, melt the butter over low heat in a heavy enamelled iron saucepan of 1 to 1·5 litre ($1\frac{3}{4}$ to $2\frac{1}{2}$ pint) capacity.

3 When the butter is melted, add all the flour, stirring constantly with a wooden spoon. Let the flour and butter bubble for 2 minutes, without ceasing to stir. Do not let the flour become coloured.

4 Turn off the heat and add the hot milk 2 tablespoons at a time, stirring it constantly into the flour-and-butter mixture. As soon as the first 2 table-spoons have been incorporated into the mixture, add another 2 tablespoons, always stirring with your trusty spoon. When you have added 8 tablespoons of milk to the mixture, you can start adding 4 tablespoons at a time, until you have added it all. (Never add more than 4 tablespoons at one time.)

5 When all the milk has been incorporated, turn on the heat to low, add salt, and stir until the sauce is as dense as double cream. If you need it thicker, cook and stir a little while longer. If you need it thinner, cook a little less.

Note When the sauce cools, it sets, and you will not be able to spread it. Therefore, as it takes so little time to prepare, it is best to make it just before you are ready to use it. If you must make it in advance, reheat it slowly, stirring constantly until it is the right consistency again. Béchamel sauce can also be refrigerated.

Salsa verde

GREEN SAUCE

This is a sharp green sauce that is always served with *bollito misto* (page 273) and often with boiled or steamed fish. If you are making it for meat, use vinegar; if for fish, lemon juice. You may vary the proportions according to taste, increasing the vinegar or lemon if you like it sharper, and adding salt when necessary.

For four servings

$2\frac{1}{2}$ tablespoons finely chopped parsley
2 tablespoons finely chopped capers
6 flat anchovy fillets, mashed in a
    mortar or bowl, **or** 1
    dessertspoon anchovy essence

$\frac{1}{2}$ clove garlic, peeled and very finely
    chopped
$\frac{1}{2}$ teaspoon strong mustard, Dijon or
    German

½ teaspoon red wine vinegar
      (approximately), if the sauce
      will be used for meat **or** 1
      tablespoon strained lemon
      juice (approximately), if the
      sauce is for fish

8 tablespoons olive oil
Salt, if necessary

1 Put the parsley, capers, mashed anchovy fillets, garlic and mustard in a bowl and stir, mixing thoroughly. Add the vinegar or lemon juice and stir again. Add the olive oil, beating it vigorously into the other ingredients.
2 Check salt and piquancy. (Add vinegar or lemon juice if you want it sharper, but add very small amounts at a time.)

Note   This sauce can be refrigerated for up to a week. Stir it well again before serving. It can also be used as dressing for *Uova sode in salsa verde* (page 40), but in that case you must reduce the quantity of the oil.

Salsa rossa

RED SAUCE

This is an alternative to green sauce as an accompaniment to *bollito misto*. It is mellower and is served warm. Also excellent with *Cotolette alla milanese* (page 228) and with grilled steaks, it can be prepared ahead of time and refrigerated for up to two weeks, but it must always be warmed up before serving.

For four servings

5 medium onions, peeled and sliced
      thin
4 tablespoons vegetable oil
2 green peppers

400 g (14 oz) tinned Italian tomatoes,
      with their juice
A pinch of chopped chilli
Salt

1 Cook the sliced onions in a saucepan with the oil over moderate heat until soft but not brown.
2 Remove the inner core and seeds from the green peppers. Peel the

peppers with a potato peeler, and cut into 12-mm ($\frac{1}{2}$-inch) slices. Add to the softened onions in the saucepan and continue cooking over moderate heat.

3 When the onions and peppers have been reduced by half in bulk, add the tomatoes, the Chilli, and salt. Continue cooking over low to moderate heat for 25 to 30 minutes, or until the tomatoes and oil separate. Check seasoning. Warm and stir just before serving.

ANTIPASTI

ANTIPASTI are the rogues of the Italian table. Nothing in all gastronomy plays so boldly upon the eye to excite the palate and set gastric juices in motion. The most appropriate place for antipasti is in a restaurant, where they are usually strategically displayed so that they can cast their spell on every arriving patron.

They are far less frequently a part of the home meal. When served at home, antipasti usually consist of one or more of the wonderful Italian pork products: prosciutto (Parma ham), *mortadella*, *coppa*, mountain salami, dried sausages. Prosciutto is sometimes served with fruit. There can be no finer antipasto than sweet prosciutto with ripe figs or cantaloupe or Ogen melon.

What is an antipasto on one occasion is not necessarily that on another. You will see more antipasti in the index than you will find in this chapter. This is because of the flexibility of many Italian dishes. For example, such an elegant antipasto as *Vitello tonnato* (page 233) can be an excellent second course, and it is among the second courses that you will find it.

Altogether, there are not as many antipasti here as in other books perhaps, or as are offered by some restaurants. There are, however, a few more than are customarily prepared in an Italian home. Too much emphasis on antipasti puts a slightly commercial stress on an Italian meal. Use antipasti liberally for parties and buffets. But in the intimacy of a family meal use them wisely – which is to say, sparingly.

Ostriche alla moda di Taranto

BAKED OYSTERS WITH OIL AND PARSLEY

For six

Coarse salt **or** well-washed pebbles
36 oysters, thoroughly washed and
    scrubbed, shelléd and each
    placed on their concave shell
1½ tablespoons fine, dry plain
    breadcrumbs

Freshly ground pepper, a twist of the
    mill for each oyster
4 tablespoons olive oil
Lemon juice

1 Preheat the oven to 250°C/500°F/Mark 10.

2 Choose enough oven dishes to accommodate the oysters in one layer.
Spread the rock salt or pebbles on the bottom of the dishes. (The salt or
pebbles serve both to keep the oysters from tipping and to retain heat.)

3 Arrange the oysters side by side in one layer in the dishes. Top each
oyster with a sprinkling of breadcrumbs, a grinding of pepper, and a few
drops of olive oil.

4 Place the oysters in the uppermost level of the preheated oven for 3
minutes. Before serving, moisten each oyster with a few drops of lemon juice.

Ostriche alla parmigiana

BAKED OYSTERS WITH PARMESAN CHEESE

For six

Coarse salt **or** well-washed pebbles
36 oysters, thoroughly washed and
    scrubbed, shelled and each
    placed on their concave shell
60 g (2 oz) freshly grated Parmesan
    cheese

1 tablespoon fine, dry plain
    breadcrumbs
Freshly ground pepper, a twist of the
    mill for each oyster
40 g (1½ oz) butter

1 Preheat the oven to 250°C/500°F/Mark 10.

2 Spread the rock salt or pebbles on the bottom of enough oven dishes to accommodate the oysters in one layer. (See explanation in Step 2 of preceding recipe.)

3 Arrange the oysters side by side in the dishes. Top each oyster with ½ teaspoon of grated cheese, a tiny pinch of breadcrumbs, a grinding of pepper, and a dot of butter.

4 Place in the uppermost level of the preheated oven for 5 minutes. Serve piping hot.

Spuma fredda di salmone
COLD SALMON MOUSSE

For six

425 g (15 oz) tinned salmon
4 tablespoons olive oil
2 tablespoons lemon juice
Salt

Freshly ground pepper, about 6 twists of the mill
325 ml (⅝ pint) very cold whipping cream

1 Drain the salmon and pick it over carefully for bones and bits of skin. Using a fork, crumble it in a mixing bowl. Add the oil, lemon juice, a little pinch of salt and the pepper, and beat them into the salmon until you have obtained a smooth, evenly blended mixture.

2 In a cold mixing bowl, whip the cream with a whisk or electric beater until it is stiff. Delicately fold the cream into the salmon mixture until it is completely incorporated. Refrigerate for at least 2 hours, but preferably not more than 24.

Note If you use left-over poached fresh salmon, you will obtain a delicious, milder result. One attractive way of presenting this is to spoon each individual serving onto a lettuce leaf, making a small, rounded mound. Decorate it by placing a black olive (not the sharp Greek variety) on the mound's peak, and standing a tomato slice and a lemon slice at divergent angles on either side of it. You can use this as a spread for canapés with cocktails or serve it as antipasto.

Cozze e vongole passate ai ferri

GRILLED MUSSELS AND CLAMS

For four to six

2 dozen clams, the tiniest you can
    find, cleaned as directed on
    pages 46–7
2 dozen mussels, cleaned as directed
    on page 49
3 tablespoons finely chopped parsley
$\frac{1}{2}$ clove garlic, peeled and finely
    chopped

6 tablespoons olive oil
60 g (2 oz) fine, dry plain
    breadcrumbs
1 tinned Italian tomato, drained and
    cut into 2 dozen small strips
Lemon wedges

1 Put the clams and mussels in separate covered pots over high heat until they open their shells. Bear in mind that mussels open up much faster than clams, and take care to remove both mussels and clams from the heat as soon as they are open, or they will become tough. Detach the clams and mussels from their shells, setting aside half the clam shells and half the mussel shells. Rinse the clams one by one in their own juice to remove all traces of sand.

2 Preheat the grill.

3 Put the parsley, garlic, olive oil and breadcrumbs in a mixing bowl and add the clams and mussels. Mix well until both clams and mussels are thoroughly coated and allow to stand for at least 20 minutes. (If you feel you will have trouble later distinguishing the clams from the mussels, divide the marinating ingredients into two parts and use two separate bowls.)

4 Wash the clam and mussel shells. In each half shell place one of its respective molluscs. Distribute the left-over marinade in the mixing bowl among all the clams and mussels and top each clam with a sliver of tomato. Place on the grilling pan and run under the hot grill for just a few minutes, until a light crust forms. Serve hot, with wedges of lemon.

Acciughe
ANCHOVIES

The heady fragrance of anchovies permeates the cooking of every Italian region, from Piedmont to Sicily. Southerners may use them with more abandon than central or northern Italians, but there is no good kitchen in Italy that gets along entirely without anchovies. The best anchovies you can use are those you fillet at home. Tinned fillets or paste are a blessed convenience when you have nothing else available, but they cannot come close to the fuller, mellower flavour of home-made fillets. Fillets are made from whole, salt-cured anchovies, and, if you have access to a Greek or Cypriot grocer, that is the ideal place to buy them, although you can find them also at some Italian and other ethnic grocers. They are sold loose, by weight, out of a large drum. If the drum has been started recently, you are in luck, because the anchovies in the upper half are always the best. The others tend to be saltier and drier. You should fillet the anchovies and steep them in oil as soon as possible, and no later than 24 hours after buying them, otherwise they will dry up.

ANCHOVIES IN OIL

Whole salt-cured anchovies
(220 g ($\frac{1}{2}$ lb) whole anchovies will
yield about four servings of
fillets as an antipasto)

Olive oil

1 Although all anchovies are not equally salty, it is best to begin by rinsing them quickly in cold running water to remove excess salt. Wipe dry with kitchen paper.

2 Spread some waxed paper or a flattened brown paper bag on the worktop. Lay the anchovies on the paper, and, grasping each by the tail, gently scrape off its skin with a knife. Remove the dorsal fin and the bones attached to it.

3 Using the knife, separate the anchovy into two halves and remove the spine. Place the fillets in a shallow rectangular dish. As soon as you have a full layer of fillets, cover with olive oil. You can build up several layers in the same dish, but make sure that they are all completely covered by oil. If you are not going to use them immediately, refrigerate them. They will keep from 10 days to 2 weeks.

Note   When the oil congeals in the refrigerator it turns into a yellowish-green solid. This does not mean it has gone bad. When it reaches room temperature again, it will return to a liquid.

MENU SUGGESTIONS

Apart from their many uses in cooking, anchovy fillets make a marvellous antipasto, the irresistible aroma of which will arouse the most indolent appetite. You may use them on canapés, of course, just as you would use tinned fillets. But these home-made fillets are perfect just by themselves. Serve them with unsalted butter, and slices of good crusty French or Italian bread. Follow with a substantial dish that will not be thrown off balance by the rather overwhelming flavour of the anchovies. Two suggestions: *Bucatini all' Amatriciana* (page 89), or *Spaghettini con le melanzane* (page 84).

Peperoni e acciughe
PEPPERS AND ANCHOVIES

Here grilled sweet peppers and anchovies are steeped together in oil until they soften and there is an exchange of flavours. The peppers acquire pungency, while letting the anchovies share in the sweetness. The result is most appetising, especially as a prelude to a robust meal.

Approximately eight servings

8 medium sweet peppers, green, yellow, or red	Salt
16 large or 20 medium flat anchovy fillets, preferably the home-prepared variety (preceding recipe)	Freshly ground pepper, Oregano 3 tablespoons capers 4 cloves garlic, lightly crushed with a heavy knife-handle and peeled Olive oil

1 Place the peppers under a hot grill. When the skin swells and is partially charred on one side, turn another side toward the flame. When all the skin is blistered and slightly charred, remove the peppers, and peel them while still hot.

2 Cut the peeled peppers lengthways into strips 37 to 50 mm ($1\frac{1}{2}$ to

2 inches) wide, removing all the seeds and the pulpy inner core. Pat the
strips dry with a cloth or kitchen paper.

3 Choose a serving dish that will hold the peppers in 4 layers. Arrange
a layer of peppers on the bottom. Place 4 to 5 anchovies over the peppers.
Add a tiny pinch of salt, a liberal grinding of pepper, a small pinch of oregano, a few capers, and one crushed garlic clove. Repeat until you have used
up all the peppers and anchovies. Add enough olive oil to cover the top
layer.

4 Put the dish in the refrigerator for 4 hours or more, then bring to room
temperature before serving. If you are preparing these peppers several days
ahead of time, remove the garlic after 24 hours.

Pomodori ripieni di tonno

TOMATOES STUFFED WITH TUNA AND CAPERS

For six

6 large, ripe, round, meaty tomatoes
Salt
2 200-g (7-oz) tins Italian of Spanish
    tuna, packed in olive oil
Mayonnaise (page 22) made using 1
    large egg yolk, 8 tablespoons
    olive oil and 2 tablespoons
    lemon juice

2 teaspoons strong mustard, Dijon or
    German
1½ tablespoons capers, the tinier the
    better
Decoration as suggested below

1 Slice off the tops of the tomatoes. Remove all the seeds and some of the
dividing walls, leaving just three or four large sections. Salt lightly and put
the tomatoes open end down on a dish, allowing their liquid to drain away.

2 In a bowl, mash the tuna to a pulp with a fork. Add the mayonnaise,
holding back 1 or 2 tablespoons, add the mustard and the capers. Mix with
a fork to a uniform consistency. Taste and check salt.

3 Shake off the excess liquid from the tomatoes, but do not squeeze them.
Stuff to the very top with the tuna mixture. Seal the tops with the remaining
mayonnaise, and decorate with an olive slice, a strip of green or red pepper,
a ring of capers, or parsley leaves. Serve at room temperature or slightly
chilled.

Pomodori coi gamberetti
TOMATOES STUFFED WITH SHRIMPS

For six

6 large, ripe, round, meaty tomatoes
325 g ($\frac{3}{4}$ lb) small shrimps
1 tablespoon red wine vinegar
Salt
Mayonnaise (page 22) made with 1
    large egg yolk, 8 tablespoons
    olive oil and $2\frac{1}{2}$ to 3
    tablespoons lemon juice

$1\frac{1}{2}$ tablespoons capers, the tinier the
    better
1 teaspoon strong mustard, Dijon or
    German
Parsley for decoration

1 Prepare the tomatoes as indicated in the preceding recipe.

2 Rinse the shrimps in cold water. Bring 2 litres ($3\frac{1}{2}$ pints) of water with
the 1 tablespoon of vinegar and salt to the boil. Drop in the shrimps and
cook for just 2 minutes after the water returns to the boil. Drain, peel the
shrimps and, if they are on the large side, remove the black intestinal tract;
set aside to cool.

3 Pick out six of the best-looking, best-shaped shrimps and set aside.
Chop the rest of the shrimps roughly. Put them in a bowl and mix with
the mayonnaise, capers and mustard.

4 Shake off the excess liquid from the tomatoes, but do not squeeze them.
Stuff to the top with the shrimp-and-mayonnaise mixture. Decorate each
tomato with a shrimp and one or two parsley leaves. Serve at cool room
temperature or slightly chilled.

Gamberetti all'olio e limone
SHRIMPS WITH OIL AND LEMON

In Italy, very tiny freshly caught shrimps are used to prepare this simple
but sublime antipasto. The shrimps are boiled very briefly with vegetables,
then steeped in olive oil and lemon juice. There is nothing more to it than

that, but I have known people whose memories turn to *gamberetti all'olio e limone* with keener joy than they feel towards anything else they had in Italy. Although elsewhere shrimps do not have the same sweetness as the tiny shrimps of the Adriatic, they can be very good all the same. For this recipe you should try to use the smallest fresh shrimps you can find.

For six

1 stick celery
1 carrot, peeled
2 tablespoons red wine vinegar
Salt
680 g (1½ lb) small fresh shrimps,
      washed in cold water but left
      unpeeled

8 tablespoons olive oil
4 tablespoons lemon juice
Freshly ground pepper to taste
    (optional)

1 Put the celery, carrot, vinegar and salt in a saucepan with 2 to 3 litres (3½ to 5¼ pints) of water and bring to a rapid boil.

2 Add the unpeeled shrimps. If very small, not over 12 mm (½ inch) in diameter, they will be cooked shortly after the water returns to the boil; medium shrimps cook in about 2 to 3 minutes.

3 When cooked, drain the shrimps, peel and, if large, remove the black intestinal tract. Put them in a shallow bowl and add the oil, lemon juice, salt to taste, and optional pepper while the shrimps are still warm. Mix well and let them marinate in the seasonings at room temperature for 1 to 1½ hours before serving. Serve with crusty French or Italian bread or with thinly sliced, good quality white bread, lightly toasted.

Note This dish is far better if never chilled, but if necessary it can be prepared a day ahead of time and kept in the refrigerator under plastic film. Always, however, return it to room temperature before serving.

Bastoncini di carota marinati
MARINATED CARROT STICKS

For four

110g ($\frac{1}{4}$ lb) carrots
1 small clove garlic, lightly crushed
    with a heavy knife-handle and
    peeled
Salt and freshly ground pepper to
    taste

$\frac{1}{4}$ teaspoon oregano
1 tablespoon red wine vinegar
Olive oil, enough to cover

1 Peel the carrots, cut them in 50-mm (2-inch) lengths, and cook them in boiling salted water for about 10 to 12 minutes. (Cooking time varies according to the thickness and freshness of the carrots. In order to cook the carrots uniformly put the thickest parts into the water first, then the thinner, tapered ends. You want the carrots tender but quite firm for this recipe because the marinade will continue to soften them.)

2 Drain the cooked carrots, and cut lengthways into small sticks about 6mm ($\frac{1}{4}$ inch) thick. Place in a small, deep serving dish.

3 Bury the garlic in the carrots. Add salt and pepper to taste, the oregano and vinegar and enough olive oil to just cover the carrots.

4 Refrigerate and allow to marinate at least overnight, removing the garlic after 24 hours. Serve at room temperature.

MENU SUGGESTIONS

This is a tasty and rustic appetiser. It can be part of an antipasto composed of such other dishes as Anchovies in oil (page 31), *Peperoni e acciughe* (page 32), and *Insalata di tonno e fagioli* (page 359).

Bagna caôda

HOT ANCHOVY DIP FOR VEGETABLES

One of the most frequent observations on Italian food is that it is based mainly on peasant cooking. Like many of the commonly held beliefs about Italian cooking, this is not entirely true, but it is a fact that some of the glories of the Italian table were first created in peasant kitchens. Typical of these is *bagna caôda*, a hot dip for raw vegetables. It is a perfect illustration of the gastronomic genius of the Italian peasant. The materials are only those most easily available to him: oil, butter, garlic, a few anchovies in brine and his own vegetables. The preparation is quick and direct: the garlic is sautéed for the briefest of moments, the anchovies are cooked just long enough to dissolve them, and the vegetables to be dipped into the sauce are raw. The result is a heartening, restorative dish of immensely satisfying flavour.

Eating *bagna caôda* is a two-handed affair. One hand takes a vegetable, the other bread, dipping them alternately in the sauce. The only interruption in this resolute rhythm is for long, slaking swallows of young, lively wine.

In peasant kitchens, *bagna caôda* is prepared in an earthenware pot, kept warm over drowsily glowing coals while everyone gathers around and dips. When the vegetables are finished, the fire is stirred up and eggs are broken into the pot and scrambled with the rest of the sauce. Today in the smart *trattorie* of Piedmont, *bagna caôda* is served in individual earthenware chafing dishes with built-in candle warmers. At home I prefer to make and serve *bagna caôda* in a single pot. It is both better for the sauce and more fun. But however you do it, it is important that the dip be kept warm for the entire time that one is eating. The heat should be kept at a minimum, at no more than candle-warmer intensity, because the dip must not continue to cook after it is prepared. An earthenware pot is all but indispensable for *bagna caôda*. If you do not already have one, this is the best of reasons for getting one.

For six to eight

180 ml ($\frac{1}{4}$ pint + 2 tablespoons) olive oil	2 cloves garlic, peeled and finely chopped
40 g ($1\frac{1}{2}$ oz) butter	8 to 10 flat anchovy fillets, chopped
	Salt to taste

Heat the oil and butter until the butter is thoroughly liquefied and barely begins to foam. (Do not wait for the foam to subside or the butter will be too hot.) Add the garlic and sauté very briefly. It must not take on any colour. Add the anchovies and cook over very low heat, stirring frequently, until the anchovies dissolve into a paste. Add the salt, stir and bring to the table along with raw vegetables, as prepared below.

The Vegetables

Cardoons   The traditional vegetable for *bagna caôda* is a very tender, sweet, dwarf cardoon found in many sections of Piedmont. The cardoon is a native of the Mediterranean and cultivated for its leaf-stalks, but it has never really caught on outside southern Europe. The outer stems and leaves are cut away and only the inner stalks and firm hearts are eaten. If you do find it in markets and shops, this trimming should already have been done. If eating the cardoon raw, remove the strings, cut the stalks into suitable lengths and the heart into sections, wash thoroughly and rub the cut parts with a lemon to prevent discoloration. (The cardoon is also delicious when cooked, for between 30 and 40 minutes, and dressed with butter, cream and Parmesan.)

Artichokes   You do not need to trim artichokes for *bagna caôda* as you do for recipes where they are cooked. Rinse the artichoke in cold water and serve it whole. One pulls off a leaf at a time, dips it and bites off just the tender part.

Broccoli   Cut off the florets and put aside for use in any recipe for cooked broccoli. Serve just the stalks, after peeling off the tough outer skin.

Spinach   Use only young, crisp spinach. Wash very thoroughly and at length in several changes of cold water until the water shows no trace of earth. Serve with the stems on because they provide a hold for dipping.

Zucchini (Courgettes)   Only very fresh, small, young, glossy-skinned zucchini are suitable. Wash thoroughly in cold water, lightly scraping the skin to remove any embedded earth. Cut lengthways into sections 25 mm (1 inch) thick.

Sweet peppers   Wash in cold water and cut into quarter sections. Remove the seeds and the pulpy inner core.

Celery   Discard any bruised or tough outer stalks. Wash very carefully in cold water.

Carrots   Scrape or peel clean and cut lengthways into sections 12 mm ($\frac{1}{2}$ inch) thick.

Radishes   Cut off the root tips, wash in cold water and serve with stems and leaves, attractive and helpful for dipping, left on.

Asparagus   This is a vegetable you will never see served with *bagna caôda* in Piedmont. The very thought scandalises my Piedmontese friends. *Bagna caôda* is a winter dish, asparagus is a spring vegetable, and never the twain, et cetera. It is a pity for them, because I have never tasted any better vegetable with this dip. Use the freshest asparagus you can find, with the crispest stalks and tightest buds. Trim it and peel it as directed on page 302. Wash it with cold water and add a generous quantity of it to the vegetable bowl because it will be very popular.

This is not necessarily a definitive list of vegetables suitable for *bagna caôda*. You should feel free to make your own discoveries. Remember, though, this is a dip for vegetables freshly picked at the peak of their development. Use only the youngest, sweetest vegetables available, and serve as wide a variety of them as possible. And before serving pat all the vegetables dry with a towel.

MENU SUGGESTIONS

Depending on the variety and quantity of vegetables you use, *bagna caôda* can be practically a meal on its own, and would need nothing more to complete it than a *Frittata al formaggio* (page 277) or *Frittata al pomodoro e basilico* (page 281). If you would like to work it into a fuller meal, however, follow it with *Stracotto al Barolo* (page 206), *Arrosto di agnello al ginepro* (page 236), *Costolettine di agnello fritte* (page 239), *Pollo alla diavola* (page 260) or *Fegatelli di maiale con la rete* (page 255). A perfect alternative to all these is a magnificent roast of beef.

Uova sode in salsa verde
HARD-BOILED EGGS WITH GREEN SAUCE

For six

6 eggs (large)
2 tablespoons olive oil
½ tablespoon chopped capers
1 tablespoon chopped parsley
1 teaspoon anchovy paste

¼ teaspoon finely chopped garlic
¼ teaspoon strong mustard, Dijon or
    German
A small pinch of salt
12 small strips of pimento

1 Put the eggs in cold water and bring to the boil. Boil slowly for 10 minutes, then set aside to cool. When cool, remove the shells, and cut the eggs in half lengthways. Carefully remove the yolks without damaging the whites. Set aside the whites.

2 Combine the egg yolks and the remaining ingredients, except for the pimento and the reserved egg whites, in a bowl. Using a fork, mash to a creamy, uniform consistency. Divide into 12 equal parts and spoon into the cavities of the reserved egg whites. Decorate each with a strip of pimento.

Note   These can be prepared ahead of time and refrigerated, but serve at room temperature.

Funghi ripieni
STUFFED MUSHROOMS WITH BÉCHAMEL SAUCE

For six

12 large mushrooms
35 g (1¼ oz) butter
1 tablespoon finely chopped shallots
    or onion
40 g (1½ oz) chopped prosciutto **or**
    ham
Salt
Freshly ground pepper, about 4 twists
    of the mill

A thick Béchamel sauce made with:
    1½ tablespoons flour, 20 g (¾
    oz) butter, salt and 250 ml
    (scant ½ pint) milk (page 23)
3 tablespoons freshly grated
    Parmesan cheese
Fine, dry plain breadcrumbs

1 Slice off the ends of the mushroom stems. Wipe the mushrooms clean with a damp cloth. If there are still traces of earth, wash each mushroom carefully under cold running water, working quickly. Dry well with a towel. Detach the stems and chop them fine.

2 Preheat the oven to 250°C/500°F/Mark 10.

3 In a frying pan, sauté the chopped shallots or onion in the butter over medium-high heat until pale gold in colour. Add the chopped prosciutto and sauté for about a minute. Add the finely chopped mushroom stems, salt and pepper and cook, stirring, for 2 to 3 minutes. Tilt the frying pan and draw off all the fat with a spoon.

4 In a bowl, mix the contents of the frying pan with the warm Béchamel. Add the grated Parmesan and mix again.

5 Place the mushroom caps, bottoms up, in a buttered baking dish. Sprinkle lightly with salt, fill with the Béchamel stuffing, sprinkle with breadcrumbs, and dot each cap with butter. Place in the upper third of the preheated oven and bake for 15 minutes, or until a slight crust has formed. Allow to settle for about 10 minutes before serving.

Insalata di funghi e formaggio
MUSHROOM AND CHEESE SALAD

In October and November, when the wild mushrooms are gathered in the woods at the foothills of the Alps, the choicest, firmest *funghi* go into delicious and wildly expensive salads with white truffles and cheese. White truffles are almost unobtainable outside Italy and fresh wild mushrooms are virtually never seen, but there is a limitless supply of excellent cultivated mushrooms and Swiss cheese. This is not a replica of the Italian original, but it can stand on its own merits as a very appealing antipasto.

For four

220 g (½ lb) very crisp, white fresh
    mushrooms
Juice of ½ lemon
100 g (7 oz) Gruyère or Emmenthal
    cheese cut into strips 25 mm
    (1 inch) long, 6 mm (¼ inch)
    wide, and 3 mm (⅛ inch) thick

3 tablespoons olive oil
Salt to taste
Freshly ground pepper, a liberal
    quantity, to taste

1 Detach the mushroom stems from the caps. Save the stems for another recipe. Wipe the caps clean with a damp cloth, then cut into slices 3 mm ($\frac{1}{8}$ inch) thick. Put the slices in a salad bowl and moisten them with some lemon juice to keep them from discolouring. (You can prepare these as much as 30 to 45 minutes ahead of time.)

2 When ready to serve, add the strips of cheese to the bowl and toss with the olive oil, salt and pepper.

Bresaola

Bresaola is a speciality of the Valtellina, a fertile valley at the northernmost edge of Lombardy. It is a whole beef fillet, cured in salt and air-dried, a little sharper yet more delicate than prosciutto. Sliced thin, it is one of the finest and most elegant of antipasti. It can precede any meal, whether hearty or light.

Although Valtellina *bresaola* is not always available, many delicatessens carry a nearly identical product, Swiss Grison or *bundesfleisch*. Grison is compressed into a rectangular loaf, while *bresaola* maintains the original round, tapered shape of the fillet. This makes Grison somewhat drier than *bresaola*, but otherwise it is a completely acceptable substitute.

It should be served as quickly as possible after it is sliced, at most within 24 hours, or else it will become dry and turn sharp.

Serve it with olive oil, enough to moisten each slice, a few drops of lemon juice and freshly ground pepper.

Bocconcini fritti

FRIED MORTADELLA, PANCETTA AND CHEESE MORSELS

This is a savoury hot antipasto that can also be served before meals with an aperitif, or as part of a buffet. In Bologna and its province it is often a prelude to the *grande fritto misto*, found on page 283.

For six

110 g ($\frac{1}{4}$ lb) Gruyère or Emmenthal cheese, in one piece
110 g ($\frac{1}{4}$ lb) *mortadella*, in one piece
110 g ($\frac{1}{4}$ lb) *pancetta*, thinly sliced
130 g ($4\frac{1}{2}$ oz) plain flour spread on a dish or on waxed paper
2 eggs, lightly beaten, in a bowl

120 g ($4\frac{1}{4}$ oz) fine, dry plain breadcrumbs, spread on a dish or on waxed paper
Vegetable oil, enough to come at least 25 mm (1 inch) up the side of the frying pan

1 Cut one-third of the cheese into 25 mm (1 inch) cubes and the rest into 12 mm ($\frac{1}{2}$ inch) cubes. Set aside.

2 Cut two-thirds of the *mortadella* into cubes whose sides are as wide as the slice is thick. Cut the rest of the slice into thin strips 50 mm (2 inches) long and about 12 mm ($\frac{1}{2}$ inch) wide.

3 Cut the *pancetta* into strips as close as possible in size to the *mortadella* strips.

4 Wrap part of the smaller cheese cubes with strips of *pancetta*, and the others with strips of *mortadella*. Fasten with toothpicks. You now have four kinds of morsels ready to coat and fry: cheese wrapped in *pancetta*, cheese wrapped in *mortadella*, cheese cubes and *mortadella* cubes.

5 Roll the morsels in flour, dip them in egg, then roll them in breadcrumbs. (You can prepare them up to this point 3 or 4 hours ahead of time, if you like.)

6 Choose not too large a frying pan, so as not to waste oil, then pour in enough oil to come at least 25 mm (1 inch) up the sides of the pan. Heat the oil over high heat.

7 When the oil is very hot, slip in as many of the morsels as will fit loosely in the pan. Fry until golden brown on both sides, then transfer to kitchen paper to drain. Continue until you have fried all the morsels. (Caution: handle them with tongs, not with a fork. The prongs of a fork might puncture the crust on the cheese and it will run out.)

Bruschetta

ROMAN GARLIC BREAD

Although it is known to foreigners as garlic bread, the most important ingredient in *bruschetta* is not garlic but olive oil. The origin of *bruschetta* in
Italy is probably nearly as old as that of olive oil itself. Each winter in ancient
Rome one's first taste of the freshly pressed, dense, green olive oil was most
likely an oil-soaked piece of bread that may or may not have been rubbed
with garlic. In modern times *bruschetta* became a staple of the poor man's
trattoria, where it went a long way in making up for the frugality of the
fare. When eating in *trattorie* became the fashionable thing to do, *bruschetta*
found its way into polite society. The name *bruschetta* comes from *bruscare*,
which means 'to roast over coals', the original and still the best way of toast-
ing the bread.

For six

12 slices Italian wholemeal bread
(*pane integrale*), 37 mm (1½
inches) thick, 80 to 100 mm
(3 to 4 inches) wide
4 to 5 cloves garlic, lightly crushed
with a heavy knife-handle and
peeled

8 tablespoons olive oil, as green and
dense as you can find,
preferably Sicilian olive oil
Salt and freshly ground pepper to
taste

1 Preheat the grill.
2 Toast the bread on both sides to a golden brown under the hot
grill.
3 Rub one side of the toast while still hot with garlic. Discard the
garlic as it dries up and take a fresh clove. Put the toast on a dish,
garlic-rubbed side facing up, and pour a thin stream of olive oil over it.
Not a few drops, but enough to soak each slice very lightly. Add a
sprinkling of salt and a generous twist or two of freshly ground pepper
per slice. The toast is best served while still warm.

FIRST COURSES

I Primi

THE first course in an Italian meal is almost always a pasta, a *risotto* or a soup. Occasionally, but not frequently, a vegetable, an antipasto or a fish course may become the first course, but no pasta or soup is ever turned into a side dish or second course. Sometimes one finds *risotto* incorporated into the second course, as when *risotto alla Milanese* (page 157) is combined with *ossobuco* (page 216). But these instances are very rare.

First courses are, justifiably, the best-known feature of Italian cooking. Into them, Italians have poured most of their culinary genius and inventiveness. Although the temptation is strong to give as many as possible of these incredibly varied and attractive dishes, it will not be done here. Rather than take a breathless junket through the whole landscape of Italian first courses, I thought it would be more profitable for those with a more than casual interest in good cooking to linger over a few selected areas and explore them in depth.

Italy's most original and important contribution to cooking is the vast repertoire of home-made pasta. However, every treatment I have seen of it has been cursory, inadequate or, even worse, misleading. The first edition of this book could claim to be the first fully detailed exposition of the subject in English and I have tried to give even the most inexperienced cook easy access to the techniques and the inexhaustible satisfactions of home-made pasta. Since I first wrote this section electric pasta-making machines have appeared on the market to make the cook's task easier (see pages 105–7). The step by step analysis of both hand-made and machine-made egg pasta should guide any willing beginner safely past the early difficulties toward a well-grounded proficiency in making pasta at home. Once you have mastered the fundamentally simple mechanics of rolling out a thin sheet of egg pasta dough, you can move on to execute any one of dozens of delicious variations on the pasta theme.

Factory-made pasta deserves and has been given whole volumes. I have given here fresh versions of some of the best-known sauces as well as several less familiar ones. There are six different tomato sauces and, altogether, twenty-seven different sauces for both home-made and commercial pasta.

Risotto, another uniquely Italian preparation that approaches pasta in variety and importance, is also examined in detail. The basic *risotto* technique is clearly set down, and you are shown how it can be developed into nine different *risotti*. With taste and ingenuity you can expand this, as Italian families do, into your own personal *risotto* repertoire.

You will also find recipes for three varieties of *gnocchi* – potato, semolina, and spinach and ricotta – along with seven different ways of serving them.

In this chapter too, are some of the heroic country soups of Tuscany, as well as several other traditional soups, including an unusual clam soup and a little-known sauerkraut soup from Trieste.

I wish there had been room for more. Perhaps you will be encouraged by what you find here to discover other dishes at their source. But even if you never go beyond the material in this chapter, you will still possess a larger variety of first courses than do most regional Italian cooks.

Zuppa di vongole

CLAM SOUP

Clams, unlike oysters and most mussels, often contain some sand. There are methods for eliminating the sand, such as allowing the clams to stand for long periods in cold water so that they can open up and disgorge it, or trapping the sand by straining the cooked juices. In terms of flavour, however, when clams are to be served in their shells, as in this soup, neither method is as satisfactory as letting the clams release their juices directly into the sauce. There may be a little sand, but this quickly settles to the bottom of the pot, and, with a little care in lifting out the clams and spooning the sauce into the soup plates, it will all be left behind.

For four

3 dozen clams in their shells, the
    tiniest you can find
1½ tablespoons finely chopped shallots
    or onion
8 tablespoons olive oil
2 cloves garlic, peeled and finely
    chopped

2 tablespoons finely chopped parsley
¼ teaspoon cornflour dissolved in
    150 ml (¼ pint) dry white wine
Toasted Italian wholemeal bread
    (*pane integrale*), 1 slice per
    serving

1 Put the clams in a large basin or sink filled with cold water. Allow to

stand for 5 minutes, then drain and refill the basin with clean water. Scrub the clams vigorously with a coarse, stiff brush or by rubbing them one against the other. When they are all scrubbed, drain and fill basin again with clean water. Repeat these steps for 20 or 30 minutes, until you see that the water in the basin remains clear. Transfer the cleaned clams to a bowl.

2 Choose a heavy casserole large enough to contain the clams later. (Remember that they more than double in volume when open.) Over medium heat sauté the shallots in the olive oil until translucent. Add the garlic. When it has coloured lightly add the parsley and stir two or three times. Add the cornflour and wine, turn the heat to high, and cook briskly for 2 minutes.

3 Drop in the clams. Stir, basting them lightly, and cover tightly. Continue cooking over high heat and stir the clams from time to time so that they all cook evenly. When their shells open they will release their juices, and they will be done.

4 Place a slice of bread in each individual soup plate. Ladle the clams and sauce over the bread, taking care not to scoop up the liquid from the bottom of the pot because it probably contains sand.

Note In Italy we bring the pot to the table and serve the shellfish a few at a time to prevent their getting cold.

Small claims of the kind found in the Adriatic are not easily obtained elsewhere but this soup can be made with other shellfish including small mussels. If you gather your own shellfish, take care to avoid polluted stretches of coast and discard any open or broken specimens.

MENU SUGGESTIONS

This is an all-purpose first course that can be followed by any fish course, giving the preference, however, to robust rather than delicate flavours. It goes well with *Pesce da taglio con salsa di prezzemolo* (page 183), *Pesce ai ferri alla moda dell' Adriatico* (page 191), *Calamari ripieni stufati al vino bianco* (page 197) or *Calamari e piselli alla livornese* (page 196).

Zuppa di vongole vellutata

VELVETY CLAM SOUP WITH MUSHROOMS

This clam soup from the northern Adriatic coast is a considerable departure from traditional Italian methods of doing shellfish. The clam broth is enriched with eggs, milk and butter, and completely eschews garlic.

For four

3 dozen clams, the tiniest you can find
2 tablespoons olive oil
1 tablespoon finely chopped shallots
    or onion
40 g (1½ oz) butter
220 g (½ lb) mushrooms, thinly sliced
Salt
3 to 4 twists of the pepper mill

3 egg yolks
6 tablespoons milk
250 ml (scant ½ pint) chicken broth, home-made or tinned
1 tablespoon cornflour dissolved in 250 ml (scant ½ pint) warm water

1 Follow the directions for washing and scrubbing clams (pages 46–7).

2 Heat the clams with the olive oil in a covered saucepan over medium-high heat until they open their shells. Give them a vigorous shake or turn them so that they will all heat evenly (some clams are more obstinate than others about opening). When most of them have opened up, it would be best to remove the open clams while waiting for the stubborn ones; otherwise they will become tough as they linger in the pan. Remove the clams from their shells and rinse off any sand on the meat by dipping them briefly one at a time in their own juice. Unless the clams are exceptionally small, cut them up into two or more pieces and set aside. Strain the clam juices through a sieve lined with kitchen paper and set aside.

3 In a frying pan, sauté the shallots in 20 g (¾ oz) of the butter over medium-high heat. When the shallots have turned pale gold, add the sliced mushrooms, salt and pepper, and sauté briskly for about 3 minutes. Remove from the heat and set aside.

4 In a small bowl beat the remaining butter until soft and creamy. Set aside.

5 Put the egg yolks in a serving bowl or soup tureen and beat them lightly with a fork or whisk, gradually adding the milk. Add the softened butter.

6 In a medium-sized stockpot or casserole bring the chicken broth to the boil. Mix in the dissolved cornflour, a little bit at a time. Add the strained clam juices, the contents of the frying pan and the clams. Pour

the hot soup, in tiny quantities at first, into the bowl or tureen containing the egg-yolk mixture. Beat rapidly with the whisk as you pour, gradually increasing the quantities of soup until it has all been added to the bowl. Serve immediately with *crostini* made from two to three slices of bread (page 75).

MENU SUGGESTIONS

Follow this soup with a fish course having a crisp, straightforward taste, such as *Spiedini di gamberoni dell' Adriatico* (page 193), *Pesce ai ferri alla moda dell' Adriatico* (page 191) or *Calamari fritti* (page 199).

Zuppa di cozze
MUSSEL SOUP

The two most important things to know about the proper preparations of mussels are, first, that you must take your time to clean them, and, second, that it takes virtually no time at all to cook them.

To get mussels clean you must scrub them thoroughly under cold running water with a coarse, stiff brush or rub them one against another until you have removed all traces of dirt and slime. It takes rather a long time because there is a surprising amount of obstinate slime on each mussel, but once you are past this tedious part the rest of the work goes quickly and the result is completely rewarding. Discard all the mussels that are not tightly closed and any that feel much lighter or heavier than the rest. With a sharp paring knife, cut off the tough, ropelike tufts that protrude from the shells. The mussels are now clean and ready.

There are cooks who let the mussels stand for a long time in a bucket of water, but since fine, fresh mussels very rarely contain sand, this step is wholly unnecessary. Not only that, but in allowing the mussels to unclench their shells in water you lose much of their precious, tasty juice.

For four

2 cloves garlic, peeled and chopped
6 tablespoons olive oil
1 tablespoon coarsely chopped parsley
225 g (8 oz) tinned Italian tomatoes, drained and cut up
$\frac{1}{8}$ teaspoon chopped chilli

900 g (2 lb) fresh mussels, cleaned and scrubbed as directed above
4 slices Italian wholemeal bread (*pane integrale*), toasted and (optional) rubbed with garlic

1 Choose a casserole large enough to contain the mussels later. Sauté the garlic in the oil over moderate heat until it has coloured lightly. Add the parsley, stir once or twice, then add the cut-up tomatoes and the chopped chilli. Cook, uncovered, at a gentle simmer for about 25 minutes, or until the tomatoes and oil separate.

2 Add the mussels, cover the casserole, raise the heat to high, and cook until the mussels open their shells, about 3 to 5 minutes. To get all the mussels to cook evenly, grasp the casserole with both hands, holding the cover down tight, and jerk it two or three times.

3 Put the 4 slices of toasted bread in 4 soup dishes and ladle the mussels, with all their sauce, over the bread. Serve piping hot.

Note Mussels are found in profusion round the coasts of Europe and can easily be gathered. Do be sure, however, that there are no sewage outlets or other sources of pollution nearby and take special care to clean them properly. If you are in any doubt, seek local advice or steer clear.

MENU SUGGESTIONS

There is as much joy for the eye as for the palate here in the delicate, amber mussel within its glossy jet-black shell balanced against the exuberance of the tomato sauce. As a first course, this can precede any fish course that is not served with a tomato sauce. Grilled or fried fish would be my first choice, but an excellent second course could also be *Scombri in tegame con rosmarino e aglio* (page 184). If you want to precede it with an antipasto, try *Peperoni e acciughe* (page 32).

Minestrina tricolore
CREAMY POTATO SOUP WITH CARROTS AND CELERY

This lovely soup is a study in delicate contrasts. The name, *minestrina tricolore*, or 'tricolor' soup, comes from the creamed potato, the orange flecks of carrot and the parsley, which recall the colours of the Italian flag. Its character comes from the interruption of its smooth, velvety consistency by the crisp specks of sautéed carrot and celery. It is quite artless and good.

For four to six

680 g (1½ lb) potatoes, peeled and
    roughly diced
40 g (1½ oz) finely chopped onion
25 g (1 oz) butter
3 tablespoons vegetable oil
40 g (1½ oz) finely chopped carrot
40 g (1½ oz) finely chopped celery

30 g (1¼ oz) freshly grated Parmesan
    cheese
250 ml (scant ½ pint) milk
450 ml (¾ pint) broth (page 8) **or** 1
    chicken stock cube dissolved
    in the same quantity of water
Salt to taste
2 tablespoons chopped parsley

1 Put the potatoes and just enough cold water to cover in a stockpot. Cover, bring to the boil, and cook at a moderate boil until the potatoes are tender. Purée the potatoes, with their liquid, through a mouli-légumes back into the pot. Set aside.

2 In a frying pan sauté the chopped onion, with all the butter and oil, over medium heat until pale gold in colour. Add the chopped carrot and celery and cook for about 2 minutes, but not long enough to let the vegetables become soft, since you want them to be crunchy in the soup.

3 Add the entire contents of the frying pan to the puréed potatoes in the pot. Turn on the heat to medium and add the grated Parmesan cheese, the milk and the broth. Stir and cook at a steady simmer for a few minutes, until the cooking fat floating on the surface is dispersed throughout the soup and the consistency of the soup is that of liquid cream. Add salt to taste. (Bear in mind that this soup will thicken as it cools in the plate. If the soup is too dense, simply add equal parts of broth and milk, as required.) When done, mix in the parsley off the heat. Serve in warm soup plates, with *crostini* (page 75) and additional freshly grated Parmesan cheese on the side.

MENU SUGGESTIONS

This is a very pleasant soup that goes well with virtually any meat or poultry second course. However, avoid dishes with cream or milk, and very sharp tomato sauces. A nice combination would be with *Cotolette alla milanese* (page 228), *Pollo coi funghi secchi* (page 262), or any of the simple roasts.

Zuppa di patate e cipolle
POTATO AND ONION SOUP

For six

680 g (1½ lb) onions, peeled and very
    thinly sliced
40 g (1½ oz) butter
3 tablespoons vegetable oil
Salt
900 g (2 lb) boiling potatoes, peeled
    and diced into 6-mm (¼-inch)
    cubes

880 ml (1½ pints) broth (page 5) **or**
    1½ beef stock cubes dissolved
    in the same quantity of water
3 tablespoons freshly grated
    Parmesan cheese

1 In an uncovered frying pan, cook the onion, with all the butter and oil and a dash of salt, over moderate heat. Cook gently and slowly, allowing the onion gradually to soften. Cook until it turns light brown. Turn off the heat and set aside. Do not remove the onion from the frying pan.

2 Boil the diced potato in 700 ml (1¼ pints) of the home-made broth or the water. Add a little salt. Do not boil too rapidly.

3 When the potato is tender add all the onion from the frying pan, together with its cooking fat. Loosen any of the cooking residue from the bottom of the frying pan with some of the hot liquid in which the potatoes have cooked and add it to the soup.

4 Add the remaining broth and bring to a gentle boil. With a wooden spoon mash part of the potatoes against the side of the pot and mix into the boiling liquid. Continue cooking for 8 to 10 minutes. Check the soup for density. If at this point it is too thick (it is supposed to be a soup, not a purée), add home-made broth or water as required.

5 Turn off the heat. Add the grated Parmesan cheese, stirring it into the soup. Check salt. Serve with a small bowl of freshly grated Parmesan cheese on the side.

MENU SUGGESTIONS

This soup goes well with meat courses that have a hearty country character. Try it with *Polpettone alla toscana* (page 211), either of the veal stews on pages 230–2, *Arrosto di maiale all' alloro* (page 241) or *Cervella fritta* (page 253).

Risi e bisi

RICE AND PEAS

No one else in Italy cooks rice in so many different ways as the Venetians. They have at least several dozen basic dishes, not counting individual variations, where rice is combined with every likely vegetable, meat, poultry, or fish. Of all of them, the one Venetians have always loved the best has been *risi e bisi*. In the days of the Republic of Venice, *risi e bisi* was the first dish served at the dinner given by the doges every 25 April in honour of St Mark. Those, of course, were the earliest, youngest peas of the season, which are the best kind to use for *risi e bisi*. But one can also make it with later, larger peas, the ones Venetians call *senatori*. You may use frozen peas, if you must, and this recipe shows you how, but until you have made it with choice fresh peas your *risi e bisi* will be a tolerable but slightly blurred copy of the original.

Risi e bisi is not *risotto* with peas. It is a soup, although a very thick one. Some cooks make it thick enough to eat with a fork, but it is at its best when it is fairly runny, with just enough liquid to require a spoon.

For four

Half onion, chopped
60 g (2 oz) butter
900 g (2 lb) fresh peas (unshelled
    weight) **or** 285 g (10 oz) frozen
    peas, thawed
Salt
850 ml (1½ pints) broth (page 8) for
    fresh peas, 700 ml (1¼ pints)
    for frozen (see note below)

200 g (7 oz) raw rice, preferably
    Italian Arborio rice
2 tablespoons chopped parsley
50 g (1¾ oz) freshly grated Parmesan
    cheese

1 Put the onion in a stockpot with the butter and sauté over medium heat until pale gold.

2 If you are using fresh peas, add the peas and salt, and sauté for 2 minutes, stirring frequently. Add 700 ml (1¼ pints) of broth, cover, and cook at a very moderate boil for 10 minutes. Add the rice, parsley and the remaining broth, stir, cover, and cook at a slow boil for 15 minutes, or until the rice is tender but *al dente*, firm to the bite. Stir from time to time while cooking, and taste and check salt.

If you are using thawed frozen peas, add the peas and salt and sauté for 2 minutes, stirring frequently. Add the broth and bring to the boil. Add the rice and parsley, stir, cover, and cook at a slow boil for 15 minutes, or until the rice is tender but *al dente*, firm to the bite. Stir from time to time while cooking and taste and check salt.

3 Just before serving, add the grated cheese, mixing it into the soup.

Note   This is one of those dishes that really demand the flavour and delicacy of home-made broth. If you absolutely must use shop-bought broth, use tinned bouillon in the following proportions: *for fresh peas*, 250 ml (scant $\frac{1}{2}$ pint) broth mixed with 550 ml (generous pint) water; *for frozen peas*, 250 ml (scant $\frac{1}{2}$ pint) broth mixed with 450 ml ($\frac{3}{4}$ pint) water.

MENU SUGGESTIONS

The ideal coupling for *risi e bisi* is that other well-known Venetian speciality, *Fegato alla veneziana* (page 250). It can also precede *Pesce ai ferri alla moda dell' Adriatico* (page 191), *Spiedini di gamberoni dell' Adriatico* (page 193) or *Petti di pollo alla senese* (page 265). Otherwise, it will go well with any meat or poultry dish, except those, of course, that incorporate peas.

Minestra di sedano e riso
RICE AND CELERY SOUP

For four

4 sticks celery, diced (see Step 1 below)	450 ml ($\frac{3}{4}$ pint) broth (page 8) **or** 1 chicken stock cube dissolved in the same quantity of water
6 tablespoons olive oil	
Half small onion, finely chopped	3 tablespoons freshly grated Parmesan cheese
25 g (1 oz) butter	
200 g (7 oz) raw rice, preferably Italian Arborio rice	2 tablespoons chopped parsley

1 Wash the celery stalks well, strip them of most of their strings with a potato peeler, and dice. Put the diced celery, olive oil and salt in a saucepan and add enough water to cover. Bring to a steady simmer, cover, and cook until the celery is tender but not soft. Turn off the heat but do not drain.

2 Put the chopped onion in another saucepan or stockpot with the butter and sauté over medium heat until pale gold but not browned.

3 Add half the celery to the saucepan with the onion, using a slotted spoon. Sauté the celery for 2 or 3 minutes, then add the rice and stir it until it is well coated. Add all the broth.

4 Purée the rest of the celery, with all its cooking liquid, through a mouli-légumes directly into the saucepan containing the rice. Bring to a steady simmer, cover, and cook until the rice is tender but firm to the bite, about 15 to 20 minutes.

5 Stir in the grated cheese, turn off the heat, add the chopped parsley, and mix. Serve promptly, before the rice becomes too soft.

MENU SUGGESTIONS

This tasty but not overwhelming soup would be a good choice if you are going to follow with *Polpettine* (page 210), *Fagioli dall'occhio con salsicce* (page 244), *Trippa alla parmigiana* (page 247) or *Coda alla vaccinara* (page 245), which has a delicious touch of celery of its own.

Zuppa di scarola e riso
ESCAROLE AND RICE SOUP

Scarola is a broad-leafed salad green from the chicory family. It is marvellous in soup as well as in salads. There are probably as many ways to cook it as there are leaves in a head of escarole, but many make it either too bland and retiring or else too aggressively flavoured. This version, where the escarole is first briefly sautéed in butter with lightly browned onions, stays at a happy distance from the two extremes.

For four

1 head of escarole (350 to 450 g [1 lb])
2 tablespoons finely chopped onion
60 g (2 oz) butter
Salt
850 ml (1½ pints) broth (page 8) **or** 2 chicken stock cubes dissolved in the same amount of water

100 g (3½ oz) raw rice, preferably Italian Arborio rice
3 tablespoons freshly grated Parmesan cheese

1 Detach all the escarole leaves from the head and discard any that are bruised, wilted or discoloured. Wash all the rest in various changes of cold water until thoroughly clean. Cut into ribbons 12 mm ($\frac{1}{2}$ inch) wide and set aside.

2 In a stockpot sauté the chopped onion in the butter over medium heat until nicely browned. Add the escarole and a light sprinkling of salt. Briefly sauté the escarole, stirring it once or twice, then add 150 ml ($\frac{1}{4}$ pint) of the broth, cover the pot, and cook over very low heat until the escarole is tender – from 25 minutes to more than three-quarters of an hour, depending on the freshness and tenderness of the escarole.

3 When the escarole is tender, add the rest of the broth, raise the heat slightly, and cover. When the broth comes to the boil, add the rice and cover. Cook for 15 to 20 minutes, stirring from time to time, until the rice is *al dente*, firm to the bite. Off the heat, mix in the Parmesan cheese. Check salt, spoon into soup plates, and serve.

Note   Do not cook the soup ahead of time with the rice in it. The rice will become mushy. If you must do it ahead of time, stop at the end of Step 2. About 25 minutes before serving, add the 700 ml ($1\frac{1}{4}$ pints) of broth to the escarole, bring to the boil, and finish cooking as in Step 3.

MENU SUGGESTIONS

Follow the suggestions for *Minestra di sedano e riso* (page 54). This dish can also precede *Arrosto di agnello al ginepro* (page 236).

Minestrina di spinaci
SPINACH SOUP

For five or six

570 g ($1\frac{1}{4}$ lb) frozen leaf spinach, thawed, **or** scant 1 kg (2 lb) fresh spinach
60 g (2 oz) butter
450 ml ($\frac{3}{4}$ pint) broth (page 8) **or** 1 chicken stock cube dissolved in the same quantity of water

450 ml ($\frac{3}{4}$ pint) milk
$\frac{1}{4}$ teaspoon nutmeg
25 g (1 oz) freshly grated Parmesan cheese
Salt, if necessary

1 Cook, squeeze dry, and chop the spinach as directed on page 130.

2 Put the chopped, cooked spinach and the butter in a stockpot. Sauté the spinach over medium heat for 2 to 3 minutes.

3 Add the broth, milk and nutmeg. Bring to a simmer, stirring frequently.

4 Add the Parmesan cheese and cook for 1 more minute, stirring two to three times. Check salt. Serve immediately, with *crostini* (page 75).

MENU SUGGESTIONS

This soup can precede any meat or poultry. It goes particularly well with any of the roasts of lamb on pages 235–8, *Costolettine di agnello fritte* (page 239), *Cervella fritta* (page 253) or *Fegato di vitello fritto* (page 252).

Minestrone di Romagna

VEGETABLE SOUP

A vegetable soup will tell you where you are in Italy almost as precisely as a map. There are the soups of the south, leaning heavily on tomato, garlic and oil, sometimes containing pasta; there are those of the centre, heavily fortified with beans; the soups of the north, with rice; those of the Riviera, with fresh herbs; and there are nearly as many variations in between as there are local cooks. In Romagna, very little is put into *minestrone* beyond a variety of seasonal vegetables, whose separate characteristics give way and inter-mingle through very slow cooking in broth. The result is a soup of mellow, dense flavour that recalls no vegetable in particular but all of them at once.

It is not necessary to prepare all the vegetables ahead of time although you may do so if it suits you. The vegetables do not go into the pot all at once, but in the sequence indicated, and while one vegetable is slowly cook-ing in oil and butter you can peel and cut another. I find this method more efficient and less tedious than preparing all the vegetables at one time, and somehow it produces a better-tasting soup. In any event, cook each vegetable 2 or 3 minutes, at least, before adding the next.

For six to eight

8 tablespoons olive oil
40 g (1½ oz) butter
3 large onions, thinly sliced

4 carrots, diced
2 sticks celery, diced
250 g (8¾ oz) potatoes, peeled, diced

200 g (7 oz) fresh white beans, if available, **or** 400 g (14 oz) tinned *cannellini* beans **or** 120 g (4¼ oz) dried white beans, cooked as directed on page 67
2 medium zucchini, diced (see note below)
100 g (3½ oz) French beans, diced
150 to 200 g (5 to 8 oz) shredded cabbage, preferably Savoy cabbage

1·5 litres (2½ pints) broth (page 8) **or** 3 beef stock cubes dissolved in the same quantity of water
The crust from a 500 g or 1 kg (1 or 2 lb) piece of Parmesan cheese, carefully scraped clean (optional)
175 g (6 oz) tinned Italian tomatoes, with their juice
40 g (1½ oz) freshly grated Parmesan cheese

1 Choose a stockpot large enough for all the ingredients. Put in the oil, butter and sliced onion and cook over medium-low heat until the onion softens and is pale gold in colour but not browned. Add the diced carrots and cook for 2 to 3 minutes, stirring once or twice. Repeat this procedure with the celery, potatoes, white beans (if you are using the fresh beans), zucchini and French beans, cooking each one a few minutes and stirring. Then add the shredded cabbage and cook for about 6 minutes, giving the pot an occasional stir.

2 Add the broth, the cheese crust, the tomatoes and their juice, and salt. (Be sparing with the salt, especially if you are using tinned broth. You can correct the seasoning later.) Cover and cook at a very slow boil for at least 3 hours. If necessary, you can stop the cooking at any time and resume it later on. (*Minestrone* must never be thin and watery, so cook until it is soupy thick. If you should find that the soup is becoming *too* thick, you can add another cup of home-made broth or water. Do not add more tinned broth.)

3 Fifteen minutes before the soup is done, add the tinned or cooked dry beans (if you are not using fresh ones). Just before turning off the heat, remove the cheese crust, stir in the grated cheese, then taste and check salt.

Note   Before dicing the zucchini, scrub thoroughly in cold water to remove all earth – and if still in doubt, peel them.

Minestrone, unlike most cooked vegetable dishes, is even better when warmed up the next day. It keeps for up to a week in the refrigerator.

MENU SUGGESTIONS

Minestrone goes very well with roasts of all kinds, particularly lamb. You can safely follow it with any meat course that does not include any vegetables.

Minestrone freddo alla milanese
COLD MINESTRONE

One of the few consolations of a hot Milan summer is this basil-scented cold *minestrone*. The *trattorie* make it fresh every morning, fill the soup plates, and set them out along with the rest of the day's specialities displayed near the entrance: fresh-picked vegetables, a poached fish, mountain prosciutto, sweet melons. By noon the *minestrone* is precisely the right temperature and consistency, and shortly thereafter it is all snapped up.

This is the most beautiful way in which one can revive left-over *minestrone*, and, of course, not only can it be made ahead of time, it *must* be made ahead of time.

For four

450 ml (¾ pint) left-over *Minestrone di Romagna* (page 57)
450 ml (¾ pint) water
100 g (3½ oz) raw rice, preferably Italian Arborio rice
Salt

Freshly ground pepper, about 8 twists of the mill
25 g (1 oz) freshly grated Parmesan cheese
8 good-sized fresh basil leaves, cut into 4 or 5 strips each

1 In a stockpot, bring the soup and 450 ml (¾ pint) of water to the boil. Add the rice, stirring it with a wooden spoon. When the soup returns to the boil, add salt and pepper, cover the pot, and turn the heat down to medium-low. Stir from time to time. Test the rice after 10 to 12 minutes. It should be very firm, because it will continue to soften as it cools in the plate. Check salt.

2 When the rice is done, ladle the soup into four individual soup plates, add the grated cheese and basil, mix well, and allow to cool. Serve at room temperature.

Note Never refrigerate the soup; always serve it the same day it is made.

MENU SUGGESTIONS

Bear in mind that this is a dish for warm weather. The second course could be a cold boiled fish with mayonnaise, *Vitello tonnato* (page 233) or *Scaloppine di vitello al limone* (page 221).

MINESTRONE, COLD OR HOT, WITH PESTO

Cold Minestrone (*Minestrone freddo*, preceding page):

When the rice is done, at the end of Step 1, stir in 1 tablespoon of *pesto* (page 119). Ladle into individual soup plates, omitting the basil in Step 2.

Hot Minestrone (*Minestrone di Romagna*, page 57):

Add 1½ to 2 tablespoons of *pesto* (page 119) at the end of Step 3. If you are making the soup ahead of time, add the *pesto* when reheating, just before serving.

Passatelli

Passatelli consists of eggs, Parmesan cheese and breadcrumbs formed into short, thick, cylindrical strands by pressing the mixture through a special tool. The strands are then boiled very briefly in home-made meat broth. The original tool can be replaced by a mouli-légumes, but the home-made broth is absolutely essential and cannot be replaced by tinned consommé or stock made from cubes.

This soup is native only to the Romagna section of Emilia, a narrow strip of territory east of Bologna, bordering on the Adriatic Sea. The *romagnoli* want their food to be satisfying but simple and delicate in taste. This soup is all these things and, moreover, extremely quick to prepare.

For six

1¾ litres (2½ pints) broth from *Bollito misto* (page 273) **or** broth (page 8)

75 g (2½ oz) freshly grated Parmesan cheese

40 g (1½ oz) fine, dry plain breadcrumbs

¼ teaspoon nutmeg (see note below)

2 eggs

1 Bring the broth to a steady, moderate boil in an uncovered pot. While the broth is coming to the boil, combine the grated Parmesan, the breadcrumbs and the nutmeg on a pastry board or large chopping block. Make a mound with a well in the centre. Break the eggs into the well and knead all the ingredients together. It should have the tender, granular consistency

Drop the passatelli *directly into the boiling broth.*

of cooked maize porridge (*polenta*). (If, as sometimes happens, the eggs are a bit on the large side, you may have to add a little more Parmesan and breadcrumbs.)

2 Put the disc with the largest holes into your mouli-légumes. When the broth boils, press the Parmesan-breadcrumb-and-egg mixture through the mouli-légumes directly into the boiling broth. Cook at a slow boil for a minute or two at the most. Turn off the heat and allow to stand for 4 to 5 minutes, then ladle into warm soup plates and serve with a bowl of freshly grated Parmesan.

Note The nutmeg quantity can be increased slightly, according to taste, but the flavour of nutmeg should never be more than hinted at.

The natural second course for *passatelli* is *Bollito misto* (page 273), which should have produced the broth for the soup. If you are making *passatelli* with other broth, you can follow it with any simple roasted meat or poultry.

Zuppa di piselli secchi e patate

SPLIT GREEN PEA AND POTATO SOUP

This is a good, simple soup. It requires so little looking after that I usually make it on the side while I am cooking other things. When it is done, I put it away in the refrigerator, where it keeps perfectly for several days, and then I have a marvellous soup on hand, all ready to heat up at a moment's notice. There is something comforting about having a robust soup like this one to fall back on, especially on a blustery winter evening. The only thing to look out for when reheating is that the soup should not become too thick. If it does, just add some more broth or water.

For six

220 g (8 oz) split green peas, washed and drained

2 medium potatoes, peeled and roughly cut up

$1\frac{1}{4}$ litres ($2\frac{1}{4}$ pints) broth (page 8) **or** 1 chicken stock cube dissolved in the same quantity of water

2 tablespoons chopped onion

3 tablespoons olive oil

40 g ($1\frac{1}{2}$ oz) butter

3 tablespoons freshly grated Parmesan cheese

Salt

1 Cook the split peas and potatoes at a moderate boil in 700 ml ($1\frac{1}{4}$ pints) of the broth until both are quite tender. Then purée the peas and potatoes, with their cooking liquid, through a mouli-légumes and into a stockpot.

2 Put the onion in a small frying pan with the oil and butter and sauté over medium-high heat until a rich golden colour.

3 Add all the contents of the frying pan to the stockpot; then add the remaining broth and bring to a moderate boil. Cook, stirring occasionally, until the oil and butter are dissolved in the broth. Just before turning off the heat, mix in the grated cheese, then taste and check salt. Serve with additional grated cheese and *crostini* (page 75).

Note If you are doing the soup in advance, add the cheese only when you reheat it. Allow the soup to cool thoroughly before refrigerating.

MENU SUGGESTIONS

Any roasted meat or poultry would make an excellent second course. Other possibilities are *Il bollito rifatto con le cipolle* (page 207), *Polpettine* (page 210), *Fagottini di vitello leccabaffi* (page 225), *Spezzatino di vitello alla salvia* (page 230), *Cotechino* (page 242), if you are not serving it with lentils, *Coniglio in padella* (page 271) or *Fegato di vitello fritto* (page 252).

Zuppa di lenticchie
LENTIL SOUP

For four

2 tablespoons finely chopped onion
3 tablespoons olive oil
40 g (1½ oz) butter
2 tablespoons finely chopped celery
2 tablespoons finely chopped carrot
30 g (1¼ oz) shredded *pancetta*,
    prosciutto or green bacon
220 g (8 oz) tinned Italian tomatoes,
    cut up, with their juice

220 g (½ lb) dried brown lentils,
    washed and drained
1 litre (1¾ pints) broth (page 8) **or** 1
    beef stock cube dissolved in
    the same quantity of water
Salt, if necessary
Freshly ground pepper, 4 to 6 twists
    of the mill
3 tablespoons freshly grated
    Parmesan cheese

1 Put the onion in a stockpot with the oil and 25 g (1 oz) of the butter and sauté over medium-high heat until a light golden brown.

2 Add the celery and carrot and continue sautéing for 2 to 3 minutes, stirring from time to time.

3 Add the shredded *pancetta*, and sauté for 1 more minute.

4 Add the cut-up tomatoes and their juice, and adjust the heat so that they cook at a gentle simmer for 25 minutes, uncovered. Stir from time to time with a wooden spoon.

5 Add the lentils, stirring and turning them two or three times, then add the broth, salt and pepper. Cover and cook, at a steady simmer, until the

lentils are tender. (Cooking time is about 45 minutes, but it varies greatly from lentils to lentils, so that the only reliable method is to taste them. Note, too, that some lentils absorb a surprising amount of liquid. If this happens add more home-made broth or water to keep the soup from getting too thick.)

6 When the lentils are cooked, check salt; then, off the heat, swirl in the remaining butter and the grated cheese. Serve with additional freshly grated cheese.

MENU SUGGESTIONS

This robust soup can precede any meat dish that does not have a strong tomato presence. Good choices would be *Stracotto al Barolo* (page 206), *Il bollito rifatto con le cipolle* (page 207), *Spezzatino di vitello alla salvia* (page 230), *Arrosto di agnello pasquale col vino bianco* (page 235), *Arrosto di maiale al latte* (page 240), *Arrosto di maiale all' alloro* (page 241), any of the roasted, grilled or fricasseed chickens (except the one with tomatoes), and *Fegato alla veneziana* (page 250).

◆

Zuppa di lenticchie e riso
RICE AND LENTIL SOUP

Lentil soup can be made in large batches and frozen. When reheating it, you can vary the basic formula by the simple and pleasant addition of rice.

For six

Zuppa di lenticchie (page 63)	100 g (3½ oz) raw rice, preferably
25 ml (⅝ pint) broth (page 8) **or** 1 beef stock cube dissolved in the same quantity of water	Italian Arborio rice Salt, if necessary

Bring the soup to the boil, then add the broth. When the soup returns to the boil, add the rice and stir with a wooden spoon. Cook at a moderate boil until the rice is tender but firm to the bite, about 15 minutes. (If the rice you are using absorbs too much liquid, add more home-made broth or water.) Taste and check salt. Serve with freshly grated Parmesan cheese.

MENU SUGGESTIONS
Follow the ones for *Zuppa di lenticchie* (preceding recipe).

La Jota

BEANS AND SAUERKRAUT SOUP

Trieste has long been the most passionately Italian of cities, but this hearty bean soup of hers with potatoes, sauerkraut and bacon speaks with an unmistakable accent from her Austro-Hungarian past.

An important step in the preparation of the soup is the slow stewing of the sauerkraut to blunt its sharpness. Although *Jota* requires much slow cooking, it can be done at your convenience because the soup should be served at least a day later to give its flavours time for full development. If you must, you can even interrupt its preparation at the end of any step, allow the soup to cool, refrigerate it, and the following day resume cooking where you left off.

When completed, *Jota* is enriched with a final flavouring called *pestà*. Although the components differ – this *pestà* contains salt pork so finely chopped that it is nearly reduced to a paste, hence the name – this procedure strongly recalls the addition of flavoured oil in Tuscan bean soups.

For eight

Scant 1 kg (2 lb) fresh cranberry
    beans (unshelled weight) (see
    note, page 69)
110 g ($\frac{1}{4}$ lb) bacon, in 25-mm (1-inch)
    strips
450 g (1 lb) sauerkraut, drained

$\frac{1}{2}$ teaspoon cumin
350 g ($\frac{3}{4}$ lb) pork cheek **or** pork rind
1 medium potato, coarsely diced
Salt
3 tablespoons cornflour

The pestà
25 g (1 oz) finely chopped salt pork
1 tablespoon chopped onion
1 clove garlic, peeled and chopped

Salt
3 teaspoons plain flour

1 Shell the beans, rinse them in cold water, and put them in a pot with 700 ml (1$\frac{1}{4}$ pints) of water. Bring to the boil, then cover and adjust the heat

so that they cook at a very slow boil. Cook until tender, about 45 minutes, depending on the beans. When done, set them aside in their own liquid.

2 While the beans are cooking, sauté the bacon in a medium saucepan over moderate heat for 2 to 3 minutes. Add the drained sauerkraut and the $\frac{1}{2}$ teaspoon cumin, mix with the bacon, and cook in the bacon fat for about 2 minutes. Then add 250 ml (scant $\frac{1}{2}$ pint) water, cover the pan, and cook at very low heat for 1 hour. At the end of an hour the sauerkraut should be very much reduced in volume and there should be no liquid in the pan. If there is still some left, uncover the pan and allow the liquid to evaporate over medium heat.

3. While the beans are cooking and the sauerkraut is stewing, put the pork cheek or pork rind in a stockpot with 1 litre ($1\frac{3}{4}$ pints) of water and bring to the boil. After it has boiled for 5 minutes, drain, discarding the cooking liquid, and cut the head or rind into 18- to 25-mm- ($\frac{3}{4}$- to 1-inch-) wide strips. (Do not be alarmed if it is very tough. It will soften away to a creamy consistency in later cooking.)

4 Return the cut-up pork to the stockpot. Add the diced potato, 700 ml ($1\frac{1}{4}$ pints) of water, and salt. Cover and cook at a slow but steady boil for 1 hour.

5 Add the beans with their cooking liquid, cover, and cook at a very slow, quiet boil for 30 minutes.

6 Add the sauerkraut, cover, and cook, always at a very slow boil, for 1 hour.

7 Add the cornflour in a thin stream, stirring it thoroughly into the soup, add 450 ml ($\frac{3}{4}$ pint) of water, cover, and cook at the same slow boil for 1 hour. Stir from time to time.

8 When the soup is nearly ready, prepare the *pestà*. Put the chopped salt pork and the onion in a small saucepan and sauté over medium heat until the onion is pale gold. Add the garlic and sauté it until it is nicely coloured. Then add salt and the flour, gradually, stirring thoroughly and cooking it until it, too, is a rich, blonde colour.

9 Add the *pestà* to the soup, stirring thoroughly, and simmer for 20 minutes more before serving.

MENU SUGGESTIONS

This is a 'heavyweight' among soups and should be balanced in the second course by grilled or roasted meat or poultry. A substantial but suitable meat course with a congenial Triestine flavour is *Lo 'schinco'* (page 219).

Cooking Dried Beans

When fresh beans are not available, most Italian cooks use dried beans rather than tinned pre-cooked beans. Dried beans are not only much more economical than tinned beans, but, when properly cooked, they have a better texture than the generally mushy tinned variety. You can buy packed dried beans in all supermarkets, but in many cities there are Greek, Italian and other shops that sell them loose, by weight. These are a still better buy than the prepacked beans, and usually offer a far broader selection.

Dried beans should always be soaked before cooking, otherwise their skins will burst before the beans become tender. There are many techniques for cooking dried beans. The following has given consistently successful results.

1 Put the desired quantity of beans in a bowl and cover them by 50 mm (2 inches) with cold water. Let them soak overnight in a warm place, such as over the pilot flame of a gas stove. (In that case be careful not to use a plastic bowl!)

2 The following day, preheat the oven to 170°C/325°F/Mark 3.

3 Rinse and drain the beans, put them in a flameproof casserole, and cover with cold water by 50 mm (2 inches).

4 Bring the beans to a moderate boil on top of the stove, then cover the pot and place in the middle level of the preheated oven. Cook until tender, about 40 to 60 minutes, depending on the beans. Keep them in their liquid until you are ready to use them.

Zuppa di cannellini con aglio e prezzemolo
BEAN SOUP WITH PARSLEY AND GARLIC

This is indeed a bean-lover's soup. It is virtually all beans, with very little liquid, and just a whiff of garlic. It is thick enough to be served as a vegetable dish next to a good roast. If you like it thinner all you have to do is add a little more broth or water.

For four to six

1 clove garlic, peeled and chopped
8 tablespoons olive oil
2 tablespoons chopped parsley
350 g (12¼ oz) dried white kidney
    beans or other white beans,
cooked as directed on page 67
and drained, **or** 1·15 kg (2½ lb)
tinned *cannellini* beans,
drained

Salt
Freshly ground pepper, about 8
    twists of the mill
250 ml (scant ½ pint) broth
    (page 8), **or** chicken
    bouillon, **or** water
Toasted Italian bread

1 Put the garlic in a large saucepan with the olive oil and sauté over medium heat until just lightly coloured.

2 Add the parsley, stir two or three times, then add the drained, cooked beans, salt and pepper. Cover and simmer gently for about 6 minutes.

3 Put about one quarter of the beans from the pan into a mouli-légumes and purée them back into the pan, together with the broth or water. Simmer for another 6 minutes, then taste and check salt. Serve over slices of toasted Italian bread.

MENU SUGGESTIONS

This needs to be balanced by a fairly substantial, forthright second course. Serve it before any roasted meat or poultry, or before *Trippa alla parmigiana* (page 247) or *Fegato alla veneziana* (page 250).

Pasta e fagioli

BEANS AND PASTA SOUP

For six

2 tablespoons chopped onion
4 tablespoons olive oil (slightly less if
    there is much fat on the pork
    you are using)
1 carrot, chopped

1 stick celery, chopped
3 or 4 pork ribs **or** a ham bone with
    some meat on them **or** 2 small
    pork chops

150 g (5¼ oz) tinned Italian tomatoes, cut up, with their juice

Scant 1 kg (2 lb) fresh cranberry beans (unshelled weight) (see note below)

700 ml (1¼ pints), approximately, broth (page 8 **or** 1 beef stock cube dissolved in the same quantity of water

Salt

Freshly ground pepper, about 6 twists of the mill

Maltagliati (page 103), made with 1 egg and 100 g (3½ oz) plain flour (basic pasta recipe, page 96), **or** 175 g (6 oz) small, tubular factory-made pasta

2 tablespoons freshly grated Parmesan cheese

1 Put the onion in a stockpot with the oil and sauté over medium heat until pale gold.

2 Add the carrot, celery and pork, and sauté for about 10 minutes, stirring the vegetables and turning the pork from time to time.

3 Add the chopped tomatoes and their juice, turn the heat down to medium-low and cook for 10 minutes.

4 If you are using fresh cranberry beans, shell the beans, rinse them in cold water and add to the pot. Stir two or three times, then add the broth. Cover the pot, adjust the heat so that the liquid is bubbling at a very moderate boil, but at a bit more than a simmer, and cook for 45 minutes to 1 hour, or until the beans are tender. (If you are using pre-cooked beans, cook the tomatoes for 20 minutes instead of 10, as in Step 3, then add the drained beans. Let the beans cook in the tomatoes for 5 minutes, stirring thoroughly, then add the broth and bring to a moderate boil.)

5 Scoop up about 8 tablespoons of beans and mash them through a mouli-légumes back into the pot.

6 Add salt and pepper.

7 Check the soup for density; add more home-made broth or water if needed, and bring the liquid to a steady boil. Add the pasta. If you are using fresh egg pasta, stop the cooking 1 minute after you have dropped it in. If you are using dried pasta, taste and stop the cooking when the pasta is very firm to the bite. (The soup should stand for about 10 minutes before serving, so if you do not stop the cooking when the pasta is very firm it will be quite mushy by the time it gets to the table.) Just before serving, add the grated cheese.

Note Cranberry beans are pink-and-white marbled beans, and they add a wonderful flavour to this soup. If they are not available use 180 g (6¼ oz) dried Borlotti beans, cooked as directed on page 67, or 600 g (21 oz) tinned *cannellini* beans or other white beans, drained. The soup can be prepared entirely ahead of time up to, but not including, Step 7. Add the pasta only when you are going to serve the soup.

This fine, comforting soup can precede any substantial dish of meat or poultry. Particularly nice would be *Bistecca alla diavola* (page 203), *Lo 'schinco'* (page 219), *Arrosto di agnello pasquale col vino bianco* (page 235), *Arrosto di maiale all'alloro* (page 241), *Pollo coi funghi secchi* (page 262), *Coniglio in padella* (page 271) or *Fegato alla veneziana* (page 250).

Zuppa di cavolo nero
RED CABBAGE SOUP

This is as much a pork-and-beans dish as it is a cabbage soup, and, along with *cassoulet*, it has an honoured place in that hearty family of Mediterranean dishes using beans and pork or beans and lamb. It is a Tuscan speciality, as are so many bean dishes in Italy, and every Tuscan cook has a personal version of it. A constant element of this and many other Tuscan soups is the garlic-and-rosemary-flavoured hot oil that is added to the soup just before serving.

You should not hesitate to take some freedom with the basic recipe, varying its proportions of sausage, beans and cabbage according to taste. In the recipe as given here, soup, meat course and vegetable are combined in one hearty dish that is a meal in itself. It can be made even heartier by increasing the quantity of sausage. On the other hand, you can eliminate the sausage altogether, substituting for it any piece of pork on a bone, and increase the quantity of broth to make a true soup that will fit as a first course into a substantial country menu.

This dish develops even better flavour when warmed up one or two days later, which means that you can prepare it entirely in advance.

For six

110 g ($\frac{1}{4}$ lb) fresh pork rind
$\frac{1}{2}$ clove garlic, peeled and chopped
2 tablespoons chopped onion
25 g (1 oz) thinly shredded *pancetta*
4 tablespoons olive oil
450 g (1 lb) red cabbage, coarsely shredded
1 large stick celery, chopped

3 tablespoons tinned Italian tomato, drained and coarsely chopped
A tiny pinch of thyme
700 ml ($1\frac{1}{4}$ pints) (approximately) broth (page 8) or $1\frac{1}{2}$ beef stock cubes dissolved in the same quantity of water
Salt

Freshly ground pepper, 6 to 8 twists
    of the mill
220 g ($\frac{1}{2}$ lb) *luganega* sausage or other
    mild sausage (see page 8)

180 g ($6\frac{1}{4}$ oz) dried *cannellini* beans or
other white beans, cooked as
directed on page 67 and
drained, **or** 600 g (21 oz)
tinned *cannellini* or other white
beans, drained

For the flavoured oil

2 large or 3 medium cloves garlic,
    lightly crushed with a heavy
    knife handle and peeled

4 tablespoons olive oil
$\frac{1}{2}$ teaspoon chopped rosemary leaves

1 Put the pork rind in a small saucepan, cover by about 25 mm (1 inch) with cold water, and bring to the boil. After it has boiled for 1 minute, drain and allow to cool. Cut into strips about 12 mm ($\frac{1}{2}$ inch) wide and 50 to 75 mm (2 to 3 inches) long and set aside.

2 Put the garlic, onion and *pancetta* in a stockpot with the oil and sauté over medium heat until the onion and garlic are very lightly coloured.

3 Add the shredded cabbage, the chopped celery, the pork rind, the tomato and a tiny pinch of thyme. Cook over medium-low heat until the cabbage has completely softened. Stir thoroughly from time to time.

4 When the cabbage has become soft, add the broth, 2 teaspoons salt, and pepper, cover the pot, and cook at very low heat for 2 to $2\frac{1}{2}$ hours. This cooking may be done at various stages, spread over two or three days. In fact the soup acquires even better flavour when reheated in this manner.

5 Off the heat, uncover the pot, tilt it slightly, and draw off as much as possible of the fat that rises to the surface.

6 Brown the sausage in a small pan for 6 to 8 minutes over medium-low heat. They need no other fat than that which they throw off, which you will discard after they are browned on all sides.

7 Return the pot to the heat and bring to a simmer. Add the browned sausages, drained of their fat. Purée half the cooked beans into the pot and stir well. Cover and simmer for 15 minutes.

8 Add the remaining whole beans and correct for desired thickness by adding more home-made broth or water. Taste and check salt. Cover and simmer for 10 more minutes. (The soup may be prepared entirely ahead of time up to and including this point. Always return it to a simmer before proceeding with the next step.)

9 Put the crushed garlic cloves and the oil in a small pan and sauté over lively heat until the garlic is nicely browned. Add the chopped rosemary, turn off the heat, and stir two or three times. Pour the oil

through a sieve into the soup pot, cover, and simmer for 15 minutes more. Serve with good, crusty Italian or French bread.

MENU SUGGESTIONS

If you are using this as a meal-in-itself dish, you might still precede it with either of the baked oyster dishes on page 28, *Cozze e vongole passate ai ferri* (page 30), *Peperoni e acciughe* (page 32), *Insalata di funghi e formaggio* (page 41) or a dish of assorted cold meats. If you decide to omit the sausages and use this as a soup, it can precede any roast of meat or poultry, and would also go well with *Polpettone alla toscana* (page 211), *Fegato di vitello fritto* (page 252) or *Fegatelli di maiale con la rete* (page 255). This would make a good, stout weekend lunch in the country, with the possibility of a long walk later to work it off.

Zuppa di ceci

CHICK PEA SOUP

This savoury soup can be made entirely ahead of time, refrigerated for as long as ten days, and it will lose none of its taste or aroma when warmed up. Many like to purée the whole soup through a mouli-légumes, in which case it may become necessary to add a little more broth until the soup has the consistency of cream. It is served then with *crostini* (page 75). If you try this soup and like it, make more than you need the next time. You will then be able to use it again as the base for *Zuppa di ceci e maltagliati* (page 74) or *Zuppa di ceci e riso* (page 74).

For four to six

140 g (5 oz) dried chick peas **or** 400 g (14 oz) tinned chick peas
4 whole cloves garlic, peeled
6 tablespoons olive oil
1½ teaspoons very finely crushed or freshly chopped rosemary leaves

140 g (5 oz) tinned Italian tomatoes, roughly chopped, with their juice
250 ml (scant ½ pint) broth (page 8) or 1 beef stock cube dissolved in the same quantity of water
Salt, if necessary
Freshly ground pepper, about 4 twists of the mill

1 If you are using dried chick peas you must first soak them over-night. Put them in a large enough bowl, add water to cover by 50 mm (2 inches), and let them soak all night in a warm corner of the kitchen. (Over the gas pilot light would be an excellent place, but do not use a plastic bowl.)

2 The following morning preheat the oven to 170°C/325°F/Mark 3. Discard the water in which the chick peas have soaked, put them in a medium-sized stockpot, add enough water to come up 25 mm (1 inch) above the chick peas (do *not* add salt), and bring them to the boil on top of the stove. Cover tightly and cook in the middle level of the oven for $1\frac{1}{2}$ hours, or until the chick peas are tender. (At this stage they are almost exactly equivalent to the tinned variety, except that they are not salted and have slightly better texture. Tinned chick peas are very con-venient, but they are also considerably more expensive. Which ones to use will have to be your decision. It does not matter to the soup, although you must watch the liquid level carefully if using cooked dried chick peas and add more broth if necessary.) I always peel chick peas before using them in soup, but it is a chore, and if you would rather put up with the skin than with the chore you can omit it.

3 Sauté the garlic cloves in the olive oil in a heavy casserole over medium-high heat. When the garlic is well browned remove it. Add the rosemary to the oil, stir, then add the chopped tomatoes with their juice. Cook over medium heat for about 20 to 25 minutes, or until the toma-toes separate from the oil.

4 Add the drained chick peas and cook for 5 minutes, turning them in the sauce. Add the broth or the dissolved bouillon cube, bring to the boil, cover, and keep at a steady, moderate boil for 15 minutes. Taste and check salt, add freshly ground pepper and allow to boil about 1 minute more, uncovered. Serve hot.

Note If you are making the soup ahead of time, add the salt and pep-per when you warm it up.

Zuppa di ceci e riso
CHICK PEA AND RICE SOUP

For eight

Zuppa di ceci (page 72)
700 ml (1¼ pints) (approximately)
    broth (page 8) **or** 2 bouillon
    cubes dissolved in the same
    quantity of water

200 g (7 oz) raw rice
Salt, if necessary

1 Purée the basic chick pea soup through a mouli-légumes into a stockpot. Add the broth and bring to the boil. Add the rice, stir, cover the pot and cook at a steady but moderate boil. Stir from time to time, and after 10 or 12 minutes check to see if more broth is required. (Some types of rice absorb more liquid than others, and the soup must be fairly liquid or it is not a soup.)

2 The soup is done when the rice is tender but firm, after 15 to more than 20 minutes, according to the type of rice you are using. Taste and check salt. Allow to stand for a minute or two, then spoon into soup plates and serve.

Note This soup, or any other that contains rice, cannot be prepared ahead of time because the rice will become mushy.

Zuppa di ceci e maltagliati
CHICK PEA AND PASTA SOUP

For eight

Zuppa di ceci (page 72)
450 ml (¾ pint) (approximately) broth
    (page 8) **or** 2 bouillon cubes
    dissolved in the same quantity
    of water

Maltagliati (page 103), made with 1
    egg and 100 g (3½ oz) of flour
    (basic pasta recipe, page 96),
    or 220 g (½ lb) small
    commercial pasta
Salt, if necessary
2 to 3 tablespoons freshly grated
    Parmesan cheese

1 Purée about one-third of the basic soup through a mouli-légumes into a stockpot. Add the rest of the soup and all the broth and bring to the boil. Add the pasta, stir, cover the pot and cook at a steady but moderate boil. If you are using freshly made pasta, watch it carefully because it cooks very rapidly, in a minute or less. Whatever pasta you may be using, stop the cooking when it is very firm to the bite, because the pasta continues to soften even after the heat is turned off. With commercial pasta you may have to add some liquid while cooking, if the soup becomes too thick.

2 Taste and check salt. Allow the soup to bubble for a few brief moments after you add salt, then turn off the heat and mix in the grated cheese. (Remember that Parmesan cheese is salty, so regulate the amount you add by the saltiness of the soup.) Allow to stand for a minute or two, spoon into soup plates, and serve.

Note   This soup cannot be prepared ahead of time because the pasta would become too soft.

MENU SUGGESTIONS

These chick pea soups, like all the bean soups, call for a substantial meat course to follow. Any of the lamb roasts on pages 235–8, or the *Arrosto di maiale all'alloro* (page 241), would be perfect. Grilled steak would be excellent too.

Crostini di pane per minestra
CROÛTONS

For four

4 slices firm-bodied, good-quality white bread	Vegetable oil, enough to come 12 mm ($\frac{1}{2}$ inch) up the side of the pan

1 Cut away the crusts from the bread and cut the slices into 12 mm ($\frac{1}{2}$ inch) squares.

2 Choose a medium-sized frying pan. (Since you need oil to a depth

of 12 mm ($\frac{1}{2}$ inch), it is wasteful to choose too broad a frying pan. If the bread does not fit in all at one time, it does not matter. Bread browns very rapidly and it can be done a few pieces at a time.) Heat the oil in the pan over moderately high heat. It should become hot enough for the bread to sizzle when it goes in. Test it first with one square. When the oil is hot, put in as much bread as will fit loosely in a single layer. Turn the heat down, because bread will burn quickly if the oil gets too hot, move the squares around in the pan, and as soon as they turn a light-gold colour transfer them with a slotted spoon or spatula to kitchen paper to drain. Finish doing all the squares, adjusting the heat as necessary so that the bread will brown lightly without burning.

Note   *Crostini* can be prepared several hours ahead of time. After more than a day, however, they acquire a stale, rancid taste.

HOW TO COOK PASTA

There is probably no single cooking process in any of the world's cuisines simpler than the boiling of pasta. This very simplicity appears to have had an unsettling effect on some writers, to judge from the curiously elaborate and often misleading procedures described in many Italian cookbooks. One book tells you to drop pasta into boiling water a little bit at a time. Another advises you to lift it painstakingly strand by strand when draining it. A third suggests you can keep pasta warm in a very low oven until you are ready to sauce it. Ah, pasta, what sins have been committed in thy name! Here is the way it is really done.

Water   It is important to cook pasta in abundant water, but it is not necessary to drown it. Italians calculate 1 litre of water per 100 grams of pasta. This works out to slightly more than 4 litres (7 pints) for 450 grams or 1 lb of pasta. Stick to just 4 litres (7 pints) of water for every pound of pasta. It will be quite sufficient.

Salt   When the water comes to the boil, add $1\frac{1}{2}$ heaped tablespoons of salt for every 4 litres (7 pints) of water. If the sauce you are going to be using is very bland, you may put in an additional $\frac{1}{2}$ tablespoon of salt.

When and how to put in the pasta   (Here we are talking of dried pasta. For fresh pasta, see page 107). Put in the pasta when the salted water has come to a rapid boil. Add all the pasta at once. When you put it in a little at a time, it cannot all cook evenly. If you are cooking long pasta, such as spaghetti or *perciatelli*, after dropping it in the pot you must bend it in the middle with a wooden spoon to force the strands entirely under water. Never, never break spaghetti in two. Stir the pasta with a wooden spoon to keep it from sticking together. Cover the pot after you put in the pasta to accelerate the water's return to the boil. Watch it, lest it boil over. When it returns to the boil, uncover, and cook at a lively but not too fierce a boil, until it is *al dente*.

Al dente   *Al dente* means 'firm to the bite', and that is how Italians eat pasta. Unfortunately, they are the only ones who do. Of course, it is not easy to switch to firm pasta when one is used to having it soft and mushy, and it is very tempting to ingratiate oneself with one's readers by not pressing the issue. The whole point of pasta, however, is its texture and consistency, and overcooking destroys these. Soft pasta is no more fit to eat than a limp and soggy slice of bread.

In the course of civilisation's long and erratic march, no other discovery has done more than, or possibly as much as, pasta has to promote man's happiness. It is therefore well worth learning how to turn it out at its best.

No foolproof cooking times for commercial pasta can be given, but you can begin by ignoring those on the box. They are invariably excessive. There are so many variables, such as the type and make of pasta, the hardness and quantity of water, the heat source, even the altitude (it is impossible to make good pasta at over 4,500 feet (1,372 metres) above sea level), that the only dependable procedure is to taste the pasta frequently while it boils. As soon as pasta begins to lose its stiffness and becomes just tender enough so that you can bite through without snapping it, it is done. You should try at first to stop the cooking when you think the pasta is still a little underdone. Do not be afraid to stop too early. It is probably already overcooked, and, in any case, it will continue to soften until it is served. Once you have learned to cook and eat pasta *al dente*, you will accept it no other way.

Draining, dressing and serving pasta   The instant pasta is done you must stop it cooking and drain it. Adding a glass of cold water to the pot as you turn off the heat is helpful, but it is not necessary if you are very quick about emptying the pot into the pasta colander. Give the colander a few vigorous sideways and up-and-down jerks to drain the pasta of all its water. Transfer the pasta without delay to a warm serving bowl. If grated cheese is called for, add it at this point and mix it into the pasta. The pasta's heat will melt it partially so that it will blend creamily with the sauce. Add the sauce and toss the pasta rapidly with two forks or a fork and spoon, coating it thoroughly with sauce. Add a thick pat of butter, unless you are using a sauce dominated by olive oil, toss briefly, and bring to the table immediately, serving it in warm soup plates.

Note   There are two important points to remember in this whole operation:

1 The moment pasta is done, drain it, toss it in the sauce, and serve with the briefest possible interval, because pasta continues to soften at every stage from the colander to the table.

2 Dress the pasta thoroughly, but avoid prolonged tossings and exaggerated liftings of strands into the air, because there is one thing worse than soft pasta and that is cold pasta.

Reheating   As a rule, pasta cannot be reheated, but some kinds of leftover pasta, such as *rigatoni* or *ziti*, can be turned into a very successful dish when baked (page 93).

Choosing pasta shapes   Although all pasta bought from a shop is made from the same, identical dough, the end result is determined by shape and size. Spaghetti is probably the most successful vehicle for the greatest variety of sauces. Thin spaghetti (spaghettini) is best for seafood sauces and for any sauce whose principal fat is olive oil. Ordinary spaghetti is ideal for butter-based white sauces or tomato sauces. The one sauce that somehow does not work very well with spaghetti is meat sauce. With meat sauce you ought to choose a substantial, stubby cut of pasta, such as *rigatoni*. Try it also with *conchiglie* (shells); their openings will trap little bits of meat. *Fusilli* and *rotelle* are splendid with dense, spicy cream and meat sauces, such as the sausage sauce on page 92, which cling deliciously to all their twists and curls. There are hundreds of pasta shapes, of which a dozen or more are easily available. You ought to experiment with all the ones you find, and develop your own favourite liaisons of pasta and sauce.

I strongly recommend that you try Italian pasta. It is vastly superior to other pastas because it really cooks to and holds that absolutely perfect degree of toothy tenderness which deserves to be called *al dente*. It also swells considerably in the cooking, which means that pound for pound it will go farther than locally made pasta. Such excellent brands as De Cecco and the commonly available Buitoni and Barilla can be found at all well-stocked Italian grocers, in a broad variety of shapes and cuts. Of non-Italian pastas the English Record brand, made by Pasta Foods in St Albans, which also turns up in supermarkets as an 'own brand', is probably the best.

Sughi di pomodoro

*FIVE TOMATO SAUCES FOR SPAGHETTI AND
OTHER PASTA*

We have all heard about the decline of the fresh tomato. To judge by the plastic-wrapped examples in the supermarkets not even the worst reports are exaggerated. The poor tomato is picked half ripe, gassed, shuttled great distances, and artificially quickened back to life. He who has never tasted a tomato honestly ripened on the vine by the heat of the summer sun cannot possibly believe that this is one of agricultural man's greatest triumphs, one of the most glorious products he has ever grown.

The situation is difficult, but not entirely hopeless. It is still possible to make a good sauce from fresh tomatoes, and it is something that everyone should experience before real tomatoes disappear altogether. You will have to limit yourself, in making these sauces, to those few weeks of the year when the tomatoes on the market are likely to be locally grown. The best tomatoes for this purpose, and those on which the recipes here are based, are the long, narrow plum tomatoes. They should feel reasonably firm, but yielding, not wooden to the touch. And they should be an even, intense red. If you use other varieties of tomatoes, you may have to increase the quantities, depending on how watery they are.

When choice, ripe, fresh tomatoes are not available, a good tomato sauce can be made with tinned imported Italian plum tomatoes. At the foot of each of the following five recipes there are instructions on how to substitute tinned tomatoes for fresh.

TOMATO SAUCE I

Of the three basic tomato sauces given here, this is the most concentrated and the most strongly flavoured. It goes well with all commercial pastas.

For six servings

Scant 1 kg (2 lb) fresh, ripe plum
    tomatoes
8 tablespoons olive oil
1 medium onion, finely chopped

1 carrot, finely chopped
1 stick celery, finely chopped
Salt
$\frac{1}{4}$ teaspoon granulated sugar

1 Wash the tomatoes in cold water. Cut them in half, lengthways.

Cook in a covered saucepan or stockpot at a steady simmer for 10 minutes. Uncover and simmer gently for 1½ hours more.

2 Purée the tomatoes through a mouli-légumes into a bowl. Discard the seeds and skin.

3 Rinse and dry the saucepan. Put in the olive oil, then add the chopped onion, and lightly sauté over medium heat until just translucent, not browned. Add the carrot and celery and sauté for another minute. Add the puréed tomato, salt and sugar, and cook at a gentle simmer, uncovered, for 20 minutes. Stir from time to time while cooking.

If using tinned tomatoes: Use a 400-g (14-oz) tin, omit Steps 1 and 2, and simmer for 45 minutes instead of 20.

TOMATO SAUCE II

Although this sauce is made with the same ingredients as Tomato Sauce I, it has a fresher, more delicate flavour. There are two reasons for this. First, the tomato is cooked much less, just enough to concentrate it, but not so long that its garden-sweet taste is altered. Second, the vegetables are cooked together with the tomato instead of undergoing a preliminary sautéing in oil. It is an excellent all-purpose sauce for every kind of pasta, from spaghettini to such thicker, stubby cuts as *penne* or *ziti*.

For six servings

Scant 1 kilo (2 lb) fresh, ripe plum tomatoes	1½ onions, chopped
	Salt
1 carrot, chopped	¼ teaspoon granulated sugar
1 stick celery, chopped	8 tablespoons olive oil

1 Wash the tomatoes in cold water. Cut them in half, lengthways. Cook in a covered stockpot or saucepan over medium heat for 10 minutes.

2 Add the carrot, celery, onion, salt and sugar, and cook at a steady simmer, uncovered, for 30 minutes.

3 Purée everything through a mouli-légumes, return to the pan, add the olive oil, and cook at a steady simmer, uncovered, for 15 minutes more. Taste and check salt.

If using tinned tomatoes: Use a 400-g (14-oz) tin and start the recipe at Step 2, cooking the tomatoes with the vegetables as directed.

TOMATO SAUCE III

This is the simplest and freshest of all tomato sauces. It has no other vegetables, except an onion. The onion is not sautéed, it is not chopped, it is only cut in two and cooked together with the tomato. Except for salt and a tiny amount of sugar, the sauce has no seasonings. It has no olive oil, only butter. What does it have? Pure, sweet tomato taste, at its most appealing. It is an unsurpassed sauce for potato *gnocchi*, and it is excellent with spaghetti, *penne* and *ziti*.

For six servings

Scant 1 kilo (2 lb) fresh, ripe plum tomatoes
110 g ($\frac{1}{4}$ lb) butter

1 medium onion, peeled and halved
Salt
$\frac{1}{4}$ teaspoon granulated sugar

1 Wash the tomatoes in cold water. Cut them in half, lengthways. Simmer in a covered stockpot or saucepan for 10 minutes.

2 Purée the tomatoes through a mouli-légumes back into the pan. Add the butter, onion, salt and sugar, and cook at a slow but steady simmer, uncovered, for 45 minutes. Taste and check salt. Discard the onion.

If using tinned tomatoes: Use a 400-g (14-oz) tin, and start the recipe at Step 2.

TOMATO SAUCE WITH MARJORAM AND CHEESE

The fragrance of marjoram and the slight piquancy of Romano cheese make this a particularly appetising sauce for summer. It is excellent with *perciatelli* and spaghetti.

For six servings

Tomato Sauce II (page 80)
2 teaspoons marjoram
2 tablespoons freshly grated Parmesan cheese

2 tablespoons freshly grated Romano *pecorino* cheese
1 tablespoon olive oil

1 Bring the tomato sauce to a simmer. Add the marjoram, stir, and simmer for 8 to 10 minutes.

2 When the pasta is ready to be dressed, mix both grated cheeses and

the olive oil into the sauce, off the heat. Stir thoroughly but rapidly and pour over the pasta. Serve the pasta with an extra bowl of grated Parmesan cheese.

TOMATO SAUCE WITH ROSEMARY AND PANCETTA

This savoury sauce is particularly good with stubby cuts of pasta, such as *maccheroncini*, *ziti* or *penne*. It is also excellent with *spaghettini*.

For six to eight servings

All the ingredients of Tomato Sauce II (page 80)

2 teaspoons finely chopped dried or fresh rosemary leaves

60 g (2 oz) thin strips of rolled *pancetta*, 3 mm ($\frac{1}{8}$ inch) wide by 50 mm (2 inches) long

1 Make Tomato Sauce II, up to and including puréeing the cooked tomatoes and vegetables. Then proceed as follows.

2 Heat up the olive oil in a small frying pan over medium-high heat. When hot, add the chopped rosemary and the *pancetta* strips. Sauté for 1 minute, stirring constantly. Transfer all the contents of the frying pan to a saucepan, together with the puréed tomatoes, and cook at a steady simmer, uncovered, for 15 minutes. Taste and check salt.

Spaghettini alla carrettiera

THIN SPAGHETTI WITH FRESH BASIL AND TOMATO SAUCE

Carretti were hand- or mule-driven carts in which wine and produce were brought into Rome from the surrounding hills. The *carrettieri*, the cart-drivers, were notoriously underpaid and had to improvise inexpensive but satisfying meals that could be quickly prepared in the intervals between treks to and from the city.

There are many versions of *spaghettini alla carrettiera*. This is evidently a spring and summer version, because it calls for a large quantity of fresh basil. It has a very fresh, unlaboured taste. Do not be put off by the amount of garlic required. It simmers in the sauce without browning so that its flavour comes through very gently. In Rome, one would use very ripe, small sauce tomatoes called *casalini*, which thicken quickly in cooking. For our purposes, a good-quality tinned Italian plum tomato is best.

For four

50 g (1¾ oz) fresh basil, preferably
    with the smallest possible
    leaves
400 g (14 oz) tinned Italian plum
    tomatoes, seeded, drained and
    coarsely chopped
5 large cloves garlic, peeled and
    chopped fine

6 tablespoons olive oil, more if
    desired
Salt
Freshly ground pepper, about 6
    twists of the mill
450 g (1 lb) *spaghettini*

1 Pull off all the basil leaves from the stalks, rinse them briefly in cold water and chop them roughly.

2 Put the chopped basil, tomatoes, garlic, olive oil, salt and pepper in an uncovered saucepan and cook over medium-high heat for 15 minutes. Check seasoning.

3 Drop the *spaghettini* in 4 litres (7 pints) of boiling salted water. Since thin spaghetti cook very rapidly, begin tasting them early. They should be truly *al dente*, very firm to the bite.

4 Drain the *spaghettini* in a large colander, giving the colander two or three vigorous upward jerks to make all the water run off, and transfer quickly to a large hot bowl. Add the sauce, mixing it thoroughly into the *spaghettini*. You may, if you wish, add a few drops of raw olive oil. Serve immediately. No grated cheese is called for.

MENU SUGGESTIONS

If you want to precede this with an antipasto, try either some cold *Funghi trifolati* (page 325) or *Peperoni e acciughe* (page 32). As a second course, serve *Arrosto di vitello* (page 213), *Arrosto di maiale all' alloro* (page 241) or *Pollo coi funghi secchi* (page 262). Avoid any second course with tomatoes.

Spaghettini con le melanzane
THIN SPAGHETTI WITH AUBERGINES

For four

1 medium aubergine (about 450 g
    [1 lb])
1 large clove garlic, peeled and finely
    chopped
3 tablespoons olive oil
2 tablespoons finely chopped parsley

340 g (12 oz) tinned Italian tomatoes
$\frac{1}{8}$ teaspoon finely chopped chilli or
    less, to taste
Salt
450 g (1 lb) *spaghettini*

1 Trim, slice, salt and fry the aubergine according to the instructions for *Melanzane fritte* (page 318). Set aside to drain on kitchen paper.

2 In a medium-sized saucepan sauté the garlic in olive oil over moderate heat just until the garlic begins to colour lightly. Stirring rapidly, add the parsley, tomatoes, chopped chilli and salt. Cook, uncovered, for about 25 minutes, or until the tomatoes have separated from the oil and turned to sauce.

3 Cut the fried aubergine slices into slivers about 12 mm ($\frac{1}{2}$ inch) wide. When the sauce is ready, add the slivers and cook for 2 or 3 minutes more. Check salt. (You can prepare the sauce three or four days in advance, if you like.)

4 Drop the *spaghettini* into 4 litres (7 pints) of boiling salted water. Since thin spaghetti cook very rapidly and continue to soften even after draining, you must be ready to stop the cooking when the *spaghettini* are still quite firm.

5 Put a small quantity of the sauce in a warm serving bowl. Add the drained *spaghettini*, mix, add the rest of the sauce quickly, mix again, and serve immediately. This dish does not call for a topping of grated cheese.

MENU SUGGESTIONS

This can precede the peppery *Bistecca alla diavola* (page 203), *Lo 'schinco'* (page 219), any roast of lamb (pages 235–8), *Pollo arrosto al forno con rosmarino* (page 259) or *Fegatelli di maiale con la rete* (page 255). If you want an appetiser, try *Insalata di funghi e formaggio* (page 41).

Spaghettini alle vongole

THIN SPAGHETTI WITH CLAM AND TOMATO SAUCE

For four

1 dozen clams, the tiniest you can
  find
1½ cloves garlic, peeled and finely
  chopped
3 tablespoons olive oil
1 teaspoon chopped anchovy fillets **or**
  anchovy paste
1½ tablespoons finely chopped parsley

400 g (14 oz) tinned Italian tomatoes,
  coarsely chopped, with their
  juice
Salt
Freshly ground pepper, about 6
  twists of the mill
450 g (1 lb) *spaghettini*

1 Wash and scrub the clams thoroughly as directed on pages 46–7. Heat them over high heat in a covered pan until they open their shells. Detach the clams from the shells and rinse off any sand on the meat by dipping them briefly, one at a time, in their own juice. Unless the clams are exceptionally small, cut them up into two or more pieces and set aside. Strain the clam juices through a sieve lined with kitchen paper and set aside.

2 In a saucepan, sauté the garlic in the olive oil over medium heat. When the garlic has coloured lightly, add the chopped anchovies or paste and stir. Add the chopped parsley, stir, then add the chopped tomatoes with their juice and the strained clam juices. Simmer, uncovered, for about 25 minutes, or until the tomatoes and oil separate. Check seasoning. Off the heat, mix in the chopped clams. (If you are preparing the sauce ahead of time, hold back the clams until after you have warmed up the sauce; otherwise they will become tough and rubbery. Brush them with a little olive oil to keep them moist.)

3 Drop the *spaghettini* into 4 litres (7 pints) of boiling salted water and cook until *al dente*, firm to the bite. (*Spaghettini* cook very rapidly and should be eaten even slightly more *al dente* than other pasta.) Drain the pasta immediately when cooked. Transfer to a warm bowl and mix in the sauce, thoroughly seasoning all the strands. Serve at once, without grated cheese.

MENU SUGGESTIONS

For an antipasto: *Pomodori coi gamberetti* (page 34) or *Cozze e vongole passate ai ferri* (page 30). As a second course, *Pesce ai ferri alla moda dell' Adriatico* (page 191) would be perfect, and so would *Calamari fritti* (page 199), or, if you have omitted the shrimp antipasto, *Spiedini di gamberoni dell' Adriatico* (page 193) or *Pesce da taglio con salsa di prezzemolo* (page 183).

Spaghettini al sugo di pomodoro e acciughe
THIN SPAGHETTI WITH ANCHOVY AND TOMATO SAUCE

For four

1 clove garlic, peeled and chopped
6 tablespoons olive oil
4 flat anchovy fillets, coarsely
    chopped
2 tablespoons chopped parsley

300 g (10½ oz) tinned Italian
    tomatoes, chopped, with their
    juice
Salt
Freshly ground pepper, 6 to 8 twists
    of the mill
450 g (1 lb) *spaghettini*

1 Put the garlic in a small saucepan with the oil and sauté over medium heat until it has coloured lightly.

2 Add the chopped anchovies and parsley, and sauté for another 30 seconds, stirring constantly.

3 Add the tomatoes, salt and pepper. Stir, and adjust the heat so that the sauce cooks at a gentle but steady simmer for 25 minutes. Stir frequently. Check salt.

4 Bring 4 litres (7 pints) of water to the boil, add 1½ tablespoons salt, drop in the *spaghettini*, and cook until *al dente*, firm to the bite. Drain, transfer promptly to a warm bowl, mix thoroughly with the sauce, and serve at once.

Note   Although the sauce takes only slightly more time to make than the pasta takes to cook, it may be prepared in advance, and reheated before using.

MENU SUGGESTIONS

Follow those given for *Spaghettini alle vongole* (page 85).

Spaghetti al tonno
SPAGHETTI WITH TUNA SAUCE

For four or five

½ clove garlic, peeled and finely
    chopped
5 tablespoons olive oil
3 tablespoons finely chopped parsley
300 g (10½ oz) tinned Italian
    tomatoes, coarsely chopped,
    with their juice

285 g (10 oz) Italian or Spanish tuna
    packed in olive oil, drained
Salt
Freshly ground pepper, about 6
    twists of the mill
40 g (1½ oz) butter
450 g (1 lb) spaghetti

1 In a frying pan, sauté the garlic, with all the olive oil over medium heat until it has coloured lightly. Add the chopped parsley, stir, and cook for another half minute. Add the chopped tomatoes and their juice, stir well, lower the heat, and cook at a steady, gentle simmer, uncovered, for about 25 minutes or until the tomatoes separate from the oil.

2 While the tomato sauce is simmering, drain the tuna and break it up into small pieces with a fork. When the tomato sauce is done, add the tuna, mixing it well into the sauce. Add just a light sprinkling of salt, bearing in mind that the tuna is already salty, add pepper, and simmer gently, uncovered, for 5 minutes. Taste and check salt, turn off the heat, and mix in the butter.

3 Drop the spaghetti into 4 litres (7 pints) of boiling salted water and cook until *al dente*, very firm to the bite. Drain and transfer at once to a warm serving bowl. Mix in all the sauce and serve immediately.

Note The sauce may be prepared entirely ahead of time and refrigerated for one or two days. Add the butter, however, only after it has been reheated. No grated cheese is called for with this sauce.

MENU SUGGESTIONS

Antipasto: *Cozze e vongole passate ai ferri* (page 30). Second course: *Sgombri in tegame con rosmarino e aglio* (page 184), *Spiedini di gamberoni dell' Adriatico* (page 193) or *Pesce ai ferri alla moda dell' Adriatico* (page 191). Avoid tomato or cream sauces.

Spaghetti 'ajo e ojo'
SPAGHETTI WITH GARLIC AND OIL

This is one of the easiest, quickest and tastiest pasta dishes you can prepare. Its humble origins are in the shanty towns of Rome, but it is now a universal favourite, especially among Rome's chic insomniacs, who depend upon a *spaghettata* in the small hours to see them through the night until their early-morning bedtime.

In most versions, crushed garlic cloves are sautéed in olive oil until they are nearly black. They are then discarded and the spaghetti is seasoned with the flavoured oil. In this recipe the garlic is chopped, sautéed lightly and left in the oil to be added to the spaghetti. The result is a fuller yet milder taste of garlic, with no trace of bitterness.

For four

9 tablespoons olive oil	450 g (1 lb) spaghetti or *spaghettini*
2 cloves garlic, peeled and very finely chopped	Freshly ground pepper, 6 to 8 twists of the mill
Salt	2 tablespoons chopped parsley

1 The sauce can be prepared in the time it takes to bring the water for the spaghetti to the boil. When you have turned on the heat under the water, put 8 tablespoons of the oil, the garlic and salt in a very small saucepan. Sauté the garlic over very low heat, stirring frequently, until it slowly becomes a rich, golden colour.

2 Drop the spaghetti into the boiling salted water and cook until tender but *al dente*, very firm to the bite. Drain immediately, transfer to a warm bowl, and add the oil and garlic sauce. Toss rapidly, coating all the strands, adding pepper and parsley. Mix the remaining tablespoon of olive oil into the spaghetti and serve.

MENU SUGGESTIONS

This dish is an easy introduction to any plain but hearty second course, whether it is fish, meat or poultry. Avoid following it with dishes that have a bold garlic taste, which would be monotonous, or a delicate sauce, which would be lost on the palate after the brashness of the spaghetti. Specially recommended would be *Fettine di manzo alla sorrentina* (page 205), *Polpette alla pizzaiola* (page 208), *Polpettine* (page 210) or *Scaloppine di vitello alla pizzaiola* (page 223).

Bucatini all'Amatriciana
BUCATINI WITH PANCETTA, TOMATOES AND CHILLI

For four

1 medium onion, chopped fine
25 g (1 oz) butter
3 tablespoons vegetable oil
1 slice rolled *pancetta*, 6 mm ($\frac{1}{4}$ inch)
    thick, cut into strips 12 mm ($\frac{1}{2}$
    inch) wide and 25 mm (1 inch)
    long
300 g (10$\frac{1}{2}$ oz) tinned Italian tomatoes
$\frac{1}{2}$ to 1 small dried chilli, chopped fine

Salt
450 g (1 lb) *bucatini* or *perciatelli*
    (thick, hollow pasta)
3 tablespoons freshly grated
    Parmesan cheese
1 tablespoon freshly grated Romano
    pecorino cheese, more if
    desired

1 Sauté the onion in a saucepan with all the butter and oil until it is pale gold. Add the strips of *pancetta* and sauté for about a minute. Add the tomatoes, chopped chilli and salt. Cook over medium heat, uncovered. The sauce is done when the tomatoes and the cooking fats separate, after about 25 minutes. Turn off the heat and check salt.

2 Drop the *bucatini* into 4 litres (7 pints) boiling salted water. Stop the cooking when very *al dente*, very firm, and drain immediately. (Although large in diameter, the *bucatini* are hollow and have very thin sides and they quickly turn from firm to soft. They will continue to soften as they are being dressed and while they stand in the serving bowl.)

3 Transfer the cooked *bucatini* to a warm serving bowl, add the sauce, and mix. Add the Parmesan and the Romano and mix very thoroughly. Check seasoning. If you like it somewhat sharper you can add a little more Romano, but not so much as to overwhelm the other flavours.

MENU SUGGESTIONS

Antipasto: ideally, good Italian salami, if you can find it. Or *Carciofi ripieni di mortadella* (page 292). A perfect second course would be *Arrosto di agnello al ginepro* (page 236). Other suggestions: *Pollo arrosto al forno con rosmarino* (page 259), *Polpettone alla toscana* (page 211) or *Fegato alla veneziana* (page 250).

Fusilli alla pappone

FUSILLI WITH CREAMY ZUCCHINI AND BASIL SAUCE

For four

450 g (1 lb) zucchini
Vegetable oil, enough to come 12 mm
($\frac{1}{2}$ inch) up the side of a
medium frying pan
450 g (1 lb) *fusilli* (spiral pasta)
40 g (1$\frac{1}{2}$ oz) butter
3 tablespoons olive oil
1 teaspoon plain flour dissolved in 6
tablespoons milk

Salt
40 g (1$\frac{1}{2}$ oz) roughly chopped fresh
basil
1 egg yolk, beaten lightly with a fork
50 g (1$\frac{3}{4}$ oz) freshly grated Parmesan
cheese
25 g (1 oz) freshly grated Romano
pecorino cheese (see note
below)

1 Wash the zucchini as directed on page 336 and cut into sticks about 80 mm (3 inches) long and 3 mm ($\frac{1}{8}$ inch) thick.

2 Heat the vegetable oil in a frying pan over medium-high heat. Fry the zucchini sticks, a few at a time, so that they are not crowded. Fry them until they are a light-brown colour, not too dark, turning them occasionally. As each batch is done, transfer to kitchen paper to drain.

3 Drop the *fusilli* into 4 litres (7 pints) of boiling salted water, stirring with a wooden spoon. It will cook while you prepare the sauce.

4 In another frying pan, melt half the butter and add all the olive oil. When the butter begins to foam, turn the heat down to medium low, and stir in the flour-and-milk mixture, a little at a time. Cook, stirring constantly, for 30 seconds. Add the fried zucchini sticks, turning them two or three times, then add salt and the chopped basil. Cook long enough to turn everything once or twice. Off the heat, stir in the remaining butter. Rapidly mix in the egg yolk, then all the grated cheese. Check salt.

5 Cook the *fusilli* until *al dente*, firm to the bite. Drain, transfer to a warm serving bowl, toss with all the sauce, and serve immediately.

Note You may increase the quantity of Romano and decrease the Parmesan if you prefer a more piquant cheese flavour.

MENU SUGGESTIONS

Antipasti: none is required. This is a rather rich sauce, and the palate should be kept fresh enough to deal with it. Second courses: *Bistecca alla diavola* (page 203), *Spezzatino di vitello alla salvia* (page 230), *Costolettine di agnello fritte* (page 239) or *Pollo arrosto in tegame* (page 257).

Penne al sugo di pomodoro e funghi secchi

PENNE WITH A SAUCE OF TOMATOES AND DRIED MUSHROOMS

For four

25 g (1 oz) dried wild mushrooms
2 tablespoons finely chopped shallots
    or onion
1 tablespoon vegetable oil
60 g (2 oz) butter
25 g (1 oz) 6-mm ($\frac{1}{4}$-inch)-wide strips
    of *pancetta*, prosciutto or green
    bacon

300 g (10$\frac{1}{2}$ oz) tinned Italian
    tomatoes, cut up, with their
    juice
Salt
Freshly ground pepper, about 4
    twists of the mill
450 g (1 lb) *penne* or other short
    tubular pasta, such as *mezzani*
    or *ziti*

1 Put the mushrooms to soak in 250 ml (scant $\frac{1}{2}$ pint) lukewarm water for about 30 minutes. When they have finished soaking, lift out the mushrooms but do not discard the water. Rinse the mushrooms in several changes of cold water and set aside. Strain the water used for the soaking through a sieve lined with kitchen paper and set aside.

2 Put the shallots in a small saucepan with the oil and butter and sauté over medium heat until pale gold.

3 Add the *pancetta*, and continue to sauté for another minute or two, stirring several times.

4 Add the cut-up tomatoes and their juice, the mushrooms, the strained liquid, salt and pepper, and cook, uncovered, at a gentle simmer for 45 minutes. Stir with a wooden spoon from time to time.

5 Drop the pasta into boiling salted water and cook until tender but *al dente*, firm to the bite. Drain, giving the colander a few vigorous up-and-down shakes to let all the water run off. Transfer to a warm serving bowl, pour all the sauce over the pasta, and mix thoroughly but rapidly. Serve immediately, with a bowl of freshly grated Parmesan cheese.

MENU SUGGESTIONS

You can follow this with any second course of meat or poultry that does not contain tomatoes or mushrooms. Particularly good choices would be grilled steak, *Arrosto di vitello* (page 213), *Arrosto di agnello pasquale col vino bianco* (page 235), *Pollo alla diavola* (page 260) or *Fegatelli di maiale con la rete* (page 255).

Conchiglie con il sugo per la gramigna
SHELLS WITH SAUSAGE AND CREAM SAUCE

Gramigna is both a kind of couch-grass and a thin, short tubular pasta with which one usually serves this sauce. *Gramigna*, to my knowledge, is not available outside Italy, but this creamy, tasty sauce is every bit as delectable with *conchiglie, fusilli* or *rotelle*: any pasta whose twists or cavities can trap little morsels of sausage and cream. Use a mild, sweet Italian sausage. Avoid any sausage containing hot peppers, fennel seeds or other pungent spices. *Luganega* is best, but you may substitute other sweet sausages if you cannot find *luganega*. German bratwurst is an acceptable alternative.

For four

175 to 220 g (6 to 8 oz) *luganega* sausage
1½ tablespoons chopped shallots **or** onion
25 g (1 oz) butter
2 tablespoons vegetable oil
Freshly ground pepper, about 4 twists of the mill
170 ml (6 fl oz) double cream
Salt
450 g (1 lb) *conchiglie* (shells), *fusilli* **or** *rotelle*

1 Skin the sausage and crumble it as fine as possible.

2 Put the shallots in a small saucepan with the butter and oil and sauté until pale gold.

3 Add the crumbled sausage meat and sauté it for 10 minutes, stirring frequently.

4 Add the pepper and cream, turn up the heat to medium high, and cook until the cream has thickened. Stir frequently while cooking. Taste and check seasoning.

5 Drop the *conchiglie* into 4 litres (7 pints) of boiling salted water and stir with a wooden spoon. When *al dente*, firm to the bite, drain, giving the colander a few vigorous up-and-down jerks to shake all the water out of the cavities. Transfer to a warm serving bowl, toss with all the sauce, and serve immediately, with a little freshly grated Parmesan cheese.

MENU SUGGESTIONS

No antipasti are recommended. Suitable second courses could be *Stracotto al Barolo* (page 206), *Arrosto di agnello pasquale col vino bianco* (page 235), *Cotolette alla milanese* (page 228) or *Pollo alla diavola* (page 260).

Rigatoni al forno col ragù
BAKED RIGATONI WITH MEAT SAUCE

For six

450 g (1 lb) *rigatoni* or similar-cut
    pasta, such as *mezzani, ziti* or
    penne
Salt
450 ml ($\frac{3}{4}$ pint) *Ragù* (Bolognese sauce,
    page 109)

A medium-thick béchamel sauce
    (page 23)
6 tablespoons freshly grated
    Parmesan cheese
25 g (1 oz) butter

1 Preheat the oven to 200°C/400°F/Mark 6.

2 Drop the pasta into 4 litres (7 pints) of boiling salted water and cook until just *al dente*, firm to the bite. (It should be a fraction firmer than you would ordinarily cook it because it will soften more as it bakes in the oven.) Drain and transfer to a large mixing bowl.

3 Add the meat sauce, the béchamel sauce and 4 tablespoons of the grated cheese to the pasta. Mix thoroughly. Transfer to a buttered oven dish. Level the top with a spatula, sprinkle it with the remaining grated cheese and dot with butter. Place in the uppermost level of the oven and bake for 10 minutes. Allow to settle a few minutes before serving.

MENU SUGGESTIONS

Follow this with *Petto di vitello arrotolato* (page 215), *Nodini di vitello alla salvia* (page 229), *Arrosto di maiale al latte* (page 240), *Coniglio in padella* (page 271) or *Piccioncini in tegame* (page 270).

La Sfoglia
(Pasta all'uovo fatta in casa)
HOME-MADE EGG PASTA

Commercial pasta is factory-made with flour and water. In home-made pasta, eggs take the place of water and hands replace machines. Ready-made pasta is widely available in packets and boxes, but it is a poor substitute for what you can make so easily at home. Although egg pasta is now produced in almost every Italian province, it is the speciality of Emilia-Romagna, and even today the pasta produced there is incontestably the finest in Italy. Until comparatively recent times, spaghetti and other commercial pastas were nearly unknown to the Emilian table. The only pasta consumed was home-made pasta, and it was made fresh every day in virtually every home. My grandmother, who died at ninety-three, made pasta for us daily until the last few years of her life. At the end, when, instead of home-made pasta, an occasional dish of bought pasta would appear on our table, she would be saddened and perplexed by our declining taste.

There is no denying that, for a beginner, making pasta at home takes time, patience and a considerable amount of physical effort. The rewards are such, however, that you should be persuaded to make the attempt. When you have mastered the art of making basic pasta dough you will have immediate access to some of the most miraculous creations in all gastronomy: *fettuccine, tagliatelle, tortellini, cappelletti, cappellacci, tortelloni, cannelloni, lasagne, garganelli* and all their glorious variations. As you become skilful, you will discover, too, that the fresh egg pasta you are making at home is not only vastly better than what you can buy in any shop, but that it is also superior to what you are likely to eat in any restaurant outside Italy.

KEEPING HOME-MADE PASTA

Uncooked flat noodle pasta, such as *tagliatelle, fettuccine, tagliolini, maltagliati* and so on, keeps for a very long time, even for as long as a month or more, without refrigeration. Allow the opened-out noodles to dry thoroughly. When dry, transfer to a tray or large soup bowl. (Handle carefully, because pasta is very brittle at this stage and breaks easily.) Put away, uncovered, in a dry, cool cupboard. Use exactly as you would fresh pasta, except that it will take somewhat longer to cook.

Although stuffed pasta can also be made ahead of time, it does not keep as long as noodle pasta. How long it keeps depends on the stuffing. Follow the suggestions at the end of each recipe.

WHAT YOU NEED TO MAKE PASTA

– A steady surface on which to work, 600 mm (24 inches) deep, 900 mm (36 inches) wide, preferably unvarnished wood, but it can well be formica or other plastic laminate. Marble is not very satisfactory.

– A rolling-pin 37 mm (1½ inches) in diameter, 820 mm (32 inches) long. This is the ideal size for pasta. You will probably not find it in any shop, but you can easily have one cut for you from a length of hardwood curtain-pole at a good timber merchant. Make sure the ends are sanded and smooth. Before using a new rolling-pin, wash it with soap and water and rinse. Dry thoroughly with a soft towel and allow to dry further in the warmth of the kitchen. Then dampen a cloth in olive oil or lightly grease your hands and rub oil over the entire surface of the pin. Do not overgrease. When the oil has been absorbed, lightly rub some flour over the pin. This procedure should be repeated every dozen or so times that the rolling-pin is used.

– A broad-bladed, well-balanced knife. The one illustrated on page 104 is ideal.

– A place protected from draughts and not overheated. Pasta dough must not dry out too quickly while you are working on it.

THE INGREDIENTS

Although no one making pasta in Italy ever really measures out flour, the traditionally accepted formula corresponds to 130 g (4½ oz) of flour for every egg, but I have been gradually revising this proportion, in batch after batch of pasta. I have found that it is possible, in fact desirable, to work with little more than half that amount of flour. It produces a far more yielding and easily stretched dough than the old proportions. The exact amount of flour will always depend, of course, on the size and flour-absorbing capacity of the eggs. It is easier for beginners to work with less rather than more flour, because the dough stays softer and easier to handle, yet if you keep it too soft, it may also become a problem, because very soft dough is likely to stick and tear. As your skills and speed develop, work with as much flour, and as tough a dough, as you can handle – the firmer the dough, the better the pasta. However, until you develop a feel for the right consistency, you are safest with these recommended proportions:

*For three or four**	*For five or six**	*For seven or eight**
2 eggs	3 eggs	4 eggs
About 200 g (7 oz) plain flour (preferably unbleached)	300 g (10½ oz) plain (unbleached) flour	400 g (14 oz) plain (unbleached) flour

* These quantities are for flat pasta only. Stuffed pasta goes further. See individual recipes for yield.

For stuffed pasta, such as *tortellini*, add 1 teaspoon of milk for each egg used. This is to make the pasta easier to seal. In Emilia-Romagna we never add oil, water or salt to pasta dough.

HAND-MADE EGG PASTA (BASIC RECIPE)

There are four steps in making a sheet of egg-pasta dough from eggs and flour. In the first step the eggs are combined with as much flour as they will take without becoming stiff and dry. In the second, the eggs and flour are kneaded to a smooth, elastic consistency. In the third, the dough is opened out with the rolling-pin to a circular sheet about 3 mm (⅛ inch) thick. In the last step the sheet is wrapped around the pin and stretched again and again until it is almost paper thin and transparent. All together, it should take a reasonably skilful person less than 25 minutes. Here is a detailed description of each step:

1 Pour out the flour on the working surface, shape it into a mound, and make a well in the centre of the mound. Put the whole eggs in the well. If you are making stuffed pasta, and the recipe calls for milk, add the milk. Beat the eggs lightly with your fingers or with a fork, for a minute or two. Start mixing flour into the eggs with a circular motion, drawing the flour from the inside wall of the well. Use one hand for mixing, the other for supporting the outside wall of the well, lest it collapse and let the eggs run through. When the eggs cease to be runny, tumble the rest of the flour over them, and, working with palms and fingertips, push and squeeze the eggs and flour until they are a well-combined but somewhat crumbly paste. If the eggs were very large, or had exceptional flour-absorption qualities, the mass may be on the moist and sticky side. Add as much flour as the mass will absorb without becoming stiff and dry, but do not exceed 130 g (4½ oz) of flour per egg.

Beat the eggs, and mix them with the flour drawn from the inside wall of the well.

Knead the dough, pressing it with the heel of your palm ...

... folding it over and turning it again and again, until smooth.

*Make the dough into a ball, and open
out the ball with the rolling-pin.
Always roll away from you, turning the
dough as it begins to flatten out.*

*Curl the far end of the pasta sheet around the end
of the rolling-pin and roll it towards you.*

*Giving the pasta sheet a final
thinning out: move hands back
and forth, quickly and lightly,
over the length of the rolling-
pin. At the same time roll the
pin backward and forward to
thin the sheet evenly.*

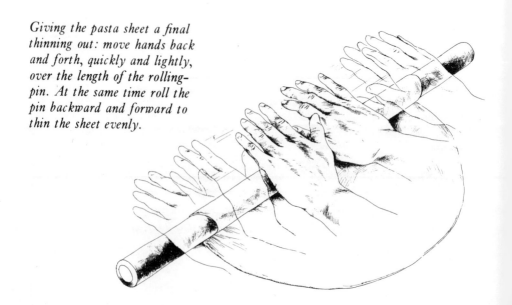

2 Set the egg and flour mass to one side and scrape off every last crumb of caked flour from the working surface and from your hands. Wash and dry your hands. Knead the mass, pressing against it with the heel of your palm, folding it over and turning it again and again. After 8 to 10 minutes it should be a smooth, compact and elastic ball of dough. Pat it into a flattish bun-like shape. (If you are making a lot of pasta and using more than 2 eggs, divide the mass in two and keep one half covered between 2 soup plates while you roll out and thin the other half. When you have become more experienced, you can try doing the entire mass at one time.)

3 Dust the work surface lightly with flour. Open out the ball of dough with the rolling-pin, starting to roll at about one-third of the way in on the ball, rolling forward, away from you. Rotate the dough one quarter turn after every roll so that it opens out into an even, circular shape. As it begins to flatten out, gradually lessen the degree of rotation after each roll, but do not lose control of the shape. It must stay as round as possible. Do not press the dough *against* the work surface. Roll it *out and away*, without putting weight on it. Stop when you have rolled out a sheet 3 mm ($\frac{1}{8}$ inch) thick.

4 This last step is the hardest one for beginners to learn. But it does not require particular skills; it is all a question of getting the right motion. Once you have it, you have mastered pasta-making, and you will never again give it a second thought. The objective is to give the pasta sheet its final thinning out by stretching it with a sideways pressure of your hands as you wrap it around the rolling-pin. Here is how you do it. Curl the far end of the pasta sheet around the centre or the rolling-pin, and roll it towards you, with both your palms cupped over the centre of the pin. When you have rolled up about a quarter of the sheet, do not roll up any more. Quickly roll the pin backward and forward, and *at the same time* slide the palms of your hands away from each other and towards the ends of the rolling-pin, dragging them against the surface of the pasta. Roll up some more of the sheet, quickly roll backward and forward while repeating the same stretching motion with the palms of your hands. By the time the sheet is completely rolled up, you should have repeated the stretching motion 12 to 14 times in 8 seconds or less. Unroll the pasta, turning the pin slightly so that the sheet does not open out to exactly the place where you rolled it up before. Flatten out any bumps or creases, and even off the edges with the rolling-pin. If the dough is a little sticky, dust very lightly with flour from time to time. Repeat the same rolling-up-and-stretching operation several times, until the pasta is almost paper-thin and transparent. The entire step must be carried out in not much more than 8 minutes, otherwise the pasta will dry, lose its elasticity and become impossible to roll thin.

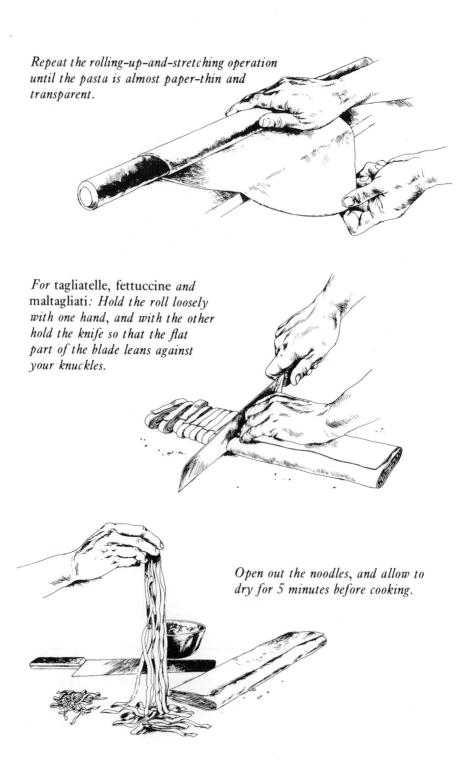

Repeat the rolling-up-and-stretching operation until the pasta is almost paper-thin and transparent.

For tagliatelle, fettuccine *and* maltagliati: *Hold the roll loosely with one hand, and with the other hold the knife so that the flat part of the blade leans against your knuckles.*

Open out the noodles, and allow to dry for 5 minutes before cooking.

For stuffed pasta, do not allow the dough to dry. Omit the next step and proceed immediately to cut and stuff it as directed in the individual recipes. If you are making more than one sheet of pasta, cut and stuff the first sheet before rolling out the second.

For *tagliatelle, fettuccine* and *maltagliati* (pages 102–3), proceed as follows:

5 Roll up the sheet of pasta on your rolling-pin. Lay a clean, dry towel on a table. Unroll the pasta on the towel, letting about a third of the sheet hang over the edge of the table. After about 10 minutes, turn it, letting another third hang over the edge. Turn it again after another 10 minutes. Pasta for noodles must be dried out so that the noodle ribbons, when cut, do not stick together. It must not be overdried, however. Before cutting, it must be folded into a flat roll, so it has to stay soft and pliable enough to fold without cracking. When the surface of the pasta begins to take on a leathery look it is ready for folding and cutting. This drying process usually takes about 30 minutes, but in a very hot room it can take as little as 15 or 20 minutes.

6 Roll up the pasta on the rolling-pin and unroll it on the worktop. Fold it over and over into a flat roll about 80 mm (3 inches) wide. Place one hand on the roll, with fingertips partly drawn back under your knuckles. Hold the knife with your other hand, crossways to the roll, leaning the flat part of the blade against your knuckles. Cut the pasta to the width desired, pulling back your knuckles after each cut and following them with the flat side of the blade. Keep your knuckles high and do not lift the knife above them. (This method gives you perfect control of the knife and is almost completely accident-proof.) When you have cut the entire roll, open out the noodles on a clean, dry towel and allow them to firm up for 5 minutes. They are then ready to cook. Gather them up with the towel and let them slide into the boiling water.

FLAT PASTA
TAGLIATELLE *AND OTHER NOODLES*

There are two broad categories of egg pasta. There is stuffed pasta, such as *tortellini, tortelloni, cannelloni* and *lasagne*, and there is non-stuffed pasta, which includes all varieties of noodles. We refer to this last category as flat pasta, and here are the most important shapes in which it is cut.

Some varieties of cut pasta, drawn to their actual size.

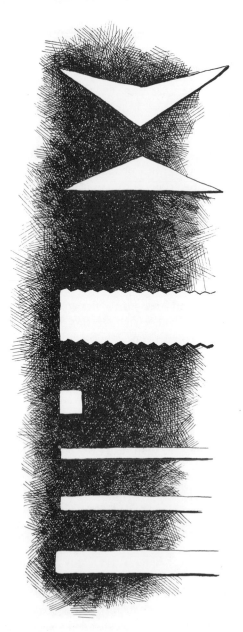

maltagliati

pappardelle

quadrucci

tagliolini

fettuccine

tagliatelle

All of the following shapes are cut from a rolled-up sheet of home-made pasta dough. (See Step 6, preceding page.)

Tagliatelle

Tagliatelle are the long, narrow noodles, and it is probably the best-known cut of all. This is the uncontested speciality of Bologna. Of all their many contributions to civilised life, there is probably none for which the Bolognese have any higher regard or greater affection than *tagliatelle*. Just as at the International Bureau of Weights and Measures in Paris the standard of the metre is deposited in the form of a platinum bar, in Bologna, at the Chamber of Commerce, there is a sealed glass case wherein the ideal width and thickness of *tagliatelle* are embodied in a solid gold noodle. According to the Accademia Italiana della Cucina, the correct dimensions of raw *tagliatelle* are: thickness, 1 millimetre (slightly more than $\frac{1}{32}$ inch), and width, 6 millimetres (slightly less than $\frac{1}{4}$ inch). This sort of precision deserves our wonder and admiration, but, inasmuch as we are not making yardsticks and are only making noodles, we can permit ourselves some elasticity.

The most desirable width, in terms of adherence to the sauce and of plumpness in the plate, hovers around 6 mm ($\frac{1}{4}$ inch). There is no need to worry, however, if you exceed it slightly. The thickness is simply that of the thinnest pasta dough you are able to produce. If you are using a pasta machine, this entire discussion is academic because the cutting blades and the rollers predetermine width and thickness.

Tagliatelle is best served as the Bolognese do it, with *Ragù* (Bolognese sauce, page 109).

Fettuccine

This is the term Romans use for noodles, and it is commonly assumed that they are precisely the same as *tagliatelle*, except for the name. The fact is, however, that *fettuccine*, as Romans are accustomed to eating them, are somewhat narrower and thicker than *tagliatelle*. I find this slightly stouter noodle ideally suited to carry sauces in which double cream is an essential ingredient.

For *fettuccine*, keep your pasta dough not quite paper thin, and cut it into noodles about 3 mm ($\frac{1}{8}$ inch) wide.

Tagliolini, Tagliarini

These are very thin noodles, best suited for use in soups, with chicken or meat broths. The dough should be as thin as possible, and cut into noodles $1\frac{1}{2}$ mm ($\frac{1}{16}$ inch) wide. The narrow blades on a pasta machine are perfect for *tagliolini*.

When even narrower, *tagliolini* are called *capellini* or *capelli d'angelo*.

Pappardelle *are cut with a fluted pastry wheel, which gives them their characteristic crimped edge.*

Maltagliati *are produced by cutting off both corners of the pasta roll and then cutting straight across. This kind of knife is especially suitable for cutting pasta.*

Capello means hair and *capelli d'angelo*, angel hair. They are indeed hair-thin. In fact, they are too thin for most people to cut by hand, so they are usually shop-bought.

Pappardelle

These are the broadest of noodles. They are cut to a width of 15 mm ($\frac{5}{8}$ inch) with a fluted pastry wheel, which gives them their characteristic crimped edge. *Pappardelle*, unlike all other noodles, are cut directly from a flat, open sheet of pasta. Allow the dough to dry for about half as long as for other noodles, then divide the pasta sheet in half, for ease of handling, before cutting it into *pappardelle*. In Tuscany, *pappardelle* are served with a sauce made from hare, whose rich, gamey taste goes well with the breadth of the noodle. Another excellent sauce for *pappardelle* is the chicken-liver sauce given on page 117).

Maltagliati

Maltagliati are used exclusively for soups, especially soups with beans or chickpeas. *Maltagliati* literally means 'badly cut'. Instead of cutting the pasta roll straight across as you would for other noodles, cut it on the bias, first cutting off one corner, then the other. This leaves the pasta roll coming to a point in the centre. Cut it straight across, thus giving the roll a straight edge again, then cut off the corners once more as before. At its broadest point, *maltagliati* should be about 12 mm ($\frac{1}{2}$ inch) wide or less, but precision, as the name indicates, is not terribly important.

There is no bean soup calling for pasta that is not immensely improved when you use home-made *maltagliati* instead of commercial pasta. Like all noodles, *maltagliati* easily keep for a month without refrigeration, so that you can always have a supply on hand.

Quadrucci

The name means 'little squares', and that is exactly what they are. They are made by first cutting the pasta into *tagliatelle* noodles, then cutting the still-folded ribbons crossways into squares. It makes a fine, delicate pasta for use with a good, clear meat or chicken broth.

HOME-MADE PASTA USING THE PASTA MACHINE

A pasta machine kneads and thins out pasta and cuts it, if you wish, into two different noodle widths. It is truly effortless, but, unfortunately, machine pasta is not really as fine as the hand-made kind. Something happens to its composition as it goes through the steel rollers that gives the dough an ever so slightly slimy texture. Moreover, the machine gives you only one degree of thinness, whereas for *fettuccine*, for example, you might want the pasta a little thicker, or for stuffed pasta a little thinner. These considerations aside, however, machine pasta can be quite good; it is certainly superior to the commercial variety, and it is far better than having no home-made pasta at all.

1 Combine the eggs and flour exactly as in Step 1 of the hand-made pasta recipe (page 96).

2 The smooth steel rollers at one end of the machine knead, roll out and thin the dough. The first setting, at which the rollers are widest apart, is for kneading. Pull off a piece of the egg and flour mass about the size of a lemon, keeping the rest of the mass covered between two soup plates. Feed the mass through the rollers 8 to 10 times, until it is smooth and elastic. Each time after you knead it, fold it over and turn it before feeding it through the rollers again, so that it will be kneaded evenly.

3 Shift the rollers to the next setting and pass the kneaded dough through. Do not fold the dough. Lower the setting again, and feed through once more. Go down all the settings, feeding the dough once through each setting until it is thoroughly thinned out. If the dough is sticky, dust it lightly with flour.

4 If you are making stuffed pasta, proceed immediately to cut the dough and stuff it as directed in the recipes. For noodles, allow the pasta to dry on a clean towel for at least 15 minutes. Before cutting, trim the dough to a workable length, no more than 600 mm (24 inches).

5 For *tagliatelle* (page 103), feed the dough through the broad cutting blades. The narrow blades are suitable only for making the *tagliolini*, very thin noodles, best served in broth. For *fettuccine* or *maltagliati*, fold the dough into a flat roll and cut it by hand, as directed in Step 6 of the hand-made pasta recipe (page 101).

NOTE ON THE ELECTRIC PASTA MACHINE

There are two types of pasta machine for home use: one is electrically driven and the other is hand cranked. The electric machine has a maddeningly noisy motor that must have been designed by a motorcycle enthusiast, but it does make better pasta than the hand-cranked model.

There are two reasons for this. The first is speed. The electric machine is dazzlingly fast, and the speed at which dough is flattened is closely related to quality in the consistency of pasta. The second reason is the material of which the rollers are made. The hand-cranked machine has smooth, polished steel rollers that produce the slithery surface characteristic of machine-made pasta. The electric model has textured nylon rollers that turn out pasta with a surface not quite so slick, almost resembling hand-rolled pasta.

Unfortunately, the electric pasta machine is much more expensive, and, although it makes unquestionably finer pasta, it is up to you to decide whether the difference is worth the higher price.

COOKING HOME-MADE PASTA

Follow the same procedure as for commercial pasta. If the pasta is to be seasoned with a very delicate sauce, add a bit more salt to the water in which it boils.

People who are doing it for the first time are always astonished to see how quickly fresh egg pasta cooks. As a general rule, fresh flat pasta is done within 5 to 10 *seconds* after the water in which it has been dropped returns to the boil. Stuffed pasta takes a while longer, and all dried home-made pasta takes much longer, several minutes at least. Taste it frequently as it boils to avoid overcooking.

Always stir pasta with a wooden spoon immediately after dropping it in the pot, or it may stick together.

Pasta verde
SPINACH PASTA

Spinach is added to pasta dough to colour it and to make it slightly softer and creamier. It does not significantly alter its flavour. You can use green pasta exactly as you would yellow pasta. It is found most frequently in the form of *lasagne* (page 122) or *tagliatelle* (page 110), but *cappelletti* (page 132), *tortelloni* (page 140) and *garganelli* (page 146) can also be very successful when made with spinach pasta. Green pasta is particularly attractive when served with a tomato and cream sauce (page 139), or any sauce in which the white of cream and béchamel or the red of tomato predominates.

Spinach pasta is made with precisely the same technique used for yellow pasta.

140 g (5 oz) frozen leaf spinach, thawed, **or** 220 g ($\frac{1}{2}$ lb) fresh spinach

Salt
2 eggs
200 g (7 oz) plain flour, approximately

1 If you are using frozen spinach, cook it with some salt in a covered pan over medium heat for 5 minutes. Drain and allow to cool. If you are using fresh spinach, try to choose young, tender spinach. Remove all the stems, and discard any leaves that are not perfectly green and crisp. Wash it in a basin of cold water, changing the water several times until it shows no traces of earth. Cook it with some salt in a covered pan over medium heat with just the water that clings to the leaves. Cook until tender, 15 minutes or more, then drain and allow to cool. Squeeze as much water as you can out of the cooked spinach with your hands, then chop it very fine.

2 Pour the flour on the worktop, shape it into a mound and make a well in the centre. Put the whole eggs and the chopped spinach in the well, and lightly beat the eggs and the spinach together, using your fingers or a fork. Add flour gradually to the egg and spinach mixture, drawing it in from the inside wall of the well. Since it is impossible to estimate in advance exactly how much flour the egg and spinach will absorb, simply work it into the egg and spinach mixture gradually until the mixture has incorporated as much flour as possible without becoming stiff and dry. When the mass is ready for kneading, proceed exactly as though it were yellow pasta. Refer to Step 2 of the basic pasta recipe (page 99), or knead it and thin it out in a pasta machine (page 106).

Note   If you are making stuffed pasta, do *not* add milk to spinach pasta. It is soft enough to seal well without it. Cooking times for spinach pasta are slightly shorter than for yellow pasta.

Ragù

BOLOGNESE SAUCE

Ragù is not to be confused with *ragoût*. A *ragoût* is a French meat stew, while *ragù* is the meat sauce the Bolognese use for seasoning their home-made pasta. The only thing they share is a common and justified origin in the verb *ragoûter*, which means 'to excite the appetite'.

A properly made *ragù* clinging to the folds of home-made noodles is one of the most satisfying experiences accessible to the sense of taste. It is no doubt one of the great attractions of the enchanting city of Bologna, and the Bolognese claim one cannot make a true *ragù* anywhere else. This may be so, but with a little care we can come very close to it. There are three essential points you must remember in order to make a successful *ragù*:
— The meat must be sautéed just barely long enough to lose its raw colour. It must not brown or it will lose delicacy.
— It must be cooked in milk *before* the tomatoes are added. This keeps the meat creamier and sweeter tasting.
— It must cook at the merest simmer for a long, long time. The minimum is $3\frac{1}{2}$ hours; 5 is better.

The union of *tagliatelle* and *ragù* (see the following recipe) is a marriage made in heaven, but *ragù* is also very good with *tortellini*, it is indispensable in *lasagne*, and it is excellent with *rigatoni*, *ziti*, *conchiglie* and *rotelle*. Whenever a menu lists pasta *alla bolognese*, that means it is served with *ragù*.

For six servings

2 tablespoons chopped onion	Salt
3 tablespoons olive oil	250 ml (scant $\frac{1}{2}$ pint) dry white wine
40 g ($1\frac{1}{2}$ oz) butter	8 tablespoons milk
2 tablespoons chopped celery	$\frac{1}{8}$ teaspoon nutmeg
2 tablespoons chopped carrot	400 g (14 oz) tinned Italian tomatoes,
350 g ($12\frac{1}{4}$ oz) minced lean beef,	roughly chopped, with their
preferably chuck or the meat	juice
from the neck	

1 An earthenware pot should be your first choice for making *ragù*. If you do not have one available, use a heavy, enamelled cast-iron casserole, the deepest one you have (to keep the *ragù* from reducing too quickly). Put in the chopped onion, with all the oil and butter, and sauté briefly over medium heat until just translucent. Add the celery and carrot and cook gently for 2 minutes.

2 Add the minced beef, crumbling it in the pot with a fork. Add salt to

taste, stir, and cook only until the meat has lost its raw, red colour. Add the wine, turn the heat up to medium high, and cook, stirring occasionally, until all the wine has evaporated.

3 Turn the heat down to medium, add the milk and the nutmeg, and cook until the milk has evaporated. Stir frequently.

4 When the milk has evaporated, add the tomatoes and stir thoroughly. When the tomatoes have started to bubble, turn the heat down until the sauce cooks at the gentlest simmer, just an occasional bubble. Cook, un-covered, for a minimum of $3\frac{1}{2}$ to 4 hours, stirring occasionally. Taste and check salt. (If you cannot keep an eye on the sauce for such a long stretch, you can turn off the heat and resume cooking it later on. But do finish cooking it in one day.)

Note *Ragù* can be kept in the refrigerator for up to 5 days, or frozen. Reheat and simmer for about 15 minutes before using. If you are using fresh tomatoes, peel and deseed them and cook in a little water for 10 to 15 minutes. Then pass through the finest blade of a mouli-légumes, or a sieve, and proceed with the recipe.

Tagliatelle alla bolognese

TAGLIATELLE WITH BOLOGNESE SAUCE

For six

450 to 550 ml ($\frac{3}{4}$ to 1 pint) *Ragù* (previous recipe)
Tagliatelle (page 103), made with 3 eggs and 300 g ($10\frac{1}{2}$ oz) plain flour (basic pasta recipe, page 96)

Salt
15 g ($\frac{1}{2}$ oz) butter
50 g ($1\frac{3}{4}$ oz) fresh grated Parmesan cheese

1 Heat 4 to 5 litres (7 to 9 pints) of water and, while it is coming to the boil, bring the sauce to a very gentle simmer, stirring it well.

2 When the water boils, add salt, then all the noodles, and stir with a wooden spoon. If the pasta is fresh, it will be done within 5 to 10 *seconds* after the water returns to the boil. Drain immediately and shake the colander well.

3 Spoon a little bit of hot sauce into a warm serving dish, add the noodles, pour the rest of the sauce over them, and toss the noodles with the sauce, the butter, and the grated cheese. Serve without delay, with an extra bowl of freshly grated cheese.

MENU SUGGESTIONS

For an authentic Bolognese meal, follow with *Cotoletta di tacchino alla bolognese* (page 267). Other second courses could be *Arrosto di vitello* (page 213), *Arrosto di agnello pasquale col vino bianco* (page 235), *Pollo arrosto in tegame* (page 257) or *Coniglio in padella* (page 271).

Fettuccine all'Alfredo

FETTUCCINE TOSSED IN CREAM AND BUTTER

There actually was an Alfredo, in whose Roman restaurant this lovely dish became famous. Alfredo had a gold fork and spoon with which he gave a final toss to each serving of *fettuccine* before it was sent to the table. Despite its southern origin, this dish has now become a fixture of those Italian restaurants abroad specialising in northern cuisine. Although it is astonishingly simple, it is not often that one finds it done well. Its essential requirements are home-made – better still, hand-made – pasta cooked very firm, and good-quality fresh double cream.

For five or six

230 ml (8 fl oz) double cream
40 g (1½ oz) butter
Salt
Fettuccine (page 103), made with
    3 eggs and 300 g (10½ oz) plain
    flour (basic pasta recipe, page
    96)

65 g (2¼ oz) freshly grated Parmesan
    cheese
Freshly ground pepper, 4 to 6 twists
    of the mill
A very tiny grating of nutmeg

1 Choose an enamelled cast-iron pan, or other flameproof dish that can later hold all the cooked *fettuccine* comfortably. Put in 140 ml (5 fl oz) of the

cream and all the butter and simmer over medium heat for less than a minute, until the butter and cream have thickened. Turn off the heat.

2 Bring 4 litres (7 pints) of water to the boil. Add 2 tablespoons of salt, then drop in the *fettuccine* and cover the pot until the water returns to the boil. If the *fettuccine* are fresh, they will be done a few seconds after the water returns to the boil. If dry, they will take a little longer. (Cook the *fettuccine* even firmer than usual, because they will be cooked more in the pan.) Drain immediately and thoroughly when done, and transfer to the pan containing the butter and cream.

3 Turn on the heat under the pan to low, and toss the *fettuccine*, coating them with sauce. Add the rest of the cream, all the grated cheese, salt, pepper and nutmeg. Toss briefly until the cream has thickened and the *fettuccine* are well coated. Check seasoning. Serve immediately from the pan, with an extra bowl of grated cheese.

MENU SUGGESTIONS

For an elegant dinner you can precede this with an antipasto of *Barchette di zucchini ripiene al forno* (page 340) or *Insalata di funghi e formaggio* (page 41). The second course may be *Stracotto al Barolo* (page 206), *Nodini di vitello alla salvia* (page 229), *Scaloppine di vitello al Marsala* (page 220), *Animelle con pomodori e piselli* (page 249), *Fegatini di pollo alla salvia* (page 256) or any roast in this book.

Paglia e fieno alla ghiotta

YELLOW AND GREEN NOODLES WITH CREAM, HAM AND MUSHROOM SAUCE

Paglia e fieno, 'straw and hay', is the bucolic, but self-effacing name of one of the most exquisite of pasta dishes. It is a combination of narrow yellow and spinach noodles, served with a cream sauce. Sautéed tiny fresh peas are usually a part of the sauce, but a less common version, using mushrooms, is given here. I think it would be a pity to limit one's enjoyment of this elegant dish to those rare occasions when very young, freshly picked peas appear on the market, and in this sauce, I much prefer the lovely, rounded taste of good mushrooms to the indifferent presence of frozen, tinned or mealy middle-aged peas. You may substitute prosciutto for the ham, but it will give you a somewhat sharper flavour and coarser texture.

For six to eight

350 g (¾ lb) crisp, white mushrooms
2 tablespoons finely chopped shallots
    or onion
90 g (3 oz) butter
Salt
Freshly ground pepper, about 6 twists
    of the mill
175 g (6 oz) unsmoked ham, shredded

180 ml (6½ fl oz) double cream
Fettuccine (page 103), made with
    2 eggs and 200 g (7 oz) plain
    flour (basic pasta recipe, page
    96)
Pasta verde (page 108), cut into
    fettuccine
50 g (1¼ oz) freshly grated Parmesan
    cheese

1 Slice off the ends of the mushroom stems. Wipe the mushrooms clean with a damp cloth. If there are still traces of earth, wash very rapidly in cold running water and dry thoroughly with a towel. Dice into 6-mm (¼-inch) cubes and set aside.

2 Choose a frying pan that can later hold all the mushrooms loosely. Put in the chopped shallots and half the butter and sauté over medium heat until the shallots have turned pale gold in colour. Turn the heat up to high and add the diced mushrooms. When the mushrooms have absorbed all the butter, briefly turn the heat down to low, add salt and pepper, and shake the pan, moving and tossing the mushrooms. As soon as the mushroom juices come to the surface, which happens quickly, turn the heat up to high and cook the mushrooms for about 3 minutes, stirring frequently. Turn the heat down to medium, add the ham, and cook it for less than a minute, stirring as it cooks. Add half the double cream, and cook just long enough for the cream to thicken slightly. Taste and check seasoning. Turn off the heat and set aside.

3 Choose an enamelled iron pan or other flameproof serving dish that can later hold all the noodles without piling them too high. Put in the rest of the butter and the cream and turn on the heat to low. When the butter is melted and incorporated into the cream, turn off the heat and proceed to boil the pasta.

4 Spinach pasta cooks faster than yellow pasta, so the two pastas must be boiled in separate pots. Bring 4 litres (7 pints) of water in each pot to the boil and add 1 tablespoon of salt to each. First drop the yellow noodles in one pot, and stir them with a wooden spoon. Immediately after, drop the spinach noodles in the other pot and stir them with the spoon. Taste the spinach noodles 5 seconds or so after the water returns to the boil. They should be really quite firm because they will continue to soften while cooking with the sauce. Drain well and transfer to the waiting pan. Immediately after,

drain the yellow noodles and transfer them to the same pan. (Be very sure not to overcook the noodles. It is safer to err on the side of underdone than overdone.)

5 Turn on the heat to low and start tossing the noodles, coating them with butter and cream. Add half the mushroom sauce, mixing it well with the noodle strands. Add the grated cheese and mix it into the noodles. (This entire step should not take more than a minute.) Turn off the heat. Make a slight depression in the centre of the mound of *fettuccine* and pour in the rest of the mushroom sauce. Serve immediately, with an extra bowl of grated cheese.

MENU SUGGESTIONS

Follow the suggestions given for *Fettuccine all' Alfredo* (page 111).

Fettuccine al gorgonzola
FETTUCCINE WITH GORGONZOLA SAUCE

This sauce is both creamy and piquant, two qualities that are seldom combined in Italian cooking. Its mild piquancy comes from gorgonzola, Italy's incomparable blue cheese. The sauce works best when the gorgonzola is creamy and mellow. Look for cheese that is warm white in colour, soft and, perferably, recently cut. Avoid dry, crumbly or yellowish cheese. You can try substituting other blue cheeses, if you are so inclined, but you will never achieve the perfectly balanced texture and flavour of this sauce with any cheese but choice Italian gorgonzola.

Garganelli (home-made macaroni, page 146) and *Gnocchi di patate* (page 167) are also absolutely lovely with gorgonzola sauce.

For six

110 g (4 oz) gorgonzola
6 tablespoons milk
40 g (1½ oz) butter
Salt
70 ml (2½ fl oz) double cream

Fettuccine (page 103) made with 3 eggs and 300 g (10½ oz) plain flour (basic pasta recipe, page 96)
30 g (1¼ oz) freshly grated Parmesan cheese

1 Choose a shallow enamelled iron pan, or other flameproof serving dish, that can later hold all the pasta. Put in the gorgonzola, milk, butter and salt, and turn on the heat to low. Mash the gorgonzola with a wooden spoon, and stir to incorporate it into the milk and butter. Cook for about 1 minute, until the sauce has a dense, creamy consistency. Turn off the heat and set aside until you are almost ready to add the pasta.

2 Bring 4 litres (7 pints) of water to the boil. Add 2 tablespoons of salt, then drop in the *fettuccine* and cover the pot until the water returns to the boil. If the *fettuccine* are fresh, they will be done a few seconds after the water returns to the boil. If dry, they will take a little longer.

3 Just seconds before the pasta is done, turn on the heat under the sauce to low, and stir in the double cream. Add the drained, cooked pasta (if you are doing *gnocchi*, add each batch as it is done) and toss it with the sauce. Add all the grated cheese and mix it into the pasta. Serve immediately, directly from the pan, with a bowl of grated Parmesan cheese.

MENU SUGGESTIONS

It would be a pity to cancel out this marvellous sauce by following it with another highly flavoured dish. A good choice for the second course would be *Arrosto di vitello* (page 213), *Cotolette alla milanese* (page 228), *Costolettine di agnello fritte* (page 239) or *Petti di pollo alla senese* (page 265).

Fettuccine al sugo di vongole bianco
FETTUCCINE WITH WHITE CLAM SAUCE

This is a tomato-less sauce that includes two ingredients rarely used in Italian clam sauces: butter and cheese. But this departure from tradition is justified and successful because it adds smoothness and delicacy to the sauce. On the Adriatic, where I first came across it, this sauce is served with the clams still in their shells. The size of full-grown Adriatic clams, however, is little more than a thumbnail. If you tried it with large clams or mussels, you might have difficulty in fitting the pasta into the same dish.

For four

2 dozen clams, the tiniest you can find
1 tablespoon chopped shallots **or**
    onion
8 tablespoons olive oil
1 clove garlic, peeled and chopped
2 tablespoons chopped parsley
¼ teaspoon chopped chilli
4 tablespoons white wine

15 g (½ oz) butter
2 tablespoons freshly grated
    Parmesan cheese
Salt
Fettuccine (page 103), made with 2
    eggs and 200 g (7 oz) plain
    flour (basic pasta recipe, page
    96)

1 Wash and scrub the clams as directed on pages 46–7, then put in a covered saucepan over high heat. As the clams open up, shell them and put them in a small bowl. When all the clams have been shelled, pour the juices from the pan over them and set aside.

2 Put the shallots in a small saucepan with the oil and sauté over medium-high heat until translucent.

3 Add the garlic and sauté until lightly coloured.

4 Add the parsley and chilli, stir three or four times, then add the wine. Allow the wine to boil until it has evaporated by half, then turn off the heat. (The sauce may be prepared several hours ahead of time up to this point.)

5 Rinse the clams one by one in their own juice and chop into small pieces.

6 Filter the clam juices through a sieve lined with kitchen paper. You should have about 150 ml (¼ pint) of liquid. If there is more, discard it. Add the liquid to the sauce and boil until it is reduced by half.

7 Add the clams, turn them quickly in the hot sauce, and turn off the heat. Add the butter and cheese, mixing thoroughly. Taste and check salt. (No salt at all may be required.)

8 Add 1½ teaspoons salt to 4 litres (7 pints) of rapidly boiling water, then drop in the pasta and drain as soon as it is tender but *al dente*, firm to the bite. (If you are using freshly made pasta, remember that it is done a few seconds after the water returns to the boil.)

9 The moment the pasta is drained, transfer it to a warm serving bowl, add the sauce (previously reheated if no longer hot), toss thoroughly but rapidly, and serve immediately. Additional grated cheese may be served if desired.

Note   The sauce is also excellent with spaghetti or with *garganelli* (home-made macaroni, page 146).

MENU SUGGESTIONS

This can be preceded by *Pomodori coi gamberetti* (page 34), *Insalata di mare* (page 363) or *Trota marinata all'arancio* (page 188). The second course could be *Pesce ai ferri alla moda dell'Adriatico* (page 191) or *Branzino al cartoccio con frutti di mare* (page 181).

Pappardelle con il ragù di fegatini

PAPPARDELLE WITH CHICKEN-LIVER SAUCE

Pappardelle are the broadest of the long noodles. In Tuscany and elsewhere they are often served with a sauce made from stewed hare. Another good seasoning for *pappardelle* is this magnificent sauce of chicken livers. The same sauce is also quite good with ordinary noodles (*tagliatelle*, page 103). In *Anello di rosotto alla parmigiana con il ragù di fegatini* (page 156), it makes a very elegant and delicious first course.

For four

220 g (½ lb) chicken livers
2 tablespoons chopped shallots **or** onion
3 tablespoons olive oil
25 g (1 oz) butter
¼ clove garlic, peeled and finely chopped
40 g (1½ oz) diced *pancetta*, prosciutto **or** green bacon
1½ teaspoons chopped sage

110 g (¼ lb) minced lean beef
Salt
Freshly ground pepper, 6 to 8 twists of the mill
1 teaspoon concentrated tomato purée dissolved in 4 tablespoons dry white vermouth
Pappardelle (page 105), made with 2 eggs and 200 g (7 oz) flour (basic pasta recipe, page 96)

1 Clean the chicken livers of any greenish spots and particles of fat, then wash them, cut them each up into 3 or 4 pieces, and dry them thoroughly on kitchen paper. Set aside.

2 Put the shallots in a small saucepan with the oil and butter, and sauté lightly over medium heat until translucent.

3 Add the garlic, but do not allow it to become coloured. Stir two or three times, then add the diced *pancetta* and the chopped sage leaves. Sauté for about half a minute and stir.

4 Add the minced meat, crumbling it with a fork, and cook until it has completely lost its raw red colour.

5 Add salt and the pepper and turn the heat up to medium high. Add the chicken livers and stir and cook until they have lost their raw colour.

6 Add the tomato purée and vermouth mixture, stir well, and cook for about 8 to 10 minutes. Taste and check salt.

7 When the sauce is nearly done, drop the pasta into 4 litres (7 pints) of boiling water containing 1 tablespoon of salt. Drain as soon as it is tender but *al dente*, firm to the bite. (If you are using fresh, moist pasta, remember that it is done just a few seconds after the water returns to the boil.)

8 The moment the pasta is drained, transfer it to a warm dish, add the sauce, toss thoroughly but rapidly, and serve immediately, with extra grated Parmesan cheese if desired.

Note You should time the preparation of this sauce so that it is ready to use the moment the pasta is cooked. If it has been prepared a bit ahead of time and has cooled, it should be reheated very gently. On no account should it be prepared long in advance or refrigerated, because the chicken livers would stiffen, lose delicacy and acquire sharpness.

MENU SUGGESTIONS

The second course should be a fine meat dish, not strongly seasoned. It can be grilled steak, *Stracotto al Barolo* (page 206), *Arrosto di vitello* (page 213), *Cotolette alla milanese* (page 228), *Arrosto di agnello pasquale col vino bianco* (page 235) or *Costolettine di agnello fritte* (page 239).

Pesto

GENOESE BASIL SAUCE FOR PASTA AND SOUP

If the definition of poetry allowed that it could be composed with the products of the field as well as with words, *pesto* would be in every anthology. Like much good poetry, *pesto* is made of simple stuff. It is simply fresh basil, garlic, cheese and olive oil, hand ground into sauce. There is nothing more to it than that, but every spoonful is loaded with the magic fragrances of the Riviera.

The Genoese, who invented it, insist that authentic *pesto* cannot be made without their own small-leaved basil and a marble mortar. This is true and it isn't. It is true that Genoese basil is particularly fragrant, partly because of the soil but, even more important, because of the very salty Mediterranean breezes that bathe it as it grows. It is also true that grinding the basil into the marble of the mortar somehow releases more of its flavour than other methods. But, with all this, *pesto* is such an inspired invention that it survives almost anything, including large-leafed basil and the electric blender.

Two recipes are given here, one for the food-processor or blender and one for the mortar. The ingredients are identical, the difference is one of procedure. You should try, at least once, to make *pesto* in a mortar, because of the greater character of its texture and its indubitably richer flavour. But *pesto* made in the blender is still so good that we should enjoy it with a clear conscience whenever we do not have the time or the patience for the mortar. Also, since fresh basil has a brief season, and *pesto* keeps quite well in the freezer, the blender is absolutely invaluable for making a large supply to keep on hand.

In Genoa, they use equal quantities of Parmesan cheese and of a special, slightly sharp Sardinian cheese made of sheep's milk. The Romano *pecorino* cheese available outside Italy is considerably sharper than Sardo *pecorino*. You must therefore increase the proportion of Parmesan to *pecorino*, or you will throw the fine equilibrium of flavours in *pesto* out of balance. The proportion I suggest is 4 parts Parmesan to 1 part Romano. As you become familiar with *pesto* you can adjust this to taste. A well-rounded *pesto* is *never* made with all Parmesan or all *pecorino*.

The old, traditional recipes do not mention pine nuts or butter. But modern *pesto* invariably includes them, and so does this recipe.

Gnocchi di patate (page 167) are delicious with *pesto*, and so is spaghetti. The Genoese use it with *fettuccine*, which they call *trenette* (page 121), and it can be a spectacular addition to cold or hot *minestrone* (page 60).

PESTO MADE IN THE BLENDER

Enough for about six servings of pasta

100 g (3½ oz) fresh basil leaves (see note below)

8 tablespoons olive oil

25 g (1 oz) pine nuts

2 cloves garlic, lightly crushed with a heavy knife-handle and peeled

Salt

50 g (1¾ oz) freshly grated Parmesan cheese

2 tablespoons freshly grated Romano *pecorino* cheese

40 g (1½ oz) butter, softened to room temperature

1 Put the basil, olive oil, pine nuts, garlic cloves and salt in the blender

and mix at high speed. Stop from time to time and scrape the ingredients down towards the bottom of the bowl with a rubber spatula.

2 When the ingredients are evenly blended, pour into another bowl and beat in the two grated cheeses by hand. (This is not much work, and it results in more interesting texture and better flavour than you get when you mix in the cheese in the blender.) When the cheese has been evenly incorporated into the other ingredients, beat in the softened butter.

3 Before spooning the *pesto* over pasta, add to it a tablespoon or so of the hot water in which the pasta has boiled.

Note   Be gentle when measuring the basil, so as not to crush it. This would discolour it and waste the first, fresh drops of juice.

PESTO MADE IN THE MORTAR

Same yield as pesto made in the blender

110 g (3½ oz) fresh basil leaves (see note for previous recipe)
25 g (1 oz) pine nuts
2 cloves garlic, lightly crushed with a heavy knife-handle and peeled
A pinch of rock salt
50 g (1¾ oz) freshly grated Parmesan cheese

2 tablespoons freshly grated Romano *pecorino* cheese
8 tablespoons olive oil
40 g (1½ oz) butter, softened to room temperature

1 Choose a large marble mortar with a hardwood pestle. Put the basil, pine nuts, garlic and rock salt in the mortar. Without pounding, but using a rotary movement and grinding the ingredients against the sides of the mortar, crush all the ingredients with the pestle.

2 When the ingredients in the mortar have been ground into a paste, add both grated cheeses, continuing to grind with the pestle until the mixture is evenly blended.

3 Put aside the pestle. Add the olive oil, a few drops at a time at first, beating it into the mixture with a wooden spoon. Then, when all the oil has been added, beat in the butter with the spoon.

4 As with *pesto* made in the blender, add 1 or 2 tablespoons of hot water from the pasta pot before using.

MAKING PESTO FOR THE FREEZER

1 Mix all the ingredients in the blender as directed in Step 1 of *Pesto*. Do *not* add the cheese or butter. Spoon the contents of the bowl into a jar. If you are doubling or tripling the recipe, divide it into as many jars. Seal tightly and freeze.

2 Before using, thaw overnight in the refrigerator. When completely thawed, beat in the grated cheeses and the butter as in Step 2 of *pesto* made in the blender. Adding the cheese at this time, rather than before freezing, is no more work and it gives the sauce a much fresher flavour.

In Genoa, *pesto* is traditionally served with *fettuccine*, which the Genoese call *trenette*. *Trenette* are cooked and served together with boiled, sliced potatoes. Here is how to make them:

Trenette col pesto
TRENETTE WITH POTATOES AND PESTO

For six

1½ tablespoons salt
3 medium potatoes, peeled and thinly
   sliced

Fettuccine (page 103), made with 2
   eggs and 200 g (7 oz) plain
   flour (basic pasta recipe, page
   96)
Pesto (previous recipes)

1 In 4 to 5 litres (7 to 9 pints) water, to which 1½ tablespoons of salt have been added, boil the sliced potatoes until nearly tender.

2 Add the *fettuccine*. If the pasta is fresh, it will be done 5 to 10 seconds after the water returns to the boil. Drain both *fettuccine* and potatoes, transfer to a warm dish and toss the *fettuccine* with the *pesto*. Serve immediately.

MENU SUGGESTIONS FOR TRENETTE, GNOCCHI, AND SPAGHETTI WITH PESTO

Pesto is compatible with fish, and any pasta seasoned with *pesto* can be followed by *Pesce ai ferri alla moda dell' Adriatico* (page 191) or *Spiedini di*

gamberoni dell' Adriatico (page 193). Other suitable second courses are *Fagottini di vitello leccabaffi* (page 225), *Rollatini di petto di pollo e maiale* (page 266), *Costolettine di agnello fritte* (page 239), *Cerrella fritta* (page 253) and *Fegato di vitello fritto* (page 252).

Lasagne verdi al forno
BAKED GREEN LASAGNE

Although this classic *lasagne* as we make it in Romagna is richly laced with meat sauce and béchamel, it is almost austere compared to the southern variety that is popular outside Italy. *Lasagne* in Romagna is not intended as a catch-all. While acting as a vehicle for a moderate amount of meat sauce, the pasta maintains its own clearly established character. The béchamel that is added should be no more than is necessary to bind the layers and maintain moistness during baking.

It is extremely important to avoid overcooking *lasagne*. Mushy *lasagne* is an abomination. And do not use commercial ready-made *lasagne* for this recipe. *Lasagne* is never, but simply never, made with anything but home-made pasta dough.

For six

500 ml ($\frac{7}{8}$ pint) *Ragù* (page 109)
Béchamel sauce (page 23), made with 700 ml ($1\frac{1}{4}$ pints) milk, 90 g (3 oz) butter, 75 g ($2\frac{1}{2}$ oz) plain flour and $\frac{1}{4}$ teaspoon salt. It should be fairly thin, with the consistency of double cream

A sheet of *Pasta verde* (page 108)
1 tablespoon salt
65 g ($2\frac{1}{4}$ oz) freshly grated Parmesan cheese
25 g (1 oz) butter

1 Prepare the ragù and béchamel sauce and set aside.

2 If you are making the pasta by hand, roll out a sheet that is not quite paper thin. Cut the dough into rectangular strips about 110 mm ($4\frac{1}{2}$ inches) wide and 270 mm (11 inches) long. Do not allow it to dry any longer than it takes to bring 4 litres (7 pints) of water to the boil. While the water is coming to the boil, lay some clean, dry towels flat on the worktop and set a bowl of cold water near the oven. When the water boils, add the salt, then drop in 4 of the pasta strips. Stir with a wooden

spoon. Cook for just 10 seconds after the water returns to the boil, then retrieve the pasta with a large slotted spoon and dip it in the bowl, rinsing with cold water. Wring each strip very gently by hand and lay it flat on the towel. Cook all the pasta in the same manner, including the trimmings. When it is all laid out on the towel, pat it dry on top with another towel.

3 Preheat the oven to 230°C/450°F/Mark 8.

4 Choose a 350-mm (14-inch) rectangular oven dish. Smear the bottom with a little bit of *ragù*, skimming it from the top, where there is more fat. Place a single layer of pasta in the pan, overlapping the strips, if necessary, no more than 6 mm ($\frac{1}{4}$ inch). (Do not prop up the edges of the pasta along the sides of the pan. It will become dry and tough there.) Spread enough sauce on the pasta to dot it with meat, then spread béchamel over the *ragù*. Before sprinkling cheese, taste the béchamel and meat sauce coating. If it is on the salty side, sprinkle the grated cheese sparsely. If it is rather bland, sprinkle the cheese freely. Add another layer of pasta and coat it as before. (Do not make more than 6 thin layers of pasta at the maximum, since *lasagne* should not be too thick, and do not build up the layers any higher than 12 mm ($\frac{1}{2}$ inch) from the top of the pan.) Use the trimmings to plug up any gaps in the layers. Coat the top layer with béchamel, sprinkle with cheese, and dot lightly with butter.

5 Bake on the uppermost rack of the oven for 10 to 15 minutes, until a light, golden crust forms on top. Do not bake for more than 15 minutes. If after 10 minutes' baking you see that no crust is beginning to form, raise the oven temperature for the next 5 minutes.

6 Allow *lasagne* to stand for 5 to 8 minutes before serving. Serve directly from the pan.

MENU SUGGESTIONS

A very nice preliminary to green *lasagne* is sweet prosciutto, served with a slice of ripe melon. A suitable second course would be *Petto di vitello arrotolato* (page 215), *Arrosto di agnello pasquale col vino bianco* (page 235), *Rognoncini trifolati al vino bianco* (page 254), *Pollo arrosto al forno con rosmarino* (page 259) or *Coniglio in padella* (page 271).

Lo scrigno di Venere

PASTA SHELLS STUFFED WITH SPINACH FETTUCCINE

This breathtakingly beautiful dish is a bonus for those who have learned to make pasta by hand. The large sheet of yellow pasta required cannot be turned out by machine. The sheet is used to form individual shells of yellow pasta to be filled with spinach *fettuccine* seasoned with a sauce of ham, béchamel and dried mushrooms, then sealed and baked. It calls for quite a bit of work, but the weight of your efforts will drop from your shoulders at the joyous surprise your family and friends will show as they unwrap their individual pasta shells.

It is very important to understand the rhythm of the recipe. Read it carefully and do not start on it until you feel you know exactly how the work is to be organised, so that everything will fall into the right place at the right time.

For six

90 g (3 oz) dried mushrooms
250 ml (scant $\frac{1}{2}$ pint) béchamel sauce (page 23) (see Step 2, below)
Pasta verde (page 108), cut by hand into *fettuccine* (page 103)
2 tablespoons chopped shallots or onion
65 g ($2\frac{1}{4}$ oz) butter
65 g ($2\frac{1}{4}$ oz) unsmoked ham, cut into 6-mm ($\frac{1}{4}$-inch) strips

Salt
230 ml (8 fl oz) double cream
A sheet of home-made pasta dough (page 96), made with 3 eggs and 300 g ($10\frac{1}{2}$ oz) plain flour
30 g ($1\frac{1}{4}$ oz) freshly grated Parmesan cheese
6 gratin dishes, about 11 mm ($4\frac{1}{2}$ inches) in diameter

1 Put the dried mushrooms in a small bowl with 325 ml ($\frac{5}{8}$ pint) luke-warm water. They must soak for at least 30 minutes.

2 Make the thin béchamel sauce (keeping it thin by cooking it little; it should have the consistency of single cream). Set aside off the heat, over a pan filled with hot water.

3 Prepare the spinach pasta, rolling it out either by hand or by machine, but cutting it into *fettuccine* by hand.

4 Remove the mushrooms from their soaking, but do not discard the water. Strain the water through a sieve lined with kitchen paper and set aside. Rinse the mushrooms in cold running water, chop each one into two or three pieces, and set aside.

5 Put shallots in a suacepan with 40g (1½ oz) of the butter and sauté over medium heat until pale gold.

6 Add the mushrooms, their water and salt. Cook at a simmer until their liquid has evaporated.

7 Add the ham, stir three or four times and add the double cream. Cook briefly until the cream thickens slightly; then turn off the heat and set aside.

8 Prepare the sheet of yellow pasta, rolling it out as thin as possible by hand. Let the dough dry for 10 minutes.

9 Choose a lid 200 mm (8 inches) in diameter. Lay the sheet of pasta flat and cut it into 6 discs with the lid. (The left-over pasta can be cut up, dried and used in a soup.)

10 Bring 4 litres (7 pints) of water to the boil, add 1 tablespoon salt and drop in the pasta discs, cooking them two at a time. While the water is coming to the boil, lay some clean, dry towels flat on your worktop and set a bowl of cold water near the stove. Cook the pasta for 20 to 30 seconds after the water returns to the boil, then retrieve it with a slotted spoon, dip it in the bowl, rinsing with cold water, wring it out gently by hand and open it up flat on a towel.

11 Bring another 4 to 5 litres (7 to 9 pints) of water to the boil, add 1 tablespoon salt and drop in the spinach *fettuccine*.

12 While the water is coming to the boil, warm up the ham-and-mushroom sauce. When it has simmered for a minute or so, turn the heat down to very low, and add all the grated cheese, mixing it thoroughly into the sauce. Turn off the heat.

13 Keep an eye on the spinach *fettuccine*. It will be done a few seconds after the water returns to the boil. When done, drain and season immediately with the ham-and-mushroom sauce. Set aside 6 single strands of *fettuccine*, and divide the rest of the *fettuccine* into 6 portions.

14 Preheat the oven to 230°C/450°F/Mark 8.

15 Take the gratin dishes and smear the remaining butter on the bottom of each; then, working on a large, flat plate, coat a pasta disc on both sides with some of the béchamel sauce. Place the disc in one of the dishes, centring it, and letting its edges hang over the sides. Put one of the portions of *fettuccine* in the centre of the disc. Make sure it has its share of sauce. Keep the *fettuccine* fairly loose – do not press them down. Pick up the disc at the edges and close it by folding the edges towards the centre. Fasten the folds at the top with a toothpick, then wrap one of the single strands of *fettuccine* around the toothpick as decoratively as you can. Repeat the operation until you have filled and sealed all 6 pasta discs. (You can prepare the shells up to this point in the morning for the evening, if you like.)

16 Put the dishes with the shells in the uppermost level of the preheated

Scrigno di Venere: *Pick up the disc of pasta dough and close it over the* fettuccine...

...gathering it in regular, pleatlike folds.

Twist the top together and fasten it with a toothpick. Wrap a single fettuccina *around the toothpick.*

oven. Bake for 5 to 8 minutes, or until a light brown crust forms on the edges of the folds.

17 Transfer each shell from its dish to a soup plate, lifting it carefully with two metal spatulas. Remove the toothpick without disturbing the decorative *fettuccina*. Serve at once. If you are nervous, and your gratin dishes are as good-looking as the ones in the illustration, serve without removing to separate plates.

MENU SUGGESTIONS

This magnificent presentation should be followed by a simple but elegant second course. My first choice would be *Piccioncini in tegame* (page 270). Other possibilities are *Costolette alla milanese* (page 226), *Nodini di vitello alla salvia* (page 229), *Petti di pollo alla senese* (page 265) or a fine whole roasted chicken. If you want to precede the pasta shells with an antipasto, serve *Ostriche alla moda di Taranto* (page 28), *Spuma fredda di salmone* (page 29) or *Bresaola* (page 42).

Cannelloni

MEAT-STUFFED CANNELLONI

This is among the few home-made egg pasta dishes that is not native to Emilia-Romagna. It may have originated in Piedmont. *Cannelloni* is one of the most elegant of pastas, but although a number of ingredients and several different steps are involved, it is not a difficult dish to produce. In fact, it is probably the easiest of all stuffed pastas to make.

The pasta for *cannelloni* is given the briefest of boils before being stuffed. It is then seasoned with a simplified meat sauce and topped with a thin béchamel sauce. The second and final cooking takes place in the oven.

For six

Béchamel sauce (page 23), made with
450 ml ($\frac{3}{4}$ pint) milk, 60 g (2 oz)
butter, 40 g ($1\frac{1}{2}$ oz) plain flour
and $\frac{1}{4}$ teaspoon salt

The Stuffing

$1\frac{1}{2}$ tablespoons finely chopped onion
2 tablespoons olive oil
175 g (6 oz) lean minced beef
Salt
50 g ($1\frac{3}{4}$ oz) chopped *mortadella* or green bacon

1 egg yolk
$\frac{1}{2}$ teaspoon nutmeg
140 g (5 oz) freshly grated Parmesan cheese
250 g ($8\frac{3}{4}$ oz) fresh ricotta

The meat sauce

1 tablespoon finely chopped onion
2 tablespoons olive oil
175 g (6 oz) lean minced beef

Salt
110 g (4 oz) tinned Italian tomatoes, chopped, with their juice

A sheet of home-made pasta dough (page 96), using 2 eggs and 200 g ($7\frac{1}{2}$ oz) plain flour
1 tablespoon salt

35 g ($1\frac{1}{4}$ oz) freshly grated Parmesan cheese
60 g (2 oz) butter

1 Make the béchamel sauce. It should be rather thin, with a consistency similar to that of cream. Set aside.

2 To make the stuffing, put the chopped onion in a saucepan or a frying pan with the olive oil and cook over medium heat until translucent but not coloured. Add the minced beef, turn the heat down to medium low and cook it without letting it brown. Crumble the meat with a fork as it cooks. When it loses its raw red colour, cook it for 1 minute more without browning. Transfer the meat with a perforated ladle or colander to a mixing bowl, carrying with it as little of the cooking fat as possible. Add salt, chopped *mortadella*, egg yolk, nutmeg, grated cheese, ricotta and 4 tablespoons of the béchamel sauce. Mix thoroughly. Check salt and set aside.

3 To make the meat sauce, put the chopped onion in a saucepan with the olive oil and sauté over medium heat until very pale gold in colour. Add the meat, turn the heat down to medium low and cook without browning, exactly as you did for the stuffing. Add salt and the chopped tomatoes and their juice and cook at the barest simmer for 45 minutes. Set aside.

4 Prepare the pasta dough, and, if you are making it by hand, make it as thin as possible. (The pasta machine has only one setting for thinness.) Cut the pasta into rectangles 75 mm (3 inches) by 100 mm (4 inches). Do not allow it to dry any longer than it takes to bring 4 litres (7 pints) of water to the boil. While the water is coming to the boil, lay one or more clean, dry towels open flat on the worktop, and set a bowl of cold water not far from the stove. When the water comes to the boil, add the salt, then drop in 5 of the pasta strips. Stir with a wooden spoon. When the water returns

to the boil, wait 20 seconds, then retrieve the pasta with a large slotted spoon, dip it and rinse it in the cold water, then spread it on the dry towel. Cook all the pasta strips, no more than 5 at a time, in the same manner. When all the pasta is laid out on the towel, pat it dry with another towel.

5 Preheat the oven to 200°C/400°F/Mark 6.

6 Take an oven dish 220 mm (9 inches) by 350 mm (14 inches) and butter the bottom. To stuff the pasta, I find a wooden chopping board very comfortable to work on, but a large dish or any clean, flat surface will do. Lay a pasta strip flat and spread a tablespoon of stuffing on it, covering the whole strip except for a 12-mm ($\frac{1}{2}$-inch) border all around. Roll the strip up on its narrow side, keeping it somewhat loose. Lay it in the oven dish with its folded-over edge facing down. Proceed until you have used up either all the pasta or all the stuffing. (Somehow it is hard to make them come out exactly even.) Squeeze the *cannelloni* in tightly, if you have to, but do not overlap them.

7 Spread the meat sauce over the *cannelloni*, coating them evenly with sauce. Spread the béchamel sauce over this. Sprinkle with the grated cheese and dot with the butter. Bake on the next-to-highest rack in the oven for 15 minutes, or until a very light, golden crust forms. (Do not in any case exceed 20 minutes, or it will be overcooked.) Allow to stand for about 10 to 15 minutes, then serve. Although the *cannelloni* are already richly seasoned, you might have some extra grated cheese available at the table.

MENU SUGGESTIONS

Bresaola (page 42) would be a fine antipasto with which to precede *cannelloni*. As a second course you could follow with *Stracotto al Barolo* (page 206), *Petto di vitello arrotolato* (page 215), *Abbacchio alla cacciatora* (page 237) or *Piccioncini in tegame* (page 270).

Il rotolo di pasta
PASTA ROLL WITH SPINACH FILLING

In this dish an entire sheet of pasta dough is rolled up with spinach stuffing, wrapped in muslin and boiled. When cool it is sliced like a roast, dressed with a béchamel and tomato sauce, and baked very briefly in a very hot oven. It is a delicious change of pace from all the familiar pasta dishes, and it lends itself to a very attractive presentation.

For six

$\frac{1}{2}$ recipe Tomato Sauce III (page 81)
600 g (21 oz) frozen leaf spinach, thawed, or scant 1 kg (2 lb) fresh spinach
Salt
2 tablespoons finely chopped onion
90 g (3 oz) butter

50 g ($1\frac{3}{4}$ oz) chopped prosciutto, green bacon **or** *mortadella*
200 g (7 oz) fresh ricotta
100 g ($3\frac{1}{2}$ oz) freshly grated Parmesan cheese
$\frac{1}{4}$ teaspoon nutmeg
1 egg yolk

A sheet of home-made pasta dough (page 96), made with 2 eggs and 200 g (7 oz) plain flour

Medium-thick béchamel sauce (page 23), made with 250 ml (scant $\frac{1}{2}$ pint) milk, 25 g (1 oz) butter, 20 g ($\frac{3}{4}$ oz) plain flour, and $\frac{1}{8}$ teaspoon salt
30 g ($1\frac{1}{4}$ oz) freshly grated Parmesan cheese

1 Prepare the tomato sauce and set aside.

2 If you are using frozen spinach, cook the thawed spinach in a covered pan with salt for 5 minutes.

If you are using fresh spinach, discard any wilted or discoloured leaves and all the stems. Wash in a basin in several changes of cold water until the water shows no trace of grit. Cook with just the water that clings to the leaves in a covered pan with salt for 15 minutes, or until tender. Drain the spinach, squeeze lightly to remove most of its moisture, and chop roughly. Set aside.

3 In a frying pan, sauté the onion, with 50 g ($1\frac{3}{4}$ oz) butter, over medium heat. When the onion turns pale gold in colour, add the chopped prosciutto and sauté for about 30 seconds more. Then add the chopped, cooked spinach and sauté it for 2 to 3 minutes. You will find that all the butter has been absorbed.

4 Transfer the contents of the frying pan to a mixing bowl, and add the ricotta, 100 g ($3\frac{1}{2}$ oz) grated Parmesan cheese, nutmeg and, last of all, the egg yolk. Mix all the ingredients with a fork until they are well combined. Check seasoning.

5 Make the pasta as directed in the basic recipe, then roll out as thin a sheet of pasta as you can and lay it flat in front of you. Spread the filling over the pasta, starting about 75 mm (3 inches) in from the edge near you. The filling should cover all but a 6 mm ($\frac{1}{4}$-inch) border all around the sheet, and the 75-mm (3-inch) border near you. Fold this 75-mm (3-

Il rotolo di pasta: *Arrange
the slices in the dish slightly
overlapping, like roof tiles.*

inch) border over the filling, and continue to fold until you have rolled
up all the pasta. Wrap the pasta roll tightly in muslin, tying the two
ends securely with string. (If you are using a pasta machine, follow
exactly the same stuffing procedure, except that you will have to make
several short rolls instead of one long one. Each roll must be wrapped in
muslin separately.)

6 If you have made a single long roll you will need a fish kettle or
other long, deep pan that can hold all the pasta and 3 to 4 litres (5 to 7
pints) of water. If you have several short rolls, a large stockpot will do.
Bring the water to the boil, add 1 tablespoon of salt, then put in the
pasta roll or rolls and cook at a gentle but steady boil for 20 minutes.
Lift out the pasta. If it is a single long roll use the fish retriever in the
kettle or two slotted spoons or spatulas, to make sure it does not split in
the middle. Unwrap the pasta while it is hot and set aside to cool.

7 Preheat the oven to 200°C/400°F/Mark 6.

8 While the pasta cools, prepare the béchamel, and when ready mix it
with the already prepared tomato sauce. When the pasta is cool, cut it like
a roast into slices about 18 mm ($\frac{3}{4}$ inch) thick.

9 Choose an oven dish that can hold all the pasta slices in a single layer.
Lightly smear the bottom of the dish with 2 to 3 tablespoons of sauce.
Arrange the slices in the dish slightly overlapping, like roof tiles. Pour the
rest of the sauce over the pasta, then sprinkle the remaining Parmesan cheese
over the sauce and dot lightly with the remaining butter. Bake on the uppermost rack of the oven for 15 minutes. Allow to stand for 6 to 8 minutes,
then serve from the baking dish.

Note   After this dish has been entirely assembled it can wait several hours
(but not overnight) at room temperature before going into the oven.

An excellent choice for a second course would be any of the three lamb roasts on pages 235–7. Also suitable would be *Pollo arrosto in tegame* (page 257), *Pollo arrosto al forno con rosmarino* (page 259) or *Coniglio in padella* (page 271). Avoid any dish that has a decided tomato presence.

Cappelletti

CAPPELLETTI FILLED WITH MEAT AND CHEESE

In the Romagna region of Emilia-Romagna, *cappelletti* served in capon broth is the traditional dish for Christmas and New Year's Day. We usually prepare all the *cappelletti* for both occasions at one time, on Christmas Eve. Since this means a production of several hundred *cappelletti*, everyone in the family, children included, moves into the kitchen to stuff and wrap dumplings. Children, in fact, are ideal for the job because their narrow, tapered fingers permit them to wrap the tightest, smallest dumplings. When you set out to make *cappelletti*, try to make a family event out of it. The work goes quickly, it is fun and it engenders respect for quality and beauty in food.

If you travel out of Romagna a dozen miles or less into the province of Bologna, the word *cappelletti* has little meaning. But the Bolognese have a virtually identical product called *tortellini*. The stuffings will vary, but then no two families make stuffing exactly the same way. The basic difference is one of shape. While the pasta for *tortellini* is cut into discs, that for *cappelletti* is cut into squares. This gives *cappelletti* its characteristic resemblance to little peaked hats, which is precisely what its name means.

Makes about 200 cappelletti (*see note below*)

25 g (1 oz) butter
110 g ($\frac{1}{4}$ lb) lean pork loin, diced into 12-mm ($\frac{1}{2}$-inch) cubes
Salt and freshly ground pepper

160 g ($5\frac{1}{2}$ oz) chicken breast, boned, trimmed of all fat and diced into 12-mm ($\frac{1}{2}$-inch) cubes
40 g ($1\frac{1}{2}$ oz) *mortadella*, finely chopped

250 g ($8\frac{3}{4}$ oz) fresh ricotta
1 egg yolk
100 g ($3\frac{1}{2}$ oz) freshly grated Parmesan
    cheese

$\frac{1}{2}$ teaspoon nutmeg
Home-made pasta dough (page 96)
    made with 4 eggs, 400 g (14
    oz) plain flour and 1
    tablespoon milk

1 Melt the butter in a frying pan over medium heat. Just as the foam begins to subside, add the pork, seasoning it with salt and 3 or 4 twists of the pepper mill. Cook gently for about 10 minutes, browning it on all sides. Remove from the frying pan with a slotted spoon and set aside to cool. Add the chicken to the frying pan, seasoning it with salt and another 3 or 4 twists of the pepper mill. Brown it on all sides, remembering that chicken breast cooks very rapidly, in about 2 to 3 minutes, depending on the thickness. Remove from the frying pan with a slotted spoon and set aside to cool, together with the pork.

2 When the pork and chicken are cool, chop them by hand as fine as possible. (Do not process them or machine-grind them. The filling should not be so homogenised that the character and texture of the meat do not come through.) Put the chopped meat into a bowl and combine it with the *mortadella*, fresh ricotta, egg yolk, grated cheese, and nutmeg. Mix thoroughly, until all the ingredients are evenly amalgamated. Check seasoning.

3 Prepare the dough as directed in the basic recipe. If you are rolling and stretching it by hand, divide the kneaded mass in two, rolling out one half while keeping the other half covered between two soup plates. (Pasta for dumplings needs no drying; on the contrary, it should be quite soft.) As soon as you have rolled out the first half of the mass into as thin a sheet of dough as possible, cut and stuff the dough as directed below. Then roll out the other half of the mass. (If you are using a pasta machine, cut and stuff each strip of dough as soon as it is thinned out.)

4 Fold the sheet of pasta dough loosely two or three times, leaving a few inches of it not rolled up. Keeping the rest of the dough under a towel, cut a continuous strip 37 mm ($1\frac{1}{2}$ inches) wide from the unfolded part. Trim the strip so that it is perfectly straight. (You can let the trimmings dry and use them on another occasion in soup.) If you are making machine pasta, cut the dough into similar 37-mm ($1\frac{1}{2}$-inch) strips. You can adjust the width of the strip about 6 mm ($\frac{1}{4}$ inch) either way so you will not have too much to trim away.

5 Cut the strip into 37-mm ($1\frac{1}{2}$-inch) squares. Put about $\frac{1}{4}$ teaspoon of the filling in the centre of each square. Fold the square in half, diagonally across, forming a triangle. The upper edges should not quite meet the lower, but should stop about 3 mm ($\frac{1}{8}$ inch) short. Press down firmly to seal the sides. Pick up the triangle at one end of its long base, holding it between your thumb and index finger with the tip of the triangle pointing upward.

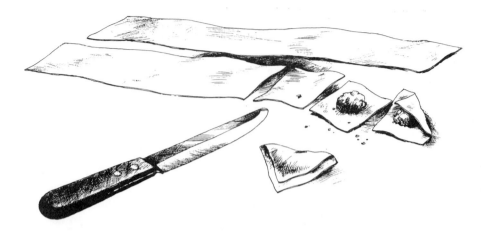

Cappelletti. *On 37-mm (1½-inch) squares of dough, put about ¼ teaspoon of filling. Fold each square diagonally, with the edges not quite meeting. Press down firmly to seal the edges.*

Bend a cappelletto *around the finger and press one corner over the other.*

Grasp the other end of the base with the other hand and wrap the base around the index finger of the first hand until the two ends meet. Press them firmly together. As you are folding the dumpling around your finger, make sure the peaked part does not hang down. Force it to fold towards you so that, as you close the dumpling, its peak points in the same direction as your fingertip.

6 As you make the dumplings, set them out in neat rows on a dry clean towel. If you are not using the *cappelletti* immediately, turn them every couple of hours until they are uniformly dry. When dry they will keep for at least a week. In Italy we keep them in a dry, cool cupboard, but, if you prefer, you can refrigerate them in an open container. Make sure they are quite dry, however, or they will stick to each other.

Note   Calculate 16 to 18 a person if served in broth, 2 dozen or more apiece if served with sauce.

Cappelletti in brodo
CAPPELLETTI IN BROTH

For six

2½ litres (4 pints) broth (page 8) (see note below)

100 *cappelletti* (page 132), approximately

Bring the broth to the boil. Drop in the *cappelletti* and stir gently from time to time with a wooden spoon. Fresh *cappelletti* cook very much faster than the dry ones; so, if fresh, taste 5 minutes after the broth returns to the boil. If dry, it may take more than three times as long. (For cooking dry *cappelletti*, it is advisable to increase the amount of broth by 150 ml (¼ pint), because some is lost through evaporation.) When the *cappelletti* are done – they should be firm but thoroughly cooked – ladle them into individual soup plates along with the broth. Serve immediately, with a bowl of grated Parmesan cheese.

Note   2½ litres (4 pints) of the broth is the amount you need for cooking the pasta. If any is left over, it can be refrigerated or frozen and used again.

MENU SUGGESTIONS
You can precede *cappelletti in brodo* with good-quality mixed cold meats such as prosciutto, *mortadella*, and Tuscan-type salami. Or you can make your own *Bocconcini fritti* (page 43). An obviously suitable second course is *Bollito misto* (page 273), but they also go well with *Stracotto al Barolo* (page 206); *Cotoletta di tacchino alla bolognese* (page 267), *Arrosto di maiale al latte* (page 240) or *Pollo coi finghi secchi* (page 262).

Cappelletti con la panna
CAPPELLETTI WITH BUTTER AND CREAM

For six

1 tablespoon olive oil
2 tablespoons salt
150 *cappelletti* (page 132)
140 ml (5 fl oz) double cream

3 tablespoons butter
50 g (1¾ oz) freshly grated Parmesan
    cheese

1 Bring 4 litres (7 pints) of water, containing 1 tablespoon of olive oil, to the boil. Add 2 tablespoons of salt, then drop in the *cappelletti*.

2 While the *cappelletti* are cooking, choose an enamelled cast-iron or other flameproof dish that will later hold all the *cappelletti* without stacking them too high. Put in half the cream and all the butter, and simmer over moderate heat for less than a minute, until the cream and butter have thickened. Turn off the heat.

3 Fresh *cappelletti* are done within 5 minutes after the water returns to the boil, while dry *cappelletti* may take 15 to 20 minutes. When done – they should be firm, but cooked throughout – transfer them with a large slotted spoon or colander to the pan containing the cream and butter and turn the heat on to low. Turn the *cappelletti* to coat them all with the cream and butter sauce. Add the rest of the cream and all the grated cheese, and continue turning the *cappelletti* until they are evenly coated and all the cream has thickened. Serve immediately from the same pan, with an extra bowl of grated cheese.

MENU SUGGESTIONS

See those for *Fettuccine all' Alfredo* (page 111).

Tortellini

Some people prefer the rounder, more compact shape of *tortellini*. If you would like to make *tortellini alla panna* or *tortellini in brodo*, follow every direction in the above recipes except for cutting the pasta. Instead of cutting the pasta into squares, cut it into 50-mm (2-inch) discs, using a glass, biscuit cutter or any circular instrument with that diameter. The discs are stuffed, folded, wrapped and sealed exactly as the squares are.

Tortellini di prezzemolo
TORTELLINI FILLED WITH PARSLEY AND RICOTTA

For four to six

20 g ($\frac{3}{4}$ oz) finely chopped parsley, preferably Italian or continental parsley
250 g ($8\frac{3}{4}$ oz) fresh ricotta
100 g ($3\frac{1}{2}$ oz) freshly grated Parmesan cheese
Salt

1 egg yolk
$\frac{1}{4}$ teaspoon nutmeg
A sheet of home-made pasta dough (page 96), made with 3 eggs, 300 g ($10\frac{1}{2}$ oz) plain flour and 1 tablespoon milk

1 Combine all the filling ingredients – parsley, ricotta, grated Parmesan cheese, salt, egg yolk and nutmeg – in a mixing bowl and mix well with a fork. Check seasoning, then set aside.

Tortellini *begin as circles.*
When stuffed and folded over,
the edges do not come exactly
together.

Bend *around the finger and*
press *one corner over the other.*

2 Prepare the pasta as directed in the basic recipe and roll out the thinnest sheet of pasta dough you can (if you are doing it by hand). Thereafter, follow all the cutting, stuffing and wrapping directions for *cappelletti* (pages 132–5). There is only one difference, and that is that the pasta is cut into discs instead of squares. This recipe calls for *tortellini* slightly larger than the meat-filled variety, which means the discs should be between 56 mm (2¼ inches) and 62 mm (2½ inches) in diameter. (If you have no cutter quite that size, you should be able to find a glass that will do.)

Note   Parsley and ricotta filling will not keep, so you should plan to cook the *tortellini* on the same day that you make them. The best way to serve these delicate dumplings is with cream and butter. Follow exactly the same method given for *Cappelletti con la panna* (page 136). Or for a soft touch of colour and a bit more flavour, try the lovely, pale *Sugo di pomodoro e panna* (see following recipe).

MENU SUGGESTIONS

Follow those given for *Fettuccine all' Alfredo* (page 111).

Sugo di pomodoro e panna
TOMATO AND CREAM SAUCE

For six servings

110 g (¼ lb) butter
½ onion, finely chopped
1 small carrot, finely chopped
1 stick celery, finely chopped

620 g (22 oz) tinned Italian tomatoes,
    with their juice
Salt to taste
¼ teaspoon granulated sugar
110 ml (4 fl oz) double cream

1 Put all the ingredients except the double cream in a saucepan and cook at the merest simmer for 1 hour, uncovered. Stir from time to time with a wooden spoon.
2 Purée the contents of the pan through a mouli-légumes (you can prepare the sauce up to this point ahead of time, and refrigerate it for a few days

or freeze it) into a saucepan and bring to a simmer, stirring with a wooden spoon. Add the double cream and cook for 1 minute more, stirring constantly. Check salt. Use immediately.

MENU SUGGESTIONS

In addition to *Tortellini di prezzemolo* (preceding recipe), this sauce is excellent with *Cappelletti* (page 132), *Tortelloni di biete* (page 140) and *Gnocchi verdi* (page 171). It is not disagreeable with factory-made pasta, but it is perhaps too delicate. Second courses following pasta seasoned with this sauce could be *Arrosto di vitello* (page 213), *Nodini di vitello alla salvia* (page 229), *Cotolette alla milanese* (page 228), *Arrosto di agnello pasquale col vino bianco* (page 235) and any of the chicken dishes that do not contain tomato.

Tortelloni di biete

TORTELLONI FILLED WITH SWISS CHARD

For five or six

2 large bunches [about 1 kg (2¼ lb)] Swiss chard (see note below)	1 egg yolk
Salt	60 g (2 oz) freshly grated Parmesan cheese
2½ tablespoons finely chopped onion	¼ to ½ teaspoon nutmeg
50 g (1¾ oz) prosciutto, rolled *pancetta* or green bacon	A sheet of home-made pasta dough (page 96) made with 2 eggs,
60 g (2 oz) butter	200 g (7 oz) plain flour and
200 g (7 oz) fresh ricotta	2 teaspoons milk

1 Pull the Swiss chard leaves from the stalks, discarding any bruised or discoloured leaves. If the chard is mature and the stalks are large and white, save them to make *Coste di biete alla parmigiana* (page 317). Wash the leaves in a basin in several changes of cold water until the water shows no earth deposit. Lift up the leaves and transfer them to a saucepan or stockpot without shaking them. (The water that clings to the leaves is all the water they need for cooking.) Add salt, cover the pot and cook over medium heat until tender, approximately 15 minutes, depending on the freshness of the chard.

Tortelloni *are laid out on a sheet of pasta by the shallow teaspoonful. The edge of the pasta is folded over...*

...and cut into squares with a fluted pastry wheel.

Drain, squeeze out all the moisture you can and chop the chard very fine. Set aside.

2 In a small frying pan sauté the chopped onion and prosciutto, in the butter, over medium heat. After less than a minute, add the chopped, cooked Swiss chard leaves and a small pinch of salt, and cook for 2 to 3 minutes more, until all the butter has been absorbed.

3 Transfer the contents of the frying pan to a mixing bowl. Add the ricotta, egg yolk, grated Parmesan cheese and nutmeg, and mix thoroughly with a fork until all the ingredients have been well combined. Check seasoning.

4 If you are hand-making the pasta, roll out the thinnest sheet of dough you can. Do not allow it to dry. Fold the sheet loosely two or three times, leaving about 125 mm (5 inches) of it extended away from you and keeping the near, folded part covered with a towel. Trim the farthest edge of the sheet so that it is perfectly straight. Dot the pasta with shallow teaspoonfuls of filling, spacing them 37 mm (1½ inches) apart, and setting them in a straight row 57 mm (2¼ inches) from the trimmed edge of the sheet. Pick up the edge and fold it towards you over the stuffing, which should then remain enclosed in the middle of a long tube. Detach this folded-over part from the pasta sheet, using a pastry cutter. Then divide it into squares, cutting straight across between each bulge of filling. Each square will have 3 cut edges. Press them firmly together, moistening them if necessary, to make sure they are tightly sealed. (If you are making pasta by machine, stuff and cut each strip of dough as it is thinned out by the machine before kneading and thinning out more pasta.) Repeat the operation until you have run out of pasta or stuffing. (It is virtually impossible to make them come out exactly the same, but left-over pasta can be cut into *maltagliati* (page 105) and used in soup. Left-over stuffing makes a tasty sandwich spread.) For cooking instructions, see following recipe.

The flavour of all cooked leaf vegetables is noticeably impaired by any attempt at conservation; therefore you must use this pasta the same day you make it.

Note Although Swiss chard has a sweeter, more delicate taste than spinach, it is not always as readily available. If you cannot find chard, spinach makes a very satisfactory substitute. Use either 550 g (1¼ lb) of frozen leaf spinach or one scant kilo (2 lb) fresh spinach.

For frozen spinach, first thaw the spinach, then cook it slowly in a covered pan for 5 minutes with salt.

For fresh spinach, remove all the stems and discard any wilted leaves. Wash in a basin in several changes of cold water until the water shows no trace of earth. Cook in a covered saucepan with salt and whatever water clings to the leaves for 15 to 20 minutes or until tender. Drain the cooked spinach, squeeze most of the moisture out of it, chop it very fine, and use it exactly as directed for Swiss chard.

Tortelloni al burro e formaggio
TORTELLONI WITH BUTTER AND CHEESE

This is the simplest way pasta is served in Italy, and it is marvellously well suited to the delicate taste of *tortelloni*. It is also an excellent way to serve spaghetti.

For five or six

1 tablespoon olive oil	110 g ($\frac{1}{4}$ lb) butter
2 tablespoons salt	100 g ($3\frac{1}{2}$ oz) freshly grated Parmesan
Tortelloni di biete (previous recipe)	cheese

1 Bring 4 litres (7 pints) water containing 1 tablespoon of oil to the boil. Add 2 tablespoons salt, then the *tortelloni*. Cover until the water returns to the boil.

2 While the *tortelloni* are cooking, cut the butter into thin strips and put in a very warm serving bowl.

3 As soon as the *tortelloni* are cooked *al dente*, firm to bite, about 5 minutes after the water returns to the boil, transfer them with a large slotted spoon or colander to the bowl containing the butter. Add the grated cheese and toss, coating all the *tortelloni* with butter and cheese. Serve immediately, with an extra bowl of grated cheese.

MENU SUGGESTIONS

There is really no meat course that is incompatible with a butter-and-cheese-seasoned pasta. The chard filling is quite delicate, however, and deserves a second course which is not too strong. I would avoid anything with sharp tomato and oregano flavouring.

TORTELLONI WITH BUTTER AND CREAM

Use the same method given for *Cappelletti con la panna* (page 136).

TORTELLONI WITH TOMATO AND CREAM SAUCE

Cook the *tortelloni* as directed above for the butter-and-cheese sauce, but season with *Sugo di pomodoro e panna* (page 139).

Cappellacci del Nuovo Mondo
CAPPELLACCI FILLED WITH SWEET POTATOES AND PARSLEY

One of the pleasantest memories of my university days in Ferrara is of the leisurely hours spent at the dinner table with friends, where food and talk gave us release from the pressures of exams and the anxieties of impending adulthood. Often these meals started with a dish of *cappellacci di zucca*, pasta filled with pumpkin. This is a speciality of Ferrara that is not made elsewhere in Italy, or even in Emilia-Romagna, except in the homes or *trattorie* of expatriate Ferrarese.

The pumpkin used in Ferrara is yellow, flat and broad, with a diameter of about 400 mm (16 inches). It has a unique, beautifully rounded taste that is difficult to describe. It is sweet, but savoury, not cloying. Some time ago, at a dinner, with my thoughts far from home, the taste of sweet potatoes suddenly brought back to me Ferrara and its *cappellacci*. The following day my long-suffering family was trying out a new dish, Italian egg pasta with a filling of sweet potato, now available in ethnic shops in many places. It went down well then, and has since become our favourite dish to spring on unsuspecting newly arrived Italian guests.

It is not, of course, Ferrara's *cappellacci*, but it makes good use of the same idea, that of combining pasta with a sweet vegetable filling. It may also encourage you to give expression to your own inventiveness and special tastes through the traditional techniques of home-made pasta.

For five or six

800 g (1¾ lb) sweet potatoes (not yams)
125 g (4¼ oz) freshly grated Parmesan cheese
3 tablespoons finely chopped parsley
25 g (1 oz) chopped *mortadella*, prosciutto **or** green bacon

1 egg yolk
½ teaspoon nutmeg
A sheet of home-made pasta dough (page 96), made with 2 eggs, 200 g (7 oz) plain flour and 2 teaspoons milk

1 Preheat the oven to 230°C/450°F/Mark 8.

2 Put the potatoes to bake in the middle level of the oven. After 20 minutes turn the thermostat down to 200°C/400°F/Mark 6. Cook for another 35 to 40 minutes, or until the potatoes are very tender when pierced with a fork.

3 Turn off the oven. Remove the potatoes and split them in half, lengthways. Return the potatoes to the oven, cut side facing up, and leave the oven door slightly ajar. Remove the potatoes after 10 minutes.

4 Peel the potatoes and purée them through a mouli-légumes into a bowl. Add all the other ingredients, except of course the pasta, and mix thoroughly with a fork until the mixture is smooth and evenly blended. Check seasoning.

5 Prepare the pasta as directed in the basic recipe and proceed to cut it and stuff it exactly as directed in Step 4 of *Tortelloni di biete* on page 140.

CAPPELLACCI WITH BUTTER AND CHEESE

Follow the directions for *Tortelloni al burro e formaggio* (page 143).

CAPPELLACCI WITH MEAT SAUCE

Cappellacci are also very good with *Ragù* (Bolognese Sauce, page 109). Calculate about 450 ml ($\frac{3}{4}$ pint) sauce for this quantity of pasta.

MENU SUGGESTIONS

Antipasti: *Bresaola* (page 42), *Bocconcini fritti* (page 43) or mixed Italian cold meats. All the roasts of veal, lamb, pork or chicken given here are suitable second courses; you can also try *Fegatelli di maiale con la rete* (page 255) or *Rognoncini trifolati al vino bianco* (page 254).

Garganelli
HOME-MADE MACARONI

Garganelli is macaroni made by hand from egg pasta. Looking somewhat like a grooved version of *penne* or *ziti*, it is native to that section of Emilia called Romagna, and it demonstrates that for the *romagnoli*, even when it comes to macaroni, there is no pasta like home-made egg pasta. I cannot justify *garganelli* to anyone who measures the advantages of a dish by the speed with which it can be prepared. But I do recommend it to those who do not regret the time spent in producing pasta whose superb texture and lovely hand-turned shape cannot be duplicated by anything bought in a box.

If you have a long, rainy afternoon on your hands, or if you have friends helping you, make a large amount of dough. *Garganelli* will keep for weeks after it dries, and you can make enough to have a supply on hand.

For six to eight

Home-made pasta dough (page 96), using 4 eggs and 400 g (14 oz) plain flour	1 tablespoon salt

1 Roll out the thinnest sheet of pasta that you can, if you are making it by hand. Fold the sheet into a loose roll and cover it, leaving just a few inches exposed. Cut this exposed part into 37-mm (1$\frac{1}{2}$-inch) squares. (If

you are making the pasta by machine, cut each thinned-out strip of dough into squares and roll into *garganelli*, as directed below, before kneading and rolling out more dough.)

2 Have ready a piece of dowelling or smooth, round pencil, 6 mm ($\frac{1}{4}$ inch) in diameter and 150 to 180 mm (6 to 7 inches) long. Take a large, absolutely clean comb, with teeth at least 37 mm ($1\frac{1}{2}$ inches) long (the closest equivalent to the original wooden tool, which is, in fact, called *pettine*, or 'comb') and lay it flat on the table, with the teeth pointing away from you. Lay a pasta square diagonally on the comb, so that one corner points in the same direction as the teeth, another towards you. Place the dowel on the square and parallel to the comb. Curl the corner of the square facing you around the dowel and, with a gentle downward pressure, push the dowel away from you and off the comb. Curled around the dowel you will have a single macaroni with a lightly ridged surface. Tip the dowel on its end and the macaroni will slide off. Proceed until all the dough has been cut and rolled into macaroni.

3 *Garganelli* are boiled like all other pasta, then served with your choice of sauce (see note below). Boil up to 6 servings of *garganelli* in 4 litres (7 pints) of water with 1 tablespoon of salt. Add more water for more servings, as needed. *Garganelli*, like all other egg pasta, will cook much faster when fresh and soft than when dry, so, if fresh, start tasting them 20 to 30 seconds after the water returns to the boil. (Do not overcook. It would be a pity to have gone to all the trouble of making *garganelli* and then ruin them by overcooking.)

Garganelli *are made by rolling pasta squares over a comb.*
Il pettine (*shown at top*) *is the Italian tool for* garganelli.

Note   The ideal sauces for *garganelli* are without doubt *Ragù* (Bolognese Sauce, page 109), and Gorgonzola (page 114). Another excellent sauce is the *Sugo di vongole bianco* on page 115. I also find *garganelli* particularly good with *Sugo di broccoli e acciughe* (page 149). This sauce is unknown in Romagna, just as *garganelli* is unknown in Apulia, where the sauce comes from. But the two hit it off beautifully together.

MENU SUGGESTIONS

If you are using meat sauce, *Lo 'schinco'* (page 219), *Fagottini di vitello lecca-baffi* (page 225), any of the three lamb roasts on pages 235–7 or *Pollo coi funghi secchi* (page 262) are good choices for the second course. If you are using the broccoli and anchovy sauce, see the suggestions under that recipe (page 150), and if white clam sauce, see the suggestions under the recipe for *Fettuccine al sugo di vongole bianco* (page 116).

Orecchiette
HOME-MADE PASTA FROM APULIA

The territory of Apulia extends over the entire heel and half the instep of the Italian boot. It is a region of glorious coastlines, of bleached, agonisingly beautiful towns and a tough, ancient race of shepherds and fishermen. They say of Bari, their principal port, that if Paris had had the sea it would have been a little Bari. There is a similar lack of understatement in Apulian food. The favourite Apulian vegetables are cabbage, cauliflower, peppers and broccoli. Chilli is used freely, anchovies appear in nearly every variety of dish short of dessert, everything is cooked in dense, fruity Apulian olive oil, and a hard, piquant ricotta is grated for seasoning pasta.

Apulia, like Emilia-Romagna, has a strong tradition of home-made pasta. It is made without eggs, just hard durum wheat flour and water, which makes a firmer, chewier, less delicate dough than the Emilian *sfoglia*. It is better suited, however, to its native, highly flavoured sauces. Like all pasta, it comes in many shapes. The best-known outside Apulia is *'recchie*, in Italian *orecchiette*, or 'little ears'. These are small discs of pasta given their ear-like shape by a rotary pressure of the thumb. The broccoli and anchovy sauce that follows this recipe is an ideal sauce for *orecchiette*.

but the inside is quite hard. Allow it to dry out before removing it from the heat, being careful that it does not stick. Spread it very thinly on a large cold dish.

2 A quarter of an hour or so before serving, melt 15 g ($\frac{1}{2}$ oz) of butter in a casserole. Add the rice and stir, coating it well with butter. Add 8 table-spoons of simmering broth and resume cooking it in the normal manner until done.

HOW MUCH BROTH TO USE

The quantity of liquid given in the following recipes for *risotto* should be considered an approximate amount. You may end up using less or slightly more than indicated, but this is not significant. There are too many variables involved to be able to establish a 'correct' amount of liquid. What is impor-tant is never to cook *risotto* with too much liquid *at one time*, and to bring it to its final tender but firm-to-the-bite stage so that it is creamy but not saturated.

Risotto alla parmigiana
RISOTTO WITH PARMESAN CHEESE

This is the purest and perhaps the finest of all *risotto*. The only major in-gredient added to the rice and broth is Parmesan cheese. In Italian cooking, you should never use anything except good-quality, freshly grated Parmesan cheese, but for this particular *risotto* you should make a special effort to obtain authentic, aged, Italian *parmigiano-reggiano* from the best supplier you know.

During the truffle season in Italy, the *risotto* is crowned at the table with thinly sliced fresh white truffles. If you should have a chance to obtain a nice large truffle, do get it for this *risotto*. It is going to set you back a con-siderable amount, but you are not likely to regret it.

Four servings

1¼ litres (2 pints) broth (page 8) **or** 2 chicken stock cubes dissolved in the same quantity of water	2 tablespoons vegetable oil
	300 g (10½ oz) raw Italian Arborio rice
2 tablespoons finely chopped shallots **or** onion	60 g (2 oz) freshly grated Parmesan cheese
40 g (1½ oz) butter	Salt, if necessary

1 Bring the broth to a slow, steady simmer.

2 Put the shallots in a heavy-bottomed casserole with 25 g (1 oz) of the butter and all the oil, and sauté over medium-high heat until translucent but not browned.

3 Add the rice and stir until it is well coated. Sauté lightly, then add 150 ml ($\frac{1}{4}$ pint) of the simmering broth. Proceed according to the basic directions for making *risotto* (page 154), adding 150 ml ($\frac{1}{4}$ pint) of simmering broth as the rice dries out, and stirring it very frequently to prevent it from sticking. (If you run out of broth, continue with water.)

4 When you estimate that the rice is about 5 minutes away from being done, add all the grated cheese and the remaining butter. Mix well. Check salt. Remember, when the cooking nears the end, not to add too much broth at one time. The *risotto* should be creamy but not runny. Serve immediately, with additional grated cheese, if desired.

MENU SUGGESTIONS

There is virtually no second course of meat, poultry or mixed meats that cannot follow this *risotto*. It can complement a delicate dish such as *Scaloppine di vitello al Marsala* (page 220) or hold its own before something as earthy as *Coda alla vaccinara* (page 245). It goes especially well before *Animelle con pomodori e piselli* (page 249) or *Fegatini di pollo alla salvia* (page 256). Do avoid any dishes with cheese. It would create monotony.

Anello di risotto alla parmigiana con il ragù di fegatini

MOULDED RISOTTO WITH PARMESAN CHEESE AND CHICKEN-LIVER SAUCE

In this elegant combination of a creamy white *risotto* with a dark and lovely sauce you have what Italians would call *un boccone da cardinale*, 'a morsel fit for a cardinal'. In Italy the church has always been known for its patronage of the arts.

For four or five

Risotto alla parmigiana (previous
    recipe), made with 25 g (1 oz)
    butter and 1 tablespoon oil
    and omitting the butter at the
    end

Ragù di fegatini (chicken-liver sauce,
    page 117), made with only 2
    tablespoons olive oil and 15 g
    ($\frac{1}{2}$ oz) butter

Lightly butter a $1\frac{1}{2}$-litre ($2\frac{1}{2}$-pint) ring mould. When the *risotto* is done, spoon it all into the ring mould and press it down. Invert the mould over a serving dish and lift it away, leaving a ring of *risotto* on the dish. Pour all the sauce in the centre of the ring, and serve immediately.

MENU SUGGESTIONS

Follow the ones given for *Pappardelle con il ragù di fegatini* (page 118).

Risotto alla milanese
MILANESE RISOTTO

For six

1 litre ($1\frac{3}{4}$ pints) broth (page 8) or 2
    chicken stock cubes dissolved
    in the same quantity of water
25 g (1 oz) diced beef marrow,
    pancetta or prosciutto
2 tablespoons finely chopped shallots
    or onion
75 g ($2\frac{1}{2}$ oz) butter
2 tablespoons vegetable oil
400 g (14 oz) raw Italian Arborio rice

$\frac{1}{3}$ teaspoon powdered saffron or $\frac{1}{2}$
    teaspoon chopped whole
    saffron, dissolved in 325 ml ($\frac{5}{8}$
    pint) hot broth or water
Salt, if necessary
Freshly ground pepper, about 4
    twists of the mill or more to
    taste
25 g (1 oz) freshly grated Parmesan
    cheese

1 Bring the broth to a slow, steady simmer.

2 In a heavy-bottomed casserole, over medium-high heat, sauté the beef marrow and shallots in 40 g ($1\frac{1}{2}$ oz) of the butter and all the oil. As soon as the shallots become translucent, add the rice and stir until it is well coated. Sauté lightly for a few moments and then add 150 ml ($\frac{1}{4}$ pint) of the simmer-

ing broth, about a ladleful. Proceed according to the basic directions for making *risotto* (page 154), adding a ladleful of hot broth as the rice dries out, and stirring it very frequently to prevent it from sticking. After 15 minutes add half the dissolved saffron. When the rice has dried out, add the rest of the saffron. (The later you add the saffron, the stronger the taste and aroma of saffron will be at the end. Herbs that call too much attention to themselves are a rude intrusion upon the general harmony of a dish, but if you like a stronger saffron presence wait another 5 to 8 minutes before adding the diluted saffron. But be careful it does not upstage your *risotto*.) When the saffron liquid has been absorbed, finish cooking the *risotto* with hot broth. (If you run out of broth, add water.)

3 When the rice is done, tender but *al dente*, firm to the bite, check salt. (If the broth was salty, you might not need any. Consider, too, the saltiness of the cheese you will be adding.) Add a few twists of pepper to taste, and turn off the heat. Add the remaining butter and all the cheese and mix thoroughly. Spoon into a hot dish and serve with a bowl of freshly grated cheese.

MENU SUGGESTIONS

Risotto alla milanese is traditionally served with *Ossobuco alla milanese* (page 216), one of the rare instances when a first course is served together with the meat course in an Italian menu. It is a well-justified exception, because the two dishes are an ideal complement to each other. This *risotto* can also be served as a regular first course when the second course is roasted or braised meat or poultry.

Risotto coi funghi secchi
RISOTTO WITH DRIED MUSHROOMS

For six

25 g (1 oz) imported dried
    mushrooms
1 litre (1¾ pints) broth (page 8) **or** 2
    chicken stock cubes dissolved
    in the same quantity of water
2 tablespoons finely chopped shallots
    or onion
60 g (2 oz) butter

3 tablespoons vegetable oil
400 g (14 oz) raw Italian Arborio rice
25 g (1 oz) freshly grated Parmesan
    cheese
Salt, if necessary
Freshly grated pepper, about 4 twists
    of the mill

1 Soak the mushrooms in 450 ml ($\frac{3}{4}$ pint) of lukewarm water for at least 30 minutes before cooking. After the liquid turns very dark, strain it through a sieve lined with kitchen paper and set aside. Continue soaking and rinsing the mushrooms in frequent changes of water until the mushrooms are soft and thoroughly free of earth.

2 Bring the broth or the bouillon to a slow, steady simmer.

3 In a heavy-bottomed casserole, over medium-high heat, sauté the chopped shallots or onion in half the butter and all the oil until translucent but not brown. Add the rice and stir until it is well coated. Sauté lightly for a few moments and then add a ladleful, 150 ml ($\frac{1}{4}$ pint), of the simmering broth. Proceed according to the basic directions for making *risotto* (page 154), adding 1 ladleful of hot liquid as the rice dries out, and stirring it very frequently to prevent it from sticking. When the rice has cooked for 10 to 12 minutes add the mushrooms and 150 ml ($\frac{1}{4}$ pint) of the strained mushroom liquid. As it becomes absorbed, add more of the mushroom liquid, 150 ml ($\frac{1}{4}$ pint) at a time. After you have used up the mushroom liquid, finish cooking the rice with hot broth. (If you run out of broth, add water.)

4 When the rice is done, turn off the heat and mix in the grated Parmesan and the rest of the butter. Check salt. (If the broth was very salty, you may not need any salt at all.) Add a few twists of pepper and mix. Spoon the rice into a hot serving dish and serve immediately with a bowl of freshly grated cheese.

MENU SUGGESTIONS

It is perhaps easier to say what second courses to avoid than to indicate which ones to choose. Stay away from any dish with mushrooms, of course, and also from other sharply competitive flavours, such as *Fettine di manzo alla sorrentina* (page 205) and *Scaloppine di vitello alla pizzaiola* (page 223) or *Arrosto di agnello al ginepro* (page 236). Otherwise, all roasts, stews and fricassees of meat and poultry are good choices. Particularly good are all the sautéed veal dishes.

Risotto col ragù

RISOTTO WITH MEAT SAUCE

For four

1¼ litres (2 pints) broth (page 8) **or**
    2 chicken stock cubes
    dissolved in the same quantity
    of water
250 ml (scant ½ pint) Ragù (Bolognese
    sauce, page 109)

300 g (10½ oz) raw Italian Arborio
    rice
Salt, if necessary
3 tablespoons freshly grated
    Parmesan cheese
15 g (½ oz) butter

1 Bring the broth to a slow, steady simmer.

2 Heat the *ragù* in a heavy, open casserole over medium heat. When it is hot and simmering, add the rice and stir until it is thoroughly mixed into the meat sauce. Cook for a few moments longer, then add a ladleful, 150 ml (¼ pint), of simmering broth. Proceed according to the basic directions for making *risotto* (page 154), adding a ladleful of simmering broth as the rice dries out, and stirring it very frequently to prevent it from sticking. (If you run out of broth, continue with water.) When the rice is done, tender yet *al dente*, firm to the bite, check salt. If you find it on the salty side, reduce or omit the grated cheese. Turn off the heat and mix in the butter. Transfer to a hot dish and serve.

MENU SUGGESTIONS

The meat sauce makes this a very substantial *risotto*. Choose a lighter second course, such as *Scaloppine di vitello al limone* (page 221) or *al Marsala* (page 220). *Pollo alla diavola* (page 260) would also be a good choice.

Risotto con la luganega

RISOTTO WITH LUGANEGA SAUSAGE

For six

Scant 1¼ litres (2 pints) broth (page 8) **or** 2 chicken stock cubes dissolved in the same quantity of water

2 tablespoons finely chopped shallots **or** onion

40 g (1½ oz) butter

2 tablespoons vegetable oil

400 g (14 oz) raw Italian Arborio rice

350 g (¾ lb) *luganega* sausage

4 tablespoons dry white wine

Salt, if necessary

Freshly ground pepper, about 5 or 6 twists of the mill

3 tablespoons freshly grated Parmesan cheese

1 Bring the broth to a slow, steady simmer.

2 In a heavy-bottomed casserole, over medium-high heat, sauté the chopped shallots with 25 g (1 oz) of butter and all the oil. When translucent, add the rice and stir until it is well coated. Sauté lightly for a few moments, then add a ladleful, 150 ml (¼ pint), of the simmering broth. Proceed according to the basic instructions for making *risotto* (page 154), adding a ladleful of hot broth as the rice dries out, and stirring it very frequently to prevent it from sticking.

3 While the rice is cooking, cut the *luganega* into 50-mm (2-inch) lengths and cook it in a frying pan over medium-high heat with the wine. After the wine has evaporated, continue browning the sausage in its own fat for 12 to 15 minutes. Remove and set aside, but do not discard the juices in the frying pan.

4 When the rice is done, tender, but *al dente*, firm to the bite, check salt. (You might not need any if the broth was salty. Consider too the saltiness of the cheese you will be adding.) Add a few twists of pepper to taste and turn off the heat. Add the remaining butter and all the cheese and mix thoroughly. Spoon into a hot dish.

5 Tip the frying pan in which the sausage was cooked and draw off all but 2 tablespoons of the fat. Add 2 tablespoons of water, turn the heat to high and, while the water boils away, scrape up and loosen any residue stuck to the pan. Return the sausages to the pan for a few moments, turning them as they warm up. Make a slight depression in the centre of the mound of *risotto* on the platter, and on it place the sausages and their sauce. Serve immediately.

Note Additional grated cheese is not usually called for with this *risotto*, but it is best to have some in a bowl at the table to suit individual taste.

MENU SUGGESTIONS

This *risotto* can precede any roasted or braised meat except pork. It is also good before chicken, if simply roasted or grilled, such as in *Pollo alla diavola* (page 260).

Risotto con gli asparagi
RISOTTO WITH ASPARAGUS

For six

450 g (1 lb) fresh asparagus
Broth (page 8) **or** 2 chicken stock cubes dissolved in water sufficient to come to $1\frac{1}{4}$ litres ($2\frac{1}{4}$ pints) liquid when added to the water in which the asparagus has cooked (see Step 3)
2 tablespoons finely chopped shallots **or** onion

75 g ($2\frac{1}{2}$ oz) butter
3 tablespoons vegetable oil
400 g (14 oz) raw Italian Arborio rice
Salt, if necessary
Freshly ground pepper, about 4 twists of the mill
25 g (1 oz) freshly grated Parmesan cheese
1 tablespoon finely chopped parsley

1 Trim, wash and boil the asparagus, following the instructions for cooking asparagus on page 302. Drain, reserving the cooking liquid, and set aside to cool.

2 When the asparagus is cool, cut into 12-mm ($\frac{1}{2}$-inch) pieces, utilising as much of the stalk as possible. If the very bottom of the stalk is tough and stringy, keep just the tender inner core, scraping it with a knife.

3 Add the broth to the water in which the asparagus cooked and bring to a slow, steady simmer.

4 In a heavy-bottomed casserole, over medium-high heat, sauté the shallots in 40 g ($1\frac{1}{2}$ oz) of the butter and all the oil until translucent. Add the cut-up asparagus and sauté lightly for 2 minutes, stirring frequently. Add the rice and stir until it is thoroughly coated. Sauté lightly for a few moments, then add a ladleful, 150 ml ($\frac{1}{4}$ pint), of the simmering broth. Proceed according to the basic directions for making *risotto* (page 154), adding a ladleful of hot broth as the rice dries out, and stirring it very frequently to prevent it from sticking. (If you should run out of broth, continue with water.)

5 When the rice reaches the proper consistency, tender but *al dente*, firm to the bite, taste it to see if it requires salt. Add a few twists of freshly ground pepper to taste. Turn off the heat and mix in the remaining butter and all the grated cheese. Add the chopped parsley and mix. Spoon the rice onto a hot serving dish and serve. At the table it can be topped with a little more freshly grated Parmesan cheese.

MENU SUGGESTIONS

Follow the suggestions for the recipe below. Of course, do not serve asparagus as a vegetable with the second course.

Risotto con le zucchine
RISOTTO WITH ZUCCHINI

For four

4 medium zucchini or 6 small ones
    (see note below)
1 small onion, coarsely chopped
5 tablespoons vegetable oil
$\frac{1}{2}$ clove garlic, peeled and finely
    chopped
Salt
Scant $1\frac{1}{4}$ litres (2 pints) broth (page
    8) **or** 2 chicken stock cubes
    dissolved in the same
    quantity of water

40 g ($1\frac{1}{2}$ oz) butter
300 g ($10\frac{1}{2}$ oz) raw Italian Arborio
    rice
Freshly ground pepper, about 4
    twists of the mill
1 tablespoon finely chopped parsley
3 tablespoons freshly grated
    Parmesan cheese

1 Carefully wash or scrape the zucchini clean and slice into discs 12 mm ($\frac{1}{2}$ inch) thick. Set aside.

2 In a medium-sized (220-mm) (9-inch) frying pan, sauté the onion with 3 tablespoons of the oil over medium-high heat. When the onion becomes translucent, add the chopped garlic, and as soon as it colours lightly, add the sliced zucchini and turn the heat down to medium low. Add a tiny pinch of salt after 10 or 12 minutes. The zucchini are done when they turn a rich golden colour, usually about 30 minutes. (You can prepare them ahead of

time, several hours or a few days, if you refrigerate them tightly covered with plastic film.)

3 Bring the broth or bouillon to a slow, steady simmer. Transfer the zucchini to a heavy-bottomed casserole, leaving behind in the pan as much of the cooking fat as possible. Add 25 g (1 oz) butter and the remaining oil to the casserole and turn the heat to high. When the fat and zucchini begin to bubble, add the rice and stir until it is well coated. Sauté lightly for about 1 minute, then add a ladleful, 150 ml ($\frac{1}{4}$ pint), of the simmering broth. Proceed according to the basic directions for making *risotto* (page 154), adding 1 ladleful of hot liquid as the rice dries out, and stirring it very frequently to keep it from sticking. (If you run out of broth, add water.)

4 When the rice is done, tender but *al dente*, firm to the bite, check salt. (If the broth was very salty, you might not need any. Bear in mind, too, that the Parmesan cheese you will add is salty.) Turn off the heat, add a few twists of pepper, the remaining butter, the chopped parsley, and the grated Parmesan and mix thoroughly. Spoon onto a hot dish and serve immediately, with a bowl of freshly grated cheese.

Note If you have made the zucchini stuffed with meat and cheese on page 341, use the chopped cores of 8 to 10 zucchini.

MENU SUGGESTIONS

Any meat or chicken roast will make a fine second course, as would *Rognoncini trifolati al vino bianco* (page 254), *Fegato di vitello fritto* (page 252) and *Fegatini di pollo alla salvia* (page 256). Avoid stews or fricassees containing vegetables, and do not accompany the second course with any vegetable dish of zucchini.

Risotto con le vongole
RISOTTO WITH CLAMS

For six

3 dozen clams, the tiniest you can find
1 tablespoon finely chopped onion
5 tablespoons olive oil
2 cloves garlic, peeled and finely chopped

2 tablespoons chopped parsley
400 g (14 oz) raw Italian Arborio rice
6 tablespoons dry white wine
Salt and freshly ground pepper to taste

1 Wash and scrub the clams thoroughly, according to the directions on page 46. Heat them over high heat in a covered pan until they open their shells, giving them a vigorous shake or turning them so that they will heat up more evenly. (Some clams are more stubborn about opening up than others.) When most of them have opened up, it is best to remove them while waiting for the tardy ones; otherwise they will become tough as they linger in the pan. Remove the clams from their shells and rinse off any sand on the meat by dipping them briefly one at a time in their own juice. Unless the clams are exceptionally small, cut them up into two or more pieces and set aside. Strain the clam juices through a sieve lined with kitchen paper and set aside.

2 Bring scant $1\frac{1}{4}$ litres (2 pints) of water to a slow, steady simmer.

3 In a heavy-bottomed casserole, sauté the chopped onion in the olive oil over medium-high heat. When translucent, add the garlic and sauté until it colours lightly. Add the parsley, stir, then add the rice and stir until it is well coated with oil. Sauté lightly for a few moments and then add the wine. When the wine has evaporated and the rice dries out, add the strained clam juices. As the rice dries out, add a ladleful, 150 ml ($\frac{1}{4}$ pint), of the simmering water. Proceed according to the basic directions for making *risotto* (page 154), adding a ladleful of simmering water as the rice dries out, and stirring it very frequently to prevent it from sticking. After 15 or 20 minutes add salt and pepper to taste.

4 When the rice is done, tender but *al dente*, firm to the bite, check seasoning. Add the clams, mixing them into the hot rice; then turn off the heat and spoon the rice onto a hot dish. Serve immediately.

Note This *risotto*, as is true of all pastas and soups with a seafood base, does not call for grated cheese.

MENU SUGGESTIONS

For a complete fish dinner, you can start with *Ostriche alla moda di Tarante* (page 28), or *Spuma fredda di salmone* (page 29), as an antipasto. Follow the risotto with *Pesce ai ferri alla moda dell' Adriatico* (page 191). Other second courses could be *Calamari ripieni stufati al vino bianco* (page 197) or *Filetti di sogliola con pomodoro e capperi* (page 187).

Riso filante con la mozzarella
RICE WITH FRESH BASIL AND
MOZZARELLA CHEESE

This is nothing more than boiled rice and fresh basil enmeshed in the fine tangles of melted mozzarella. It is another example of how, in Italian cooking, simple handling of the simplest ingredients results in a dish interesting in texture, lovely to look at, and, best of all, delicious.

For four

Salt

300 g (10½ oz) raw rice, preferably
    Italian Arborio rice

90 g (3 oz) butter, cut up

2 tablespoons shredded fresh basil **or**
    1 tablespoon chopped parsley

250 g (8½ oz) mozzarella cheese,
    shredded on the largest holes
    of the grater

60 g (2 oz) freshly grated Parmesan
    cheese

1 Bring 3 litres (5 pints) of water to the boil, add salt, then the rice, and mix with a wooden spoon. Cover the pot and cook at a moderate but steady boil until the rice is tender but *al dente*, firm to the bite. (Depending on the rice, it should take about 15 to 20 minutes.) While cooking, stir from time to time with a wooden spoon.

2 Drain and transfer the rice to a warm serving bowl. Mix in the cut-up butter; then add the basil (or parsley) and mix.

3 Add the shredded mozzarella and mix quickly and thoroughly. (The heat of the rice melts the mozzarella, forming a soft, fluffy skein of cheese and rice flecked with green.)

4 Add the grated Parmesan cheese, stir two or three times, and serve immediately.

MENU SUGGESTIONS

This would be very nice before a second course of *Fettine di manzo alla sorrentina* (page 205), *Scaloppine di vitello alla pizzaiola* (page 223), *Rollatini di vitello al pomodoro* (page 224), *Spezzatino di vitello coi piselli* (page 232) or *Pollo alla cacciatora* (page 261). Actually, it can precede any kind of meat or poultry – roasted, braised, fried or sautéed – as long as it is not made with cheese or milk.

Gnocchi di patate
POTATO GNOCCHI

Most recipes for potato *gnocchi* call for one or more egg yolks. I find that the eggless version produces finer *gnocchi*. Eggs may make them easier to handle, but they also make them tough and rubbery. Eggless *gnocchi* are light, fluffy and less filling. *Gnocchi* can be seasoned with almost any sauce. Three particularly happy combinations are *gnocchi* with Tomato Sauce III (page 81), with *Pesto* (page 118) or *al gorgonzola* (page 114).

For four to six

680 g (1½ lb) boiling potatoes (not King Edward or new potatoes; see note below)
120 g (4½ oz) plain flour

Tomato Sauce III (page 81), or Pesto (page 118), **or** Gorgonzola Sauce (page 114)
60 g (2 oz) freshly grated Parmesan cheese, more if necessary

1 Boil the potatoes, unpeeled, in abundant water. (Do not test them too often while cooking by puncturing them with a fork or they will become waterlogged.) When cooked, drain them, and peel as soon as you can handle them. Purée them through a mouli-légumes while still warm.

2 Add most of the flour to the mashed potatoes and knead into a smooth mixture. (Some potatoes take more flour than others, so it is best not to add all the flour at once.) Stop adding flour when the mixture is soft, smooth and still slightly sticky. Shape it into sausage-like rolls about as thick as your thumb, then cut the rolls into 18-mm (¾-inch) lengths.

3 This step is more complicated to explain than it is to execute. At first, just go through the motions until you feel you have understood the mechanics of the step. Then start on the *gnocchi* – but without losing heart if the first few do not turn out quite right. You will soon acquire the knack and do a lot of *gnocchi* in two or three minutes. (And, in working with *gnocchi*, it will make your life much easier if you remember to dust repeatedly with flour the *gnocchi*, your hands and any surface you are working on.)

Take a fork with long, rounded, slim prongs. Working over a flat surface hold the fork sideways – that is, with the prongs pointing from left to right (or right to left) and with the concave side facing you. With the other hand, place a dumpling on the inside curve of the fork just below the points of the prongs and press it against the prongs with the tip of the index finger pointing directly at and perpendicular to the fork. While pressing the dumpling with your finger, flip it away from the prong tips and towards the handle

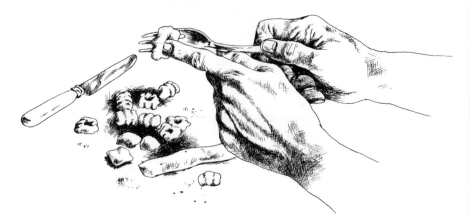

Place gnocchi *on the inside curve of a fork and press against the prongs with the tip of the index finger, pointing directly at and perpendicular to the fork. While pressing the dumpling with your finger, flip it away from the prong tips, towards the fork handle, and as it rolls let it drop to the worktop.*

of the fork. Do not drag it, flip it. As it rolls to the base of the prongs, let it drop to the worktop. The dumpling will then be somewhat crescent-shaped, with ridges on one side formed by the prongs, and a deep depression on the other formed by your fingertip. (This is not just a capricious decorative exercise. It serves to thin out the middle section of the dumpling so that it will cook more evenly, and to create little grooved traps in its surface for the sauce to sink into and make the *gnocchi* tastier.)

4 Drop the *gnocchi*, about 2 dozen at a time, into 5 litres (8 pints) or more of boiling salted water. In a very short time they will float to the surface. Let them cook just 8 or 10 seconds more, then lift them out with a slotted spoon and transfer to a heated dish. Dress with a little of the sauce you are using. (If you are using the tomato sauce, add a light sprinkling of grated cheese.) Drop more *gnocchi* in the boiling water and repeat the whole process until they are cooked. When all the *gnocchi* are done, pour the rest of the sauce over them and mix in all the grated cheese. Serve hot.

Note   In Britain, Desirée potatoes are the best for making *gnocchi* without eggs. If you want to use King Edward potatoes, you will find if easier if you mix an egg in with the purée and the flour. White potatoes do not make good *gnocchi*.

If dressed with pesto, see the suggestions for *Trenette col pesto* (page 121). If dressed with tomato sauce, *Stracotto al Barolo* (page 206), *Lo 'schinco'* (page 219), *Petto di vitello arrotolato* (page 215), *Arrosto di agnello al ginepro* (page 236), *Fegato alla veneziana* (page 250) or *Rollatini di petto di pollo e maiale* (page 266) are some suitable second courses. If dressed with gorgonzola, see the suggestions for *Fettuccine al gorgonzola* (page 114).

Gnocchi alla romana
SEMOLINA GNOCCHI

Although many Romans will maintain that *semolino gnocchi* are not *alla romana*, this dish can be traced back directly to Imperial Rome. Apicius gives a recipe for *gnocchi* made of *semolino* milk exactly like these, then fried and served with honey. All that has changed substantially since then is the cooking method and the seasoning.

For four to six

1 litre (1¾ pints) milk	Salt
200 g (7 oz) semolina, preferably imported Italian *semolino*	2 egg yolks
100 g (3½ oz) freshly grated Parmesan cheese	100 g (3½ oz) butter

1 Heat the milk in a heavy saucepan over moderate heat until it is just short of boiling. Lower the heat and add the *semolino*, pouring it in a thin, slow stream and beating it steadily into the milk with a whisk. Continue beating until it forms a thick mass on the whisk as it turns (about 10 minutes). Remove from the heat.

2 Add 60 g (2 oz) of the grated cheese, salt, the 2 egg yolks and 25 g (1 oz) of butter to the *semolino*. Mix rapidly, to avoid coagulating the egg, until all the ingredients are well blended.

3 Moisten a formica or marble surface with cold water and spoon out the *semolino* mixture, using a metal spatula or a broad-bladed knife to spread it to a thickness of approximately 9 mm (⅜ inch). (Dip the spatula or knife into the cold water from time to time.) Let the *semolino* cool completely, about 30 to 40 minutes.

4 Preheat the oven to 230°C/450°F/Mark 8.

5 With a 37-mm (1½-inch) biscuit cutter, or with a small glass of approxi-

mately the same diameter, cut the *semolino* mixture into discs, moistening the cutting tool from time to time in cold water to make the cuts easier and neater.

6 Smear the bottom of a rectangular or oval oven dish with butter. Lift off the small four-sided sections of *semolino* in between the discs and lay them on the bottom of the baking dish. Dot with butter and sprinkle with grated Parmesan. Over this arrange all the discs in a single layer, overlapping them like roof tiles. Dot with butter and sprinkle with the remaining grated cheese. Place on the uppermost rack of the oven and bake for 15 minutes or until a light golden crust has formed. If after 15 minutes the crust has not formed, turn the oven thermostat up to 250°C/500°F/Mark 10 and bake for 5 more minutes. Allow to stand a few minutes before serving.

Note The entire dish can be prepared up to two days ahead of time before baking if it is refrigerated and covered with plastic film.

MENU SUGGESTIONS

This is a dish of uncomplicated taste and texture that can precede any meat or poultry dish. It is a particularly fitting first course when the second course is *Abbacchio alla cacciatora* (page 237). *Animelle con pomodori e piselli* (page 249) or *Rollatini di petto di pollo e maiale* (page 266) are also excellent choices. For an antipasto you might have *Carciofi alla romana* (page 286) or *Insalata di funghi e formaggio* (page 41).

Gnocchi alla romana

Gnocchi verdi
SPINACH AND RICOTTA GNOCCHI

For four

1 tablespoon finely chopped onion
25 g (1 oz) butter
25 g (1 oz) very finely chopped
    mortadella, pancetta **or**
    green bacon
300 g (10 oz) frozen leaf spinach,
    thawed, **or** 450 g (1 lb) fresh
    spinach, prepared as directed
    on page 130

Salt
150 g (5¼ oz) fresh ricotta
90 g (3 oz) plain flour
2 egg yolks
100 g (3½ oz) freshly grated Parmesan
    cheese
¼ teaspoon nutmeg

1 Put the onion in a frying pan with the butter and sauté over medium heat until pale gold.

2 Add the chopped *mortadella* and continue sautéing just long enough to stir 3 or 4 times, combining the *mortadella* well with the onion and butter.

3 Add the spinach and salt, and sauté for 5 to 6 minutes, stirring frequently. (The spinach will absorb all the butter, but it is not necessary to add any more.)

4 Transfer the entire contents of the frying pan to a mixing bowl. Add the ricotta and flour, mixing thoroughly with a wooden spoon. Add the egg yolks, grated cheese and nutmeg, and incorporate them thoroughly into the mixture with the spoon. Check salt.

5 Make small pellets out of the mixture, shaping them quickly in the palm of your hand. Ideally they should be about 12 mm (½ inch) in diameter, but if this size is too small for you to handle, or the job too tedious, you can make them as large as 18 mm (¾ inch). (The smaller the better, however, because they cook more quickly and stay softer.) When the mixture begins to stick to your hands, dust your hands lightly with flour.

6 Cook the *gnocchi* as indicated in the three recipes that follow.

Note A recipe for home-made ricotta appears on page 13.

Gnocchi verdi al burro e formaggio
BAKED GREEN GNOCCHI

For four

1½ tablespoons salt
Gnocchi verdi (preceding recipe)
65 g (2¼ oz) butter

50 g (1¾ oz) freshly grated Parmesan
cheese

1 Preheat the oven to 190°C/375°F/Mark 5.

2 Bring 4 litres (7 pints) of water to the boil. Add the salt, then drop in the *gnocchi*, a few at a time. Two to three minutes after the water returns to the boil, retrieve the *gnocchi* with a slotted spoon and place in a buttered oven dish. Add more *gnocchi* to the boiling water, repeating the above procedure, until all the *gnocchi* are cooked and in the baking dish.

3 Melt the butter in a small pan and pour it over the *gnocchi*.

4 Sprinkle all the grated cheese over the *gnocchi*. Place the dish on the uppermost rack of the oven for about 5 minutes, until the cheese has melted. Allow to stand for a few minutes before serving, then serve directly from the baking dish, with an extra bowl of grated cheese.

MENU SUGGESTIONS

Follow with any roast: beef, veal, lamb, pork, or poultry. Other excellent choices for the second course would be *Stracotto al Barolo* (page 206), *Rollatini di vitello al pomodoro* (page 224), *Pollo alla cacciatora* (page 261), *Fegato alla veneziana* (page 250) or *Fegato di vitello fritto* (page 252).

Gnocchi verdi in brodo
GREEN GNOCCHI IN BROTH

If you have very good home-made broth on hand, made from beef, veal and/or chicken, you can make a delicious and elegant soup with green *gnocchi*. Served as soup, *gnocchi* go quite a bit further, so calculate about

6 ample servings, using the same quantity of *gnocchi* produced with the basic recipe.

For six

2 litres (3½ pints) home-made broth
Gnocchi verdi (page 171)

Bring the broth to the boil. Drop in all the *gnocchi* and cook for 3 to 4 minutes after the broth has returned to the boil. Ladle into soup plates and serve with a bowl of freshly grated Parmesan cheese.

MENU SUGGESTIONS

If the broth comes from meat boiled for the occasion, a dish of *Bollito misto* (page 273) would be the ideal second course. Otherwise, follow the suggestions given for the preceding recipe (page 172); especially suitable would be a substantial dish, such as *Stracotto al Barolo* (page 206).

Gnocchi verdi con sugo di pomodoro e panna
GREEN GNOCCHI WITH TOMATO AND CREAM SAUCE

For four

Sugo di pomodoro e panna (Tomato and Cream Sauce, (page 139)

2 tablespoons salt
Gnocchi verdi (page 171)

1 Keep the sauce warm as you prepare the rest of the dish.

2 Bring 4 litres (7 pints) of water to the boil. Add the salt, then the *gnocchi*, a few at a time. Three to four minutes after the water returns to the boil, retrieve the *gnocchi* with a slotted spoon and place on a hot dish. Season with a little bit of sauce. Add more *gnocchi* to the boiling water, repeating the above procedure, until all the *gnocchi* are cooked and dressed. Pour any remaining sauce over the *gnocchi* and serve immediately, with a bowl of freshly grated Parmesan cheese.

MENU SUGGESTIONS

The perfect second course would be a roast of veal, either *Arrosto di vitello* (page 213) or *Petto di vitello arrotolato* (page 215). Also suitable is *Pollo arrosto in tegame* (page 257) or *Pollo arrosto al forno con rosmarino* (page 259). Avoid any second course that is especially strong or includes tomatoes.

POLENTA

For the past three centuries *polenta* has been the staff of life in much of Lombardy and all of Venetia, particularly in Friuli, that northern region of Venetia which arches towards Yugoslavia.

To call *polenta* a maize porridge is a most indelicate use of language. In country kitchens, *polenta* was more than food, it was a rite. It was made daily in an unlined copper kettle, the *paiolo*, which was always kept hanging at the ready on a hook in the centre of the fireplace. The hearth was usually large enough to accommodate a bench on which the family sat, warming itself at the fire, talking, watching the glittering meal stream into the boiling kettle, encouraging the tireless stirring of the cook. When the *polenta* was done, there was a moment of joy as it was poured out in a steaming, golden circle on the beechwood top of the *madia*, a cupboard where bread and flour were stored. Italy's great nineteenth-century novelist, Alessandro Manzoni, described it as looking like a harvest moon coming out of the mist. The image is almost Japanese.

The uses of *polenta* are infinite, and although it is always listed among the first courses, it cannot be neatly labelled a first course, second course or vegetable dish. It can be any of the three. When piping hot it can be eaten alone, with butter and cheese. Or it can accompany any stewed, braised or roasted meat or poultry. With game birds it is divine. When it has cooled and hardened, it can be fried, grilled or sliced and baked with a variety of fillings.

There are two basic types of *polenta* flour. One is fine-grained, the other coarse. The coarse-grained is the one used in these recipes because of its more interesting, robust texture. Some traditional Italian recipes tell you to stir *polenta* for an hour or even more. But with a modern stove this is completely unnecessary. In the method given below, 20 minutes' stirring after all the corn meal has been added will produce absolutely perfect *polenta*. Never use pre-cooked polenta flour.

BASIC METHOD FOR MAKING POLENTA

For four to six

Salt

300 g (10½ oz) coarse-grained corn meal

1 Bring 1½ litres (3 pints) of water to the boil in a large, heavy saucepan.

2 Add salt, turn the heat down to medium low so that the water is just simmering, and add the corn meal in a very thin stream, stirring with a stout, long wooden spoon. The stream of corn meal must be so thin that you can see the individual grains. A good way to do it is to let a fistful of corn meal run through nearly closed fingers. Never stop stirring, and keep the water at a slow, steady simmer.

3 Continue stirring for 20 minutes after all the corn meal has been added. The *polenta* is done when it tears away from the sides of the pot as you stir.

4 When done, pour the *polenta* onto a large wooden block or a flat dish. Allow it to cool first if you are going to slice it in preparation for subsequent cooking. Otherwise, serve it piping hot.

Note It may happen that some of the *polenta* sticks to the bottom of the pot. Cover the bottom with water and let it soak for 25 minutes. The *polenta* will then wash away easily.

Polenta con la luganega
POLENTA WITH SAUSAGES

For four to six

2 tablespoons chopped onion
3 tablespoons olive oil
1 carrot, chopped
1 stick celery, chopped
110 g (¼ lb) sliced *pancetta*, cut into strips 12 mm (½ inch) wide

450 g (1 lb) *luganega* sausage **or** other mild sausage, cut into 75-mm (3-inch) lengths
220 g (8 oz) tinned Italian tomatoes, cut up, with their juice
Polenta (previous recipe)

1 Put the onion in a saucepan with the oil and sauté over medium heat until pale gold.

2 Add the carrot, celery and *pancetta*. Sauté for 3 to 4 minutes, stirring frequently.

3 Add the sausages and cook for 10 minutes, always at medium heat, turning them from to time.

4 Add the tomatoes and their juice and cook at a gentle simmer for 25 minutes, stirring from time to time. Cover the pan and transfer to a very low oven to stay warm while you prepare the *polenta*.

5 When the *polenta* is done, pour it onto a large dish. Make a depression in the centre and pour in the sausages and all their sauce. Serve immediately.

MENU SUGGESTIONS

This is a second course, but *polenta* takes the place of pasta or rice, so you can omit the first course. It is quite appropriate to precede this with a plate of mixed Italian cold meats such as prosciutto, good salami and *mortadella*. Another excellent antipasto would be *Peperoni e acciughe* (page 32).

Polenta al burro e formaggio
POLENTA WITH BUTTER AND CHEESE

For four to six

Polenta (page 175), cooked with an additional 150 ml ($\frac{1}{4}$ pint) of water to keep it a little thinner

110 g ($\frac{1}{4}$ lb) butter
40 g ($1\frac{1}{2}$ oz) freshly grated Parmesan cheese

Pour the *polenta* onto a warm dish and mix with the butter and cheese. Serve promptly.

MENU SUGGESTIONS

In this case *polenta* is served as a first course, and may be followed by any meat or poultry. Particularly suitable are roasts of lamb, pork or chicken.

Polenta fritta
FRIED POLENTA

For four to six or more, depending on how it is used

Polenta (page 175)

Vegetable oil, enough to come 18 mm ($\frac{3}{4}$ inch) up the side of a frying pan

1 Prepare the *polenta* as directed in the basic recipe and allow it to cool completely and become firm. Divide it into four parts, then cut these into slices 12 mm ($\frac{1}{2}$ inch) thick. (The traditional way to cut *polenta* is with a tautly held thread.)

2 Heat the oil in a frying pan over high heat. When the oil is very hot, slide in as many slices of *polenta* as will fit comfortably. Fry until a transparent, not coloured, crust forms on one side, then turn them and do the other side. Transfer to kitchen paper to drain.

MENU SUGGESTIONS

Fried *polenta* is ideal as a component of *Il grande fritto misto* (page 283). It can also accompany *Fegato alla veneziana* (page 250) or any roasted meat or poultry. In that case, a soup rather than pasta or rice would be preferable as a first course.

Polenta col gorgonzola
POLENTA WITH GORGONZOLA

Polenta prepared in this manner is excellent as an antipasto or as a nourishing snack.

Polenta (page 175), allowed to cool and sliced as in *Polenta fritta* (previous recipe)

Gorgonzola or any ripe, strong cheese

1 Preheat the grill to its maximum setting.

2 Toast the *polenta* slices under the grill until they are a light, mottled brown on both sides. Spread the cheese on one side of the hot, toasted slices and serve immediately.

Polenta pasticciata
BAKED POLENTA WITH MEAT SAUCE

For six

Béchamel sauce (page 23) (see Step 2, below)
Polenta (page 175), allowed to cool
450 ml ($\frac{3}{4}$ pint) *Ragù* (Bolognese sauce, (page 109)

60 g (3 oz) freshly grated Parmesan cheese
15 g ($\frac{1}{2}$ oz) butter

1 Preheat the oven to 230°C/450°F/Mark 8.

2 Make the béchamel, keeping it on the thin side by cooking it less. It should have the consistency of double cream. Set aside.

3 Slice the cold *polenta* horizontally into 3 layers, each about 12 mm ($\frac{1}{2}$ inch) high. Watch both sides of the *polenta* mass as you cut to make sure you are slicing evenly.

4 Lightly butter a 270-mm (11-inch) rectangular oven tin. Cover with a layer of *polenta*, patching where necessary to cover uniformly.

5 Spread béchamel sauce over the *polenta*, then spread the meat sauce and sprinkle with Parmesan cheese. Cover this with another layer of *polenta* and repeat the operation, leaving just enough béchamel, meat sauce and Parmesan cheese for a light topping over the next and final layer of *polenta*. Dot the top lightly with butter.

6 Bake in the uppermost level of the preheated oven for 10 to 15 minutes, until a light crust has formed on top. Remove from the oven and allow to stand for about 5 minutes before serving.

Note You may prepare this entirely ahead of time up to the point where the dish is ready for the oven. It may be refrigerated overnight, but it should be returned to room temperature before baking.

MENU SUGGESTIONS

Follow the ones given for *Lasagne verdi al forno* (page 122), which this dish strongly resembles.

SECOND COURSES

I Secondi

WHILE Italian first courses owe their luxuriance to the fertile imagination of the home cook, the austerity of the second courses is the legacy of the hunter and the fisherman. Cross out everything grilled or roasted from a list of Italian second courses and you would be left with a very brief list indeed. This should be no cause for regret, however. If the second courses were as exuberant as the pastas, an Italian meal would exhaust both our enjoyment and our digestion.

Next to grilling and roasting, sautéing and frying are the most important cooking methods, and they are all amply represented in this chapter.

The section on fish is relatively brief, which may startle anyone familiar with the excellence and (before polluted waters) the abundance of Italian fish. This is because many of the varieties of fish and, particularly, of shellfish and crustaceans found in the Adriatic and Mediterranean are difficult or impossible to find outside Italy and southern Europe. Alan Davidson's *Mediterranean Seafood* and *North Atlantic Seafood* are invaluable guides to edible fish species and have useful lists of local regional names.

Some generally available varieties of ocean fish, however, do lend themselves to an Italian taste in cooking. There is a beautiful recipe for baked sea bass stuffed with shellfish and sealed in foil that would not turn out any better with any Italian fish. Fresh young halibut and bream are other excellent fish for which specific recipes are given. There is a general recipe for grilling fish that will give an Italian flavour to the fish already mentioned, as well as to such other varieties as mackerel and mullet. Fish soup is, by definition, a collection of what fish is available. There is a recipe for it in this chapter that should be successful wherever you might be, as long as it is close to a source of good salt-water fish.

The quality of Italian meat is often, but unjustly, maligned. It is true that beef in the south and certain parts of the north can be perfectly terrible, but in those regions cattle are used first for labour, then for food. For meat the people raise lambs, and the delectable *abbacchi* of Rome or kids of Apulia can make one forget filet mignon. Lamb can be butchered at various ages, and the flavour and cooking methods vary accordingly. There are three substantially different lamb roasts in this chapter. One is for baby lamb, which is nearly as young as Roman *abbacchio*, another is for slightly older spring lamb, and the third is for the more mature, generally available standard lamb.

There is superb beef in Italy, and it is found in Tuscany. Beef from Val di Chiana cattle can hold its own with the Burgundian Charolais, Japan's Wadakin or Aberdeen Angus. The most famous cut of beef in Italy is the Florentine T-bone steak, known as *bistecca alla fiorentina*, whose simple but special cooking method is given here. Piedmont also produces good beef, and the *Stracotto al Barolo* (Beef Braised in Red Wine) in this chapter is a Piedmontese speciality.

Piedmont, along with Lombardy, produces marvellous, milky veal. Italy's veal dishes are probably its best-known contribution to meat courses, and in this chapter there are, in fact, more recipes for veal than for any other meat. Veal when cut into *scaloppine* has its own special tempo of cooking. It is done very briefly, and at quick, high heat. The Dutch veal we can now buy in England can be very successfully used in all these recipes. With care in the buying and cooking, it is now possible to produce veal dishes of a very high order.

Italian chicken dishes have always had a universal appeal. They are uncomplicated, easygoing and invariably charming. Here there are two simple roasts, a tasty, peppery grilled chicken, and two typically Italian fricassees with vegetables. Chicken and turkey breast fillets are very much an Italian speciality. You will find a clear and detailed explanation of a technique for making fillets that can be adapted for any recipe calling for chicken or turkey breasts. This is followed by three examples of how the technique is used in Italian cooking, including the famous turkey breast fillets with ham, cheese and truffles of Bologna. Near the end of the chapter, there is a section on offal. Those who already include them in their cooking will find some newly edited classic dishes, and some less familiar ones.

Italians make an excellent omelette which is called a *frittata*, but they have kept the secret of it at home. Restaurant *frittata* is more often than not stiff and leathery, which has led travellers to conclude that Italians cannot cook eggs. In the last section of this chapter you will find a full explanation of the method – practically the opposite of that of a French omelette – and six excellent examples of *frittate*. If you follow the instructions carefully, you will find that a *frittata* can be every bit as delectable as an omelette, but with more of a country flavour. With a *frittata* it is easier to serve a number of people than with omelettes, which are difficult to make with a large quantity of eggs. If you already know how to make omelettes, learn how to make *frittate*, and your repertoire will have been doubled.

Branzino al cartoccio con frutti di mare

BAKED SEA BASS AND SHELLFISH
SEALED IN FOIL

This fish is stuffed with mussels, shrimps and oysters, sealed in heavy foil, and cooked in the oven. Its flesh remains extraordinarily juicy and becomes delicately flavoured with a fresh sea fragrance. The ideal way to prepare it is to completely remove the bones while leaving the fish intact. At the table you will then be able to cut it into neat, boneless slices, which makes it so much more attractive to serve and agreeable to eat. Here is how you do it:

There is a slit in the fish's belly made by the fishmonger when he cleans out its intestinal cavity. With a sharp knife, extend this slit for the whole length of the fish from head to tail. This will expose the entire backbone, from the upper half of which extend the rib bones embedded in the belly. Using your fingers and a small knife pry these rib bones loose and detach them. With the same technique, loosen the backbone, separating it from the flesh around it. Now carefully bend the head, snapping off the backbone at that end, then do the same with the tail. At this point you will be able to lift away the entire backbone. If you do not feel up to doing this yourself, you should be able to persuade your fishmonger to do it for you. But make sure he slits open the fish on only one side, the belly side.

If you wish, you can substitute sea bream or red snapper for the bass.

For six

12 mussels, cleaned as directed on page 49	40 g (1½ oz) fine, dry plain breadcrumbs
6 medium or 12 tiny shrimps	2 tablespoons thinly sliced onion
6 oysters, unshelled	Juice of 1 medium lemon
2 tablespoons chopped parsley	Salt
2 cloves garlic, lightly crushed with a heavy knife-handle and peeled	Freshly ground pepper, 5 or 6 twists of the pepper mill
8 tablespoons olive oil	1 sea bass or sea bream (1.35 to 1.5 kg) (3 to 3½ lb), boned as directed above

1 Put the mussels in a covered pan over high heat until their shells open, just a few minutes. Detach the mussels from their shells and put them in a mixing bowl large enough to hold all the ingredients except the fish. Strain the juices from the mussels left in the pan into the mixing bowl, using a sieve lined with a sheet of kitchen paper.

2 Peel the shrimps and, if they are on the large side, remove the black intestinal track. Wash them thoroughly in cold water and pat dry. If they are extra large, slice them in half lengthways. Drop them into the mixing bowl.

3 Open the oysters and add them and their juices to the mixing bowl. Add all the other ingredients, except for the fish, to the bowl. Mix thoroughly, but not roughly, so as not to bruise the shellfish.

4 Preheat the oven to 240°C/475°F/Mark 9.

5 Wash the fish in cold running water inside and out. Pat thoroughly dry with kitchen paper.

6 Spread a double thickness of aluminium foil on the bottom of a long, shallow baking dish, remembering that the piece of foil must be large enough to close over the fish at all points. Spread some of the liquid from the mixture in the bowl on the bottom of the foil. Place the fish in the centre and stuff it with all the ingredients from the bowl, reserving some of the liquid, with which you will now coat the outside of the fish. Fold the foil over the fish and seal it tightly with a double lengthways fold, making sure the corners are tightly tucked in. Place in the upper third of the oven and bake for about 40 minutes. When cooked the fish will be very tender and soaked in cooking juices.

7 Allow the fish to stand for 10 minutes in the sealed foil, then place the whole package on a serving dish. (Unveiling the fish at the table can be very dramatic, but it can also be quite messy. Do not do it unless you have a little serving table on the side. Also, do not lift the fish out of the foil, because it has no bones and will break up.) Cut the foil open and trim it with scissors down to the edge of the dish. Bring the fish to the table whole and slice it as you would a roast.

MENU SUGGESTIONS

You can build a very fine fish dinner around this dish. For antipasti you can start with *Spuma fredda di salmone* (page 29), *Insalata di mare* (page 363) or *Pomodori ripieni di tonno* (page 33). Choose a first course with *pesto*, either *Trenette col pesto* (page 121) or *Gnocchi di patate* (page 167). No vegetable dish is required. Follow the fish with a green salad or *Fagiolini verdi in insalata* (page 355).

Pesce da taglio con salsa di prezzemolo
POACHED HALIBUT WITH PARSLEY SAUCE

For four

The fish

$\frac{1}{2}$ medium onion, sliced thin
1 stick celery
2 or 3 sprigs parsley
1 bayleaf
$\frac{1}{8}$ teaspoon fennel seeds

250 ml (scant $\frac{1}{2}$ pint) dry white wine
Salt
900 g (2 lb) halibut, cut in one slice,
　　bone removed

The sauce

1 tablespoon finely chopped onion
30 g ($1\frac{1}{4}$ oz) butter
2 tablespoons olive oil
2 tablespoons finely chopped parsley
$\frac{1}{2}$ clove garlic, peeled and finely
　　chopped
1 tablespoon chopped capers
2 teaspoons anchovy paste

2 teaspoons plain flour dissolved in 8
　　tablespoons broth **or**, with 1
　　bouillon cube, in 8 tablespoons
　　hot water
2 tablespoons red wine vinegar
Salt to taste
Freshly ground pepper, about 4
　　twists of the mill

The decoration

2 hard-boiled eggs, sliced
1 lemon, sliced into 6-mm ($\frac{1}{4}$ -inch)
　　discs
Parsley leaves

Gherkins, sliced lengthways but left
　　whole at one end so they can
　　be fanned out

1 Put the sliced onion, the celery stick, parsley sprigs, bayleaf, fennel seeds, white wine, salt and 1 litre ($1\frac{3}{4}$ pints) water in a deep saucepan. Bring to the boil and let bubble at a moderate pace for about 15 minutes. There must be enough liquid to cover the fish; if you feel it is insufficient, add more water. Meanwhile, wash the fish in cold water and pat dry. When the poaching liquid has bubbled for 15 minutes, add the fish, cover the pan and simmer slowly for 10 to 12 minutes. Turn off the heat, but do not remove the fish from the pan. Let it stand in the poaching liquid while you prepare the sauce.

2 In a small saucepan sauté the chopped onion, with 15 g ($\frac{1}{2}$ oz) of the butter and all the oil, over medium heat until translucent but not browned. Add the chopped parsley, garlic, capers and anchovy paste. Stir well and sauté lightly for a few moments. Add the flour-broth mixture a tablespoon at a time, stirring thoroughly, then add the vinegar. Stir and keep at a

moderate boil for 2 minutes. Check salt, then add the pepper. Off the heat, mix in the remaining butter.

3 Remove the fish from the pan, lifting it carefully so that it does not break up (try using two metal spatulas), and place it on a warm serving dish. Pour the sauce over it and decorate with hard-boiled egg slices, lemon slices topped with parsley leaves, and fanned-out sliced gherkins. Serve immediately.

MENU SUGGESTIONS

For antipasto, *Spuma fredda di salmone* (page 29) or *Ostriche alla parmigiana* (page 28). First course: *Risotto con le vongole* (page 164) or *Fettuccine al sugo di vongole bianco* (page 115). No vegetable dish, just a green salad after the fish.

Sgombri in tegame con rosmarino e aglio
MACKEREL WITH ROSEMARY AND GARLIC

In the small fishing towns along the Adriatic coast this is a very popular way of cooking mackerel; the slow cooking in oil keeps its firm flesh tender and juicy and the subdued taste of rosemary and garlic make mackerel's robust flavour gentler and very appealing.

For four

6 tablespoons olive oil
4 cloves garlic, peeled
4 mackerel (about 350 g ($\frac{3}{4}$ lb) each), cleaned but with heads and tails on

1 80-mm (3-inch) sprig fresh rosemary **or** 1 teaspoon dried rosemary, crumbled
Salt and freshly ground pepper to taste
Juice of $\frac{1}{2}$ lemon
Lemon wedges

1 Wash the mackerel under cold running water and pat dry.
2 Heat the oil in a casserole and lightly sauté the garlic.
3 Add the mackerel and rosemary and lower the heat to medium. Brown the fish well on each side but take care that it does not stick to the pan.

(Should it stick, be careful as you turn it so that it does not break up.) Season each side with salt and pepper.

4 When the fish is nicely browned add the lemon juice, cover with a tight-fitting lid, turn the heat down to low, and cook slowly for approximately 15 minutes, or until tender. Serve piping hot with wedges of lemon.

MENU SUGGESTIONS

As a first course, *Zuppa di vongole* (page 46). *Spaghettini alla vongole* (page 85), *Spaghettini al sugo di pomodoro e acciughe* (page 86) or *Risotto con le vongole* (page 164). No vegetables. Follow the fish with *Insalata mista* (page 351) or *Insalata di zucchini* (page 357).

Pagello con i funghi trifolati
SEA BREAM or RED SNAPPER WITH SAUTÉED MUSHROOMS

In this recipe the fish is slowly simmered in wine and broth with a flavour base of sautéed vegetables, anchovy, parsley and bayleaves. It is then combined with mushrooms sautéed in the classic Italian manner with oil, garlic and parsley. Although the flavourings in this dish are numerous, they are used in minuscule quantities, and are calculated to set off rather than cloak the delicacy and sweetness of the fish.

For four

The sautéed mushrooms
3 tablespoons olive oil
$\frac{1}{2}$ clove garlic, peeled and chopped
220 g ($\frac{1}{2}$ lb) crisp, fresh mushrooms

3 teaspoons chopped parsley
Salt

The fish
3 tablespoons olive oil
15 g ($\frac{1}{2}$ oz) butter
2 tablespoons finely chopped onion
2 tablespoons finely chopped carrot

1 large clove garlic, peeled and lightly crushed with a heavy knife-handle
1 teaspoon chopped flat anchovy fillet
2 teaspoons chopped parsley

$\frac{1}{2}$ bayleaf, crumbled
6 tablespoons dry white wine
1 sea bream or red snapper [1 kg (2
    to $2\frac{1}{2}$ pounds)], cleaned, scaled
    and washed, but with head
    and tail left on
Salt

Freshly ground pepper, 4 to 6 twists
    of the mill
8 tablespoons home-made meat broth
    (page 8) or $\frac{1}{2}$ bouillon cube
    dissolved in 8 tablespoons
    warm water

1 Using the ingredients listed above, prepare and cook the mushrooms as directed on page 325. Set aside after cooking.

2 In a frying pan just large enough for the fish, put the olive oil, butter, onion and carrot. Cook over medium-low heat until the onion is translucent but not browned.

3 Add the garlic and chopped anchovy. Cook, stirring, for a minute or two, until the anchovy has dissolved and the garlic has released some of its fragrance; then add the parsley and cook long enough to stir everything once or twice.

4 Add the bayleaf and the wine. Cook, stirring frequently, until the wine has evaporated by half.

5 Add the fish, salt, half the pepper and all the broth, and put a cover on the frying pan, setting it slightly askew. Cook, keeping the heat always at medium low, and after about 10 minutes, slightly longer if the fish is larger, turn the fish over carefully (possibly using two metal spatulas) so that it stays intact, and add more salt and pepper. After it has cooked another 10 minutes on the second side, add the mushroom mixture, drained of its oil. Cover the pan and let the mushrooms and fish cook together for no more than a minute. Serve piping hot.

MENU SUGGESTIONS

Antipasto to precede this dish could be *Ostriche alla moda di Taranto* (page 28), *Spuma fredda di salmone* (page 29) or *Pomodori coi gamberetti* (page 34). Avoid the ones that are very salty or highly flavoured. As a first course after the antipasto, an excellent choice would be *Fettuccine al sugo di vongole bianco* (page 115), *Spaghettini* with the same sauce or with a clam and tomato sauce (page 85) or *Risotto con le vongole* (page 164). No vegetable accompaniment is required. Follow the fish with *Insalata mista* (page 351).

Filetti di sogliola con pomodoro e capperi
FILLET OF SOLE WITH PIQUANT TOMATO SAUCE

Crisply fried Adriatic sole is simply one of the best things it is possible to eat, and can be matched by using the very best Dover sole but I would not ideally try it with plaice or other flatfish. The best one can do with plaice is to take the edge off its awkwardness through the graces of a seductive sauce. The following version relies on the unabashed charms of a tasty tomato sauce.

For six

1 onion, thinly sliced	225 g (8 oz) tinned Italian tomatoes,
5 tablespoons olive oil	cut up, with their juice
2 small cloves garlic, peeled and	Salt to taste
finely chopped	Freshly ground pepper, about 6
1 teaspoon oregano	twists of the mill
2 tablespoons very tiny capers, or	Scant 1 kg (2 lb) fresh sole fillets,
larger capers roughly chopped	preferably Dover sole

1 Put the sliced onion in a frying pan with the olive oil and cook over medium heat until soft and pale gold in colour. Add the garlic, and when it has coloured lightly add the oregano and capers, stirring once or twice. Add the cut-up tomatoes and their juice, salt and pepper. Stir well and cook at a steady simmer for 15 to 20 minutes, or until the tomatoes and the oil separate.

2 Preheat the oven to 230°C/450°F/Mark 8.

3 Rinse the fish fillets in cold water and blot dry. The fillets are going to be arranged in a single layer in a baking dish, folded over end to end and slightly overlapping. Choose an oven dish just large enough for the job, and smear the bottom with about a tablespoon of the tomato sauce. Dip each fillet on both sides in the sauce in the frying pan, then fold it and arrange it in the baking dish as directed above. Pour the remaining sauce over the fillets, and place the dish in the uppermost level of the oven. Cook for no more than 5 to 8 minutes, depending upon the thickness of the fillets. (Do not overcook, or the fish will become dry.)

4 When you remove the dish from the oven you may find that the fish has thrown off liquid, thinning out the sauce. If this happens, tilt the dish and spoon all the sauce and liquid into a small pan. Boil it rapidly until

it is sufficiently concentrated, then pour it back over the fish. Serve immediately.

MENU SUGGESTIONS

The first course could be *Risotto con le vongole* (page 164), *Fettuccine al sugo di vongole bianco* (page 115) or *Spaghetti 'ajo e ojo'* (page 88). If you want an antipasto, serve *Gamberetti all'olio e limone* (page 34). Follow the fish with *Insalata mista* (page 351) or *Fagiolini verdi in insalata* (page 355).

Trota marinata all'arancio
COLD SAUTÉED TROUT IN ORANGE MARINADE

Long ago Italian lakes and rivers were busy with trout and other delicious
small fish. A day's catch used to result in a large concoction of fried fish
for dinner, and marinating was a genial way to cope with the left-overs. Fish
treated this way is so remarkably good that soon people started to fry it
especially for the purpose of marinating it.

There are many widely different marinades. That most frequently published is the one in which garlic, vinegar and herbs are the principal
ingredients. It is very popular, but I find it rather aggressive. The marinade
given here is elegantly flavoured with orange, lemon and vermouth. It settles
fragrantly but gently into the delicate flesh of trout, perch or other fresh-
water fish.

For six

3 trout, perch **or** other fresh-water
    fish [about 350 g ($\frac{3}{4}$ lb) each],
    cleaned and scaled, but with
    heads and tails left on
8 tablespoons olive oil
60 g (3 oz) or less plain flour, spread
    on a dish or on waxed paper
2 tablespoons finely chopped onion
250 ml (scant $\frac{1}{2}$ pint) dry white Italian
    vermouth

2 tablespoons chopped orange peel
8 tablespoons freshly squeezed orange
    juice
Juice of 1 lemon
Salt
Freshly ground black pepper, about 6
    twists of the mill
1$\frac{1}{2}$ tablespoons chopped parsley
Unpeeled orange slices (optional)

1 Wash the trout in cold water and pat dry thoroughly with kitchen paper.

2 Heat the oil in a frying pan over medium heat. When the oil is hot, dip both sides of the trout lightly in flour and slip into the frying pan. (If all the trout will not fit into the frying pan at one time, dip in flour just the ones you are ready to fry.)

3 Brown the fish well on one side, then on the other, calculating about 5 minutes for the first side and 4 minutes for the other. Transfer the fish to a deep dish large enough to contain them in a single layer. Reserve the oil in the frying pan.

4 With a very sharp knife, make two or three small diagonal cuts in the skin on both sides of each fish. Be careful not to tear the skin apart, and do not cut into the flesh.

5 Put the chopped onion in the frying pan in which you fried the fish and sauté it in the same oil, over medium heat, until pale gold. Add the vermouth and the orange peel and let the vermouth boil for 15 or 20 seconds. Stir, then add the orange juice, lemon juice, salt and pepper. Let everything bubble for about 30 seconds, stirring two or three times. Add the chopped parsley, stir again once or twice, then pour the entire contents of the pan over the trout.

6 Plan to serve the trout no earlier than the following day. Let the fish soak in the marinade for at least 6 hours at room temperature, then refrigerate. (They will keep in the refrigerator for 3 to 4 days; after that they lose their fresh taste.) Take them out sufficiently ahead of time to serve them at room temperature. If you like, you may decorate them with unpeeled orange slices.

MENU SUGGESTIONS

This is a fine antipasto for an elegant fish dinner. It can be followed by *Fettuccine al sugo di vongole bianco* (page 115) or *Trenette col pesto* (page 121), and then by *Pesce ai ferri alla moda dell' Adriatico* (page 191) or *Branzino al cartoccio con frutti di mare* (page 181). You can also promote the trout to a second course, preceded by *Spuma fredda di salmone* (page 29) and/ or *Gnocchi di patate* (page 167) with *Pesto* (page 118), or *Zuppa di vongole vellutata* (page 48). Follow with *Fagiolini verdi in insalata* (page 355) or *Insalata mista* (page 351).

Salame di tonno

TUNA SALAMI

In this recipe tuna is combined with mashed potatoes and eggs to form a salami-like roll, which is then slowly simmered with vegetables, herbs and white wine. It is served cold, sliced, with a caper and anchovy mayonnaise. The tuna completely loses its tinned, salty taste and acquires an elegance of texture and flavour that is enhanced but not overwhelmed by the seasonings.

For six

1 medium potato
400 g (14 oz) tinned imported Italian or Spanish tuna packed in olive oil, drained
25 g (1 oz) freshly grated Parmesan cheese

1 whole egg plus 1 white
Freshly ground pepper, about 6 twists of the mill
Muslin

The flavoured broth
$\frac{1}{2}$ medium onion, sliced thin
1 stick celery
1 carrot

6 parsley sprigs, stems only
Salt
250 ml (scant $\frac{1}{2}$ pint) dry white wine

A mayonnaise (page 22) made with
1 egg yolk
2 tablespoons lemon juice

generous 150 ml ($\frac{1}{4}$ pint) olive oil
Salt

When the mayonnaise is made, incorporate the following
2 tablespoons chopped capers
$\frac{1}{4}$ teaspoon anchovy paste

Sliced black olives

1 Boil the potato, unpeeled, until it is tender. Drain, peel and mash through a mouli-légumes.

2 Mash the tuna in a bowl. Add the grated cheese, the whole egg plus the egg white, the pepper and the mashed potato.

3 Moisten a piece of muslin, wring it until it is just damp, and lay it out flat on the worktop. Place the tuna mixture at one end of the cloth, shaping it into a salami-like roll about 72 mm (2$\frac{1}{2}$ inches) in diameter. Wrap it in the muslin, covering it with at least two layers. Tie the ends securely with string.

4 Put the sliced onion, celery stick, carrot, parsley stems, salt and the

wine in a saucepan or oval casserole, together with the tuna roll. Add enough water to cover by about 25 mm (1 inch). Cover the pot and bring to the boil. When it reaches the boil, adjust the heat so that it cooks at the gentlest of simmers. Cook for 45 minutes.

5 When cooked, remove the tuna roll and, as soon as you can handle it, unwrap it gently. Set aside to cool completely.

6 While the tuna loaf is cooling, make a mayonnaise with the egg yolk, lemon juice, olive oil and salt, according to the directions on page 22. Incorporate the chopped capers and anchovy paste.

7 Cut the cold tuna roll into slices 18 mm ($\frac{3}{8}$ inch) thick. Arrange the slices on a dish, overlapping them very slightly. Cover the slices with the caper-and-anchovy-flavoured mayonnaise and garnish with black olive slices running the length of the dish, over the centre of each slice of tuna.

MENU SUGGESTIONS

This is a very attractive dish for a buffet. It can also be combined with a salad to make a very light meal for a hot summer day, and it can be presented as a lovely antipasto before the recipe below.

Pesce ai ferri alla moda dell'Adriatico
GRILLED FISH FROM THE ADRIATIC

Grilling fish over a charcoal or wood fire is the favourite way of doing fish along the Adriatic. Before grilling, the fish is steeped in a marinade of olive oil, lemon juice, salt and breadcrumbs for an hour or more. This not only enhances the flavour of the fish, but keeps it from drying out while cooking.

For four

1·1 to 1·35 kg (2$\frac{1}{2}$ to 3 lb) fish, either whole, with head and tail left on, or thick slices of larger fish
Salt
4 tablespoons olive oil
2 tablespoons lemon juice
6 tablespoons fine, dry plain breadcrumbs

$\frac{1}{2}$ teaspoon dried rosemary **or** a sprig of fresh rosemary (optional; for use only on such dark fleshed fish as mackerel)
1 or 2 bayleaves (optional)
Lemon wedges

1 If you are using a whole fish, scale and clean it, wash it in cold water, and dry it thoroughly on kitchen paper.

2 Sprinkle the fish with salt on both sides, put it on a dish, and add the olive oil and lemon juice. Turn the fish two or three times to coat it well. Add the breadcrumbs, turning the fish again until it is well coated. If you are preparing a dark-fleshed fish, add the rosemary. Marinate for 1 to 2 hours at room temperature, turning and basting the fish from time to time. Save the marinade.

3 If you are doing the fish in the grill, preheat it to the maximum at least 15 minutes before cooking. If you are doing the fish over charcoal, the fire must also be ready 15 minutes ahead of time. Throw a bayleaf or two in the fire just before setting the fish on the charcoal grill.

4 Put the fish in the grill at a distance of 100 to 125 mm (4 to 5 inches) from the source of heat. Grill on both sides, until done. (Cooking times vary greatly, depending on the thickness of the fish and the intensity of the heat. You must learn to judge it time by time. A 1·35-kg (3-lb) sea bass, for example, should be done in about 20 minutes. Do not overcook or it will become dry, nor undercook, because partly done fish is most disagreeable. The flesh should come away easily from the bone and show no traces of translucent, raw pink colour.) Baste the fish occasionally while it grills with the left-over marinade. Serve piping hot, with lemon wedges.

MENU SUGGESTIONS

You can precede grilled fish with any pasta or rice with a seafood sauce. Other suggestions for a first course: *Zuppa di cozze* (page 49), *Zuppa di vongole* (page 46) or *Zuppa di vongole vellutata* (page 48), *Minestrone freddo alla milanese* (page 59), *Spaghettini al sugo di pomodoro e acciughe* (page 86), *Spaghetti* with *Pesto* (page 118), or *Trenette col pesto* (page 121), *Spaghetti* 'ajo e ojo' (page 88) or *Spaghetti* with Tomato Sauce III (page 81). You can accompany it, if you like, with *Dadini di patate arrosto* (page 332), but with no other vegetables. Follow with any raw salad or with *Insalata di zucchine* (page 357). If you would like an antipasto, choose among *Pomodori coi gamberetti* (page 34), *Insalata di mare* (page 363) and *Ostriche alla moda di Taranto* (page 28).

Spiedini di gamberoni dell'Adriatico
PRAWN BROCHETTES FROM THE ADRIATIC

I have tasted many versions of this very simple dish in seafood and Italian restaurants in England and America, but I have never come across any that recall the delicate balance of flavours and the juicy texture of the prawns that fishermen cook all along the Adriatic. You must start, of course, with very good-quality prawns from a reputable fish market, fresh if possible. Do not try to make do with the bags of frozen prawns from the supermarket freezer. Apart from the prawns, however, the success of this dish depends upon how you apply the coating of oil and breadcrumbs. There must be just enough oil to coat the prawns, but not so much as to drench them. There must be enough breadcrumbs to retain the oil and to form a light protective covering over the delicate flesh, but not so much as to bury the prawns under a thick, gross crust. Follow the proportions indicated below, but bear in mind that the quantities are approximate. If you use larger prawns you will need less oil and crumbs because there is less total surface to be coated. Also, some breadcrumbs go further than others, depending upon how absorbent they are. An essential ingredient is your good judgment.

For six

680 g (1½ lb) small prawns
3½ tablespoons olive oil
3½ tablespoons vegetable oil
80 g (2¾ oz) fine, dry plain
    breadcrumbs
½ clove garlic, peeled and very finely
    chopped

2 teaspoons finely chopped parsley
Salt
Freshly ground pepper, 5 or 6 twists
    of the mill
Lemon wedges

1 Preheat the grill to its maximum setting. (The grill must be heated at least 15 minutes before the prawns are to be cooked.)

2 Shell the prawns, and, if they are on the large side, remove the black intestinal tract. Wash in cold water and pat thoroughly dry with kitchen paper.

3 Put the prawns in a comfortably large mixing bowl. Add as much of the two oils (mixed in equal parts) and of the breadcrumbs as you need to obtain an even, light, creamy coating on all the prawns. (Do not add it all at once because it may not be necessary, but if you are working with very tiny prawns, you may need even more. In that case, always use 1 part olive oil to 1 part vegetable oil.) When the prawns are well coated, add the chopped

garlic, parsley, salt and pepper and mix well. Allow the prawns to steep in the marinade for at least 20 minutes at room temperature.

4 Have ready some flat, double-edged skewers. Skewer the prawns lengthways, 5 or more prawns per brochette, depending upon the size. As you skewer each prawn, curl and bend one end inwards so that the skewer goes through the prawn at three points. This is to make sure that the prawns do not slip as you turn the skewer.

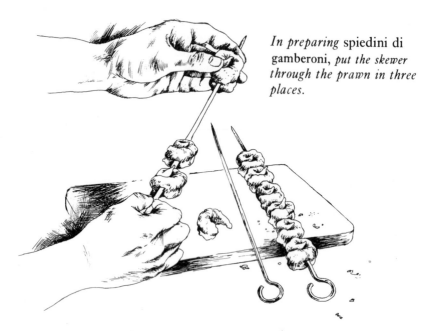

In preparing spiedini di gamberoni, *put the skewer through the prawn in three places.*

5 These prawns require brisk, rapid cooking. Wait until the grill has been on for 15 minutes. Cook the prawns no more than 3 minutes on one side and 2 minutes on the other, and even less if the prawns are very small. Each side is done as soon as a crisp, golden crust forms.

6 Serve piping hot, on the skewers, with lemon wedges.

MENU SUGGESTIONS

Very tiny prawns grilled in this manner are a frequent part of Italian 'shore dinners', served together with a mixture of grilled and fried fish. The dish can be preceded by *Risotto con le vongole* (page 164), *Zuppa di vongole* (page 46), *Zuppa di cozze* (page 49) or *Trenette col pesto* (page 121). Generally no vegetable is served with it, but *Funghi trifolati* (page 325) can be a very agreeable accompaniment. Follow the prawns with *Insalata mista* (page 351).

Calamari
SQUID

It is odd how many people who will happily eat oysters and mussels dread the thought of eating another excellent mollusc, the squid. Actually, the flesh of the squid, when properly cooked, is delicate and tender, and it is no accident that fish-loving countries from Italy to Japan regard the squid and its numerous relatives as one of the sea's most delectable offerings. If you are open minded about experimenting with food, you will be well rewarded by the taste of squid.

The sac of the large Italian squid, *calamari* and *calamaroni*, exclusive of tentacles, measures from 75 to 150 or 180 mm ($3\frac{1}{2}$ inches to 6 or 7 inches) in length. It is available either fresh or frozen, and both are good. In Italy, freshly caught large squid is kept in the refrigerator one or two days before cooking, to relax its rigid flesh. Away from the sea it is probably already that old before it reaches the market. Use squid only when it is a pure, milky white in colour. The tastiest, sweetest squid, whether fresh or frozen, comes to the markets in early spring. Smaller squid are called *calamaretti*.

HOW TO CLEAN SQUID

Your fishmonger will clean squid if you ask him, but he rarely does a thorough job. It is much better to do the whole thing at home rather than to pick up where he has left off.

Hold the sac in one hand and, with the other, firmly but gently pull off the tentacles. If you are not too abrupt, all the pulpy contents of the sac should come away attached to the tentacles. Cut the tentacles above the eyes. Reserve the tentacles, discarding everything else from the eyes down, and squeezing out the small bony beak.

Remove the quill-like bone from the sac, and thoroughly wash out the inside of the sac, removing anything it may still contain. Peel off the sac's outer skin, which comes off quite easily if the job is done under cold running water. Also under running water, peel off as much of the skin on the tentacles as will come off. Rinse both sac and tentacles in several changes of cold water, until the water runs clear. Dry thoroughly. The squid is now ready for cooking.

Calamari e piselli alla livornese
STEWED SQUID WITH TOMATOES AND PEAS

For four to six

1½ tablespoons finely chopped onion
3 tablespoons olive oil
1 to 2 cloves garlic, peeled and finely chopped
1 tablespoon finely chopped parsley
175 g (6 oz) tinned Italian tomatoes, coarsely chopped, with their juice

Scant 1 kg (2 lb) smallest possible squid, cleaned and prepared for cooking as directed above
Salt and freshly ground pepper to taste
Scant 1 kg (2 lb) fresh peas (unshelled weight) **or** 300 g (10½ oz) frozen peas, thawed

1 Put the onion in a flameproof casserole with the olive oil and sauté over medium heat until it begins to turn pale gold. Add the garlic and sauté until it colours lightly but does not brown. Add the parsley, stir once or twice, then add the tomatoes. Cook at a gentle simmer for 10 minutes.

2 Slice the squid sacs into rings about 18 to 25 mm ($\frac{3}{4}$ to 1 inch) wide. Divide the tentacle cluster into two parts. Add all the squid to the casserole; then add the salt and pepper, stir, cover, and cook at a gentle simmer for 30 minutes.

3 If you are using fresh peas, add them to the casserole at this point. Cover and continue cooking until the squid is tender, about another 20 minutes. (Cooking times, however, vary considerably, depending on the size and toughness of the squid, so test from time to time with a fork. When the squid is easily pierced, it is done.) If you are using thawed frozen peas, add them to the casserole when the squid is practically done, because they need only a few minutes' cooking. Check seasoning.

Note This stewed squid can be prepared entirely ahead of time and refrigerated for up to 2 days. Warm up slowly just before serving.

MENU SUGGESTIONS

Serve *Cozze e vongole passate ai ferri* (page 30), *Peperoni e acciughe* (page 32) or even some *Spiedini di gamberoni dell'Adriatico* (page 193) as an antipasto. Omit the first course because you will be sopping up lots of bread with the tasty sauce. No vegetables, of course. Follow with *Insalata di carote* (page 350).

Calamari ripieni stufati al vino bianco
STUFFED SQUID BRAISED IN WHITE WINE

For six

6 large squid [the sac should measure 110 to 125 mm ($4\frac{1}{2}$ to 5 inches), not including the tentacles]

The stuffing

1 tablespoon olive oil, approximately
2 tablespoons finely chopped parsley
$\frac{1}{2}$ clove garlic, peeled and finely chopped, or more to taste
1 whole egg, lightly beaten
$2\frac{1}{2}$ tablespoons freshly grated Parmesan cheese

30 g (2 oz) fine, dry, plain breadcrumbs
Salt
Freshly ground pepper, about 6 twists of the pepper mill

The braising liquid

Olive oil, enough to come 6 mm ($\frac{1}{4}$ inch) up the side of the frying pan

4 whole cloves garlic, peeled

110 g (4 oz) tinned Italian tomatoes, coarsely chopped, with their juice

$\frac{1}{2}$ clove garlic, peeled and finely chopped

4 tablespoons dry white wine

1 Clean and prepare the squid as directed on page 196.

2 Chop the squid tentacles very fine. In a bowl, mix them with all the stuffing ingredients until you have a smooth, even mixture. There should be just enough olive oil in the mixture to make it slightly glossy. If it does not have this light surface gloss, add more olive oil.

3 Divide the stuffing into 6 equal parts and spoon it into the squid sacs. (Do not overstuff, because the squid shrinks as it cooks and too much stuffing may cause it to burst.) Sew up each opening tightly with a darning needle and thread – and be sure to put the needle safely away as soon as you have finished using it or it may disappear into the sauce.

4 Choose a frying pan large enough to hold the squid in a single layer and coat the bottom with just enough olive oil to come 6 mm ($\frac{1}{4}$ inch) up the side of the pan. Heat the oil over medium-high heat and sauté the garlic cloves until golden brown. Discard the garlic and put in the stuffed squid. Brown the squid well on all sides, then add the chopped tomatoes with their juice, the chopped garlic and the wine. Cover tightly and cook over low heat for 30 to 40 minutes. The squid is done when it feels tender when pricked with a fork.

5 Remove the squid to a chopping board and allow to stand for a few minutes. Slice away just enough from the sewn-up end to remove the thread and cut the rest into slices 12 mm ($\frac{1}{2}$ inch) thick. Arrange the slices on a warm serving dish so that each squid sac is recomposed. Warm up the sauce in the frying pan, pour over the sliced squid, and serve immediately.

Note   This dish can be prepared 4 or 5 days ahead of time and refrigerated. Warm it up as follows: Preheat the oven to 150°C/300°F/Mark 2. Transfer the squid and the sauce to an oven dish, add 2 to 3 tablespoons of water, and place in the middle level of the oven. Turn and baste the slices as they warm up, being careful that they do not break up. Serve when warm.

MENU SUGGESTIONS

If you wish to serve a vegetable dish with the squid, the most suitable would be steamed potatoes. It is quite sufficient, however, to serve *Insalata di zucchine* (page 357) or mixed greens afterwards. It can be preceded by *Fettuccine al sugo di vongole bianco* (page 115) or *Risotto con le vongole* (page 164). I have found that *Bresaola* (page 42), with its sharp, clean taste, makes an ideal prelude to this rather robust dish.

Calamari fritti

FRIED SQUID

One of the most prized delicacies along the Adriatic is very tiny squid (*calamaretti*), often no more than 37 mm ($1\frac{1}{2}$ inches) long, fried whole in hot oil. They are incredibly tender and sweet, and, should you find yourself on the Adriatic coast, do not miss your chance to eat them. Although not quite so tender and delicate, larger squid can be very good indeed when fried, but it must first be cut up into rings.

For four

1·35 kg (3 lb) squid	120 g ($4\frac{1}{4}$ oz) plain flour, spread on
Vegetable oil, enough to come 25 mm	waxed paper or on a dish
(1 inch) up the side of the pan	Salt
	Lemon wedges

1 Clean the squid as directed on page 196, drying it thoroughly on kitchen paper. Cut the squid sacs into rings about 9 mm ($\frac{3}{8}$ inch) wide and separate the tentacle cluster into two parts. Make sure it is all very thoroughly dried.

2 Heat the oil over high heat.

3 When the oil is very hot, dip the squid in the flour, shake off the excess and slip into the pan. Do not put in any more at one time than will fit loosely in the frying pan. Cover the frying pan with a wire mesh, if you have one, since squid has a tendency to burst and spatter while frying.

4 As soon as the squid is fried to a tawny gold on one side, turn it. When both sides are done, transfer to kitchen paper to drain. Sprinkle with salt and serve with lemon wedges.

MENU SUGGESTIONS

Fried squid can be preceded by *Cozze e vongole passate ai ferri* (page 30), *Insalata di mare* (page 363), *Zuppa di vongole* (page 46) or *Spaghettini* or

Fettuccine al sugo di vongole bianco (page 115), *alle vongole* (page 85) or *al tonno* (page 87). Follow with *Insalata mista* (page 351) or *Insalata di zucchine* (page 357).

Il brodetto di papi
MY FATHER'S FISH SOUP

Fish soup is one of the most ancient dishes of the Mediterranean. In Italy, every coastal town has its own traditional version. On the Tuscan coast it is called *cacciucco*, on the Adriatic side it is called *brodetto* ('little broth'), and elsewhere simply *zuppa di pesce*. To describe every variety of *cacciucco* or *brodetto* would take a larger volume than this one because it changes not just from town to town but from family to family. One of the best soups I have ever tasted is my father's, for which he acquired a considerable reputation in his lifetime. It has the merit of achieving an over-all hearty flavour without the individual delicacy and character of each fish being overwhelmed. My father would use a large variety of small fish, nine or more different kinds, but away from the Mediterranean we have to make do with a smaller variety of larger fish. Deep-sea fish is quite different from that of the Adriatic, but this is no cause for despair. The very idea behind fish soup is that it can turn virtually any combination of fish into a succulent and satisfying dish. This particular soup does it as well as any I have ever tried.

You need at least 3 to 4 heads for this recipe, so buy as many small whole fish as you can find; otherwise, your fishmonger can probably supply you with a few heads. The greater the variety, the tastier and more interesting the soup becomes. If you use dark-fleshed, fatty fish such as mackerel, or fresh-water eel, it adds to the flavour of the soup, but use it in small quantities. I have been very successful with monkfish, sea bass, sea bream, halibut, baby cod and bass. Plaice or flounder adds very little to the soup, and it always has a most disagreeably submissive consistency.

For six to eight

1·35 to 1·8 kg (3 to 4 lb) assorted
    fresh fish, cleaned and scaled
220 g ($\frac{1}{2}$ lb) or more large shrimps **or**
    prawns in their shells

450 g (1 lb) squid, cleaned and
    prepared for cooking as
    directed on page 196
$\frac{1}{2}$ dozen clams

$\frac{1}{2}$ dozen mussels
3 tablespoons finely chopped onion
6 tablespoons olive oil
1$\frac{1}{2}$ cloves garlic, peeled and chopped
3 tablespoons chopped parsley
8 tablespoons dry white wine

225 g (8 oz) tinned Italian tomatoes, cut up, with their juice
Salt
Freshly ground pepper, about 10 twists of the mill

1 Wash all the fish under cold running water. Cut off the heads and set aside. Cut the larger fish into slices 80 to 95 mm (3 to 3$\frac{1}{2}$ inches) wide and set aside. (Fish no longer than 200 mm (6$\frac{1}{2}$ inches) can be kept whole.) Wash the shrimps very thoroughly in cold water, but do not remove the shells. Set aside.

2 Divide the squid's tentacle cluster into 2 or 3 parts. Slice the sacs into rings 25 mm (1 inch) wide. Set aside.

3 Wash and scrub the clams and mussels very thoroughly, according to the directions on pages 46–7 and 49. Heat the clams and mussels in separate, covered pans over medium-high heat until they open. Remove the clams from their shells, filter their juices through a sieve lined with kitchen paper and set aside. Remove the mussels from their shells. Tipping the pan, gently draw off with a spoon all but the bottom, murky part of the mussel juices and set aside.

4 Choose a frying pan large enough to contain all the fish later in one layer. Lightly sauté the onion in the olive oil over medium heat until translucent, then add the chopped garlic and continue sautéing until it colours lightly. Add the chopped parsley and stir two or three times, then add the wine and raise the heat to high. When the wine has boiled briskly for about 30 seconds, add the chopped tomatoes with their juice. Stir, turn the heat down to a gentle simmer, and cook for about 25 minutes, or until the tomatoes and oil separate.

5 Add the fish heads, salt and the ground pepper, then cover the pan and cook for 10 to 12 minutes over medium heat, turning the heads over after 5 or 6 minutes. Remove the heads from the pan and pass them through a mouli-légumes. Add the puréed heads to the pan, together with the sliced squid and their tentacles. Cover and cook at a slow, steady simmer for 30 or 40 minutes, or until the squid are tender and easily pierced by a fork. Add the fish, holding back the smallest and tenderest pieces for 1 or 2 minutes, then add more salt and all the juices from the clams and mussels. Cover and cook over medium heat for 10 minutes, turning and basting the fish once or twice. After 5 minutes' cooking add the whole, unshelled shrimps. Add the clams and mussels at the very end, giving them just enough time to warm up. Check seasoning. Serve hot, with plenty of good country bread for dipping into the broth.

Note   The ideal pot for *brodetto* is dark red earthenware. It cooks the soup to perfection and is charming to serve from at the table. If your pot is not suitable for serving, transfer the fish with some delicacy (otherwise it will break up into unattractive bits) to a hot soup tureen. Spoon all the sauce and shellfish over it.

MENU SUGGESTIONS

This is both soup and second course, a meal in itself. If you want to make more of an event out of it, precede it with *Spiedini di gamberoni dell'Adriatico* (page 193), *Gamberetti all'olio e limone* (page 34) or *Insalata di funghi e formaggio* (page 41). Follow the soup with *Fagiolini verdi in insalata* (page 355) or *Insalata di zucchine* (page 357).

La fiorentina
GRILLED FLORENTINE STEAK

Beans and beef are Tuscany's most celebrated contributions to the Italian table. Even before the discovery of America, Florence was famous for its T-bone steak, known in Italy simply as a *fiorentina*. Although the particular flavour and texture of a *fiorentina* cannot be duplicated with any other meat but that of Tuscan-raised Val di Chiana beef, a fine Scotch or Australian beefsteak, prepared the Florentine way, can be spectacularly good.

Nothing could be more straightforward than the preparation of a *fiorentina*, but it is often misunderstood outside Tuscany, even by Italians. The error that is made most frequently is to marinate the steak in oil before grilling, which will make even the finest meat taste of tallow. Here is how the Florentines do it.

For two

$\frac{1}{2}$ teaspoon peppercorns, crushed in a mortar or inside a cloth with a heavy blunt object

1 T-bone steak, 37 mm ($1\frac{1}{2}$ inches) thick
Salt
Olive oil

1 Rub the peppercorns into both sides of the meat.
2 Grill the steak, over a very hot hardwood or charcoal fire, until cooked

as desired. (A *fiorentina* should be very rare.) Sprinkle the steak with salt on the grilled side as you turn it.

3 When the steak is done, but while it is still on the grill, moisten it very lightly on both sides with a few drops of olive oil. Serve immediately.

MENU SUGGESTIONS

In an Italian menu a *fiorentina* might be preceded by any of the bean or chick pea soups, by *Pappardelle con il ragù di fegatini* (page 117), *Risotto alla parmigiana* (page 155), or, omitting the first course, by *Carciofi alla romana* (page 286) or *Fave alla romana* (page 306). The vegetable accompaniment (if you started with soup or pasta) can be *Pisellini alla fiorentina* (page 328), *Spinaci saltati* (page 332) or *Zucchine all'aglio e pomodoro* (page 339). In Florence, in the spring, the salad would be *Fagiolini verdi in insalata* (page 355).

Bistecca alla diavola

STEAK WITH MARSALA AND CHILLI SAUCE

While Italians may have anticipated by a few centuries Americans' predilection for steaks grilled over coals, they have not overlooked the virtues of pan-grilling. It often gives brilliant results, as in this fiery steak whose own cooking juices are turned into a peppery sauce with a little help from such Italian ingredients as Marsala, garlic, fennel seeds, tomato purée, and, of course, *peperoncino rosso*, chilli.

For four persons

4 rump steaks or any other good
    cut of steak [about 1·35 kg
    [3 lb)], 18 mm ($\frac{3}{4}$ inch) thick
4 tablespoons olive oil
Salt and freshly ground pepper to
    taste
8 tablespoons dry Marsala
8 tablespoons dry red wine

1$\frac{1}{2}$ cloves garlic, peeled and finely
    chopped
1 teaspoon fennel seeds
1 tablespoon concentrated tomato
    purée diluted in 1
    tablespoon water
$\frac{1}{4}$ teaspoon chopped chilli (see note
    below)
2 tablespoons chopped parsley

1 Choose a frying pan large enough to hold all the steaks in a single layer. Put in the olive oil, and tilt the pan in several directions so that the bottom is well coated. Heat the oil over high heat until a haze forms over it, then put in the meat. Cook the steaks 3 minutes on one side and 2 to 3 minutes on the other, for rare meat. Regulate the heat to make sure the oil does not burn. When done, transfer the steaks to a warm dish, and season with salt and pepper.

2 Tip the pan and, with a spoon, remove all but $1\frac{1}{2}$ to 2 tablespoons of fat. Turn on the heat again to high and add the Marsala and the red wine. Boil the wine for about 30 seconds, while scraping the pan with a wooden spoon to loosen any cooking residue.

3 Add the garlic, cook just long enough to stir 2 or 3 times, then add the fennel seeds and stir again for a few seconds.

4 Add the diluted tomato purée and the chopped chilli. Turn the heat down to medium and cook, stirring constantly, for about 1 minute, until the sauce is thick and syrupy.

5 Return the steaks to the pan, just long enough to turn them in the hot sauce. Transfer steaks and sauce to a hot dish, sprinkle the parsley over the meat, and serve immediately.

Note Do not use the crushed chilli in jars, unless you absolutely cannot find the tiny, dried, whole chilli.

MENU SUGGESTIONS

As a first course choose either a vegetable *risotto* (pages 162–3), or *Risotto alla parmigiana* (page 155), or *Fusilli alla pappone* (page 90), or any of the stuffed pastas on pages 132–140, as long as they are not dressed with tomato or meat sauce. Or you can have a vegetable first course, such as *Carciofi alla romana* (page 286) or *Barchette di zucchine ripiene al forno* (page 340). If you are not having pasta, *Patate sponose* are a good accompaniment. Other vegetable suggestions: *Zucchine fritte con la pastella* (page 337), *Fagiolini verdi al burro e formaggio* (page 308) and *Topinambur gratinati* (page 301).

Fettine di manzo alla sorrentina
THIN STEAKS WITH TOMATOES AND OLIVES

This tasty southern dish utilises thin slices of beef and can be quite successful with inexpensive cuts of meat. It takes 25 minutes or less if you start from scratch and no more than 5 minutes if the sauce has been prepared ahead of time.

For four

$\frac{1}{2}$ medium onion, sliced thin
Olive oil, sufficient to come 6 mm ($\frac{1}{4}$ inch) up the side of the pan
2 medium cloves garlic, peeled and diced
140 g (5 oz) tinned Italian tomatoes, roughly chopped, with their juice
1 dozen black Greek olives, pitted and quartered

$\frac{1}{4}$ teaspoon oregano
Salt to taste
Freshly ground pepper, 6 to 8 twists of the mill
450 g (1 lb) beef steak, preferably chuck **or** feather steak, sliced 6 mm ($\frac{1}{4}$ inch) thick, pounded, and edges notched to keep from curling

1 In a good-sized frying pan (the broader the frying pan, the faster the sauce will thicken), slowly sauté the sliced onion in the olive oil, letting it soften gradually. As it takes on a pale gold colour, add the diced garlic. Continue sautéing until the garlic has coloured lightly, then add the tomatoes, olives, oregano, salt and pepper. Stir and cook at a lively simmer until the tomatoes and oil separate, about 15 minutes or more. (The sauce may be prepared ahead of time up to this point.) Turn the heat down, keeping the sauce at the barest simmer.

2 Heat up a heavy iron frying pan until it is smoking hot. Quickly grease the bottom with an oil-soaked cloth or kitchen paper. Put in the beef slices and cook just long enough to brown the meat well on both sides. As you turn the meat, season it with salt and pepper. (Do not overcook or the thinly sliced steaks will become tough). Transfer the browned meat first to the simmering sauce, turning it quickly and basting it with sauce, then to a hot dish, pouring the sauce over the meat. Serve immediately.

MENU SUGGESTIONS

An excellent first course would be *Spaghetti 'ajo e ojo'* (page 88) or *Gnocchi alla romana* (page 169). Avoid any pasta with either tomato or cream sauce. *Zuppa di scarola e riso* (page 55) and *Zuppa di lenticchie e riso* (page 64) are also good choices for the first course. For the vegetable, *Carciofi e piselli stufati* (page 295) or *Carciofi e porri stufati* (page 297) would temper nicely the piquancy of the tomatoes and olives.

Stracotto al Barolo
BEEF BRAISED IN RED WINE

For six

Vegetable oil
1 beef joint [1·8 kg (4 lb)], preferably chuck
15 g ($\frac{1}{2}$ oz) butter
1 small onion, coarsely chopped
1 small carrot, coarsely chopped
1 small stick celery, coarsely chopped
325 ml ($\frac{5}{8}$ pint) dry red wine (see note below)

250 ml (scant $\frac{1}{2}$ pint) broth (page 8) **or** tinned beef bouillon, more if necessary
1$\frac{1}{2}$ tablespoons tinned Italian tomatoes, chopped
A pinch of thyme
$\frac{1}{8}$ teaspoon marjoram
Salt and freshly ground pepper to taste

1 Preheat the oven to 180°C/350°F/Mark 4.

2 Pour enough oil into a heavy, medium-sized frying pan to just cover the bottom. Turn on the heat to moderately high, and when the oil is quite hot slip in the meat. Brown well on all sides. Transfer the meat to a dish and set aside.

3 Choose a casserole, with a tight-fitting lid, just large enough to contain the meat. Put in 2 tablespoons of vegetable oil, the butter and the chopped vegetables, and over moderate heat sauté the vegetables lightly, stirring from time to time. The vegetables should soften and colour lightly, but should not brown. Turn off the heat and put in the well-browned meat.

4 Tip the frying pan, and with a spoon draw off and discard as much of the fat as possible. Add the wine, turn the heat to high, and boil for less than a minute, scraping up and loosening the browning residue stuck to the pan. Add this to the meat in the casserole.

5 Add the broth or tinned bouillon to the casserole. It should come two-thirds up the side of the meat; add more if it does not. Add the tomatoes, thyme, marjoram, salt and pepper. Turn the heat to high and bring to the

boil, then cover the pot and place it in the middle level of the preheated oven. Braise for about 3 hours, every 20 minutes or so turning the meat and basting it with its liquid, and making sure it is cooking at a steady, slow simmer. (If it is not, regulate the heat accordingly.) At times, either because the cover does not fit tightly or because of the texture of the meat, you will find all the liquid has evaporated or been absorbed. If this happens before the meat is cooked, add 3 or 4 tablespoons of warm water. The meat is cooked if it feels very tender when pricked with a knife or fork.

6 Remove the meat to a chopping board. If the cooking liquid is too thin and has not reduced to less than 150 ml ($\frac{1}{4}$ pint), place the casserole on the stove and boil the liquid over high heat until it has thickened, loosening any residue that may be stuck to the pot. Taste the sauce, adding salt and pepper if necessary. Slice the meat and place on a warm dish, with the slices slightly overlapping. Pour all the sauce over the meat and serve promptly.

Note The ideal wine to use is Barbera or Barolo, which have the right amount of acidity combined with full-bodied flavour.

MENU SUGGESTIONS

Any first course that is not too strong in flavour, and does not have fish, can precede this substantial beef dish. All three varieties of *gnocchi* (pages 167, 169 and 171) are suitable, as are some of the more delicate pastas, such as *Tortelloni di biete* (page 140) and *Fettuccine all' Alfredo* (page 111). *Risotto alla parmigiana* (page 155) or either of the vegetable *risotti* (pages 162–3) are excellent. Or try the nice little *Minestrina tricolore* (page 50) or *Zuppa di lenticchie* (page 63). For vegetables, any of the butter and cheese ones will do, such as *Coste di biete alla parmigiana* (page 317), or the fried vegetables, such as *Carciofi alla giudia* (page 293) or *Asparagi fritti* (page 305).

Il bollito rifatto con le cipolle
LEFT-OVER BOILED BEEF WITH ONIONS

The art of serving left-overs is not a highly developed one in Italy, perhaps because portions tend to be small and appetites large. An exception is this savoury way to brighten up left-over boiled beef. It comes from Florence, where, from the time Florentines have been Florentines, nothing has ever been thrown away.

For four

6 onions, thinly sliced
4 tablespoons olive oil
450 g (1 lb) boiled beef
    (approximately), cut into slices
      9 mm ($\frac{3}{8}$ inch) thick
Salt
Freshly ground pepper, 4 to 6 twists
    of the mill

1 bouillon cube dissolved in 8
    tablespoons home-made meat
    broth (page 8) or in 8
    tablespoons water
1 or 2 tablespoons left-over juices
    from any beef or veal roast
    (optional)

1 Put the sliced onions in a frying pan with the olive oil and cook slowly over medium-low heat until a light brown colour.

2 Add the sliced beef, salt, the pepper, broth and the optional roasting juices. Cover the pan and cook at a gentle simmer for 10 minutes. Uncover, raise the heat to medium, and cook until the broth has completely evaporated. Check seasoning. Serve piping hot.

Note   This method is also successful with left-over grilled steak.

MENU SUGGESTIONS

Precede this with hearty *Zuppa di ceci* (page 72) or any of the good country soups, such as *Zuppa di cannellini con aglio e prezzemolo* (page 67) or *Pasta e fagioli* (page 68). Follow with a salad.

Polpette alla pizzaiola

RISSOLES WITH ANCHOVIES AND MOZZARELLA

Although it is very far from being a national dish, Italians do eat 'hamburger'. This is particularly true of some areas of the south where the beef is rather tough and it is chopped to make it tender. The following version of 'hamburger', in its frank, zesty taste, in the simplicity of its approach and in its decorative appearance, is undeniably Italian.

For six

1 80-by-80-mm (3-by-3-inch) piece white bread, crust removed	$\frac{1}{4}$ cup vegetable oil
3 tablespoons milk	6 tinned Italian tomatoes, opened flat, without seeds and juice
680 g (1$\frac{1}{2}$ lb) lean beef, preferably chuck, minced	1 teaspoon oregano
1 egg	6 slices mozzarella, 100 mm (4 inches) square, 6 mm ($\frac{1}{4}$ inch) thick
Salt	12 flat anchovy fillets
90 g (3 oz) fine, dry plain breadcrumbs, spread on a plate or on waxed paper	

1 Preheat the oven to 200°C/400°F/Mark 6.

2 In a saucer or small bowl, soak the bread in the milk and mash it to a cream with a fork. Put the meat in a bowl, add the bread and milk mush, the egg and salt, and knead with your hands until all the ingredients are well mixed.

3 Divide the meat mixture into 6 rissoles 37 mm (1$\frac{1}{2}$ inches) high and turn them over in the breadcrumbs.

4 Over medium heat, heat the oil in a frying pan until the meat sizzles when it is slipped in. Add the rissoles and cook 4 minutes on each side, handling them delicately when you turn them over so that they do not break up. When done, transfer to a buttered baking dish.

5 Cover each rissole with a flattened tomato, reserving a small strip of each tomato, no larger than 12 mm ($\frac{1}{2}$ inch), to be used for decoration. Season lightly with salt and a pinch of oregano. Over each tomato place a slice of mozzarella, and over the mozzarella place two anchovy fillets in the form of a cross. Where the anchovies meet place the reserved strip of tomato. Put the dish in the uppermost level of the oven and bake for 15 minutes, or until the mozzarella melts.

Note   These rissoles can be prepared several hours ahead of time before they are put in the oven.

MENU SUGGESTIONS

Zuppa di piselli secchi e patate (page 62), *Zuppa di lenticchie* (page 63), *Risotto alla parmigiana* (page 155) and *Spaghettini alla carrettiera* (page 82) are all good choices for the first course. An excellent vegetable accompaniment would be any of the ones sautéed with garlic, such as *Spinaci* (page 332), *Broccoli* (page 310), *Funghi* (page 325), *Melanzane* (page 320) or *Topinambur* (page 300).

Polpettine

MEATBALLS

For four

6 tablespoons milk
1 slice firm, fine-quality white bread, crust removed
450 g (1 lb) lean beef, preferably from the neck, minced
1 tablespoon finely chopped onion
1 tablespoon chopped parsley
1 egg
A tiny pinch of nutmeg or marjoram

15 g ($\frac{1}{2}$ oz) freshly grated Parmesan cheese
Vegetable oil
Salt
Freshly ground pepper, 3 to 4 twists of the mill
Fine, dry plain breadcrumbs
225 g (8 oz) tinned Italian tomatoes, cut up, with their juice

1 Put the milk and the bread in a saucepan and bring to the boil. Mash the bread with a fork and blend it uniformly into the milk. Set aside and allow to cool before proceeding with the next step.

2 In a mixing bowl put the chopped meat, onion, parsley, egg, nutmeg or marjoram, grated Parmesan, 1 tablespoon of oil, the bread and milk mush, salt and the pepper. Mix everything thoroughly but gently by hand. Check seasoning.

3 Gently, without squeezing, shape the mixture into small round balls about 25 mm (1 inch) in diameter. Roll the meatballs lightly in the breadcrumbs.

4 Choose a frying pan large enough to hold all the meatballs in a single layer, with a cover. Pour in oil until it is 6 mm ($\frac{1}{4}$ inch) deep. Turn on the heat to medium high, and when the oil is quite hot slip in the meatballs. (Sliding them in with a broad spatula is a good way of doing it. Dropping them in will splatter hot oil over you and your kitchen floor.) Brown the meatballs on all sides, turning them carefully so that they do not break up or stick to the pan.

5 When well browned turn off the heat, tip the pan slightly, and remove as much of the fat that floats to the surface as you can with a spoon. Turn on the heat to medium, add the chopped tomatoes with their juice and salt, and turn the meatballs over once or twice with care, so that they do not break up. Cover the frying pan and cook until the tomato has thickened into sauce, about 25 minutes. While cooking, turn the meatballs over from time to time and check seasoning.

Note The meatballs can be prepared entirely ahead of time and refrigerated for several days.

Minestrina tricolore (page 50), *Zuppa di patate e cipolle* (page 52), *Minestra di sedano e riso* (page 54) or *Zuppa di scarola e riso* (page 55) would be a good first course here. For vegetables serve *Pisellini alla fiorentina* (page 328), or any of the fried vegetables (pages 294, 305, 324 and 337).

Polpettone alla toscana

MEAT LOAF BRAISED IN WINE WITH DRIED MUSHROOMS

This juicy and beautifully flavoured meat loaf is from Tuscany, whose Val di Chiana beef is the best in Italy. It should be made with a fine, lean cut of beef, all of whose fat has been removed before chopping. The loaf should be firmly packed, not loose and crumbly, so that when it is cooked it can be cut into thin, elegant, compact slices.

For four to five

30 g (1 oz) imported dried mushrooms
450 g (1 lb) lean beef, minced
A 50-by-50-mm (2-by-2-inch) square piece good-quality white bread, crust removed
1 tablespoon milk
1 tablespoon finely chopped onion
Salt
Freshly ground pepper, about 6 twists of the mill
2 tablespoons chopped prosciutto **or** *pancetta* **or** *mortadella*, **or** if you really cannot obtain any of these, green bacon

30 g (1 oz) freshly grated Parmesan cheese
$\frac{1}{2}$ small clove garlic, peeled and finely chopped
1 egg yolk
90 g (3 oz) fine, dry plain breadcrumbs, spread on a dish or waxed paper
15 g ($\frac{1}{2}$ oz) butter
2 tablespoons vegetable oil
6 tablespoons dry white wine
2 tablespoons concentrated tomato purée

1 Put the dried mushrooms in a small bowl or large tumbler with 250 ml (scant $\frac{1}{2}$ pint) of lukewarm water. Let them soak for at least 20 minutes.

2 Put the chopped meat in a bowl, loosening it up with a fork.

3 Put the bread and milk in a small pan. Over medium heat, mash it

with a fork until it is creamy. Add it to the meat in the bowl, along with the chopped onion, salt, pepper, chopped prosciutto, grated cheese and chopped garlic. Mix gently but thoroughly by hand until all the ingredients have been incorporated into the meat. Add the egg yolk, mixing it into the other ingredients. Shape the meat into a single, firmly packed ball. Place the ball of meat on any flat surface, a wooden board or large dish, and roll it into a compact salami-like loaf about 62 mm ($2\frac{1}{2}$ inches) thick. Tap it with the palm of your hand to drive out any air bubbles. Roll the loaf in the breadcrumbs until it is evenly coated.

4 Drain the mushrooms, reserving the water in which they have soaked. (Remember that they should have soaked for at least 20 minutes.) Strain the dark liquid through a fine sieve lined with kitchen paper and set aside. Rinse the mushrooms in several changes of clean, cold water. Chop them roughly and set aside.

5 Choose a heavy-bottomed, preferably oval casserole, just large enough for the meat. Over medium heat, heat all the butter and oil. When the butter foam subsides, add the meat loaf and brown it well on all sides, handling the meat carefully at all times lest the loaf break up.

6 When the meat has been evenly browned, add the wine and raise the heat to medium high. Boil the wine briskly until it is reduced by half. Turn the loaf carefully once or twice.

7 Turn the heat down to medium low and add the chopped mushrooms. Warm up the strained mushroom liquid in a small pan and stir the tomato purée into it. When the tomato purée is thoroughly diluted, add to the meat. Cover and cook at a steady simmer, turning and basting the meat once or twice. After 30 minutes, set the cover slightly askew and cook for another 30 minutes, turning the meat at least once.

8 Transfer the meat loaf to a chopping board and allow to rest for a few minutes before cutting into slices about 9 mm ($\frac{3}{8}$ inch) thick. Meanwhile, if the sauce in the pot is a little too thin, boil it rapidly, uncovered, over high heat until it is sufficiently concentrated. Spoon a little sauce over the bottom of a warm serving dish, arrange the meat loaf slices in the dish, partly overlapping, then pour the rest of the sauce over the meat.

MENU SUGGESTIONS

This deserves a robust Tuscan soup as a first course. Choose any of the chick pea soups (pages 72–4), *Zuppa di cannellini con aglio e prezzemolo* (page 67), *Pasta e fagioli* (page 70) or *Zuppa di cavolo nero* (page 68). Also suitable are *Gnocchi alla romana* (page 169) or *Risotto alla parmigiana* (page 155). For a vegetable, accompany with *Finocchi fritti* (page 324), *Zucchine fritte con la pastella* (page 337) or *Carciofi alla giudia* (page 293).

Vitello

VEAL

Italy's finest veal comes from entirely milk-fed calves less than three months old. The meat is faintly rosy, nearly white, extraordinarily fine-grained and almost perfectly lean. Up to a few years ago, comparable veal was not marketed outside Italy. But if you buy Dutch veal you can attempt with confidence any of the delicious preparations to which veal lends itself.

Arrosto di vitello

ROAST VEAL

If there is any dish in Italy that comes close to being a part of every family's repertoire, it is probably this exquisitely simple pot-roasted veal. There is an infinite number of ways of roasting veal more elaborately, but there is none that produces more savoury or succulent, tender meat. The success of this method lies in slow supervised cooking, carefully regulating the amount of liquid so that there is just enough to keep the veal from drying out but not so much as to saturate it and dilute its flavour.

The best-looking roast comes from the top round, which some butchers will prepare for you. Rolled, boned shoulder of veal also makes an excellent and considerably less expensive roast.

For six

Scant 1 kg (2 lb) joint of veal, boned
3 medium cloves garlic, lightly crushed with the handle of a knife and peeled
1 teaspoon dried rosemary leaves **or a** sprig of fresh rosemary

Freshly ground pepper, about 8 to 10 twists of the mill, **or** $\frac{1}{4}$ teaspoon crushed peppercorns
2 tablespoons vegetable oil
30 g (2 oz) butter
Salt
170 ml ($\frac{1}{4}$ pint + 4 tablespoons) dry white wine

1   If the roast is to be rolled, spread on it the garlic, rosemary and pepper while it is flat, then roll and tie it securely. If it is a solid piece, pierce it

at several points with a sharp, narrow-bladed knife and insert the rosemary and garlic. (You will season it with pepper later.) Tie it securely.

2 Choose a heavy-bottomed saucepan or casserole, preferably oval, just large enough for the meat. Heat the oil and butter over medium-high heat, and when the butter foam begins to subside add the meat and brown it well on all sides for about 15 minutes. Sprinkle the meat with salt and, if it was omitted before, pepper.

3 Cook just long enough to turn the roast once and then add the wine. As soon as the wine comes to the boil, lower the heat so that it is barely simmering, place the lid askew, and cook until the meat is tender when pierced by a fork, about $1\frac{1}{2}$ to 2 hours. Turn the roast from time to time, and if the cooking liquid dries up, add 1 or 2 tablespoons of warm water.

4 When the roast is done, transfer it to a chopping board. If there is no liquid left in the pot, put in 8 tablespoons of water. Evaporate the water rapidly over high heat while loosening the cooking residue stuck to the pot. Altogether you should have about a spoonful of sauce per serving, so, if there is too much liquid left, concentrate it quickly over high heat. Cut the roast into slices no more than 6 mm ($\frac{1}{4}$ inch) thick. Arrange them on a warm dish, spoon the sauce over them and serve immediately.

MENU SUGGESTIONS

This roast really presents no problems over the choice of a first course. I would exclude none, except those with fish or with a very spicy sauce. Particularly nice with roast veal is *Tagliatelle alla bolognese* (page 110). Other pasta suggestions: *Spaghettini alla carrettiera* (page 82) or *Cappellacci del Nuovo Mondo* (page 144). Most vegetables are also a suitable accompaniment. *Cipolline agrodolci* (page 327) would be ideal. Other suggestions: *Pisellini alla fiorentina* (page 328), either of the sautéed mushrooms (pages 325–326), *Spinaci saltati* (page 332), or any of the vegetables with butter and cheese, such as the *Carote* on page 311.

Petto di vitello arrotolato

STUFFED BREAST OF VEAL

Roast boned breast of veal is an ideal way to enjoy the tenderness and delicate taste of veal without paying its usually steep price. It is an attractive-looking dish, and not at all complicated to prepare. If you are irredeemably opposed to dressing your own cuts of meat, you can persuade the butcher to bone the breast for you. But be sure to take the bones home with you, as they make an excellent veal stock or addition to meat broth. Boning it yourself, however, is quite simple, it keeps the cost down and it can even be enjoyable.

Lay the piece of breast on the worktop, ribs down, and, slipping the blade of a sharp knife between the meat and the bones, work carefully, detaching all the meat in a single, flat uninterrupted piece. Remove all gristly bits and loose patches of skin, leaving just the single layer of skin that adheres to and covers the meat.

For four to six

1 piece breast of veal [2 to 2½ kg (4½ to 5 lb) with bones, about 800 g (1¾) boned], bones removed as directed above

Salt

Freshly ground pepper, about 4 to 6 twists of the mill

110 g (¼ lb) rolled *pancetta* (see note below)

2 whole cloves garlic, peeled

½ teaspoon dried rosemary leaves **or** sprig of fresh rosemary

35 g (1¼ oz) butter

1 tablespoon vegetable oil

250 ml (scant ½ pint) dry white wine, approximately

1 Remove the bones from the veal as directed above, then lay the boned meat flat. Sprinkle lightly with salt, add pepper, cover with a layer of sliced *pancetta*, place on it the two garlic cloves spaced apart, and sprinkle the rosemary leaves over all. Roll the meat up tightly, like a Swiss roll, and fasten securely with string.

2 Heat the butter and oil over medium heat in a heavy-bottomed casserole just large enough to contain the veal. When the butter foam subsides, add the meat and brown well on all sides. Season lightly with salt, add enough wine to come one-third of the way up the side of the meat, and turn the heat up to high. Let the wine boil briskly for about 10 seconds, turning the meat in it, then turn the heat down to medium low and put the lid on, slightly askew. Cook until tender when pierced by a fork, about 1¾ to 2 hours. Turn and baste the meat from time to time. If it is sticking, add a couple of tablespoons of warm water.

3 Transfer the veal to a chopping board. Allow it to stand for a minute or two and then cut into slices 9 mm ($\frac{3}{8}$ inch) thick. (As you slice, look for the garlic cloves and remove them.) Arrange the slices on a warm dish.

4 Tilt the casserole and remove all but 2 or 3 tablespoons of fat. Add 2 tablespoons of water, turn the heat on to high, and while the water evaporates scrape up and loosen any cooking residue stuck to the pan. Pour over the sliced veal and serve immediately.

Note If *pancetta* is not available, green bacon, prosciutto or cooked ham are acceptable, although not equally satisfactory, substitutes.

MENU SUGGESTIONS

The same general observations hold true for this roast that were made for the pot roast on page 214. In addition, one should bear in mind that this one has *pancetta* (or prosciutto), so it would be better to avoid any first course or vegetable accompaniment that is thickly laced with either *pancetta* or proscuitto. Particularly ideal first courses here would be *Risi e bisi* (page 53), *Rigatoni al forno col ragù* (page 93), *Risotto alla parmigiana* (page 155), or either vegetable *risotto* (pages 162–3).

Ossobuco alla milanese (oss bus)
BRAISED SHIN OF VEAL FROM MILAN

Ossobuco, oss bus in Milanese dialect, literally means 'bone with a hole', or hollow bone. It is made with the shins of milk-fed veal, very slowly braised in broth with vegetables and herbs, and it turns, when done, into one of the most tender morsels of meat one can eat. A properly cooked *ossobuco* needs no knife; it can be broken up with a fork. The hind shins are better than the front ones for *ossobuco* because they are meatier and more tender. When the butcher prepares your shins, ask him to saw off the two ends, which contain mostly bone and little meat (you can use them in a broth). Ask him to cut the shins into pieces no more than 50 mm (2 inches) long, the size at which *ossobuco* cooks best, making sure he does not remove the skin enveloping the shins. It helps to hold the *ossobuco* together, and it has a delectable, creamy consistency when cooked.

For six

3 medium onions, finely chopped
2 carrots, finely chopped
2 sticks celery, finely chopped
50 g (1¾ oz) butter
1 clove garlic, peeled and finely
  chopped
2 strips lemon peel
8 tablespoons vegetable oil
2 shins of veal, sawed into 8 pieces
  about 50 mm (2 inches) long,
  each securely tied around the
  middle
90 g (3 oz) plain flour, spread on a
  plate or on waxed paper

250 ml (scant ½ pint) dry white wine
325 ml (⅝ pint) broth (page 8) **or** 1
  chicken stock cube dissolved
  in the same quantity of water
300 g (10½ oz) tinned Italian
  tomatoes, coarsely chopped,
  with their juice
¼ teaspoon dried thyme
4 leaves fresh basil (optional)
2 bayleaves
2 or 3 sprigs parsley
Freshly ground pepper, about 6
  twists of the mill
Salt, if necessary

1 Preheat the oven to 180°C/350°F/Mark 4.

2 Choose a heavy casserole with a tight-fitting lid that is just large enough to contain the veal pieces later in a single layer. (If you do not have a casserole large enough for all the veal, use two small ones, dividing the chopped vegetables and butter in two equal parts, but adding 15 g (½ oz) extra butter per casserole.) Put in the onion, carrot, celery and butter, and cook over medium heat for 8 to 10 minutes, until the vegetables soften. Add the chopped garlic and lemon peel at the end. Remove from the heat.

3 Heat the oil in a frying pan over medium-high heat. Turn the pieces of veal in the flour, shaking off any excess. When the oil is quite hot (test it with the corner of one of the pieces of veal: a moderate sizzle means the heat is just right), brown the veal on all sides. (Brown the veal as soon as it has been dipped in flour, otherwise the flour may dampen and the meat will not brown properly.) Stand the pieces of veal side by side on top of the vegetables in the casserole.

4 Tip the frying pan and draw off nearly all the fat with a spoon. Add the wine and boil briskly for about 3 minutes, scraping up and loosening any browning residue stuck to the pan. Pour over the pieces of veal in the casserole.

5 In the same frying pan, bring the broth to a simmer and pour into the casserole. Add the chopped tomatoes with their juice, the thyme, basil, bayleaves, parsley, pepper and salt. (Do not add salt until after cooking if you are using tinned beef broth. It is sometimes very salty.) The broth should come up to the top of the veal pieces. If it does not, add more.

6 Bring the contents of the casserole to a simmer on top of the stove. Cover tightly and place in the lower third of the preheated oven. Cook for about 2 hours, carefully turning and basting the veal pieces every 20 minutes.

When done, they should be very tender when pricked with a fork, and their sauce should be dense and creamy. (If, while the veal is still cooking, there is not enough liquid in the casserole, you may add up to 6 tablespoons warm water. If the reverse is true, and the sauce is too thin when the veal is done, remove the meat to a warm dish, place the uncovered casserole on top of the stove, and over high heat briskly boil the sauce until it thickens.) Pour the sauce over the veal and serve piping hot.

Note   When transferring the veal pieces to the serving dish, carefully remove the trussing strings without breaking up the shins.

Gremolada

The traditional recipe for *ossobuco* calls for a decoration of herbs, grated lemon peel and garlic called *gremolada*, which is added to the veal shanks as they finish cooking. Tradition deserves respect, but art demands sincerity, and cooking is, above all else, an art. In the light of modern taste, I find that the *gremolada* overloads with unnecessary sharpness a beautifully balanced and richly flavoured dish. I never serve *ossobuco* with *gremolada*. If you feel, however, that you absolutely must try it for yourself, here are the recommended ingredients:

1 teaspoon grated lemon peel   1 tablespoon finely chopped parsley
$\frac{1}{2}$ small clove garlic, peeled and very
     finely chopped

Some old recipes also include sage and rosemary, but that, I think, is going too far. *Gremolada* is sprinkled over the veal just as it finishes cooking.

MENU SUGGESTIONS

The natural accompaniment for *ossobuco* is *Risotto alla milanese* (page 157), as was noted under that recipe. It is not served separately, but together with *ossobuco*. If you would just as soon not have *risotto*, you can precede *ossobuco* with *Gnocchi di patate* (page 167) *al gorgonzola* (page 114), or with *Carciofi alla romana* (page 286). *Ossobuco* can be served without any vegetables but if you are willing to make the effort, *Pisellini alla fiorentina* (page 328) make a very happy accompaniment. Follow *ossobuco* with a fine salad. An excellent one would be *Insalata di spinaci e topinambur* (page 349).

Lo 'schinco'

BRAISED SHIN OF VEAL FROM TRIESTE

This is the same cut that in Milan is sawed into 50-mm (2-inch) pieces and called *ossobuco*. In Trieste the shins are cooked whole and flavoured with anchovies, which give the dish a decidedly different texture and character from *ossobuco*, although still every bit as tender. It is served whole, in all its magnificence, and carved at the table.

As in *ossobuco*, the hind shins are to be preferred because they are more tender. Ask the butcher to saw off the two joints at the end where there is no meat.

For six

2 onions, chopped
3 tablespoons olive oil
40 g ($\frac{1}{2}$ oz) butter
2 veal shins
2 cloves garlic, crushed lightly with a
        knife-handle and peeled
Salt

Freshly ground pepper, about 6
        twists of the mill
6 tablespoons dry white wine
4 large or 6 medium flat anchovy
        fillets
325 ml ($\frac{5}{8}$ pint) broth (page 8) **or** 1
        chicken stock cube dissolved in
        the same quantity of water

1 Preheat the oven to 180°C/350°F/Mark 4.

2 Choose a heavy casserole, preferably oval, just large enough for the shins. Put in the onion with the oil and butter, and sauté over medium heat until pale gold.

3 Add the shins, garlic, salt, pepper and wine. Simmer the wine for about 1 minute, turning the shins once or twice. Add the anchovies and the broth, cover, and bring to the boil. Transfer the casserole to the preheated oven and cook for 2 hours, or until the meat is extremely tender. (It should come easily off the bone.) Turn and baste the shins every 20 minutes. (While the meat is cooking, if you find that the cooking liquids have dried up, you may add 8 tablespoons of warm water. If, on the contrary, the meat is done but the cooking juices are too thin, return to the stove, uncover, turn on the heat to high and boil until the juices are concentrated.)

Note This dish can be prepared entirely ahead of time, refrigerated, and reheated like *ossobuco*.

Another speciality of Trieste is *La Jota* (page 65), which makes an ideal choice for a first course here. Also excellent would be *Gnocchi di patate* (page 167) *al gorgonzola* (page 114), or *Risotto alla parmigiana* (page 155). Any of the fried vegetables, such as *Zucchine fritte con la pastella* (page 337) or *Carciofi alla giudia* (page 293), is a suitable accompaniment, and so is *Cipolline agrodolci* (page 327).

SCALOPPINE

The perfect *scaloppina* is cut across the grain from the top round. It is cut a shade more than 6 mm ($\frac{1}{4}$ inch) thick and flattened to a shade less than 6 mm ($\frac{1}{4}$ inch). It is a solid slice of meat without any muscle separations and the problems lies in finding a butcher to cut it. Look for the kind of butcher who is willing to cooperate with you, and give you what you want – at a price. It may be expensive, but it will save you much heartache.

Once you have found this paragon, make sure not only that he cuts the *scaloppine* from a single muscle but also that he cuts them across the grain. If *scaloppine* are cut any other way, the muscle fibres will contract in the cooking, producing a wavy, shrunken tough slice of meat.

Scaloppine di vitello al Marsala
VEAL SCALOPPINE WITH MARSALA

For four

3 tablespoons vegetable oil	Salt
450 g (1 lb) veal *scaloppine*, very thinly sliced and pounded flat	Freshly ground pepper, 5 to 6 twists of the mill
90 g (3 oz) plain flour, spread on a plate or waxed paper	8 tablespoons dry Marsala
	40 g (1$\frac{1}{2}$ oz) butter

1 Heat the oil over medium-high heat in a heavy frying pan.

2 Dip the veal *scaloppine* in flour, coating them on both sides and shaking off any excess. When the oil is quite hot slip the *scaloppine* into the pan and quickly brown them on both sides, which should take less than a minute for each side if the oil is hot enough. (If you cannot get all of them into your frying pan at one time, do them a few at a time but dip them in flour only as you are ready to brown them, otherwise the flour will get soggy and the *scaloppine* will not brown properly.) Transfer the browned meat to a warm dish and season with salt and pepper.

3 Tip the frying pan and draw off most of the fat with a spoon. Turn the heat on to high, add the Marsala and boil briskly for less than a minute, scraping up and loosening any cooking residue stuck to the pan. Add the butter and any juices that may have been thrown off by the *scaloppine* in the dish. When the sauce thickens, turn the heat down to low and add the *scaloppine*, turning them and basting them with sauce once or twice. Transfer meat and sauce to a warm dish and serve immediately.

MENU SUGGESTIONS

An elegant first course would be *Crespelle alla fiorentina* (page 152), *Cannelloni* (page 127) or *Paglia e fieno alla ghiotta* (page 112). *Risotto alla parmigiana* (page 155) or either vegetable *risotto* (pages 162–3) would also be a good choice. For the vegetable: *Fagiolini verdi al burro e formaggio* (page 308) or *Finocchi al burro e formaggio* (page 322).

Scaloppine di vitello al limone
VEAL SCALOPPINE WITH LEMON SAUCE

For four

2 tablespoons vegetable oil
60 g (2 oz) butter
450 g (1 lb) veal *scaloppine*, thinly sliced and pounded flat
90 g (3 oz) plain flour, spread on a dish or on waxed paper

Salt and freshly ground pepper to taste
2 tablespoons lemon juice
2 tablespoons finely chopped parsley
½ lemon, thinly sliced

1 Heat the oil and 25 g (1 oz) of the butter in a frying pan, over medium-high heat. (It should be quite hot. Thinly sliced veal must cook quickly or it will become leathery.)

2 Dip both sides of the *scaloppine* in flour and shake off the excess. Slip the *scaloppine*, no more than will fit comfortably in the frying pan at one time, into the pan. If the oil is hot enough the meat should sizzle.

3 Cook the *scaloppine* until they are lightly browned on one side, then turn and brown the other side. (If they are very thin they should be completely cooked in about 1 minute.) When done, transfer to a warm dish and season with salt and pepper.

4 Off the heat, add the lemon juice to the frying pan, scraping loose the cooking residue. Mix in the remaining butter. Add the parsley, stirring it into the sauce.

5 Add the *scaloppine*, turning them in the sauce. Turn on the heat to medium very briefly, just long enough to warm up the sauce and *scaloppine* together – but do not overdo it, because the *scaloppine* are already cooked.

6 Transfer the *scaloppine* to a warm dish, pour the sauce over them, decorate with the lemon slices and serve immediately.

MENU SUGGESTIONS

These exquisite *scaloppine* should be preceded by a first course that has both delicacy and character. It could be *spaghetti* with Tomato Sauce III (page 81), *Fettuccine all'Alfredo* (page 111), *Tortelloni di biete* (page 140), with either butter and cheese (page 143) or *Sugo di pomodoro e panna* (page 139), *Risotto con gli asparagi* (page 162), *Risi e bisi* (page 53) or *Gnocchi verdi* (page 171), with either of the two sauces recommended. Some of the vegetables that can accompany the *scaloppine* are *Carciofini fritti* (page 294), *Topinambur gratinati* (page 301), *Fagiolini verdi al burro e formaggio* (page 308), *Cavolfiore gratinato al burro e formaggio* (page 313) and *Zucchine fritte con la pastella* (page 337).

Scaloppine di vitello alla pizzaiola
VEAL SCALOPPINE WITH TOMATOES

For four

2½ tablespoons vegetable oil
3 cloves garlic, peeled
450 g (1 lb) veal *scaloppine*, very thinly
    sliced and pounded flat
90 g (3 oz) plain flour, spread on a
    plate or waxed paper
Salt
Freshly ground pepper, 4 to 5 twists
    of the mill

6 tablespoons white wine
3 teaspoons concentrated tomato
    purée diluted in 8 tablespoons
    warm water
½ teaspoon oregano
2 tablespoons capers

1 In a heavy-bottomed frying pan heat the oil over high heat and sauté the garlic cloves. When they are browned, remove them.

2 Dip both sides of the veal *scaloppine* in the flour, shake off the excess, and sauté very rapidly on both sides in the hot oil. (Do not overcook. It is sufficient to brown them lightly, which should take a minute or less each side. And never dip the *scaloppine* in flour until you are just ready to cook them. If you do it ahead of time the flour becomes damp and they will not brown properly.) Transfer the *scaloppine* to a warm dish and season with salt and pepper.

3 Tip the frying pan and draw off most of the fat with a spoon. Turn on the heat to moderately high, add the wine, and scrape up and loosen the cooking residue in the pan. Then add the diluted tomato purée, stir, add the butter, stir, and continue cooking for a few minutes, until the liquids thicken into sauce. Add the oregano and the capers, stirring them into the sauce. Cook for another minute, then add the sautéed *scaloppine*, turning them quickly once or twice in the sauce. Transfer to a warm dish, pouring the sauce over the veal, and serve immediately.

MENU SUGGESTIONS

This is a tasty but amiable second course that can follow practically any soup or *risotto* and any pasta that does not carry a cream-based sauce or a tomato sauce. It is ideally accompanied by green vegetables sautéed in oil such as *Spinaci* on page 332 or *Finocchio* on page 323.

Rollatini di vitello al pomodoro
VEAL ROLLS IN TOMATO SAUCE

For four

450 g (1 lb) veal *scaloppine*, very thinly
    sliced and pounded flat
110 g ($\frac{1}{4}$ lb) rolled *pancetta*, sliced very
    thin
30 g (1 oz) freshly grated Parmesan
    cheese
60 g (2 oz) butter

2 tablespoons vegetable oil
Salt to taste
Freshly ground pepper, about
    4 twists of the mill
8 tablespoons dry white wine
1 tablespoon concentrated tomato
    purée with just enough warm
    water to dilute it

1 If the *scaloppine* are unusually large, cut them down to about 125 mm (5 inches) in length and 80 to 100 mm ($3\frac{1}{2}$ to 4 inches) in width. (If some pieces are irregular it does not really matter; it is better to use them than to waste them.) Over each *scaloppina* lay enough *pancetta* to cover. Sprinkle with grated cheese and roll up into a tight, compact roll. Fasten each roll with one or two toothpicks. Insert the toothpicks not across the roll, but into it along the length, so that the roll can turn in the pan.

2 In a heavy frying pan, heat up 40 g ($1\frac{1}{2}$ oz) of butter and all the oil over medium-high heat. When the butter foam subsides, add the veal rolls and brown quickly on all sides. Transfer the veal to a warm dish, remove the toothpicks, and season with salt and pepper.

3 Add the wine to the frying pan, turn the heat to high, and boil briskly for about 2 minutes, scraping up and loosening any browning residue stuck to the pan. Add the diluted tomato purée, stir, turn the heat down to medium, and cook for several minutes, until the tomato separates from the cooking fat. Return the veal rolls to the frying pan and warm them up for a minute, turning them in the sauce. Off the heat, mix in the remaining butter. Transfer to a very warm serving dish and serve without delay.

Note   This dish can be prepared entirely ahead of time and refrigerated for a few days in its sauce. When doing this, do not remove the toothpicks at the end of Step 2. You will need them to hold the veal rolls together while they warm up.

To reheat, remove the meat from the sauce and allow time to return to room temperature, meanwhile preheating the oven to 170°C/325°F/Mark 2. Add 1 tablespoon of water to the sauce and bring it to a simmer on the stove. Return the meat to the pan, cover, and warm up in the oven. Turn the rolls once or twice while reheating. *Rollatini* take some time to heat up inside. They must be hot through and through before serving. Remove from the oven when they feel quite hot at the touch of a finger.

MENU SUGGESTIONS

First course: *Tortelloni al burro e formaggio* (page 143), *Crespelle alla fiorentina* (page 152), *Trenette col pesto* (page 121) or *Risi e bisi* (page 53). Choose white vegetables, such as *Topinambur gratinati* (page 301), *Finocchi fritti* (page 324) or *Coste di sedano alla parmigiana* (page 314).

Fagottini di vitello leccabaffi
VEAL 'BUNDLES' WITH ANCHOVIES AND CHEESE

These veal 'bundles' are made of very thin *scaloppine* coated with a sauce of anchovies and tomato and a layer of cheese. The cheese should be bland to balance the sharpness of the anchovies. The *scaloppine* are then rolled and tightly trussed up and cooked very rapidly over high heat, first with butter, then with a little Marsala.

For six

75 g (2½ oz) butter
8 large or 10 medium flat anchovy fillets
15 g (½ oz) chopped parsley
6 tinned Italian tomatoes, drained and seeds removed
Freshly ground pepper, about 12 twists of the mill
680 g (1½ lb) veal *scaloppine*, very thinly sliced and pounded flat

Salt
220 g (8 oz) mozzarella, preferably smoked mozzarella, **or** Bel Paese cheese, cut into slices 3 mm (⅛ inch) thick or grated on the largest holes of the grater
60 g (2 oz) plain flour, spread on a dish or on waxed paper
250 ml (scant ½ pint) dry Marsala

1 Put 30 g (1 oz) of the butter and all the anchovies in a very small saucepan, and, over very low heat, mash the anchovies to a pulp with a fork.

2 Add the chopped parsley, the tomatoes and the pepper, turn the heat

up to medium, and cook, stirring frequently, until the tomato thickens into sauce.

3 Lay the veal *scaloppine* flat, sprinkle them with salt, spread the sauce over them, and cover, except for a 6 mm ($\frac{1}{4}$-inch) edge all around, with a layer of cheese. Roll up the *scaloppine*, push the ends in, and truss tightly, running the string both around the rolls and over the ends.

4 In a frying pan that can later hold all the bundles without crowding, melt the remaining butter over medium-high heat. When the butter foam begins to subside, roll the *scaloppine* lightly in the flour, shaking off the excess, and slide them into the frying pan. Brown on all sides for about 2 minutes. (If a little cheese oozes out of the rolls, it is quite all right. It enriches the sauce, and the floating white shreds of cheese are very attractive.) When the meat is well browned, add the Marsala and turn the heat up to high. While the wine boils, turn the veal rolls, and scrape up any browning residue in the pan. Cook for 2 to 3 minutes, stirring constantly, until the wine and other cooking juices have turned into a creamy sauce. Transfer the meat and sauce to a warm dish and serve immediately.

MENU SUGGESTIONS

This can be part of a meal that starts with a fish antipasto, such as *Cozze e vongole passate ai ferri* (page 30), *Gamberetti all'olio e limone* (page 34) or *Ostriche alla moda di Taranto* (page 28). The first course can be *Spaghetti 'ajo e ojo'* (page 88) or *Trenette col pesto* (page 121). For vegetable: *Finocchi fritti* (page 324), *Topinambur trifolati* (page 300) or *Melanzane al funghetto* (page 320).

Costolette alla milanese
MILANESE VEAL CHOPS

A breaded veal chop *alla milanese* is, at its best, the most perfect thing that one can do with veal. When skilfully done, the tender, juicy eye of the chop is enveloped by a delectable crust, very thin and very crisp. It is cooked entirely in butter, and the trick one must learn is to keep the butter hot enough long enough to cook the meat all the way through, but not so hot that it will burn.

The greatest problem we have in doing this dish is that of getting the right kind of chop. The only correct cut is the rib chop. In Italy, where veal comes from a very small animal, each rib yields a single chop, which is flattened to make it broad and thin. Only the eye is left on the bone, and a sufficient length of the rib is left on to give the appearance of a handle. Here, in England, you should buy Dutch veal. The tail of the chop should be trimmed away, leaving a clean, round eye. Since you must pay for the trimmings, take them home and use them for broth. The chops should be pounded flat, but first the butcher must knock off the corner where the rib meets the backbone.

It will be a rather expensive cut of meat, and it will not be quite a Milanese-looking chop, but you will have a beautiful piece of veal. If you give its preparation the necessary care, the result should amply reward your efforts and expense.

For six

6 veal rib chops, pounded flat	200 g (7 oz) fine, dry plain
2 eggs, lightly beaten with salt, in a	breadcrumbs, spread on a dish
soup plate	or on waxed paper
	90 g (3 oz) butter

1 Dip each chop in the beaten eggs, coating both sides, and letting excess egg flow back into the plate as you pull the chop away. Dredge the chops in the breadcrumbs, pressing the crumbs with your hands into the surface of both sides of the chops.

2 Choose a frying pan that can later contain the chops in a single layer. Put in the butter and melt it over medium-low heat. When the butter foam subsides, slip the chops into the frying pan. Cook for 3 minutes on one side, until a dark golden crust has formed, then turn and cook for another 3 minutes on the other side, watching the butter to make sure it does not burn and adjusting the heat if necessary. When done, transfer the chops to a warm dish and serve immediately.

MENU SUGGESTIONS

Veal chops in breadcrumbs will fit with complete assurance into any menu, whether plain and sturdy or delicately balanced. They make an especially nice second course when preceded by one of the fine home-made pastas, such as *Tortellini di prezzemolo* (page 137) with *Sugo di pomodoro e panna* (page 139), or by *Risotto con le zucchine* (page 163) or *Risotto con gli asparagi* (page 162). *Gnocchi di patate* (page 167) or *Gnocchi verdi* (page 171) are also excellent choices for the first course. But you can just as easily serve a substantial soup, such as *Pasta e fagioli* (page 68), or commercial pasta, such as *Fusilli alla pappone* (page 90). There is simply no vegetable that will not go with these chops. The tastiest accompaniment is *Melanzane fritte* (page 318) combined with *Pomodori al forno* (page 333). Other good pairings are *Funghi trifolati* (page 325), *Cipolline agrodolci* (page 327), *Pisellini alla fiorentina* (page 328) and *Fagiolini verdi al burro e formaggio* (page 308).

Cotolette alla milanese
MILANESE VEAL CUTLETS

In Italian cooking, *cotolette*, or cutlets, are not so much the cut of meat as the method by which it is cooked. A *cotoletta* is often a slice of veal, cut like a *scaloppina*, but it can also be a slice of turkey or chicken breast, or beef, or even aubergine. It is dipped in beaten egg, dredged in breadcrumbs and fried in very hot oil.

For six

680 g (1½ lb) veal *scaloppine*, sliced 6 mm (¼ inch) thick and pounded flat

2 whole eggs, lightly beaten, in a soup plate

240 g (8½ oz) fine, dry plain breadcrumbs, spread on a plate or on waxed paper

Vegetable oil and butter, just enough to come 9 mm (⅜ inch) up the side of the frying pan (see note below)

Salt

Lemon wedges

1 Dip each veal slice very lightly on both sides in the eggs and then into the breadcrumbs. As you turn the cutlet over in the breadcrumbs, tap it into the breadcrumbs with the palm of your hand to get a better adherence of the crumbs to the meat. Shake off all excess loose crumbs and pile the breaded slices on a dish until you are ready to cook them. (You may prepare them up to this point a few hours ahead of time.)

2 Heat the oil and butter in a heavy frying pan over medium-high heat. (To make sure the fat is hot enough, test it with the end of a cutlet. If it sizzles, it is ready.) Cook as many cutlets at one time as will fit in a single layer in the frying pan. When they brown on one side, quickly turn them

over. Remove them just as soon as they are brown and crisp on both sides, which will be very quickly. (Do not cook any longer than it takes to brown them or the meat will become dry.) Place the browned cutlets on kitchen paper, which will absorb any excess fat, and sprinkle with salt. Serve piping hot with lemon wedges, or with *Salsa rossa* (Red Sauce, page 25).

Note The quantity of cooking fat obviously depends upon the size of the pan, but the proportions are always 2 parts of vegetable oil to 1 part of butter.

MENU SUGGESTIONS

Follow the ones given for *Costolette alla milanese* (previous recipe), but avoid tomatoes in the first course or vegetables if you are using the *Salsa rossa*.

Nodini di vitello alla salvia
VEAL CHOPS WITH SAGE AND WHITE WINE

For four

3 tablespoons vegetable oil	Salt
4 veal loin chops, cut 18 mm ($\frac{3}{4}$ inch) thick	Freshly ground pepper, about 4 twists of the mill
90 g (3 oz) plain flour, spread on a plate or on waxed paper	6 tablespoons dry white wine
12 dried sage leaves	30 g (1 oz) butter

1 Heat the oil in a heavy-bottomed frying pan over medium-high heat.

2 Turn the chops over in the flour, coating both sides, and shake off any excess. (Do not coat meat with flour until you are ready to sauté it. The flour becomes damp and the meat does not brown properly.)

3 Slip the chops and the sage into the hot oil. Cook for about 8 to 10 minutes altogether, turning the chops two or three times so that they cook evenly on both sides. (Veal should not cook too long or it will become

dry. The meat is done when it is rosy pink on the inside when cut.) When cooked, remove to a warm dish and add salt and pepper.

4 Tilt the frying pan and draw away most of the fat with a spoon. Add the wine and turn the heat to high. Boil rapidly until the liquid has almost completely evaporated and become a little syrupy. While boiling, loosen any cooking residue in the pan and add what juice the chops may have thrown off in the dish. When the wine has almost completely evaporated and thickened, turn the heat to very low and mix in the butter. Return the chops to the frying pan for a few moments, turning them over in the sauce. Transfer them to a warm serving dish, pour the remainder of the sauce over them, and serve immediately.

MENU SUGGESTIONS

First course: *Rigatoni al forno col ragù* (page 93), *Cannelloni* (page 127), *Lasagne verdi al forno* (page 122), *Garganelli* (page 146) with *Ragù* (page 109), *Gnocchi verdi* (page 171) or *Crespelle alla fiorentina* (page 152). A lovely vegetable accompaniment would be *Carciofi e piselli stufati* (page 295), *Asparagi alla parmigiana* (page 303) or *Barchette di zucchine ripiene al forno* (page 340).

Spezzatino di vitello alla salvia
VEAL STEW WITH SAGE AND WHITE WINE

The preferred cuts for Italian veal stew are the shoulder and the shin. Avoid the round, which makes a dry and uninteresting stew.

For four

2 tablespoons finely chopped shallots or onion	90 g (3 oz) plain flour, spread on a plate or on waxed paper
2 tablespoons vegetable oil	18 medium dried sage leaves
25-mm (1-inch) cubes	150 ml ($\frac{1}{4}$ pint) dry white wine
680 g (1$\frac{1}{2}$ lb) shin or shoulder of veal, boned and rather lean, cut into 25 mm (1-inch) cubes	Salt
	Freshly ground pepper, about 4 twists of the mill

1 In a deep frying pan, sauté the shallots in the oil and butter over medium-high heat until translucent but not browned.

2 Dip the pieces of veal in the flour, coating them on all sides and shaking off excess flour. Add to the frying pan, together with the sage leaves, and brown well on all sides. (If all the meat does not fit into the frying pan at one time you can brown a few pieces at a time, but dip them in the flour only when you are ready to put them in the frying pan or the flour coating will get soggy and the meat will not brown properly.) Transfer the meat to a warm dish when browned.

3 When all the meat has been browned, turn up the heat to high, add the wine to the frying pan, and boil briskly for about 30 seconds, scraping up and loosening any cooking residue in the pan. Turn the heat down to medium and add the browned meat, salt and pepper. Cover and cook gently for about 1 hour, turning and basting the meat from time to time, adding a little warm water if necessary. The meat is done when it is tender when pricked by a fork. Serve immediately.

Note This stew can be prepared entirely ahead of time and refrigerated for several days in a Pyrex or enamel container with a cover. It can then be warmed up, covered, in the same container, in an oven preheated to 170°C/325°F/Mark 2. Add 2 tablespoons of water when warming it up.

MENU SUGGESTIONS

Follow the first-course suggestions for *Nodini di vitello alla salvia* (page 230). Also suitable would be *Risotto con gli asparagi* (page 162) or *Risotto con le zucchine* (page 163). An ideal vegetable is *Funghi alla panna* (page 326), which, after cooking, can be mixed with the veal stew. The combination also makes a fine hot buffet dish.

Spezzatino di vitello coi piselli
VEAL STEW WITH TOMATOES AND PEAS

For four

2 tablespoons chopped shallots
    or onion
3 tablespoons vegetable oil
25 g (1 oz) butter
680 g (1½ lb) boneless veal for stewing
    (see preceding recipe), cut into
    37 mm (1½-inch) cubes
Salt

Freshly ground pepper, about 6 twists
    of the mill
225 g (8 oz) tinned Italian tomatoes,
    coarsely chopped, with their
    juice
Scant 1 kg (2 lb) fresh peas (unshelled
    weight) **or** 300 g (10½ oz) frozen
    petits pois, thawed

1 Put the chopped shallots in a heavy casserole with the oil and butter and sauté over medium heat until pale gold.

2 Put in the pieces of veal, browning them well on all sides. (There are two points to bear in mind when browning the meat: it should be thoroughly dry, and it should not be crowded in the pot. If it does not all fit in at once, do a few pieces at a time. Remove the first batch as it is done and then add the others.)

3 Return all the meat to the pot, add salt, the pepper and the chopped tomatoes with their juice. When the tomatoes begin to boil, cover the pot and adjust the heat so that the tomatoes are barely simmering. Cook until the veal is very tender when pricked with a fork, as little as 1 hour from the time you have covered the pot if it is very young, fine veal. (More often, however, it will be closer to 1½ hours. Actually, a little extra slow cooking does not do it any harm.)

4 The peas must be added to the stew before it is completely cooked. If you are using fresh peas, calculate 15 or more minutes' cooking time for the peas, depending on their size and freshness. Add them when the meat has begun to turn tender but is still rather firm. If you are using thawed frozen peas, add them when the veal is tender nearly right through. Frozen peas take only about 5 minutes or less to cook. Check seasoning.

Note   The stew can be prepared completely ahead of time and refrigerated for several days. Reheat over medium heat when ready to serve.

MENU SUGGESTIONS

A perfect choice for the first course is *Risotto alla parmigiana* (page 155). Also to be recommended is *Riso filante con la mozzarella* (page 166). If the occasion seems to call for a soup, try either *Zuppa di patate e cipolle* (page 52 or *Passatelli* (page 60). No vegetable is required.

Vitello tonnato

COLD SLICED VEAL WITH TUNA SAUCE

This is one of the loveliest and most versatile of all cold dishes. It is an ideal second course for a summer menu, a beautiful antipasto for an elegant dinner, a very successful party dish for small or large buffets. It requires quite some time and patience in the preparation, but, since it must be prepared at least 24 hours in advance, you can set your own pace and make it at your convenience.

Vitello tonnato is common to both Lombardy and Piedmont, and there are many ways of making it. Most recipes call for braising the veal either partly or wholly in white wine. You may try it if you like. I find it gives the dish a sharper flavour than it really needs. In this recipe, do not under any circumstances use prepared, commercial mayonnaise.

Veal tends to be dry. To keep it tender and juicy, cook it in just enough water to cover (the method indicated below – put the meat in, add water to just cover, and then remove the meat – is the simplest way to gauge the exact amount); add veal to its cooking liquid only when the liquid is boiling; *never* add salt to the liquid; allow the meat to cool in its own broth.

For six to eight

900 g to 1·125 kg (2 to 2½ lb) lean, boneless veal joint, preferably top round, firmly tied	1 stick celery, without leaves
	1 medium onion
	4 sprigs parsley
1 medium carrot	1 bayleaf

The tuna sauce

Mayonnaise (page 22), made with 2 egg yolks, 300 ml (½ pint) olive oil, 2 to 3 tablespoons lemon juice, ¼ teaspoon salt	5 flat anchovy fillets
	300 ml (½ pint) olive oil
	3 tablespoons lemon juice
	3 tablespoons tiny capers
200 g (7 oz) tinned Italian or Spanish tuna in olive oil	Salt, if necessary

1 In a pot just large enough to contain the veal, put in the veal, carrot, celery, onion, parsley, bayleaf and just enough water to cover. *Now remove the veal and set aside.* Bring the water to the boil, add the meat, and when the water comes to the boil again, cover the pot, reduce the heat and keep at a gentle simmer for 2 hours. (If you are using a larger piece or veal, cook proportionately longer.) Remove the pot from the heat and allow the meat to cool in its broth.

2 Prepare the mayonnaise according to the recipe on page 22, remembering that all ingredients for the mayonnaise must be at room temperature.

3 In a blender mix the tuna, anchovies, olive oil, lemon juice and the capers at high speed for a few seconds until they attain a creamy consistency. Remove the mixture from the bowl and fold it carefully but thoroughly into the mayonnaise. Taste to see if any salt is required. (None may be necessary, depending upon how salty the anchovies and capers are.)

4 When the meat is quite cold, transfer it to a chopping board, remove the strings, and cut into thin and uniform slices.

5 Smear the bottom of a serving dish with some of the tuna sauce. Arrange the veal slices over this in a single layer, edge to edge. Cover the layer well with sauce. Lay more veal over this and cover again with sauce; set aside enough sauce to cover well the topmost layer. (The more layers you make the better. It prevents the veal from drying.)

6 Refrigerate for 24 hours, covered with plastic film. (It keeps beautifully for up to 2 weeks.) Before serving you may decorate it with lemon slices, olive slices, whole capers and parsley leaves.

MENU SUGGESTIONS

If you are using this as a second course, precede it with *Minestrone freddo alla milanese* (page 59), *Risi e bisi* (page 53) or *Trenette col pesto* (page 121). No vegetable, but follow it with a simple salad, such as *Fagiolini verdi in insalata* (page 355). As an introduction to a memorable meal, follow it with *Anello di risotto alla parmigiana con il ragù di fegatini* (page 156), and follow the *risotto* with *Piccioncini in tegame* (page 270).

Arrosto di agnello pasquale col vino bianco
ROAST LAMB WITH WHITE WINE

In most of Italy, lamb is a seasonal dish. It is usually consumed at Easter time, when it is around four months old. The following traditional Easter recipe from Emilia-Romagna is not quite as highly flavoured as *Abbacchio alla cacciatora* (page 237), but it brings out all the tenderness and delicacy of spring lamb.

For four

750 to 900 g (1¾ to 2 lb) spring lamb, preferably shoulder, including some chops
3 tablespoons vegetable oil
25 g (1 oz) butter
3 whole cloves garlic, peeled

½ teaspoon dried rosemary leaves, or a sprig of fresh rosemary
Salt
Freshly ground pepper, about 6 twists of the mill
150 ml (¼ pint) dry white wine

1 If the lamb is too large to fit into your largest saucepan in one piece, cut it in two or three parts. Wash in cold running water, and pat thoroughly dry with kitchen paper.

2 Heat the oil and the butter in the saucepan over medium-high heat. When the butter foam begins to subside, add the lamb, garlic and rosemary. Brown the lamb well on all sides. (Make sure the garlic does not become too brown. If you see that it is darkening too fast, put it on top of the lamb.)

3 When the lamb is nicely browned, especially on the skin side, add salt, pepper and all the white wine. Turn the heat up to high for a minute or less, enough to turn the lamb over twice. Cover the pan, turn the heat down to low, and cook the lamb at a very gentle simmer for 1½ or 2 hours, turning the lamb from time to time. (If you find that there is not enough cooking liquid in the pan and the meat is sticking to the bottom, add 2 or 3 tablespoons of warm water.)

4 The lamb is done when it feels very tender when pierced by a fork and the meat begins to come away from the bone. Transfer the lamb to a warm serving dish. Tip the pan, drawing off with a spoon all but 1 or 2 tablespoons of fat. Add 2 tablespoons of water, raise the heat to high, and while the water evaporates scrape up and loosen all the cooking residue in the pan. Pour this over the lamb and serve immediately.

As a first course, if you want to omit the pasta, you can serve *Carciofi alla romana* (page 286), *Carciofi ripieni di mortadella* (page 292) or *Fave alla romana* (page 306). If you are having pasta, these can be either antipasti or vegetable dishes. For pasta, choose something robust, such as *Bucatini all' Amatriciana* (page 89), *Orecchiette* (page 148) with *Sugo di broccoli e acciughe* (page 149), *Spaghettini con le melanzane* (page 84), *Fusilli alla pappone* (page 90) or *Lasagne verdi al forno* (page 122). Apart from the vegetables mentioned above, other suitable vegetables are *Finocchi fritti* (page 324) or *Zucchine fritte con la pastella* (page 337).

Arrosto di agnello al ginepro

CASSEROLE-ROASTED LAMB WITH JUNIPER BERRIES

In this recipe the meat is simmered right from the start with the vegetables, wine and flavourings. There is no browning and no liquid or cooking fat to add, because the meat supplies its own fat and juices as it cooks. There is practically nothing to do but watch the pot occasionally. Juniper berries, which are easily found at most spice counters, are absolutely essential to the full-bodied flavour of this dish. Most of the lamb commonly available throughout the year is mature lamb, and this method is particularly successful with it, because it transforms it into meat as tender as that of baby lamb or kid. Allow at least $3\frac{1}{2}$ hours' cooking time.

For four

1·1 kg ($2\frac{1}{2}$ lb) leg of lamb, preferably butt end, bone in
1 tablespoon chopped carrot
2 tablespoons chopped onion
1 tablespoon chopped celery
250 ml (scant $\frac{1}{2}$ pint) dry white wine
2 cloves garlic, lightly crushed with a knife-handle and peeled

$\frac{1}{2}$ teaspoon dried rosemary or a sprig of fresh rosemary leaves
$1\frac{1}{2}$ teaspoons juniper berries
Salt
Freshly ground pepper, 4 to 6 twists of the mill

1 Put all the ingredients into a heavy casserole. Cover and cook on top of the stove at low heat for 2 hours, turning the meat every 45 minutes.

2 At this point the lamb should have thrown off a considerable amount of liquid. Set the lid askew, and cook for another 1½ hours at slightly higher heat. The meat should now be very tender when pricked with a fork. If there is still too much liquid, uncover completely, raise the heat to high, and boil it until it is a little more concentrated. At the end the meat must be a rich brown in colour.

3 Off the heat, tilt the casserole and draw off as much of the fat as you can with a spoon. (You can use it as cooking fat for *Dadini di patate arroste* on page 332.) If you are not serving the roast immediately, do not degrease until after you have reheated it.

MENU SUGGESTIONS

This is the most highly flavoured of the three lamb roasts and requires a first course that is interesting but not too aggressive. I suggest *Minestrone di Romagna* (page 57), *Anello di risotto alla parmigiana con il ragù di fegatini* (page 156), *Cappellacci del Nuovo Mondo* (page 144) or *Zuppa di cannellini con aglio e prezzemolo* (page 67). As a vegetable: *Cavolfiore fritto* (page 314), *Asparagi fritti* (page 305), *Spinaci saltati* (page 332) or *Broccoli all'aglio* (page 310).

Abbacchio alla cacciatora
SPRING ROMAN LAMB

Abbacchio is very young, milk-fed lamb, taken when it is just one month old. Its flesh is nearly as pale as veal, and it is so delicate and tender that in texture it is almost closer to chicken than to lamb. In this recipe it is slowly pot roasted, and flavoured with sage, rosemary, a faint amount of garlic, and anchovies. It is one of Rome's most celebrated specialities.

Such young lamb is never available in England, but very young English spring lamb is a good substitute. Cook it as directed here and you will come remarkably close to the taste of the best Roman *abbacchio*. You must avoid the coarser, stronger-tasting meat of mature lamb.

For six

25 g (1 oz) cooking fat, preferably
  lard
1·35 kg (3 lb) shoulder and/or leg of
  very young lamb, boned and
  cut into 50-mm (2-inch) cubes
Salt
Freshly ground pepper, 6 to 8 twists
  of the mill
½ teaspoon chopped dried sage leaves

1 small clove garlic, peeled and finely
  chopped
1 teaspoon chopped dried rosemary
  leaves or sprig of fresh
  rosemary
2 teaspoons plain flour
8 tablespoons vinegar
6 tablespoons water
4 large anchovy fillets, chopped

1 In a saucepan, melt the lard over medium-high heat. Put in the lamb
pieces and brown well on all sides.

2 Add the salt, pepper, sage, garlic and rosemary, and continue to cook
briskly for another minute or so, long enough to turn all the pieces once.

3 Dust the lamb with flour, sifting it through a sieve. Continue cooking
at lively heat, turning each piece once. The meat will have turned a rather
dark colour.

4 Add the vinegar and boil it briskly, turning up the heat, for 30 seconds.
Add the water, cover the pan, lower the heat, and cook at a very gentle
simmer for about 1 hour. (The exact cooking time depends entirely on the
age of the lamb. When done, it should be very tender when pricked with a
fork.) Turn the meat from time to time as it cooks. If there is not sufficient
cooking liquid, add 2 to 3 tablespoons of water.

5 When the lamb is done, take 2 or 3 tablespoons of sauce from the pan
and put it in a small bowl, together with the chopped anchovies. Mash the
anchovies with a spoon or a pestle, then spoon over the lamb in the pan.
Turn and baste the lamb with its sauce over very low heat for about
30 seconds. Transfer to a warm dish and serve immediately.

MENU SUGGESTIONS

First course: *Gnocchi alla romana* (page 169), *Il rotolo di pasta* (page 129),
Spaghetti 'ajo e ojo' (page 88) or *Pappardelle con il ragù di fegatini* (page
117). For vegetable: *Carciofi alla giudia* (page 293), *Fave alla romana* (page
306) or *Dadini di patate arrosto* (page 332).

Costolettine di agnello fritte

LAMB CHOPS FRIED IN PARMESAN CHEESE BATTER

You will never know how succulent lamb chops can be until you have fried them in this egg-and-cheese batter. The crust, which is crisp and delicious, seals in all the sweetness and tenderness of young lamb. The younger the lamb you use, the sweeter and more delicate will be its flavour and texture in frying. But this recipe can be executed also with standard lamb. The chops must be no more than one rib thick. Get the butcher to knock off the corner bone and remove the backbone, leaving just the rib. Ask him to flatten the eye of the chop for you or do it yourself at home with a meat pounder or cleaver.

For six

12 single rib chops, boned and flattened as directed above
50 g (1¾ oz) freshly grated Parmesan cheese, spread on a dish or on waxed paper
2 eggs, lightly beaten in a deep dish
120 g (4¼ oz) fine, dry plain breadcrumbs, spread on a dish or on waxed paper

Vegetable oil, enough to come 6 mm (¼ inch) up the side of the frying pan
Salt
Freshly ground pepper, about 6 twists of the mill

1 Turn both sides of the chops in the Parmesan cheese, then give the chops a tap to shake off the excess. Dip them immediately into the beaten eggs, letting any excess egg flow back into the dish. Then turn the chops in the breadcrumbs, coating both sides and tapping them again to shake off all excess. (You can prepare the chops up to this point as much as an hour ahead of time, or, if you refrigerate them, even 3 or 4 hours. If refrigerated, allow to return to room temperature before frying.)

2 Heat the oil in the frying pan over medium heat until it is very hot. Fry as many chops at one time as will fit loosely in the frying pan. As soon as they have formed a nice crust on one side, season with salt and pepper and turn them. Add salt and pepper to the other side. Transfer to a warm dish as soon as the second side has formed a crust and do the next batch. (If it is truly young lamb and cut very thin, it should take, altogether, 4 to 5 minutes to cook. If the lamb is a little older or the chops are a bit thick, it may take a few moments longer.) Serve piping hot.

Home-made pastas are ideal with these crisp, tender chops, but any soup, *risotto* or commercial pasta will make a suitable first course, as long as it has no fish in it. Almost all vegetables are a suitable accompaniment, but particularly nice are *Pisellini alla fiorentina* (page 328). *Fave alla romana* (page 306), *Sedano e patate all'olio* (page 316) and *Zucchine fritte all'aceto* (page 338).

Arrosto di maiale al latte

LOIN OF PORK BRAISED IN MILK

Whenever I teach this dish I am greeted by more or less polite scepticism, which usually turns to enthusiasm at the first taste. Pork cooked by this method turns out to be exceptionally tender and juicy. It is quite delicate in favour because it loses all its fat and the milk, as such, disappears, to be replaced by clusters of delicious, nut-brown sauce.

For six

25 g (1 oz) butter	Salt
2 tablespoons vegetable oil	Freshly ground pepper, 3 or 4 twists
Scant 1 kg (2 lb) loin of pork in one	of the mill
piece, with some fat on it,	550 ml (1 pint) milk
securely tied	

1 Heat the butter and oil over medium-high heat in a casserole large enough to just contain the pork. When the butter foam subsides add the meat, fat side facing down. Brown thoroughly on all sides, lowering the heat if the butter starts to turn dark brown.

2 Add salt, pepper and milk. (Add the milk slowly, otherwise it may boil over.) Shortly after the milk comes to the boil, turn the heat down to medium, cover, but not tightly, with the lid partly askew, and cook slowly for about $1\frac{1}{2}$ to 2 hours, until the meat is easily pierced by a fork. Turn and baste the meat from time to time, and, if necessary, add a little milk. By the time the meat is cooked the milk should have coagulated into small nut-brown clusters. If it is still pale in colour, uncover the pot, raise the heat to high and cook briskly until it darkens.

3 Remove the meat to a chopping board and allow to cool off slightly for a few minutes. Remove the trussing string, carve into slices 9 mm ($\frac{3}{8}$ inch) thick and arrange them on a warm dish. Draw off most of the fat from the pot with a spoon and discard, being careful not to discard any of the coagulated milk clusters. (There may be as much as 250 to 325 ml (scant to generous $\frac{1}{2}$ pint) of fat to be removed.) Check seasoning. Add 2 or 3 tablespoons of warm water, turn the heat to high, and boil away the water while scraping and loosening all the cooking residue in the pot. Spoon the sauce over the sliced pork and serve immediately.

MENU SUGGESTIONS

Arrosto di maiale al latte originates from Bologna and is often preceded by dishes with a Bolognese sauce, *Tagliatelle alla bolognese* (page 110) or *Lasagne verdi al forno* (page 122). If this appears to be too substantial, try *Gnocchi alla romana* (page 169) or an assortment of Italian cold meats. As a vegetable, *Carciofini fritti* (page 294) or *Carciofi alla giudia* (page 293) are excellent accompaniments.

Arrosto di maiale all'alloro

ROAST PORK WITH BAYLEAVES

For six

Scant 1 kg (2 lb) boneless loin of pork	1 teaspoon whole peppercorns
40 g (1½ oz) butter	3 bayleaves, medium size
2 tablespoons vegetable oil	8 tablespoons red wine vinegar
Salt	

1 Choose a good heavy pot, preferably enamelled cast iron, just large enough to contain the meat, and provided with a close-fitting lid. Heat the butter and oil together at medium–high heat. When the butter foam begins to subside, put in the meat and brown it well on all sides.

2 When the meat is well browned, salt it on all sides, then add the peppercorns, bayleaves and vinegar. Turn up the heat for as long as it takes to scrape up all the cooking residue from the bottom. (Do not allow the vinegar

to evaporate more than slightly.) Turn the heat down to low, cover the pot, and cook slowly for at least 2 hours, until a fork easily pierces the meat. (Check from time to time to make sure that the liquid in the pot has not completely dried up. If it has you can add, as required, 2 or 3 tablespoons of water.)

3 Place the meat on a chopping board and cut into slices 6 to 9 mm ($\frac{1}{4}$ to $\frac{3}{8}$ inch) thick. Arrange the slices, slightly overlapping, on a warm serving dish.

4 Tip the pot, removing most, but not all, of the fat with a spoon. Remove the bayleaves and pour the sauce from the pot over the meat. (If there should be any cooking residue in the bottom of the pot, put in 2 tablespoons of water and scrape it loose over high heat. Add to the sauce.)

MENU SUGGESTIONS

This goes well with *Zuppa di scarola e riso* (page 55), *Minestrone di Romagna* (page 57), *Pasta e fagioli* (page 68), or any of the chick pea soups on pages 72–4. If you want a factory-made pasta, try *Spaghettini alla carrettiera* (page 82), *Penne al sugo di pomodoro e funghi secchi* (page 91) or *Bucatini all' Amatriciana* (page 89). Accompany with *Topinambur trifolati* (page 300), *Carciofi e porri stufati* (page 297) or any of the fennel dishes on pages 322–4.

Cotechino con le lenticchie

BOILED COTECHINO SAUSAGE WITH LENTILS

Cotechino has always been a speciality of that section of Emilia called Romagna, but now it is also made in other Emilian provinces, Modena especially. It is a large, fresh pork sausage about 75 mm (3 inches) in diameter and 200 to 230 mm (8 to 9 inches) long. The name *cotechino* comes from *cotica*, the Italian word for pork rind, which is an essential ingredient in this sausage. It also contains meat from the shoulder, cheek and neck, and it is seasoned with salt, pepper, nutmeg and cloves. There are slight variations, of course, according to the maker. In the finest *cotechino* only the pork rind is ground; the meat is mashed in a special mortar. A skilfully made *cotechino* when properly cooked is exquisitely tender, with an almost creamy texture, and it is more delicate in taste than you might expect from any pork sausage. *Cotechino* with lentils makes a wonderful country dish for family and friends, and it is especially heartening on a cold winter day.

For six

1 *cotechino* sausage	180 g (6 oz) lentils, rinsed in cold water and drained
1 tablespoon chopped onion	
2 tablespoons vegetable oil	Salt
1 tablespoon chopped celery	Freshly ground pepper, 4 twists of the mill

1 Let the *cotechino* soak overnight, or for at least 4 hours, in abundant cold water.

2 Put the *cotechino* in a stockpot large enough to contain it comfortably. Add at least 3 litres (5 pints) of cold water, cover, and bring to the boil. Cook at a very slow boil for 2½ hours. (Do not prod it with a fork. You must not puncture the skin while it cooks.) When the *cotechino* is done, turn off the heat and allow it to stand in its cooking liquid for 30 minutes before serving. Do not remove it from its liquid until you are ready to slice it.

3 Start doing the lentils about 1½ hours after the *cotechino* has been cooking. Bring 1 litre (1¾ pints) of water to a simmer. Meanwhile, in a heavy-bottomed casserole, sauté the chopped onion, in the oil, over medium-high heat until pale gold in colour. Add the chopped celery and sauté it for about 1 minute.

4 Add the lentils and stir until they are well coated with oil. Add enough simmering water to cover the lentils, turn the heat down to medium low so that the lentils cook at the gentlest simmer, cover the pot, and cook for 30 to 40 minutes, or until the lentils are tender. Add water from time to time so that the lentils are always just covered. (It will improve the taste of the lentils if, in addition to water, you use a ladleful or two of the liquid in which the *cotechino* is cooking.)

5 When the lentils are nearly done, do not add any more water. They must absorb all their cooking liquid before serving. Do not be concerned if some of the lentils burst their skins and become a bit mashed-looking. If there is still some liquid in the pot when they are cooked, uncover, turn up the heat, and quickly evaporate it while stirring the lentils. Add salt and pepper to taste.

6 Transfer the *cotechino* to a chopping board and cut into slices 12 mm (½ inch) thick. Spoon the lentils onto a heated dish and arrange the *cotechino* slices on top.

Note If the lentils should cook much faster than anticipated and the *cotechino* is not yet ready, set them aside and warm them up before serving, over medium heat, uncovered, adding a small amount of *cotechino* broth.

MENU SUGGESTIONS

All this needs is a good soup to go before it: *Passatelli* (page 60), *Minestra di sedano e riso* (page 54) or *Zuppa di scarola e riso* (page 55).

Fagioli dall'occhio con salsicce

BLACK-EYED BEANS AND SAUSAGES WITH TOMATO SAUCE

For four

2 tablespoons chopped onion
4 tablespoons olive oil
½ small clove garlic, peeled and chopped
1 carrot, chopped
1 small stick celery, chopped
225 g (8 oz) tinned Italian tomatoes, coarsely chopped, with their juice

450 g (1 lb) *luganega* sausage or other mild continental type of sausage
180 g (6 oz) dried black-eyed beans, soaked in lukewarm water for at least 1 hour before cooking
Salt and freshly ground pepper, if necessary

1 Use an earthenware casserole if you have one. Otherwise, choose a heavy saucepan, preferably of enamelled cast iron. Put in the chopped onion, along with the olive oil, and sauté over medium heat until pale gold. Add the garlic and sauté until it has coloured lightly. Add the carrot and celery and cook for about 5 minutes, stirring occasionally. Add the chopped tomatoes with their juice, turn the heat down to medium low, and cook at a gentle, slow simmer for 20 minutes.

2 Preheat the oven to 180°C/350°F/Mark 4.

3 Puncture the sausage skins in several places with a fork. If you are using *luganega*, cut it into 62-mm (2½-inch) lengths. Add the sausage to the pot and cook at a slow simmer for 15 minutes.

4 Add the beans and enough water to cover them well. Cover and bring

to a steady simmer. Transfer to the middle level of the preheated oven and cook for 1½ hours, or until the beans are tender, remembering that cooking times vary according to the beans: some beans do cook faster than others. Look into the pot from time to time to make sure that there is enough cooking liquid. If there is not, you can add 150 ml (¼ pint) of warm water at a time, as needed. (If, on the contrary, the beans are cooked and the cooking liquid is too watery, return the pot to the stove, uncover, turn on the heat to high, and boil until the liquid is concentrated.)

5 Tip the pot and draw off most of the fat with a spoon. Taste the beans and check salt and pepper. (Seasoning varies greatly, according to the sausage.)

Note If you are not serving it immediately, you can prepare the entire dish ahead of time. It keeps in the refrigerator for several days. Reheat either on the stove at low heat or in a 130°C/250°F/Mark ½ oven.

MENU SUGGESTIONS

Precede with a hot vegetable soup, as suggested for the previous recipe (page 244).

Coda alla vaccinara

OXTAIL BRAISED WITH WINE AND VEGETABLES

If you go to Rome and want to eat as the Romans do, you might include in your plans a meal at one of the *trattorie* near the slaughterhouse where they specialise in this dish. *Coda alla vaccinara* is as genuinely Roman as its name. *Vaccinaro*, although now it means 'tanner', was the old local name for 'butcher'. And truly it is a hearty butcher's dish. Oxtail is not for choosy filet mignon eaters, but it will satisfy those who appreciate the flavour and body that meat always has when it comes from next to the joints and bones.

For four to five

220 g (½ lb) pork rind
6 tablespoons olive oil
15 g (½ oz) cooking fat, preferably lard

3½ tablespoons chopped parsley
½ clove garlic, peeled and chopped
1 large onion, chopped

1½ carrots, chopped
1·125 kg (2½ lb) oxtail, cut at the joints and, if frozen, thawed overnight in the refrigerator
325 ml (⅝ pint) dry white wine

120 g (4 oz) tinned Italian tomatoes, seeded, drained, and coarsely chopped
Salt
Freshly ground pepper, 8 to 10 twists of the mill
3 sticks celery, very coarsely chopped

1 Rinse the pork rind in cold water. Bring water to the boil in a pan. Drop in the pork rind. When the water returns to the boil, drain and let the rind cool. When cool, cut it into 25-mm (1-inch) long strips and set aside.

2 Preheat the oven to 180°C/350°F/Mark 4.

3 Choose a heavy casserole, large enough to contain all the ingredients in the recipe. Put in the olive oil, lard, parsley, garlic, onion and carrot. Sauté lightly over medium heat for 10 minutes, stirring frequently.

4 Raise the heat to medium high, then add the oxtail pieces and the pork rind. Brown the meat well on all sides for about 8 minutes.

5 Add the wine, but pour it in gradually, or it may boil over. Boil the wine for 2 to 3 minutes, turning the meat once or twice.

6 Add the chopped tomatoes, 250 ml (scant ½ pint) water, salt and pepper. When the contents of the casserole have come to a steady simmer, cover the pot and place it in the middle level of the preheated oven. Cook for 1½ hours, turning the meat every 30 minutes.

7 Add the cut-up celery to the casserole, mixing it well in the meat and juices. Cook for 45 minutes more in the oven, turning the contents of the pot at least twice. At this point, the meat should be very tender and come easily off the bone. (Some cooks cook the meat much longer and boil the celery before adding it to the meat. I find that 2¼ to 2½ hours are quite sufficient to make oxtail tender enough to cut with a fork. And boiling the celery results in a partial loss of the flavour that is characteristic of the dish.)

8 Before serving, tip the casserole and draw off as much fat as possible with a spoon.

Note   This dish can be prepared entirely ahead of time and warmed up on top of the stove at medium heat just before serving. It will keep in the refrigerator for several days.

MENU SUGGESTIONS

A good country soup is the best first course here: *Zuppa di lenticchie* (page 63), *Zuppa di cannellini con aglio e prezzemolo* (page 67) or *Pasta e fagioli* (page 68). If you would rather have a pasta, choose either *Spaghetti 'ajo e ojo'* (page 88) or *Bucatini all' Amatriciana* (page 89). No vegetables need accompany this dish, but follow it with a nice cleansing *Insalata mista* (page 351) or *Finocchio in insalata* (page 350).

Trippa alla parmigiana

HONEYCOMB TRIPE WITH PARMESAN CHEESE

To a great many people tripe is not a particularly appealing dish. Actually, it is just a muscle, the stomach muscle, and a delicious one at that. Little of the meat we routinely eat is so savoury, so succulently tender, or has such an appetising fragrance as a well-prepared dish of tripe. To those who can approach a new experience without tension or preconceptions, I firmly recommend it. The greatest drawback to making tripe at home – its long and tedious scrubbing, soaking and preliminary blanching – has never been a problem in England, where traditionally tripe has always been sold ready-prepared, and elsewhere has been completely overcome by the appearance of ready-to-cook frozen honeycomb tripe. This is an excellent product with which you can confidently prepare any of the great regional Italian tripe dishes.

For six

Scant 1 kg (2 lb) frozen honeycomb tripe, thawed
1 small carrot
1 small onion
1 stick celery
8 tablespoons olive oil
40 g (1½ oz) butter
1 onion, chopped
1 stick celery, chopped
1 medium carrot, chopped
2 cloves garlic, lightly crushed with a knife-handle and peeled
1 tablespoon chopped parsley

¼ teaspoon chopped rosemary
150 ml (¼ pint) dry white wine
225 g (8 oz) tinned Italian tomatoes, with their juice
Freshly ground pepper, about 8 to 10 twists of the mill
Salt
250 ml (scant ½ pint) home-made meat broth (page 8) or ½ beef stock cube dissolved in the same quantity of water
75 g (2½ oz) freshly grated Parmesan cheese

1 Rinse the tripe thoroughly under cold running water and set aside.
2 Bring 3 litres (5 pints) of water to the boil with the whole carrot, onion

and celery. Add the tripe, cover, and cook at a moderate boil for 15 minutes. Drain and place the tripe in a bowl with enough cold water to cover. Soak until the tripe is thoroughly cool, then cut it into strips 12 mm ($\frac{1}{2}$ inch) wide by 75 to 100 mm (3 to 4 inches) long. Set aside.

3 Preheat the oven to 170°C/325°F/Mark 3.

4 In a heavy casserole put the olive oil, 15 g ($\frac{1}{2}$ oz) of the butter, and the chopped onion, celery and carrot, and cook slowly over medium-low heat for about 5 minutes, or until the vegetables have slightly softened. Add the crushed garlic, parsley and rosemary, and cook just long enough to stir everything well two or three times.

5 Add the tripe, stirring it into the vegetables and seasonings, and cook it for 5 minutes. Add the white wine and raise the heat to medium high, boiling the wine for 30 seconds.

6 Add the tomatoes and their juice, the pepper, salt and broth, and bring to a light boil. Cover the pot and bake in the middle level of the preheated oven for 2 to $2\frac{1}{2}$ hours. (Check the tripe from time to time to make sure there is sufficient liquid in the pot. If the liquid is drying too fast, add 2 to 3 tablespoons of water.) Taste the tripe after 2 hours. It should be very tender but pleasantly chewy and easily cut with a fork.

7 When done, remove from the oven and mix in the remaining butter and the grated cheese. Serve piping hot.

Note   A more fiery version of the same dish can be achieved by adding $\frac{1}{4}$ teaspoon of chopped chilli, or slightly more, to taste, before the tripe goes into the oven.

Tripe is just as delicious when reheated. It keeps perfectly in the refrigerator for 4 to 5 days.

MENU SUGGESTIONS

The earthy flavour of tripe goes best with a hearty soup such as *Pasta e fagioli* (page 68), any of the chick pea soups on pages 72–4 or *Minestrone di Romagna* (page 57). If you want pasta, choose *Spaghetti 'ajo e ojo'* (page 88). No vegetables are needed. Follow with *Insalata mista* (page 351), *Finocchio in insalata* (page 350) or *Cavolfiore lesso in insalata* (page 356).

Animelle con pomodori e piselli
SWEETBREADS WITH TOMATOES AND PEAS

In the Italian preparation of sweetbreads you must have a firm, light, patient hand to peel off the thin membrane in which they are wrapped. It is not necessary to soak them in water for several hours to whiten them because the Italian approach rarely alters or tones down the natural characteristics of an ingredient. In the version below, the sweetbreads are very briefly blanched, sautéed in butter and oil, then cooked slowly with tomatoes and peas. They are quite tender when cooked and very delicate in flavour, somewhat tastier and firmer than brains. They are perfectly complemented by the sweet taste of very young peas.

For four to six

680 g (1½ lb) sweetbreads	150 g (5¼ oz) tinned Italian tomatoes,
½ carrot, peeled	coarsely chopped, with their
1 stick celery	juice
1 tablespoon vinegar	Scant 1 kg (2 lb) fresh, young peas
Salt	(unshelled weight) **or** 300 g
2½ tablespoons chopped shallots **or**	(10 oz) frozen *petits pois*,
onion	thawed
60 g (2 oz) butter	Freshly ground pepper, 2 to 3 twists
1 tablespoon vegetable oil	of the mill

1 Working under cold running water, peel off as much of the membrane surrounding the sweetbreads as you can. If you are patient and careful you should be able to pull virtually all of it off. When finished, rinse the sweetbreads under cold running water.

2 In a saucepan put enough cold water to cover the sweetbreads later and add the carrot, celery, vinegar and a pinch of salt. Bring the water to the boil, add the sweetbreads, and cook at a very gentle simmer for 6 minutes. Drain the sweetbreads and, while still warm, pull off any remaining bits of membrane. (The sweetbreads may be prepared a day ahead of time up to this point and refrigerated under plastic film.) When cold, cut the sweetbreads into small chunks, about 25 mm (1 inch) thick.

3 In a deep frying pan or casserole, sauté the shallots, in the butter and oil, over medium heat until pale gold but not browned. Add the sweetbreads and sauté until lightly browned on all sides. Add the chopped tomatoes with their juice and continue cooking over low heat.

4 After 20 minutes add the shelled fresh peas, salt and pepper, mixing well with the sweetbreads and tomato. (If you are using frozen peas wait

another 15 minutes before adding the thawed peas.) Cover and cook at a
gentle simmer for 20 more minutes. Check seasoning, and serve while hot.
(If the sauce is too thin, transfer the sweetbreads with a slotted spoon to
a warm dish and rapidly reduce the sauce over high heat, then pour the
sauce and peas over the sweetbreads and serve immediately.)

MENU SUGGESTIONS

Sweetbreads may also be served in individual vol-au-vents or over slices
of toasted fine white bread. They can follow a first course of soup, pasta
or *risotto* that does not have a strong tomato presence. *Risotto alla parmigiana*
(page 155) would be an excellent choice. Avoid any spicy or very hearty
first course that would be out of balance with the delicate taste of the sweetbreads.

Fegato alla veneziana

CALVES' LIVER WITH ONIONS

What you need for *Fegato alla veneziana* is, above all else, a butcher able
and willing to slice calves' liver to an even thinness of 6 mm ($\frac{1}{4}$ inch). The
thinner the liver is, the faster it cooks, and the faster it cooks, the sweeter
it tastes. This is the whole point of *Fegato alla veneziana*. Another essential
requirement is that the liver comes from a very young, milk-fed animal, less
than three months old. Liver from young calves is of a pale, clear, rosy
colour. As the animal gets older, the liver becomes darker, tougher and
sharper in taste. Of course, you can use the technique of *Fegato alla veneziana* with what calves' liver you have available. But if you ever discover
a source of younger liver and a cooperative butcher, do not pass up the
opportunity to discover what a joy this dish can be at its best.

For four

680 g (1$\frac{1}{2}$ lb) calves' liver, very thinly   Salt
    sliced   Freshly ground pepper, about 6
3 tablespoons vegetable oil   twists of the mill
6 medium onions, thinly sliced

1 Remove the thin skin around the liver slices and any large gristly tubes. (Traditionally, liver for *Fegato alla veneziana* is cut at this point into bite-sized pieces about 37 mm ($1\frac{1}{2}$ inches) wide. You may do this if you like. I find the larger slices easier to turn while cooking, and I omit this step, unless I am having Venetians to dinner.)

2 Choose a frying pan that can later hold all the liver in a single layer without crowding. Put in all the oil and sliced onion and cook over medium-low heat for about 15 to 20 minutes. The onion should be limp and nicely browned. (You can prepare everything several hours ahead of time, up to and including this point.)

3 Remove the onion from the frying pan with a slotted spoon or spatula, and set aside. Do not be concerned if two or three slivers of onion are left in the frying pan. What is important is that you should still have oil in the frying pan.

4 Turn the heat to high, and when the oil is very hot put in the liver. (The oil should be very hot in order to cook the liver rapidly.) As soon as the liver loses its raw, reddish colour, turn it, add a large pinch of salt and some pepper, and return the onions to the frying pan. Give everything one more turn, transfer to a warm dish and serve immediately.

Note   It takes almost longer to read this than to cook the liver. If it is cut thin the liver is done in less than a minute.

MENU SUGGESTIONS

For a first course, it would be hard to improve on *Risi e bisi* (page 53). *Zuppa di lenticchie e riso* (page 64), *Risotto con le zucchine* (page 163) and *Risotto con gli asparagi* (page 162) are also good choices. If you want a vegetable, *Pomodori fritti* (page 335) go well with liver.

Fegato di vitello fritto

FRIED CALVES' LIVER

For four

Vegetable oil, enough to thickly coat
    the bottom of the frying pan
25 g (1 oz) butter
680 g (1½ lb) thinly sliced calves' liver

90 g (3 oz) fine, dry plain
    breadcrumbs, spread on a dish
    or on waxed paper
Salt and freshly ground pepper to
    taste
Lemon wedges

1 Heat the oil and the butter in a frying pan over high heat.

2 Press the slices of liver into the breadcrumbs with the palm of your hand, turning to coat both sides. Shake off excess crumbs. As soon as the butter foam subsides, slip the liver into the frying pan.

3 When the liver is lightly and crisply browned on one side, turn it and do the other side. (If it is as thin as recommended, it should take about 30 seconds for each side. If it is thicker, it will take just a little longer.) When done, the liver should be pink and very tender inside.

4 As each slice is done, place on kitchen paper to drain and season with salt and pepper. Serve piping hot, with lemon wedges.

MENU SUGGESTIONS

First course: any *risotto* with vegetables (pages 162–3) or *Risotto alla parmigiana* (page 155). Other possibilities are *Crespelle con il ragù* (page 153), *Conchiglie con il sugo per la gramigna* (page 92), *La gota* (page 65) or *Minestrina di spinaci* (page 56). For a vegetable, choose *Melanzane al funghetto* (page 320) or *Pomodori al forno* (page 333).

Cervella fritta

FRIED CALVES' BRAINS

This is the favourite way of doing brains in Italy. The brains are first cooked with vegetables, then sliced and fried. Frying emphasises their lovely texture. As one bites, the thin, golden armour of their crust gives way to yield the delectable core in all its tenderness.

For four

1 set of brains [about 450 g (1 lb)]
$\frac{1}{2}$ carrot, peeled
$\frac{1}{2}$ onion, peeled
$\frac{1}{2}$ stick celery
1 tablespoon vinegar
Salt
1 egg, lightly beaten with salt, in a bowl

120 g ($4\frac{1}{4}$ oz) fine, dry plain breadcrumbs, spread on a dish or on waxed paper
Vegetable oil, enough to come 12 mm ($\frac{1}{2}$ inch) up the side of the pan
Lemon wedges

1 Wash the brains thoroughly in cold water, then let them soak in cold water for 10 minutes. Drain, and carefully remove as much as possible of the surrounding membrane and the protruding blood vessels.

2 Put the carrot, onion, celery, vinegar and salt in a saucepan with $1\frac{1}{2}$ litres ($2\frac{1}{2}$ pints) of water and bring to the boil.

3 Drop in the brains and, when the water has returned to the boil, cover the pan and adjust the heat so that the liquid bubbles very slowly but steadily. Cook for 20 minutes.

4 Drain, and let the brains cool completely. When cool, refrigerate for about 10 minutes, or until they are very firm. (You may even prepare them ahead of time, in the morning, and refrigerate until shortly before you are ready to fry. If refrigerating brains for several hours, cover them with plastic film.)

5 Cut the brains into broad pieces, about 12 mm ($\frac{1}{2}$ inch) thick.

6 First dip the slices in egg, letting the excess flow back into the bowl, then turn them in breadcrumbs.

7 Heat the oil in a frying pan over high heat. When the oil is very hot, slip the coated slices into the pan. (Do not put in any more at one time than will fit loosely). Fry until golden brown on one side, then do the other side. When a nice crust has formed on both sides, transfer to kitchen paper to drain. When all the slices are done, serve immediately with lemon wedges.

Fried brains can be one of the components of *Il grande fritto misto* (page 283). If it is going to be a second course on its own, it can be preceded by a soup, such as *Zuppa di scarola e riso* (page 55) or *Minestrina di spinaci* (page 56),or by *Fettuccine all'Alfredo* (page 111), *Cannelloni* (page 127), *Risi e bisi* (page 53) or any *risotto*, except those with chicken livers or with clams. It can then be accompanied by any one of the fried vegetables, and *Fagiolini verdi al burro e formaggio* (page 308), *Funghi trifolati* (page 325) or *Broccoli all'aglio* (page 310).

Rognoncini trifolati al vino bianco
LAMBS' KIDNEYS WITH WHITE WINE

For four to six

20 lambs' kidneys
3 tablespoons vinegar
4 tablespoons vegetable oil
2 tablespoons finely chopped shallots
    or onion
$\frac{1}{2}$ clove garlic, peeled and finely chopped

2 tablespoons finely chopped parsley
Salt to taste
Freshly ground pepper, 6 to 8 twists
    of the mill
$\frac{1}{2}$ teaspoon cornflour
150 ml ($\frac{1}{4}$ pint) dry white wine

1 Split the kidneys in half and wash briefly under cold running water. To a china or earthenware bowl of water large enough to contain them add the vinegar, then the kidneys. Let the kidneys soak for at least 30 minutes, then drain and pat dry with kitchen paper. Cut them into very thin slices and try to remove as many of the small white tubes as possible.

2 Heat the oil in a heavy-bottomed frying pan and sauté the shallots until pale gold. Add the chopped garlic, stir two or three times, add the parsley and, immediately after, add the sliced kidneys.

3 Raise the heat to high, add salt and pepper, and stir so that the kidneys are well coated with the sautéed shallots and with the garlic and parsley. As soon as the kidneys have lost their raw red colour, transfer them to a warm dish. (It is very important not to overcook kidneys. Tiny lambs' kidneys, in particular, cook very rapidly.)

4 Mix the cornflour into the wine and add to the frying pan. Bring to a rapid boil over high heat, taking care to scrape up all the cooking residue stuck to the bottom of the pan. Add any juice the kidneys may have left in their dish. When the sauce starts to thicken, add the kidneys and stir quickly, cooking them just a moment more. Serve with their sauce while still hot.

MENU SUGGESTIONS

Any first course that has character but is not overbearingly sharp goes well with kidneys. Any of the following makes a good choice: *Gnocchi di patate* (page 167), with either Tomato Sauce III (page 81) or *al gorgonzola* (page 114), *Cappelletti con la panna* (page 136), *Crespelle alla fiorentina* (page 152), *Risi e bisi* (page 53). For vegetable: *Carciofi e porri stufati* (page 297) or *Carciofi e piselli stufati* (page 295).

Fegatelli di maiale con la rete

GRILLED PORK LIVER WRAPPED IN CAUL FAT

This is a classic Tuscan dish, and it is delicious. Like all Tuscan grills it is extremely simple. The one important point to remember is not to overcook the liver. Perfectly grilled liver is pink, juicy and sweet tasting. Caul fat, or pork net, is a fatty reticulated membrane enveloping the intestines. It acts as a self-baster for the liver. It is so inexpensive that it is well worth buying a large piece and utilising the best parts of it for the wrappers. In Italy, liver is sold ready-wrapped in its *rete*.

For six

A large piece of caul fat (about 450 g (1 lb)
680 g (1½ lb) pork liver

Salt and freshly ground pepper to taste
Bayleaves

1 Preheat the grill to its maximum.
2 Soak the caul fat in lukewarm water for 2 or 3 minutes, until it loosens up. Change the water a few times to rinse and clean the membrane. Lay

the membrane on a dry cloth and carefully open it up. Cut the best parts of it into rectangles 120 by 180 mm (5 by 7 inches). (Do not bother to patch small pieces together.)

3 Remove any skin or tough, exposed vessels from the liver. Wash the liver in cold water and pat thoroughly dry. Cut it into sections about 75 mm (3 inches) long, 50 mm (2 inches) wide and 15 mm ($\frac{5}{8}$ inch) thick.

4 Season the sections of liver with a good pinch of salt and at least a grinding of pepper each. Place a bayleaf on each section and wrap each section with one of the caul-fat wrappers, tucking the ends under as you wrap. Fasten each piece of liver with a toothpick.

5 Place in the hot grill, which should have been on for at least 15 minutes, so that it is searing hot when you put in the liver. Turn the liver after $2\frac{1}{2}$ to 3 minutes. Do not cook for more than 4 or 5 minutes all together. Serve piping hot.

MENU SUGGESTIONS

This dish is absolutely sensational cooked outdoors over charcoal. It can be part of a mixed grill with steaks and chops. Indoors, precede it with *Zuppa di cannellini con aglio e prezzemolo* (page 67); *Zuppa di patate e cipolle* (page 52) or *Zuppa di piselli secchi e patate* (page 62). Accompany the liver with *Cavolfiore gratinato al burro e formaggio* (page 313), *Coste di biete alla parmigiana* (page 317) or *Carciofi e porri stufati* (page 297).

Fegatini di pollo alla salvia
CHICKEN LIVERS WITH SAGE

For six

680 g (1½ lb) chicken livers
2 tablespoons finely chopped shallots
    or onion
60 g (2 oz) butter
1 dozen dried sage leaves **or** a
    handful of fresh sage

6 tablespoons dry white wine
Salt to taste
Freshly ground pepper, about 4
    twists of the mill

1 Examine the livers carefully for green spots and cut them out. Remove any bits of fat and wash the livers thoroughly in cold water. Dry well on kitchen paper.

2 In a frying pan, sauté the shallots in the butter over medium heat. When they turn pale gold, raise the heat and add the sage leaves and chicken livers. Cook over high heat for just a few minutes, stirring frequently, until the livers lose their raw, red colour. Transfer the livers to a warm dish.

3 Add the wine to the frying pan and boil briskly until it has almost completely evaporated. Scrape up and loosen any cooking residue in the pan. Add any liquid the livers may have thrown off in the dish, and allow it to evaporate.

4 Return the chicken livers to the pan, turn them rapidly for a few moments over high heat, add salt and pepper, and transfer to a warm serving dish. Serve immediately.

MENU SUGGESTIONS

These chicken livers go so well with *Purè di patate* (page 329) that you can dispense with a pasta first course without any regrets. You can precede them with *Funghi ripieni* (page 40), *Carciofi alla romana* (page 286) or *Barchette di zucchine ripiene al forno* (page 340). If you want to vary this arrangement, choose *Minestra di sedano e riso* (page 54) or *Minestrina di spinaci* (page 56) as a first course and accompany the livers with *Carote al burro e formaggio* (page 311).

Pollo arrosto in tegame

POT-ROASTED CHICKEN WITH GARLIC, ROSEMARY AND WHITE WINE

Reliable ovens are only a recent addition to the Italian kitchen and, consequently, traditional roasts are done either on the spit or in a heavy casserole on top of the stove. In this recipe the chicken is entirely pot roasted, with just enough liquid to keep it from drying out. As in almost all Italian roasts, it is flavoured with garlic and a hint of rosemary. It is one of the simplest and tastiest ways of doing chicken, and, if you use a young roasting chicken, you should have it on the table in less than 45 minutes from the time you start preparing it.

For four

30 g (1 oz) butter	A small sprig of fresh rosemary, cut
2 tablespoons vegetable oil	in two, **or** $\frac{1}{2}$ teaspoon dried
2 to 3 cloves garlic, peeled	rosemary leaves
1 roasting chicken [1·15 kg (2$\frac{1}{2}$ lb)],	Salt
washed in cold water,	Freshly ground pepper, about 6
quartered, and thoroughly	twists of the mill
dried in a towel	8 tablespoons dry white wine

1 Heat the butter and oil in a heavy casserole over medium-high heat. When the butter foam begins to subside, add the garlic and the chicken quarters, skin side down. When the chicken is well browned on one side, turn the pieces over and add the rosemary. If the garlic starts to blacken, remove it. If, however, it stays a deep golden brown, leave it in until the chicken is cooked. Control the heat so that the cooking fat stays hot but does not burn.

2 When you have browned the chicken well on all sides, add a large pinch of salt, the pepper and the wine. Allow the wine to bubble rapidly for 2 to 3 minutes, then lower the heat until it is just simmering and cover the pan. Cook slowly until the chicken is tender when pricked with a fork. (A young roasting chicken should take about 30 to 35 minutes.) Turn the chicken two or three times while cooking. (If you see that the cooking liquid has dried up, you can add 1 to 2 tablespoons of water as needed.)

3 Transfer the chicken to a warm serving dish, removing the garlic from the casserole if you have not done it earlier. Tilt the casserole, drawing off all but 2 tablespoons of fat with a spoon. Return the casserole to high heat, adding 2 to 3 tablespoons of water, and scraping up the cooking juices in the pot. Pour these over the chicken and serve.

MENU SUGGESTIONS

You can precede this with soup, such as *Minestra di sedano e riso* (page 54), *Zuppa di scarola e riso* (page 55) or *Minestrina di spinaci* (page 56). If you would like a pasta or risotto, any of these would be a good choice: *Penne al sugo di pomodoro e funghi secchi* (page 91), *Rigatoni al forno col ragù* (page 93), *Tagliatelle alla bolognese* (page 110), *Cannelloni* (page 127), *Risotto alla parmigiana* (page 155), *Risotto col ragù* (page 160), *Risi e bisi* (page 53). If the first course was soup, you can accompany the chicken with *Dadini di patate arrosto* (page 332) or *Purè di patate* (page 329). If you had pasta, a good vegetable accompaniment would be *Fagiolini verdi al burro e formaggio* (page 308), *Pisellini alla fiorentina* (page 328) or *Carote al burro e formaggio* (page 311).

Pollo arrosto al forno con rosmarino
ROAST CHICKEN WITH ROSEMARY

For four

3 cloves garlic, peeled
A sprig of chopped fresh rosemary **or**
    1 heaped teaspoon dried
    rosemary leaves
1 roasting chicken [about 1·15 kg (2½
    lb)], washed and thoroughly
    dried in a towel

Salt
Freshly ground pepper, about 8 twists
    of the mill
4 tablespoons vegetable oil

1 Preheat the oven to 190°C/375°F/Mark 5.

2 Put all the garlic and half the rosemary into the cavity of the bird. Add a large pinch of salt and a few grindings of pepper.

3 Rub about half the oil over the outside of the chicken, and sprinkle with salt, more pepper and the rest of the rosemary.

4 Put the chicken and the rest of the oil in a roasting pan and place it in the middle level of the preheated oven. Turn the chicken and baste it with the fat and cooking juices in the pan every 15 minutes. Cook for about 1 hour, or until the skin is well browned and crisp.

5 Transfer the chicken to a warm dish. Tip the pan and draw off all but 1 tablespoon of fat with a spoon. Place the pan on the stove, turn on the heat to high, add 1 or 2 tablespoons of water, and while it boils away scrape up all the cooking residue. Pour over the chicken and serve immediately.

MENU SUGGESTIONS

Follow the ones given for the preceding chicken recipe.

Pollo alla diavola

CHARCOAL-GRILLED CHICKEN MARINATED IN PEPPER, OIL AND LEMON

This peppery chicken should be very satisfying to an outdoor appetite. It is a famous Roman speciality that has now become popular in most of Italy. The chicken is opened out flat, rubbed liberally with crushed peppercorns, and marinated in oil and lemon juice. Many cooks omit the lemon juice until the chicken is cooked, but I find that it enhances the texture and fragrance of the chicken if it is included in the marinade. If you are picnicking, you can prepare the chicken at home, put it in a plastic bag, stow it in a portable refrigerator or insulated food bag, and when your charcoal fire is ready, the chicken is ready. Do not skimp on the pepper, or it will not be *alla diavola*, 'hot as the devil'.

Although charcoal is the ideal fire for chicken *alla diavola*, it is delicious even when cooked on an indoor grill. Preheat the grill to its maximum setting at least 15 minutes ahead of time.

For four

1 roasting chicken [about scant 1 kg (2 lb)]	1 tablespoon crushed peppercorns
6 tablespoons lemon juice	3 tablespoons olive oil
	Plenty of salt

1 Lay the chicken on a flat surface with the breast facing down and split it open along the entire backbone. Crack the breastbone from the inside. Spread the chicken as flat as you can with your hands. Turn it over so that the breast faces you. Cut the wings and legs where they join the body, but without detaching them – just enough to spread them flat. Turn the chicken over again, with the inside of the carcass facing you, and pound it as flat as possible, using a cleaver or large meat flattener. It should have something of a butterfly shape.

2 Put the chicken in a deep dish. Pour the lemon juice over the chicken, then add the peppercorns and the olive oil. Cover the dish and let it marinate for at least 2 hours. Uncover and baste from time to time.

3 When the fire is ready, sprinkle the chicken with salt and place on the grill (which should be about 5 inches above the charcoal), skin side towards the fire. Grill until the skin has turned light brown, then turn it over on the other side, basting with marinade liquid from time to time. Turn it over after about 10 minutes and cook briefly once again on each side, until the thigh is tender when pricked with a fork. (Altogether, it should take about

35 minutes.) If the marinating liquid should run out before the chicken is done, baste with a teaspoonful of olive oil from time to time. Season with a pinch of crushed pepper before serving.

MENU SUGGESTIONS

If cooked outdoors, some or all of the *Verdura mista in graticola* (page 344) would be lovely with this chicken. Indoors, a first course can be any soup, *risotto* or pasta that does not have fish or cream in it. You cannot go wrong with any vegetable, but a good combination is *Fagiolini verdi con peperoni e pomodoro* (page 309) or *Melanzane fritte* (page 318), together with *Pomodori al forno* (page 333).

Pollo alla cacciatora

CHICKEN FRICASSEE WITH GREEN PEPPERS AND TOMATOES

For four or five

Roasting chicken [1·15 to 1·35 kg (2½ to 3 lb)], cut into 4 to 6 pieces
3 tablespoons vegetable oil
120 g (4¼ oz) plain flour, spread on a plate or on waxed paper
Salt
Freshly ground pepper, 4 to 6 twists of the mill
150 ml (¼ pint) dry white wine
½ medium onion, thinly sliced

1 green pepper, with seeds removed, cut into thin strips
1 medium carrot, sliced very thin
½ stick celery, cut into thin strips
1 clove garlic, peeled and chopped very fine
150 g (5 oz) tinned Italian tomatoes, coarsely chopped, with their juice

1 Wash the chicken pieces in cold running water and pat dry very thoroughly with kitchen paper.

2 Choose a frying pan large enough to contain all the chicken pieces comfortably, without crowding. Heat the oil in the frying pan over moderately high heat. Turn the chicken pieces in the flour, coating both sides and shaking off the excess, and put in the frying pan, skin side down. When one

side has turned golden brown, turn the pieces over and brown the other side. When nicely browned on all sides, transfer them to a warm dish and add salt and pepper.

3 Tip the frying pan and draw off most of the fat with a spoon. Turn the heat to high, add the wine and boil rapidly until it is reduced by half. Scrape up and loosen any cooking residue in the pan. Lower the heat to medium, add the sliced onion, and cook for about 5 minutes, stirring two or three times. Add the browned chicken pieces, all but the breasts. (Breasts cook faster, so they can be added later.) Add the sliced pepper, carrot, celery, garlic and the chopped tomatoes and their juice. Adjust to a slow simmer and cover. After 9 to 10 minutes add the breasts and continue cooking until tender, about 30 minutes. Turn and baste the chicken a few times while cooking.

4 Transfer the chicken to a warm serving dish. If the sauce in the pan is too thin, raise the heat to high and boil it briskly until it thickens, stirring as it boils. Pour the sauce over the chicken and serve immediately.

Note   If prepared ahead of time, let the chicken cool in its sauce. When reheating, simmer very slowly, covered, for a few minutes, just until the chicken is hot.

MENU SUGGESTIONS

A good choice for a first course would be a simple *Risotto alla parmigiana* (page 155). Other possibilities are *Pasta e fagioli* (page 68), *Gnocchi di patate* (page 167) with *Pesto* (page 118), *Riso filante con la mozzarella* (page 166) or *Tagliatelle alla bolognese* (page 110). No vegetable is required, but instead of the usual raw salad you might serve *Insalatone* (page 358).

Pollo coi funghi secchi

CHICKEN FRICASSEE WITH DRIED MUSHROOMS

The key ingredient in this succulent dish is dried wild boletus mushrooms, on which a note will be found on page 9).

For four

25 g (1 oz) imported dried wild boletus
    mushrooms
1 roasting chicken [about 1·15 kg
    (2½ lb)]
3 tablespoons vegetable oil
40 g (1½ oz) butter

Salt and freshly ground pepper to
    taste
8 tablespoons dry white wine
3 tablespoons tinned Italian tomatoes,
    coarsely chopped

1 Place the mushrooms in 150 ml (¼ pint) lukewarm water. Allow to soak for at least 15 to 20 minutes.

2 Wash the chicken under cold running water. Cut into quarters and pat thoroughly dry.

3 Remove the mushrooms, reserving the water in which they have soaked. Filter the water by straining it through kitchen paper placed in a fine sieve, and set aside. Rinse the mushrooms in cold running water three or four times, then chop them roughly and set aside.

4 In a heavy-bottomed frying pan heat all the oil and 25 g (1 oz) of the butter. When the butter foam subsides, add the chicken quarters and brown them well on all sides over medium heat. Add salt and pepper, turning the chicken once or twice. Add the wine.

5 When the wine has evaporated add the chopped mushrooms, the water they were soaked in and the chopped peeled tomatoes. Cover the frying pan and cook at gentle heat for about 30 minutes, or until the chicken is tender. Turn the chicken pieces over from time to time.

6 Transfer the chicken to a warm dish. Tip the pan and draw off most of the fat with a spoon. If the sauce in the pan is too thin, boil it over high heat until it is concentrated. Off the heat, mix in the remaining butter and pour the sauce over the chicken.

MENU SUGGESTIONS

A perfect first course would be *Crespelle alla fiorentina* (page 152). Other good choices: *Lasagne verdi al forno* (page 122), *Fettuccine al gorgonzola* (page 114), *Conchiglie con il sugo per la gramigna* (page 92), *Minestrina tricolore* (page 50). *Cappellacci del Nuovo Mondo* (page 144) or *Risotto con la luganega* (page 161). For a vegetable: *Finocchi fritti* (page 324), *Carciofi alla giudia* (page 293) or one of the vegetables with butter and cheese, such as *Carote al burro e formaggio* (page 311).

Petti di pollo

FILLETS OF BREAST OF CHICKEN

This is the Italian method of filleting chicken breasts. It produces very thin slices of chicken that cook very rapidly and remain extraordinarily juicy and tender. Once you have acquired the knack of separating the two muscles that make up each side of the breast, the whole procedure becomes very simple. The result in terms of texture and flavour is so fine that you will probably adopt this method of filleting for any recipe calling for suprêmes of chicken.

To fillet a chicken breast, after skinning, run a finger along the broad upper part of the breast from the centre bone towards the side and feel for an opening. You will find a spot where the finger enters easily. Detach the muscles from the bone with a small sharp knife.

When slicing the larger piece, make sure the side that was next to the bone is facing down. Hold it flat with the palm of one hand, and slice the breast parallel to the chopping board, dividing the piece into two even slices.

1 Slip your fingers underneath the skin and pull it entirely away from the breast. It comes off quite easily. Be sure you also remove the thin membrane that adheres to the breast underneath the skin.

2 Run a finger along the broad upper part of the breast from the centre bone towards the side and feel for an opening. You will find a spot where the finger enters easily without resistance. This is where the two muscles meet, and the probing, lifting action of your fingers has separated them. Detach them from the bone with a small sharp knife. You will obtain from each side of the breast two separate pieces, one small and tapered, the other flatter, larger and somewhat triangular in shape.

3 The smaller piece has a white tendon that must be pulled out. With one hand grasp the tendon where it protrudes, with the other take a knife and push with the blade against the flesh where it meets the tendon. Pull the tendon out. It should come easily. Nothing else needs to be done to this piece.

4 Lay the larger piece on a chopping board with the side that was next to the bone facing down. Hold it flat with the palm of one hand. With the other hand take a sharp knife and slice the breast with the blade moving parallel to the chopping board, thus dividing the piece into two even slices of half the original thickness. Watch both sides of the piece while slicing to make sure you are slicing it evenly.

You now have from each half breast three tender fillets ready for cooking.

Petti di pollo alla senese

CHICKEN BREAST FILLETS WITH LEMON AND PARSLEY

For four or five

1 tablespoon vegetable oil	Freshly ground pepper, about 4 twists
75 g (2½ oz) butter	of the mill
3 whole chicken breasts, filleted as	Juice of 1 lemon
directed above	3 tablespoons chopped parsley
Salt to taste	1 lemon, thinly sliced

1 Heat the oil and 40 g (1½ oz) of the butter in a frying pan over medium-high heat. When the butter foam begins to subside, sauté the chicken fillets on both sides very briefly. (They will be cooked in 2 minutes at most.)

2 Remove the fillets to a warm dish and add salt and pepper.

3 Add the lemon juice to the frying pan and turn on the heat to medium. Loosen all the cooking residue from the bottom of the pan, adding 1 or 2 tablespoons of water if necessary. Add the parsley and the remaining butter to the cooking juices. Stir three or four times. Lower the heat to a minimum and add the cooked chicken fillets, turning them over quickly in the sauce once or twice.

4 Transfer the fillets to a warm serving dish and pour the cooking juices from the frying pan over them. Serve, decorated with lemon slices.

MENU SUGGESTIONS

First course: *Tortellini di prezzemolo* (page 137), with *Sugo di pomodoro e panna* (page 139), *Risotto coi funghi secchi* (page 158) or *Gnocchi verdi* (page 171). For vegetable: *Pisellini alla fiorentina* (page 328), *Fave alla romana* (page 306) or *Funghi trifolati* (page 325).

Rollatini di petto di pollo e maiale
BREAST OF CHICKEN FILLETS STUFFED WITH PORK

For four to six

2 cloves garlic, lightly crushed with a heavy knife-handle and peeled	1 teaspoon dried rosemary leaves **or** a sprig of fresh rosemary
3 tablespoons vegetable oil	2 large whole breasts of chicken, filleted as directed on page 265
225 g (½ lb) any lean cut pork, minced	
Salt	25 g (1 oz) butter
Freshly ground pepper, about 6 twists of the mill	8 tablespoons dry white wine

1 In a frying pan, sauté the crushed garlic cloves in the oil over medium heat. When the garlic has coloured lightly, add the minced pork, a large pinch of salt, the pepper and rosemary. Stir, and sauté the meat for 10 minutes, crumbling it with a fork as it cooks. Then, with a perforated ladle or slotted spoon, transfer the meat to a dish and allow to cool. Discard all but $2\frac{1}{2}$ to 3 tablespoons of fat from the frying pan.

2 Lay the chicken breast fillets flat and sprinkle very lightly with salt and pepper. Spread the sautéed minced pork on the fillets, and roll each fillet up tightly. Tie up each roll securely with string as though you were preparing miniature roasts. (You can prepare the dish up to this point several hours ahead of time.)

3 Add the butter to the frying pan in which you cooked the pork and turn the heat up to medium high. When the butter foam begins to subside, put in the stuffed chicken rolls. Brown well on all sides, but do not overcook. Remember, it takes about 2 minutes to cook filleted chicken breasts. When the rolls are well browned, transfer them to a warm dish and remove the strings. Add the wine to the frying pan, turn the heat to high, and loosen any cooking residue in the pan. When the wine has evaporated, pour the sauce over the chicken rolls and serve hot.

MENU SUGGESTIONS

A first course that goes well here is *Risotto coi funghi secchi* (page 158). Other possibilities are *Gnocchi alla romana* (page 169), *Rigatoni al forno col ragù* (page 93) or *Penne al sugo di pomodoro e funghi secchi* (page 91). A good choice for vegetables would be *Cavolfiore gratinato al burro e formaggio* (page 313) or *Topinambur gratinata* (page 301).

Cotoletta di tacchino alla bolognese
TURKEY BREAST FILLETS WITH HAM, CHEESE AND WHITE TRUFFLES

This is Bologna's most celebrated meat course, in which the delicate, almost neutral taste of veal or breast of turkey is used as a foil for perhaps the three finest products in the Italian larder: aged Parmesan cheese, sweet

Parma ham and the fresh white truffles of Alba. No one who has tasted this dish in Bologna in late autumn, when the white truffles are in season, could possibly forget it.

The old recipes call for thinly sliced veal or turkey breast to be lightly sautéed, then bound to slices of ham, truffles and cheese, and simmered in beef stock or tomato sauce in a covered pan. Today the last step is omitted and the cutlet is put briefly into the oven just long enough to melt the cheese. This is an improvement over the old method, which tended to produce a flabbier texture and a less fresh-tasting liaison of the ingredients.

Fresh white truffles are virtually unobtainable outside Italy. Tinned white truffles, although expensive, are available throughout the year at all gourmet shops or from Italian groceries and some department stores. Some tins contain marvellous truffles, while others, unfortunately, are nearly taste-less. The tin should release a powerful fragrance when you open it, and the truffle should be a creamy beige colour. It is a rather blind item, but you must take your chances, because the presence of truffles, however weakened by tinning, is absolutely essential to *Cotoletta alla bolognese*. Without it the dish is banal, and you would be better advised to invest time and effort in something more promising.

For four to five

550 g (1¼ lb) turkey breast, thawed if frozen	6 tablespoons dry Marsala or dry white wine
1 tablespoon vegetable oil	2 tablespoons freshly grated Parmesan cheese
60 g (2 oz) butter	
90 g (3 oz) plain flour, spread on a dish or on waxed paper	110 g (4 oz) thinly sliced prosciutto
Freshly ground pepper, about 4 twists of the mill	175 g (6 oz) Parmesan cheese (approximately), cut into slivers or shavings using a potato peeler
25 g (1 oz) tinned white Alba truffles, or more, if you are not daunted by the price	15 g (½ oz) butter

1 Fillet the turkey breast, using the same method suggested for chicken breasts (page 265). Cut the fillets into slices 6 mm (¼ inch) thick.

2 Melt the butter and oil in a frying pan over medium-high heat.

3 When the butter foam begins to subside, turn the turkey slices in the flour, coating both sides and shaking off any excess, and slip the turkey into the frying pan. If the slices are no more than 6 mm (¼ inch) thick, they should cook very quickly, about 1 to 1½ minutes per side. Sauté as many slices at one time as will fit comfortably into the frying pan, coating them with flour just before putting them in. As they are done, transfer to a warm dish and add the pepper.

4 Preheat the oven to 200°C/400°F/Mark 6.

5 Open the tin of truffles and pour the liquid it contains into the frying pan. Turn on the heat to medium and stir for a minute or so, scraping up and loosening the cooking residue in the pan.

6 Add the Marsala or wine and partly evaporate it for a minute or two over medium heat. Stir it as it thickens.

7 Choose a baking dish that can hold all the turkey slices in a single layer. Smear the bottom with about 1 tablespoon of sauce from the frying pan, then put in the turkey slices, laying them close together but not overlapping.

8 Distribute the grated cheese over the turkey, sprinkling a little over each slice, then cover each slice with prosciutto. Slice the truffles very thin, using a potato peeler, and distribute over the prosciutto. Cover each turkey slice with the slivered Parmesan cheese. (Some recipes suggest Fontina or Bel Paese cheese, but only Parmesan is part of an authentic *Cotoletta alla bolognese*.) Pour the rest of the sauce from the frying pan over the cheese and put a tiny dot of butter on each slice.

9 Place the dish in the uppermost level of the preheated oven for 6 to 8 minutes, or until the cheese melts. Serve piping hot from the same dish.

Note The prosciutto and cheese should be sufficiently salty to make any addition of salt unnecessary. If, as sometimes happens, either prosciutto or the Parmesan, or both, lack salt, it can be added at the table.

MENU SUGGESTIONS

Tagliatelle alla bolognese (page 110) is a natural combination with this dish, but other excellent choices would be *Cappelletti con la panna* (page 136) or *Gnocchi verdi* (page 171). One or two fried vegetables would complete it to perfection: *Carciofini fritti* (page 294) and *Pomodori fritti* (page 335).

Piccioncini in tegame

POT-ROASTED SQUAB

For four to six (see note below)

4 fresh squab [about 450 g (1 lb) each], cleaned and plucked
2 dozen medium-dried sage leaves
4 strips of *pancetta*, 37 mm (1½ inches) long, 12 mm (½ inch) wide and 6 mm (¼ inch) thick

Salt and freshly ground pepper
40 g (1½oz) butter
2 tablespoons vegetable oil
150 ml (¼ pint) dry white wine

1 Remove all the organs from the insides of the birds. Reserve the livers but discard the hearts and gizzards (or keep them for a *risotto*). Wash the squab in cold running water and pat dry thoroughly inside and out. Stuff the cavity of each bird with 2 sage leaves, 1 strip of *pancetta* and 1 liver, and season with 2 pinches of salt and a twist of pepper.

2 In a pot large enough to hold all the squab, heat up the butter and oil over medium-high heat. When the butter foam subsides, add the remaining sage leaves and then the squab. Brown the squab evenly on all sides and season with salt and pepper. Add the wine. Turn the heat up to high, allowing the wine to boil briskly for 30 to 40 seconds. While the wine is bubbling, turn and baste the squab, then lower the heat to medium low and cover the pot. Turn the birds every 15 minutes. They should be tender and done in 1 hour.

3 Transfer the squab to a warm dish. If you are serving ½ bird per person, halve them with poultry shears. Tip the pan and draw off some of the cooking fat with a spoon. Add 2 tablespoons of warm water, turn the heat to high, and while the water evaporates scrape up and loosen any cooking residue in the pan. Pour over the squab and serve.

Note A generous portion would be 1 whole squab per person. If you are having a substantial first course, however, ½ squab per person is quite adequate. The remaining squabs can be divided up for second helpings among the hungrier guests.

MENU SUGGESTIONS

The happiest accompaniment for squab and for any game is *Polenta* (page 175). When serving *polenta* you do not serve pasta as a first course. You can start the meal with very good-quality prosciutto, sliced thick, or with

Carciofi alla romana (page 286) or *Carciofi alla giudia* (page 293). If you are not serving *polenta*, an excellent first course would be *risotto*, either *Risotto coi funghi secchi* (page 158) or *Anello di risotto alla parmigiana con il ragù di fegatini* (page 156), *Cappelletti in brodo* (page 135) or *Tortelloni al burro e formaggio* (page 143). A good vegetable dish would be *Pisellini alla fiorentina* (page 328), *Cipolline agrodolci* (page 327), *Finocchi al burro e formaggio* (page 322) or *Topinambur trifolati* (page 300).

Coniglio in padella

STEWED RABBIT WITH WHITE WINE

Now that factory chicken has completely replaced free-range chicken, one of the best-tasting 'fowls' you can eat is rabbit. Rabbit meat is lean and not as flabby as most chicken, and its taste is somewhere in between very good breast of chicken and veal. Frozen young rabbit of excellent quality is now widely available cut up in ready-to-cook pieces. It is so good that there is really little need to bother dismembering whole fresh rabbit. I recommend it without reservation.

In France and Germany rabbit is sometimes subjected to a lengthy preliminary marinade which gives it somewhat the taste of game and partly breaks down its texture. The method given here is very straightforward. Without sautéing, rabbit is stewed in practically nothing but its own juices. It is then simmered in white wine with a little rosemary and a touch of tomato. It is a familiar northern Italian approach, and it succeeds marvellously well in drawing out the delicate flavour of rabbit and in maintaining its fine texture intact.

For six

1·35 to 1·6 kg (3 to 3½ lb) frozen cut-up rabbit, thawed overnight in the refrigerator (see note below)	Salt
	Freshly ground pepper, 6 to 8 twists of the mill
8 tablespoons olive oil	1 bouillon cube
1 small stick celery, finely diced	2 tablespoons concentrated tomato purée
1 clove garlic, peeled	
150 ml (¼ pint) dry white wine	¼ teaspoon sugar
A sprig of fresh rosemary **or** 1½ teaspoons dried rosemary	

1 Rinse the rabbit pieces in cold running water and pat thoroughly dry with kitchen paper.

2 Choose a deep covered frying pan large enough to contain all the rabbit pieces in a single layer. Put in the oil, celery, garlic and the rabbit, cover, and cook over low heat for 2 hours. Turn the meat once or twice, but do not leave uncovered.

3 After 2 hours, you will find that the rabbit has thrown off a great deal of liquid. Uncover the pan, turn up the heat to medium, and cook until all the liquid has evaporated. Turn the meat from time to time. When the liquid has evaporated, add the wine, rosemary, salt and pepper. Simmer, uncovered, until the wine has evaporated. Dissolve the bouillon cube, tomato purée and sugar in 150 ml ($\frac{1}{4}$ pint) of warm water, pour it over the rabbit, and cook gently for another 12 to 15 minutes, turning and basting the rabbit two or three times. Serve immediately or reheat gently before serving.

Note   Do not use wild rabbit in this recipe, only domestic rabbit.

If using fresh rabbit, soak in abundant cold water for 12 hours or more, then rinse in several changes of cold water and thoroughly pat dry. It may be refrigerated while soaking.

The rabbit may be prepared entirely ahead of time. When reheating, add 2 to 3 tablespoons of water and warm up slowly in a covered pan over low heat, turning the meat from time to time.

MENU SUGGESTIONS

Although this goes well with most soups – and *risotti*, except those with fish – your best choice for first courses is among the home-made pastas: *Tagliatelle alla bolognese* (page 110), *Lasagne verdi al forno* (page 122) or *Cappelletti in brodo* (page 135). A fine soup would be *Passatelli* (page 60). For vegetables, the most congenial are *Finocchi fritti* (page 324), *Zucchine fritte con la pastella* (page 337) or *Carciofini fritti* (page 294).

Bollito misto

MIXED BOILED MEATS

When friends and acquaintances about to go to Italy ask what dishes they should eat, among my recommendations, especially if they are going to be in Emilia, Lombardy or Piedmont, is *bollito misto*, mixed boiled meats. *Boiled* meat?' they say, their incredulity soon overtaken by disdain. I am afraid it is a piece of advice that has done little to advance my reputation for culinary sagacity.

This makes me think of an episode in *La vie et le passion de Dodin-Bouffant*, Marcel Rouff's legend of that prodigious gastronome. Dodin had been the guest of the Prince of Eurasia, who, in his anxiety to parade the richness of his table before this most discerning of gourmets, overwhelmed him with a vulgar and grandiloquent display of pretentious courses. Dodin countered by inviting the Prince and some friends to dine with him at home. When his guests were seated, trembling in anticipation of the feast that awaited them, Dodin announced his menu. Not only was it astonishingly brief, but its principal course was to be a 'boiled beef garnished with its own vegetables'. The Prince was at first inwardly outraged at being served a dish he regarded as only fit for servants. But this is what followed:

At last this formidable boiled beef arrived, reviled, despised, an insult to the Prince and to the whole of gastronomy: Dodin-Bouffant's boiled beef—monstrously imposing, borne on a huge long platter which the head chef held so high at arm's length that the anxious guests could at first catch no glimpse of it. But when it was lowered with straining caution on to the table, there were several minutes of stunned silence. Each guest recovered his composure in a way which was entirely characteristic. Rabaz and Magot inwardly berated themselves for having doubted the Master; Trifouille was seized with panic in the face of such genius; Beaubois trembled with emotion; as for the Prince of Eurasia, his reaction wavered between the worthy desire to make a duke of Dodin-Bouffant, as Napoleon had wished to make a duke of Corneille, a wild longing to offer the gastronome half of his fortune and of his throne if only he would agree to oversee his banquets, annoyance at being taught such an obvious lesson, and impatience to taste the heady enchantments of the culinary marvel set out before him.

The boiled beef, to give it its real name, lightly rubbed with saltpetre and sprinkled with salt, was carved in slices so tender that its deliciously melting texture created an air of expectancy. The aroma it gave off came not just from the beef juice, smoking like incense, but from the powerful smell of tarragon with which it was impregnated and from a very small number of transparent and extremely lean cubes of bacon with which it was larded. The slices, fairly thick and with a velvety texture that had already set every mouth watering, rested gently on a pillow consisting of a large slice of coarsely chopped sausage, made from pork mixed with the more delicate flesh of veal and with thyme and chervil. But this delicate pork mixture, cooked in the same liquid as the beef, was itself supported by an ample carving of white meat taken from the fillets and wings of a chicken boiled in its own juice with a shin of veal and rubbed with mint and wild thyme.

And, to prop up this triple-tiered magical edifice, behind the white chicken flesh (it had been reared exclusively on bread soaked in milk) had daringly been slipped in the plump, sturdy support of a comfortable bed of fresh goose liver simply cooked in Chambertin. The dish continued upwards in the same sequence of clearly defined layers, with each one being wrapped in a parcel of assorted vegetables cooked in the broth and glazed with butter; and each guest had only to extract at one stroke, between fork and spoon, the fourfold enchantment that was his share and then carry it to his plate. . . .

They could control their mounting excitement no longer. There were no more doubts. He had set their minds at rest. They could abandon themselves in total bliss to the pleasures of the palate and to that sweet and intimate companionship which gentlemen affect after meals really worthy of the name.

An Italian dish of mixed boiled meats, although not as profusely aromatic as Dodin's boiled beef, has many points in common with it. Like Dodin's dish it includes veal, chicken and a pork sausage, the *zampone* from Modena. But what a sausage it is! No pork product in the world can approach its miraculously creamy texture or the poise of its perfectly balanced delicacy and tastiness. Dodin would have been enraptured. There is no *foie gras*, of course, but there is a calf's head, which yields a very fine, tender, gelatinous supplement to the corpulence of the other meats.

Restaurants that feature *bollito misto* present it in a special trolley, somewhat resembling an English roast beef trolley, which carries the different meats in separate compartments filled with steaming broth. The meat is carved at the table, as roast beef is in England, and served with a piquant sauce or a red tomato and pepper sauce or both. In Italy, a proper *bollito misto* is the mark of a top-class restaurant.

The recipe given below is for a complete *bollito misto*. It is a fine recipe if you are serving at least eighteen people. If you are not, you will want to scale it down. You can reduce it by more than half simply by omitting the tongue and the *cotechino*. If any of the beef, chicken, or veal is left over, it can be cut up and used in a salad. The beef can also be used in the recipe on page 207.

For eighteen or more

2 medium carrots, peeled
2 sticks celery
1 medium onion, peeled
1 medium potato, peeled
½ green pepper, cored and seeded
1 beef tongue [about 1·35 to 1·6 kg (3 to 3½ lb)]
Scant 1 kg (2 lb) beef brisket, rump or chuck steak in one piece
Salt

3 tablespoons tinned Italian tomatoes
Scant 1 kg (2 lb) shoulder of veal, boned and in one piece
½ calf's head
1 chicken [1·15 kg (2½ lb)]
1 *cotechino* sausage, boiled separately, as directed on page 243, and kept warm in its own broth

1 Choose a stockpot or saucepan large enough to hold all the above ingredients, except for the *cotechino*. (It is very important in a *bollito misto* for all the meats to cook together because each lends part of its flavour to the others. However, if you just cannot manage in one pot, divide the vegetables in two parts, and cook the beef and tongue in one pot, and all the other meats in another.) Since in an Italian *bollito* the meat is put into liquid that is already boiling, begin by putting all the vegetables, except the tomatoes, into the pot and enough water to cover the meat later. Bring to the boil.

2 Add the tongue and beef brisket, cover, and return to the boil. Adjust the heat so that the liquid is just barely simmering. Skim off the scum that comes to the surface for the first few minutes. Add salt and the tomatoes.

3 After 2 hours of very slow simmering, remove the tongue for peeling. It is easier to peel the tongue if you can handle it while it is still very hot; otherwise wait a few moments for it to cool off slightly. Slit the skin all around the top of the tongue and peel it away with your fingers. (There is a second skin beneath this that does not peel off. It will be cut off later in one's own dish after the tongue has been sliced.) Trim away all the fat and gristle from the root of the tongue, and return it to the pot.

4 Add the veal, then, when the veal has simmered for 1 hour, add the calf's head.

5 After another 45 minutes' simmering, add the chicken. When the chicken has simmered for 45 minutes to 1 hour, the *bollito* is done. Leave it in its broth, and it will stay warm enough to serve for 1 hour after you turn off the heat. If you are serving it much later, reheat by bringing the

CIC–J

broth to a slow simmer for about 10 minutes. Turn the pieces of meat once or twice, changing their position in the pot.

6 A steaming dish with an arrangement of all the boiled meats in slices is a beautiful and enticing thing to see. The juicy texture of boiled meat, however, is very short-lived once out of its broth. There are two solutions. One, slice only part of the meat and serve it, keeping the rest in the pot until you are ready for another round. Or, even more successful, if less elegant, bring the pot to the table (or transfer all the meat and enough broth to cover to a large tureen), pull out one piece at a time, carving as much of it as desired, and then return it to the protection of its broth. The *cotechino*, as mentioned earlier, should be kept in its own broth until it is time to slice and serve it. Serve *bollito misto* with one of two sauces: *Salsa verde* (Green Sauce) (page 24) or *Salsa rossa* (Red Sauce) (page 25), or both, if you like.

Note   Calves' heads are usually sold whole, but if you are on good terms with your butcher he should be willing to let you have a half. In case you have never used it before, a calf's head is sold completely boned and ready for cooking. If the brains are included they should be removed. Use them for *Cervella fritta* (page 253).

The following are approximate cooking times for the meats in this recipe, calculated from the moment the liquid they are in comes to a simmer:

beef – $4\frac{1}{2}$ hours   calf's head – $1\frac{1}{2}$ hours
tongue – $4\frac{1}{2}$ hours   chicken – 45 minutes
veal – $1\frac{3}{4}$ hours

MENU SUGGESTIONS

Any light soup with a vegetable can precede *bollito misto*. An ideal combination is *Passatelli* (page 60), cooked in part of the *bollito*'s broth, or *Cappelletti in brodo* (page 135).

Frittate
ITALIAN OMELETTES

In some texts, the Italian *frittata* has become partly confused with French omelettes. Actually, the technique for *frittata* differs in three very important ways from that for making omelettes.

– Whereas an omelette is cooked very briefly over high heat, a *frittata* is cooked slowly over very low heat.
– An omelette is creamy and moist, just short of runny. A *frittata* is firm and set, although by no means stiff and dry.
– An omelette is rolled or folded over into an oval, tapered shape. A *frittata* is flat and perfectly round.

Because a *frittata* is cooked over low heat, there is less danger of it sticking. You do not need to set aside a special pan for *frittate*, but it is essential to use a very good, heavy-bottomed frying pan that transmits and retains heat evenly.

A *frittata* must be cooked on both sides. To do this, some people flip it in mid-air like a pancake. Others turn it over on a dish and then slide it back into the pan. I have found that the least perilous and most effective way is to run it under the grill for about 20 seconds to cook the top side, once the underside is done.

You can incorporate into *frittate* an endless number of fillings, such as cheese, vegetables, herbs and ham. The following *Frittata al formaggio* illustrates the basic *frittata* technique, which remains exactly the same no matter what filling you use.

Frittata al formaggio
ITALIAN OMELETTE WITH CHEESE

For four

7 large eggs	100 g (3½ oz) freshly grated Parmesan
Salt	cheese or Swiss cheese
Freshly ground pepper, about 4 twists of the mill	40 g (1½ oz) butter

1 Beat the eggs in a bowl until the yolks and whites are blended. Add salt, pepper and grated cheese, beating them into the eggs.

2 Melt the butter in a 300-mm (12-inch) frying pan over medium heat. When the butter begins to foam, well before it becomes coloured, add the eggs and turn the heat down as low as possible. When the eggs have set and thickened and only the top surface is runny, after about 15 minutes of very slow cooking, run the frying pan under the grill for 30 seconds to 1 minute, or until the top face of the *frittata* has set. (When done the *frittata* should be set, but soft. It should not be browned either on the bottom or top side.)

3 Loosen the *frittata* with a spatula and slide it onto a warm round dish. Cut it into four pie-like wedges and serve.

MENU SUGGESTIONS

In Italy, a *frittata* usually appears at the evening meal, which is the light meal of the day. It takes the place of meat or poultry and is preceded by a light soup, or a dish of prosciutto or assorted cold meats. Here the situation is reversed, and *frittata* obviously makes a fine dish around which you can plan a light lunch. For a hearty country meal, however, this dish can be a satisfying second course when preceded by *Bagna caôda* (page 37).

Frittata di carciofi

ITALIAN OMELETTE WITH GLOBE ARTICHOKES

For four

1 large or 2 medium globe artichokes	Freshly ground pepper, 6 twists of
1 clove garlic, peeled and finely	the mill
chopped	6 large eggs
2 tablespoons olive oil	3 tablespoons freshly grated
2 tablespoons finely chopped parsley	Parmesan cheese
Salt	40 g (1½ oz) butter

1 Trim the artichokes as directed on page 287. Then cut them lengthways into the thinnest possible slices.

2 In a frying pan, sauté the garlic, with all the oil, over medium heat

until it has coloured lightly. Add the sliced artichokes, the parsley, a small pinch of salt and half the pepper, and sauté for about 1 minute, or long enough to turn the artichokes two or three times. Add 6 tablespoons water, cover the pan, and cook until the artichokes are very tender. If they are young and fresh, it may take just 15 minutes or less. (In this case there might be some water left in the pan. Uncover the pan and evaporate the water over high heat while stirring the artichokes.) If the artichokes are tough, it may take twice as long to cook them. (In which case, if all the water evaporates before they are done, add 2 or 3 tablespoons of water.) When done, drain all the oil out of them and set aside to cool.

3 Beat the eggs in a bowl until the yolks and whites are blended. Add the artichokes, another small pinch of salt, the rest of the pepper and all the grated cheese, and mix thoroughly.

4 In a 300-mm (12-inch) frying pan, melt the butter over medium heat. When it begins to foam, and well before it becomes coloured, add the egg-and-artichoke mixture, turn the heat down as low as possible, and proceed exactly as directed in Steps 2 and 3 of *Frittata al formaggio* (page 278).

Frittata di asparagi

ITALIAN OMELETTE WITH ASPARAGUS

For four

450 g (1 lb) asparagus	60 g (2 oz) freshly grated Parmesan
6 large eggs	cheese
Salt	40 g (1½ oz) butter
Freshly ground pepper, 4 to 6 twists	
of the mill	

1 Trim, peel and boil the asparagus as directed on page 302; then drain and allow to cool.

2 Cut the cooled asparagus into 12-mm (½-inch) lengths, utilising as much of the stalk as possible.

3 Beat the eggs in a bowl until the yolks and whites are blended. Add the cut asparagus, salt, pepper and grated cheese, and mix everything thoroughly.

4 In a 250- or 300-mm (10- or 12-inch) frying pan, melt the butter over medium heat. When it begins to foam, and well before it becomes coloured, add the egg-and-asparagus mixture, turn the heat down as low as possible, and proceed exactly as directed in Steps 2 and 3 of *Frittata al formaggio* (page 278).

Frittata con fagiolini verdi

ITALIAN OMELETTE WITH FRENCH BEANS

For four

6 large eggs
Salt
Freshly ground pepper, 6 to 8 twists
    of the mill

175 g (6 oz) coarsely chopped boiled
    French beans (see page 307)
100 g (3½ oz) freshly grated Parmesan
    cheese
40 g (1½ oz) butter

1 Beat the eggs in a bowl until the yolks and whites are blended.

2 Add salt, pepper, beans and grated cheese, and mix thoroughly.

3 Melt the butter in a 300-mm (12-inch) frying pan over medium heat. When it begins to foam, and well before it becomes coloured, add the egg-and-French-bean mixture, making sure the beans are evenly distributed, not bunched up all at one end. Turn the heat down as low as possible and proceed exactly as directed in Steps 2 and 3 of *Frittata al formaggio* (page 278).

Frittata al pomodoro e basilico
ITALIAN OMELETTE WITH TOMATO, ONIONS AND BASIL

For four

6 medium onions, thinly sliced
6 tablespoons olive oil
225 g (8 oz) tinned Italian tomatoes, drained and roughly chopped
Salt
6 large eggs

2 tablespoons freshly grated Parmesan cheese
Freshly ground pepper, 6 twists of the mill
25 g (1 oz) roughly chopped fresh basil
40 g (1½ oz) butter

1 Cook the sliced onion, with all the oil, in a medium frying pan over low heat until it is completely softened and has turned a rich golden-brown colour.

2 Add the tomatoes and salt. Raise the heat to medium and cook for 8 minutes, stirring frequently. Turn off the heat and tilt the pan, gathering the tomatoes and onion at the up-ended side of the pan to drain them of oil. When the oil has drained off, transfer the vegetables to a bowl and allow to cool.

3 Beat the eggs in a bowl until the yolks and whites are blended. Using a slotted spoon, add the tomatoes and onion, and then add more salt, the grated cheese, pepper and chopped basil, and beat everything into the eggs.

4 Melt the butter in a 300-mm (12-inch) frying pan over medium heat. When the butter begins to foam, and well before it becomes coloured, add the eggs, turn the heat down to minimum, and proceed exactly as directed in Steps 2 and 3 of *Frittata al formaggio* (page 278).

Frittata di zucchine
ITALIAN OMELETTE WITH ZUCCHINI

For four

3 onions, thinly sliced
4 tablespoons vegetable oil
3 medium zucchini (**or** zucchini
    cores; see note below)
Salt
5 large eggs
60 g (2 oz) freshly grated Parmesan
    cheese

Freshly ground pepper, 7 or 8 twists
    of the mill
6 fresh basil leaves, roughly chopped,
    or, if basil is not in season, 1
    tablespoon finely chopped
    parsley
40 g (1½ oz) butter

1 Cook the sliced onion, with all the oil, in a medium frying pan over low heat until it is completely soft and has turned a rich golden-brown colour.

2 While the onion is cooking, cut off the ends of the zucchini and wash thoroughly in cold water. If not absolutely fresh, with very smooth glossy skin, peel the skin to remove all traces of embedded grit. Slice into discs 6 mm (¼ inch) thick. If you are using zucchini cores, chop them roughly.

3 When the onion is cooked, add the zucchini and salt. Cook over medium heat until lightly browned – or, if you are using the cores, until they have turned into a light-brown, creamy paste. When done, turn off the heat and tilt the pan lightly, pushing the zucchini and onion towards the up-ended side of the pan. When the oil has drained off, remove the vegetables to a bowl to cool.

4 Beat the eggs in a bowl until the yolks and whites are blended. Add the grated cheese and, with a slotted spoon, the zucchini and onion. Beat everything into the eggs, adding the pepper and basil or parsley at the end.

5 Melt the butter in a 250-mm (10-inch) frying pan over medium heat. When the butter begins to foam, and well before it becomes coloured, add the egg-and-zucchini mixture, turn the heat down as low as possible, and proceed exactly as described in Steps 2 and 3 of *Frittata al formaggio* (page 278).

Note   If you have made *Zucchini con ripieno di carne e formaggio* (page 341) you can use the left-over cores of 6 or 7 zucchini for this recipe.

Il Grande Fritto Misto
MIXED FRIED MEATS, VEGETABLES, CHEESE, CREAM AND FRUIT

Brillat-Savarin has given the very best description of frying, defining its action as that of a surprise. Perfectly fried food is 'surprised' in hot fat, which quickly imprisons its natural flavour and texture intact within a crisp, light crust. Successful frying requires a generous quantity of very hot fat. Never add fat after you have started frying. Butter, even when clarified, does not tolerate very high temperatures, and it is not, as a rule, suitable for quick frying. The most convenient medium to use is vegetable oil.

Italians are the masters of the frying pan, and fried cheese, meat, vegetables, fruit, taken singly, are frequent components of an Italian meal. Moreover, in some sections of Italy, and in Emilia-Romagna in particular, an entire meal, from first course to fruit, can be based exclusively on fried dishes. This tour de force is known as *il grande fritto misto*. It is a menu that requires from its creator not just skill, but great self-abnegation. Fried foods must be consumed hot, and while the cook fries, the guests eat. In Naples it is called *frienno magnanno*, 'frying and eating', which is also used idiomatically as an equivalent of 'said and done'.

For obvious reasons, a *grande fritto misto*, like a *bollito misto*, is consumed more frequently these days in a restaurant than at home. But if you have help in the kitchen and feel like trying it, here is a list of recipes scattered throughout this book that you can pull together into a truly memorable meal.

The first course
Bocconcini fritti (page 43)

The second course
An assortment of as many as possible of the following, in reduced quantities:

Cotolette alla milanese (page 228), served cut into small squares
Costolettine di agnello fritte (page 239)
Fegato di vitello fritto (page 252), served cut into small squares
Cervella fritta (page 253)
Carciofini fritti (page 294)
Asparagi fritti (page 305)
Pomodori fritti (page 335)

Finocchi fritti (page 324)
Zucchine fritte con la pastella (page 337) and/or *Fiori di zucchine fritti* (page 343)
Cavolfiore fritto (page 314)
Crema fritta (page 381), an absolutely indispensable part of any *fritto misto*
Polenta fritta (page 177)

Desserts and fruit

Frittelle di mele renette (page 373)

VEGETABLES

Le Verdure

I CANNOT imagine Italy without its vegetable stalls, filling ancient squares and animating dusty side streets with mounds of fabulous forms in purple, green, red, gold and orange. In a land heavy with man's monuments, these are the soil's own masterpieces. Perhaps one day the vitality of these still-flourishing markets will be replaced by the pallor of deep-freeze counters, those cemeteries of food, where produce is sealed up in waxed boxes marked, like some tombstones, with photographs of the departed. But I hope it never happens. I would sooner be deprived of all the marvels of Michelangelo.

The quality of Italy's produce is matchless. Only that of France comes close. It is not surprising that, in Italian cooking, the richness and variety of vegetable dishes approach that of the first courses. Sometimes a vegetable will even take the place of a first course, or of the second. Frequently a boiled vegetable, such as green beans or asparagus, is used as salad. Most often the vegetable is a side dish. Except when fish is served, it is always an essential part of every meal.

In Italian cooking, vegetables can be boiled, braised, fried, sautéed, gratinéed, baked and even grilled. Every one of these procedures is illustrated in this chapter, including a recipe for charcoal-grilled vegetables.

In a typically Italian approach, the vegetable is first boiled, then given a finish in the frying pan or in the oven with butter and Parmesan cheese. Sometimes, instead of the butter-and-cheese treatment, a boiled vegetable such as spinach or broccoli is sautéed with garlic and olive oil. Frying is another favourite treatment for vegetables, and several examples are given, with different batters.

Trifolare is an expression you will find in all Italian cookbooks, and vegetables *trifolati* appear on nearly every restaurant menu. When vegetables are *trifolati*, they are thinly sliced and sautéed with garlic, oil and parsley, a method very successful with mushrooms. You will find the recipe for it here, as well as a similar one for Jerusalem artichokes.

The Jerusalem artichoke, not to be confused with the globe artichoke, is a native American tuber that is now happily settled in Europe, where it is highly prized. In the following chapter you will be shown how it can be used in a salad.

There are three recipes for fennel, a vegetable universally popular in Italy.

Very good fennel is available here, it is not terribly difficult to prepare, and it can be an enjoyable addition to your vegetable repertoire.

The longest single section of this chapter deals with globe artichokes. Italians take great pleasure in this extraordinary relative of the thistle, and have found many fascinating ways to cook it. Among the recipes for artichokes given here you will find one of the oldest and still one of the best, *carciofi alla giudia* (crisp-fried whole artichokes), which dates back to Jewish cooking in the ghetto of ancient Rome.

Preparing and cooking vegetables take time, patience and care. Do not waste your efforts on second-rate materials. Buy carefully, avoiding any vegetable that is wilted, badly bruised, ill assorted, tired-looking, soggy, flabby or overgrown. Shopping for good fresh vegetables in this country may be frustrating at times, but that does not mean that we must deliver ourselves up in thrall to the frozen-food shelves. On any one market day there are always available two or more fresh vegetables of respectable quality. Limit yourself as much as possible to vegetables that are in season. They are more likely to be locally grown and fresher, or, at any rate, richer in flavour. Try not to decide in advance what you are going to cook but, rather, buy the best-quality vegetables you can find and then choose a recipe to suit them.

Carciofi alla romana

BRAISED GLOBE ARTICHOKES

In Italy one finds two basic types of artichokes. One is purplish in colour, with long, narrow, tapered leaves spiked at the tips. It is well worth looking out for if you are travelling in the northern and central part of Italy in the winter and spring because it is truly extraordinary in flavour and texture. However, it is seldom available outside Italy and the South of France, so we will not discuss it further. The other type of artichoke is very common in the south, where it is called *mammola*. It has a stout, globe-like shape, it is green and is very similar to the artichokes grown elsewhere in Europe. One of the most attractive and appetising ways of preparing these artichokes is *alla romana*.

For four

4 large globe artichokes	$\frac{1}{2}$ teaspoon crumbled mint leaves
$\frac{1}{2}$ lemon	Salt
3 tablespoons finely chopped parsley	8 tablespoons olive oil
$1\frac{1}{2}$ cloves garlic, peeled and finely chopped	

1 Artichokes *alla romana* are served with the stems attached, so be careful not to snap them off while trimming the artichokes. Begin preparing an artichoke by bending back and snapping off the outer leaves. Do not pull the leaves off all the way to the base, because the whitish bottom of the leaf is tender and edible. As you get deeper into the artichoke, the leaves will snap off farther and farther from the base. Keep pulling off leaves until you expose a central cone of leaves that are green only at the tips and whose paler, whitish base is at least 37 mm $1\frac{1}{2}$ inches) high.

Slice at least 25 mm (1 inch) off the top of the entire central cone, eliminating all the green part. Do not be afraid to trim too much – you are eliminating only the tough, inedible portions. Rub with half a lemon, squeezing juice over the cut portions of the artichoke so that they will not discolour.

You can now look into the centre of the artichoke, where you will find at the bottom some very small, pale leaves with prickly tips curving inward. Cut off all the little leaves and scrape away the fuzzy 'choke' beneath them, being careful not to cut away any of the heart or the other tender parts. (A rounded point on the knife can be helpful.) Return to the outside of the artichoke and pare away the green parts of the leaves at the base, leaving only the white.

All there is left to trim now is the outer part of the stem. Turning the artichoke upside down, you will note from the bottom of the stem that the stem has a whitish core surrounded by a layer of green. Trim away all the green up to the base of the artichoke, keeping only the white part. Be careful not to detach the stem, and always rub the cut portions with lemon juice so that they will not discolour.

2 In a bowl, mix the chopped parsley, chopped garlic, mint leaves and salt. Set aside one-third of the mixture and press the rest into the cavity of each artichoke, rubbing it well into the sides of the cavity.

3 Choose a heavy-bottomed casserole just large enough to contain the artichokes, which are to go in standing, and provided with a tight-fitting lid. Place the artichokes, tops facing down and stems pointing upward, in the casserole. Rub the rest of the parsley, garlic and mint mixture on the outside of the artichokes. Add all the oil and enough water to cover one third of the artichoke leaves, *not* the stems. Soak two thicknesses of kitchen

paper in water. (Since the moist paper helps to keep steam, which cooks the stems, inside the pot, it must be wide enough to cover the casserole.) Place the paper over the casserole and put the lid over the kitchen paper. Bend the corners of the paper back over the lid. Cook over medium heat for about 35 to 40 minutes, or until tender and easily pierced by a fork.

Cooking times vary according to the freshness and tenderness of the artichokes. (If the artichokes are tough and take long to cook, you may have to add 2 or 3 tablespoons of water from time to time. If they cook rapidly and there is too much water left in the pot, uncover and boil it away rapidly. Do not worry if the edges of the leaves next to the bottom of the pot start to brown; it improves their flavour.)

4 Transfer the artichokes to a serving dish, arranging them always with the stems pointing up. (Bear in mind that the stems are not merely decorative. They have an excellent flavour and they are to be eaten along with the rest of the artichoke.) Reserve the oil and juices from the pot and pour them over the artichokes just before serving. They should be served either luke-warm or at room temperature. The ideal temperature at which to serve them, if you can arrange it, is when they are no longer hot, but have not quite completely cooled off.

Note   Try to prepare them the same day they are going to be eaten because, like most cooked greens, they lose part of their flavour when refrigerated.

MENU SUGGESTIONS

This is one of many vegetable dishes that Italians use primarly as an antipasto or even a first course, rather than a side dish. As an antipasto, it goes with practically anything, preceding either a simple dish of spaghetti with tomato sauce or the elegant *Fettuccine all' Alfredo* (page 111). As a first course it can lead to any roast, from beef to poultry.

PREPARING AN ARTICHOKE

1 *Taking care not to break the stem off, begin bending back and snapping off the outer green part of the leaves, letting only the whitish, tender bottom of each leaf remain – the edible portion. Use half a lemon to squeeze juice over the cut portions so that they will not discolour.*

2 *As you get deeper into the artichoke, the leaves will snap off farther from the base. Keep snapping off leaves until you expose a central cone of leaves that are green only at the tips. The paler, whitish base of the leaves should be at least 37 mm ($1\frac{1}{2}$ inches) high.*

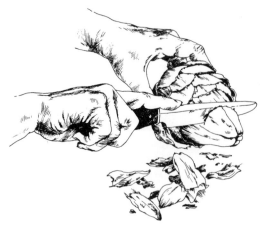

3 *Slice about 25 mm (1 inch) off the top of the central cone, enough to eliminate all the green part.*

4 *In the centre of the artichoke, you will see at the bottom some very small, pale leaves with purple, prickly tips curving inward. Using a knife with a rounded end, cut off all these little leaves and scrape away the fuzzy 'choke' beneath them. Be careful not to cut away any of the heart or the other edible parts.*

5 *Pare away the green outer parts of the leaves at the base of the artichoke, leaving the white and continuing to rub the cut portions with half a lemon.*

6 *Taking care not to break the stem, trim away its outer green layer, leaving only the whitish core.*

7 *The finished product.*

Carciofi ripieni di mortadella
BRAISED GLOBE ARTICHOKES WITH MORTADELLA STUFFING

For four

4 medium globe artichokes	1 egg
½ lemon	A small pinch of nutmeg
½ clove garlic, peeled and finely chopped	Salt
1 tablespoon chopped parsley	Freshly ground pepper, about 4 twists of the mill
50 g (1¾ oz) chopped *mortadella*	2½ tablespoons fine dry breadcrumbs
30 g (1 oz) freshly grated Parmesan cheese	5 tablespoons olive oil

1 Clean and trim the artichokes exactly as directed in Step 1 of the preceding recipe (page 287), leaving the stems *on*. (Remember to rub with lemon, squeezing juice over the cut parts.)

2 In a mixing bowl, combine the garlic, parsley, *mortadella*, Parmesan cheese, egg, nutmeg, salt, pepper and 1½ tablespoons of the breadcrumbs. Mix thoroughly and divide into 4 equal parts.

3 Stuff the artichokes with the *mortadella* mixture, sealing the tops with the remaining breadcrumbs.

4 Choose a deep casserole that can later hold all the artichokes standing. Put in all the olive oil and the artichokes, laying them on their sides. Turn on the heat to medium, and slowly brown the artichokes on all sides. When nicely browned, stand the artichokes with their stems pointing up, put in 5 tablespoons of water, and cover the casserole, placing between the cover and the pot a double thickness of water-soaked kitchen paper. Turn the heat down to low and cook for about 30 minutes. Test the hearts with a fork. If easily pierced, the artichokes are done. (If they are still firm, and there is no liquid left in the pot, add 1 or 2 tablespoons of water as needed. And do not worry if the leaves next to the bottom of the pot stick and darken.) When done, transfer the artichokes to a serving dish, pouring over them any juices left in the pot. Serve warm. Do not refrigerate or reheat.

MENU SUGGESTIONS

Follow the suggestions given for *Carciofi alla romana* (page 288).

Carciofi alla giudia

CRISP-FRIED WHOLE GLOBE ARTICHOKES

There is a substantial tradition of native Jewish cooking in Italy, centred mainly on Ferrara in the north and Rome in the south. That of Rome goes back to the days of the Empire, which must make it, no doubt, the oldest Jewish cuisine in Europe. One of the dishes prized by both ancient and modern visitors to the ghetto is *Carciofi alla giudia*. These are young Roman artichokes, trimmed of any hard leaves, flattened, and fried to a golden brown. The finished product is particularly beautiful, looking somewhat like an opened, dried chrysanthemum.

The frying is done in two stages. The artichokes are first fried at a lower temperature, to give the heat time to cook them thoroughly. They are then transferred to a pan with hotter oil, which is excited further by being sprinkled with cold water. This is what gives the leaves their crisp finish, while the heart remains moist and tender.

The best artichokes to use for this recipe are very young, tender artichokes.

For six

6 medium globe artichokes	Vegetable oil, enough to come 37 mm
½ lemon	(1½ inches) up the sides of
Salt	both pans
Freshly ground pepper, 6 twists of	
the mill	

1 Trim the artichokes exactly as directed in Step 1 of *Carciofi alla romana* (page 287), but now leaving only a short stump of a stem. Keep the inside rows of leaves progressively longer, giving the artichoke the look of a thick, fleshy rosebud. Make sure, however, to cut off all the tough part of each leaf, because no amount of cooking will make it edible, and remember to rub all the cut edges of the artichoke with lemon juice to keep them from discolouring.

2 Turn the artichokes with their bottoms up, gently spread their leaves outward, and press them against your work surface to flatten them as much as possible without cracking them. Turn them right side up and season them with salt and pepper.

3 Heat the oil in a deep frying pan (preferably earthenware) over medium heat. When it is hot, add the artichokes, with their leaves facing down. Cook for about 5 to 6 minutes, then turn the artichokes, adjusting the heat to make sure they do not fry too rapidly. Turn them every few

minutes as they cook, until their bottoms feel tender when pricked with a fork. Times vary greatly, depending on the artichokes, but it may take about 15 minutes if they are very young.

4 When the artichokes are tender, turn them so that their leaves face the bottom of the pan and press firmly on them with a wooden spoon to flatten them further.

5 Meanwhile, heat the oil in another deep frying pan over high heat. When it is very hot, transfer the artichokes from the other pan, with the leaves always facing down. After they have fried at high heat for about 5 minutes, turn them so that the leaves face up, dip your hand in cold water, and shake the water into the hot oil, keeping at a distance from the pan because the oil will spatter.

6 Transfer the artichokes to kitchen paper to drain. Serve them piping hot, with the leaves facing up.

MENU SUGGESTIONS

This can be not only a vegetable dish but also a hot antipasto or even a first course in any meal whose second course is meat or poultry. It goes particularly well with *Abbacchio alla cacciatora* (page 237) and *Rognoncini trifolati al vino bianco* (page 254).

Carciofini fritti

FRIED GLOBE ARTICHOKE WEDGES

For four to six

3 medium globe artichokes **or** 300 g (10 oz) frozen artichoke hearts, thawed
$\frac{1}{2}$ lemon
1 tablespoon lemon juice
1 egg, lightly beaten, in a bowl

120 g ($4\frac{1}{4}$ oz) fine, dry plain breadcrumbs, spread on a dish or on waxed paper
Vegetable oil, sufficient to come 18 mm ($\frac{3}{4}$ inch) up the side of the frying pan
Salt

1 If you are using fresh artichokes, detach and discard the stems; then prepare as directed on page 287, but cutting them into smaller wedges (about

18 mm ($\frac{3}{4}$ inch) thick at the broadest point) and remembering to rub with lemon as you cut, to keep the artichoke from discolouring. Drop into boiling water containing the 1 tablespoon lemon juice. Cook for 5 to 7 minutes, or until tender but not too soft. Drain and set aside to cool. (If you are using frozen artichokes, simply pat dry when thoroughly thawed.)

2 Dip the artichoke wedges into the egg, letting the excess flow back into the dish, then roll in the breadcrumbs. (The artichokes may be prepared up to and including this point as much as 3 or 4 hours ahead of time.)

3 Heat the oil in a frying pan until a haze forms over it. Slip the artichokes into the pan, frying them on one side until a golden crust forms, then turning them until a crust has formed on all sides.

4 Transfer to kitchen paper to drain; then add salt. Serve while still hot.

MENU SUGGESTIONS

Fried artichoke wedges are a perfect accompaniment for any fried meat, such as *Cotolette alla milanese* (page 288), *Costolettine di agnello fritte* (page 239) or *Fegato di vitello fritto* (page 252). Like all fried vegetables, they fit beautifully into any type of *fritto misto*. They are also a good accompaniment to *Bistecca alla diavola* (page 203), *Polpettone alla toscana* (page 211), *Arrosto di maiale al latte* (page 240), *Petti di pollo alla senese* (page 265), or *Coniglio in padella* (page 271).

Carciofi e piselli stufati
BRAISED GLOBE ARTICHOKES AND PEAS

For six

2 large **or** 3 or 4 small medium-small
    globe artichokes
$\frac{1}{2}$ lemon
2 tablespoons chopped onion
3 tablespoons olive oil
$\frac{1}{2}$ clove garlic, peeled and finely
    chopped

scant 1 kg (2 lb) fresh peas
    (unshelled weight) **or** 300 g
    (10 oz) frozen *petits pois*,
    thawed
1 tablespoon chopped parsley
Salt
Freshly ground pepper, about 4
    twists of the mill

1 For this recipe you need to cut the artichokes lengthways into wedges about 25 mm (1 inch) thick at their widest point. It may be easier, therefore, first to trim away the hard outer leaves and the green tips as in Step 1 of *Carciofi alla romana* (page 287). Then cut the artichoke into wedges and from there proceed to remove the choke and the soft, white curling leaves directly above it. (You may discard the stems, if you are so inclined, but it would be a pity, because they have a sharp, interesting flavour and can be quite tender. If you use the stems, cut away the green outer layers, leaving just the white inner core.) Remember as you prepare each artichoke to rub it with the lemon, squeezing juice over the cut portions, or it will discolour.

2 Put the chopped onion in a casserole with the olive oil and sauté over medium heat until translucent. Add the garlic and continue sautéing until it becomes lightly coloured but not brown. Add the artichokes and 5 table-spoons of water, cover, and cook over medium heat.

3 After 10 minutes add the shelled fresh peas, chopped parsley, salt, pep-per and, if there is no more water in the pot, 4 tablespoons of warm water. Turn and mix the peas and artichokes. (If you are using frozen peas, add them only after the artichokes are almost completely tender, because they take only about 5 minutes to cook.) Cover and continue cooking over medium heat until the artichokes are tender all the way through. Test with a fork or, even better, taste, and check salt. (If there is too much water in the pot when the vegetables are cooked, uncover, raise the heat to high, and boil the water away rapidly.)

MENU SUGGESTIONS

This dish is a perfect accompaniment to grilled and roasted meats, roasted poultry, sautéed veal *scaloppine*, and to *Cotolette alla milanese* (page 228). It does not go well with meats that are cooked in a cream- or milk-based sauce.

Carciofi e porri stufati

BRAISED GLOBE ARTICHOKES AND LEEKS

For six

3 large globe artichokes **or** 5 or 6
   small ones
½ lemon
4 large leeks, about 40 mm (1¾ inches)
   in diameter, **or** 6 smaller ones

4 tablespoons olive oil
Salt
Freshly ground pepper, about 4
   twists of the mill

1 Prepare the artichokes as directed in the previous recipe (page 296), remembering to rub the lemon over the cut portion of each artichoke as you finish preparing it, or it will discolour.

2 Cut off the roots of the leeks, remove any leaves that are withered and discoloured, and slice off a small part of the green tops. Slice the leeks lengthways into two sections and wash thoroughly under cold running water.

3 Choose a casserole with a tight-fitting lid. Lay the leeks in the casserole, and add the oil and enough water to come 25 mm (1 inch) up the side of the pot. Cover and cook over moderate heat for 10 minutes. Add the artichoke sections, salt, pepper and, if necessary, a little warm water. Continue cooking over moderate heat, turning the vegetables from time to time. The vegetables are cooked when they are tender. (Cooking times vary greatly according to the freshness and quality of the vegetable. The only way to tell is by piercing them with a fork or tasting a small piece. If they take long to cook, you will have to add a little warm water from time to time, but all the water must be absorbed by the time they finish cooking.)

MENU SUGGESTIONS

This dish is an ideal accompaniment to roasted meats and poultry, to *Petti di pollo alla senese* (page 265), or *Scaloppine di vitello al limone* (page 221) or *al Marsala* (page 220). Do not pair them with a second course carrying a cream- or milk-based sauce.

Carciofi e patate

BRAISED GLOBE ARTICHOKES AND POTATOES

For four to six

3 medium potatoes [about 350 g
    ($\frac{3}{4}$ lb)]
2 medium globe artichokes **or** 3 or 4
    small ones
$\frac{1}{2}$ lemon
$\frac{1}{2}$ onion, coarsely chopped
5 tablespoons olive oil

$\frac{1}{2}$ small clove garlic, peeled and finely
    chopped
Salt
Freshly ground pepper, about 4
    twists of the mill
1 tablespoon chopped parsley

1 Peel the potatoes and wash in cold water. Cut lengthways into wedges about 18 mm ($\frac{3}{4}$ inch) thick at the broadest point.

2 Prepare the artichokes for cooking as directed in *Carciofi e piselli stufati* (page 296), remembering to rub the lemon over the cut portion of each artichoke as you finish preparing it or it will discolour.

3 Choose a casserole just large enough for the artichokes and potatoes. Over medium heat sauté the onion in the olive oil until translucent. Do not let it colour. Add the garlic and sauté until it colours lightly. Add the potatoes, artichokes, salt, pepper and parsley, and sauté long enough to turn everything two or three times.

4 Add 4 tablespoons of water, cover the pot, turn the heat down to medium low, and cook, turning the artichokes and potatoes from time to time, for about 40 minutes, or until the artichokes and potatoes are tender when pierced by a fork. (If, while they are still cooking, there is no liquid left in the pot, add 2 tablespoons of water as needed.) When done, taste and check salt. Serve warm.

MENU SUGGESTIONS

Follow those given for *Carciofi e piselli stufati* (page 296). In Italy you would use this as a vegetable dish in a light evening meal, where the first course would not be pasta but a vegetable soup, or a rice-and-vegetable soup.

Topinambur
JERUSALEM ARTICHOKES

The Jerusalem artichoke is not an artichoke nor did it come from Jerusalem. It is a tuber, the edible rootstock of a variety of the sunflower plant, native to Canada and the northern United States. Jerusalem is apparently a corruption of *girasole*, the Italian word for 'sunflower'. It is much prized in the Piedmont and Friuli regions of northern Italy, where it shares a variant of the French name *topinambour*. It has an exquisite texture and a delicate flavour that faintly recalls that of artichoke hearts. It is delicious raw in salads (page 349), sautéed or gratinéed. Jerusalem artichokes are available usually during late autumn and throughout the winter. If you find them at your market, buy one or two pounds of them, even though you might not be ready to cook them immediately. They keep easily for a week or more in the refrigerator. They look somewhat like ginger root, so be careful that what you are buying are Jerusalem artichokes. It is not easy to use up two pounds of ginger root, as I once found out to my dismay.

When buying Jerusalem artichokes, make sure they are as firm as possible, not spongy. Dig into one or two with your fingernail: if the colour under the skin is pinkish, not the creamy white it should be, do not buy them. And peeling them will take half the time if you choose the least gnarled and twisted roots.

Topinambur (*Jerusalem Artichokes*)

Topinambur trifolati
SAUTÉED JERUSALEM ARTICHOKES

For six

680 g (1½ lb) Jerusalem artichokes
4 tablespoons olive oil
1 clove garlic, peeled and finely
    chopped

Salt
Freshly ground pepper, about 6
    twists of the mill
1 tablespoon finely chopped parsley

1 Peel the artichokes with a potato peeler, or, if you do not object to the peel, scrub them thoroughly under cold running water with a stiff brush. Drop them into boiling salted water, the largest pieces first, the smallest last. As the water comes to the boil again, remove the artichokes and drain. Cut them into very thin slices, about 6 mm ($\frac{1}{4}$ inch) thick. They should still be fairly hard.

2 In a frying pan sauté the chopped garlic in the olive oil over medium heat. When the garlic has coloured lightly, add the artichokes and stir. Add salt, the pepper and the chopped parsley, and stir again. Turn the artichokes a few times while cooking. They are done if quite tender when pricked with a fork. Taste and check salt, and serve hot.

MENU SUGGESTIONS

Sautéed Jerusalem artichokes are a natural accompaniment for all roasts of veal or chicken, and they make a fine vegetable dish with grilled meat. Try them also with *Fagottini di vitello leccabaffi* (page 225), *Costolette alla milanese* (page 226), *Cervella fritta* (page 253), or *Petti di pollo alla senese* (page 265).

Topinambur gratinati
GRATINÉED JERUSALEM ARTICHOKES

For four

450 g (1 lb) Jerusalem artichokes	25 g (1 oz) freshly grated Parmesan cheese
Salt	
Freshly ground pepper, about 4 twists of the mill	35 g (1¼ oz) butter

1 Preheat the oven to 190°C/400°F/Mark 6.

2 Peel or scrub the artichokes as directed in the preceding recipe. Drop them into boiling salted water, holding back the smaller pieces for a few moments. Cook until tender but firm when pricked with a fork. (Jerusalem artichokes tend to go from very firm to almost mushy in a brief span of time, so watch them carefully.) When done, drain and allow to cool.

3 Cut the artichokes into slices 12 mm (½ inch) thick. Arrange them in a buttered oven dish so that they slightly overlap. Add salt and pepper, sprinkle the grated cheese over them, dot with butter, and place in the uppermost part of the preheated oven. Bake until a nice golden crust forms. Allow to stand briefly before serving.

MENU SUGGESTIONS

Gratinéed vegetables take easily to all roasts and grilled meats. They are also an excellent accompaniment to *Bistecca alla diavola* (page 203), *Stracotto al Barolo* (page 206), *Scaloppine di vitello al limone* (page 221) or *al Marsala* (page 220). There is actually no dish which they cannot accompany gracefully, but to avoid monotony, try not to pair them with those already containing cheese.

Asparagi

ASPARAGUS

HOW TO PREPARE AND BOIL ASPARAGUS

To have good cooked asparagus, you must first buy good raw asparagus. The surest sign that asparagus is beyond its best is an open, droopy tip. It should always be tightly closed and firm. The stalk should feel crisp and look moist. You can buy early asparagus, if you do not mind the price, but avoid it at the end of its season, in late June.

Preparation.   Asparagus must be trimmed so as to make the entire spear edible. At the tip it is very tender, but it can be very tough at the base, with differing degrees of tenderness in between. The parts that must be eliminated are the very end and a thin layer of fibres surrounding the lower half of the spear.

Start by slicing off about 25 mm (1 inch) at the butt end. If, in cutting, you find the flesh hard, fibrous and somewhat dry, slice off more of the stalk until the exposed end is tender and moist. (If the asparagus is very young, it will not need to have much of the base sliced off. If it is older and drier you might have to cut off as much as 37 to 50 mm ($1\frac{1}{2}$ to 2 inches).) Now, using a sharp paring knife, trim away the tough, outer fibres. Start your cut at the base, going about a millimetre ($\frac{1}{16}$ inch) deep and gradually tapering to nothing midway between the tip and the base. Remove any small leaves sprouting below the tip. Soak the trimmed asparagus in a basin of cold water for 10 minutes, then rinse in 2 or 3 fresh changes of cold water. It is now ready for cooking.

Cooking.   In Italy we partially boil and partially steam asparagus in a special cooker. Inside the cooker there is a separate, perforated liner that holds the spears upright and lifts out to remove the asparagus when it is cooked. While the butt of the spear is under boiling water, the tip is cooked by the rising steam. This method compensates for the difference between the butt and the tip so that both are cooked to an even degree of tenderness. The Italian asparagus cooker is available in most good houseware shops and departments, and I heartily recommend it to you. You can, however, cook asparagus almost equally well, as the French have always done, in a fish-kettle, or in a deep, oval pot large enough to hold the spears horizontally. Here are directions for both methods.

Asparagus cooked in the Italian asparagus cooker

1 Make a bundle of the asparagus, tying it in two places, one above the butts, the other below the tips.

2 Put enough cold water in the cooker to come 62 mm (2½ inches) up the side of the pot. Add salt. Put in the asparagus bundle, cover, and cook at a steady, moderate boil for 15 to 20 minutes. Test the base of the asparagus with a sharp-pronged fork. If it is easily pierced, it is done.

3 Transfer the asparagus bundle to an oval dish and remove the ties. Prop the dish up 25 mm (1 inch) at one end so that the liquid thrown off by the asparagus runs down to the opposite end. This liquid is to be discarded when the asparagus has been well drained.

Asparagus cooked without an asparagus cooker

1 Make a bundle of the asparagus exactly as in Step 1 above.

2 Bring at least 4 litres (7 pints) of water to the boil in a fish-kettle or in a deep oval pot large enough to contain the asparagus horizontally. Add salt. Wait a moment for the water to return to a rapid boil, then put in the asparagus. Cook the asparagus at a steady, moderate boil, uncovered, for 15 to 20 minutes. After 15 minutes test the base of the asparagus with a sharp-pronged fork. It is done when easily pierced.

3 Hook one or two forks under the strings and transfer the bundle to an oval dish. Remove the string, loosening the asparagus, and proceed to drain it of its liquid as in Step 3 above.

Asparagi alla parmigiana
ASPARAGUS WITH PARMESAN CHEESE

One of spring's most exquisite gifts to the Italian table is young asparagus, first boiled, then briefly baked with fragrant, grated aged Parmesan cheese. Of all the many dishes called *alla parmigiana* this is an authentic speciality of Parma, which does not keep it from being a great favourite all over Italy, or even in France, where, curiously, it is called *à la milanaise*.

For four

Scant 1 kg (2 lb) asparagus	60 g (2 oz) freshly grated Parmesan
Salt	cheese
	75 g (2½ oz) butter

1 Preheat the oven to 230°C/450°F/Mark 8.

2 Trim, peel and boil the asparagus as directed on pages 202–3.

3 Smear the bottom of a rectangular oven dish with butter. Arrange the boiled asparagus in the dish side by side, in slightly overlapping rows, setting the tips of the spears in one row over the butt ends of the ones in the row ahead. (Never cover the tips.) Sprinkle each row with salt and grated cheese, and dot with butter before arranging the next row over it.

4 Bake on the uppermost rack of the oven for about 15 minutes, until a light, golden crust forms. Allow to stand a few minutes before serving.

MENU SUGGESTIONS

This is often served as a first course. It goes well before *Petto di vitello arroto-lato* (page 215), *Rollatini di vitello al pomodoro* (page 224), *Arrosto di agnello pasquale col vino bianco* (page 235), *Abbacchio alla cacciatora* (page 237) or *Pollo arrosto al forno con rosmarino* (page 259). If you are using it as a first course, you can dispense with green vegetables later and serve instead *Dadini di patate arrosto* (page 332).

Asparagi alla parmigiana con uova fritte

ASPARAGUS WITH PARMESAN CHEESE AND FRIED EGGS

Serving asparagus *alla parmigiana* with fried eggs is a succulent enrichment of an already delectable dish. It can no longer, in fact, be considered a side dish. It has all the substance of a full second course and should be employed as such.

For four

Scant 1 kg (2 lb) asparagus	Freshly ground pepper, about 8 twists
8 eggs	of the mill
60 g (2 oz) butter	

1 Prepare the asparagus as directed in the previous recipe.

2 After you remove the asparagus from the oven, fry the eggs in the butter.

3 Divide the asparagus into four equal parts and place on individual dishes. Slide two fried eggs over each portion of asparagus; then spoon the juices left in the baking dish over the asparagus and eggs. Grind pepper over the eggs and serve immediately.

Note   Eat the asparagus with your fingers, holding it by the stem and swirling it in the eggs.

MENU SUGGESTIONS

Like a *frittata*, this can be the mainstay of a light but elegant lunch, preceded by a clear soup or *Bresaola* (page 42).

Asparagi fritti

FRIED ASPARAGUS

The sweet inner core under the crusty exterior of fried asparagus makes this one of the most delectable of all fried vegetables. Virtually no trimming is required because only the tips and the most tender part of the stalk are used.

For four

450 g (1 lb) crisp, fresh asparagus
Vegetable oil, enough to come 12 mm ($\frac{1}{2}$ inch) up the side of the frying pan
1 egg, well beaten, in a deep, oval dish

120 g ($4\frac{1}{4}$ oz) fine, dry plain breadcrumbs, spread on a dish or on waxed paper
Salt

1   Snap off the bottoms of the stems of the asparagus, leaving a stalk about 100 to 120 mm (4 to 5 inches) long, including the tips. Remove all the tiny leaves below the tips and wash the asparagus thoroughly in cold water. Pat dry with kitchen paper.

2   Heat the oil in a frying pan over high heat. When the oil is very hot, dip the asparagus in the beaten egg, roll it in breadcrumbs, and slide it into the frying pan, doing just a few stalks at a time so that they are not crowded

in the pan. When the asparagus has formed a crust on one side, turn it. When it has formed a crust on the other side, transfer with a slotted spatula to kitchen paper to drain, and add salt. When all the asparagus is done, taste and salt, and serve immediately.

MENU SUGGESTIONS

See *Carciofini fritti* (page 294). Fried asparagus is a particularly nice vegetable dish for *Stracotto al Barolo* (page 206).

Fave alla romana
BROAD BEANS FROM ROME

Broad beans usually appear in the vegetable markets from the middle of May until the end of June. They are best at the very beginning of their season when they are young and sweet and very small. In Italy, when they are at their peak, they are often served raw. The pods are brought whole to the table, and everyone shells his own and eats the beans, dipping them in salt. When eaten raw, broad beans are usually served at the end of the meal, replacing fruit. The raw broad bean has an intriguing bitter-sweet taste that usually turns very mellow and sweet when cooked. The Romans claim to have the best broad beans. There the beans are cooked with pork cheek (*guanciale*), and you will find them listed in the menus as *Fave al guanciale*. Since pork cheek, as the Romans know it, is hard to come by outside Italy, I use *pancetta*, which is a totally successful substitute and is easily available in all Italian food shops.

For four

1·35 kg (3 lb) small, young broad beans (unshelled weight)	1 slice rolled *pancetta*, 12 mm ($\frac{1}{2}$ inch) thick, cut into strips 6 mm ($\frac{1}{4}$ inch) wide
2 tablespoons olive oil	Salt
2 tablespoons finely chopped onion	Freshly ground pepper, 3 or 4 twists of the mill

   1 Shell the broad beans and wash in cold water.

   2 Heat the oil in a casserole and sauté the onion until translucent. Add the *pancetta* and sauté 30 seconds more.

3 Add the broad beans, salt and pepper, and stir, coating them well. Add 6 tablespoons water and cover the pot.

4 Cook over low heat. If the beans are very young and fresh they will cook in 6 or 8 minutes. (If there is any water left, uncover the pot and raise the heat until it has evaporated.) Serve immediately.

MENU SUGGESTIONS

This dish makes a very tasty antipasto. An unconventional but happy pairing is with *Bresaola* (page 42). As a vegetable dish it goes beautifully with roasts of lamb, especially *Abbacchio alla cacciatora* (page 237), and with *Costolettine di agnello fritte* (page 239).

Fagiolini verdi

FRENCH BEANS

Very fresh, properly cooked French beans, used either as salad or vegetable, are one of the finest pleasures of the table. When you can appreciate the virtues of a salad of crisp beans, seasoned with nothing more than salt, olive oil and lemon juice, you have understood Italian eating at its best – simple, direct and inexhaustibly good.

When buying French beans, the best ones to look for are the smallest, youngest beans. They should be vividly green and should break with a snap, revealing a moist, meaty interior with very tiny, undeveloped seeds. Vegetable markets, in their tireless efforts to frustrate good cooking, often lump together beans of assorted sizes. These are practically impossible to cook evenly. If you have a choice, buy beans that are uniform in size.

COOKING FRENCH BEANS

All it takes to cook French beans properly is plenty of salted boiling water and a readiness to drain them the moment they are tender but still crisp.

1 Snap both ends off the beans, pulling away any possible strings. Soak the beans in a basin of cold water for a few minutes, then drain.

2 For 450 g (1 lb) of beans, bring 4 litres (7 pints) of water to the boil. Add salt. After a moment, when the water is boiling rapidly again, drop in the French beans. After the water has returned to the boil, regulate the heat so that the beans cook at a moderate boil. Do not cover. Since cooking times vary, depending on the size and freshness of the beans (very young, fresh beans may cook in 6 or 7 minutes, while larger, older ones may take 10 or 12), start tasting them after 6 minutes and drain them the moment they are tender but firm and crisp to the bite.

Boiled French beans can be used for salad (see page 355) or in the following recipe, which requires further cooking.

Fagiolini verdi al burro e formaggio

SAUTÉED FRENCH BEANS WITH BUTTER AND CHEESE

For six

450 g (1 lb) fresh, crisp French beans
60 g (2 oz) butter

25 g (1 oz) freshly grated Parmesan cheese
Salt, as required

1 Prepare and cook the French beans as directed above, being certain to drain them when they are tender but still crisp.

2 Put the French beans in a frying pan with the butter and lightly sauté over medium heat for 2 minutes. Add the grated cheese and stir. Taste and check salt. Stir once or twice more, transfer to a warm dish and serve immediately.

MENU SUGGESTIONS

Follow those for *Topinambur gratinati* (page 301). These green beans go particularly nicely with veal dishes, especially *Costolette alla milanese* (page 226) or *Cotolette alla milanese* (page 228).

Fagiolini verdi con peperoni e pomodoro
FRENCH BEANS WITH PEPPERS AND TOMATOES

For four to six

450 g (1 oz) French beans
1 green pepper
3 tablespoons olive oil
1 medium onion, cut into slices about
    6 mm ($\frac{1}{4}$ inch) thick

140 g (5 oz) tinned Italian tomatoes,
    coarsely chopped, with their
    juice
Salt
Freshly ground pepper, 3 or 4 twists
    of the mill

1 Snap off the ends of the French beans, pulling off any strings they may have. Wash in cold water and set aside.

2 Wash the green pepper in cold water and, if you find the peel as disagreeable as I do, remove it with a potato peeler. Remove the core with all the seeds and slice the pepper into strips a little less than 12 mm ($\frac{1}{2}$ inch) wide. Set aside.

3 Heat the oil in a casserole and sauté the onion until translucent.

4 Add the strips of green pepper and the chopped tomatoes and cook over medium heat until the tomatoes separate from the oil and thicken into sauce, about 25 minutes.

5 Add the French beans, stir a few times until they are all well coated, and add 6 tablespoons water, salt and pepper. Cover and cook until tender, about 20 to 30 minutes, depending on the freshness and size of the beans. Add 1 or 2 tablespoons of water from time to time if required. (If, however, at the end there is too much liquid in the pot, uncover, raise the heat to high, and boil it away quickly.) Taste and check salt.

Note These French beans maintain their excellent flavour also when prepared ahead of time and warmed up.

MENU SUGGESTIONS

These beans are a tasty accompaniment for grilled or roasted meats and for veal cutlets and other veal dishes, as long as these are not dressed with cream or with tomato.

Broccoli all'aglio
SAUTÉED BROCCOLI WITH GARLIC

For four to six

680 g (1½ lb) fresh broccoli
Salt
2 cloves garlic, peeled and finely
    chopped

4 tablespoons olive oil
2 tablespoons chopped parsley

1 Cut off the tough butt end of the broccoli stalks, about 12 mm (½ inch). With a sharp paring knife, peel off all the dark-green skin on the stalks and stems. (The skin is thicker around the larger part of the stalk, so you will have to cut deeper there.) Split the larger stalks in two, or if extremely large, in four, without cutting off the florets. Rinse well in 3 or 4 changes of cold water.

2 Bring 4 litres (7 pints) of water to the boil, adding salt. Drop in the broccoli and boil slowly until the stalks can be pierced easily by a fork, about 7 to 10 minutes, depending on the freshness of the broccoli. Drain and set aside. (You can prepare the broccoli several hours ahead of time up to this point, but do not refrigerate, because refrigeration impairs the flavour.)

3 Choose a frying pan large enough to hold all the broccoli without much overlapping. Sauté the garlic in the olive oil over medium heat. As soon as the garlic colours lightly, add the broccoli, salt and the chopped parsley, and sauté lightly for about 2 to 3 minutes. Turn the broccoli two or three times while cooking. Serve hot.

MENU SUGGESTIONS

Follow those for *Topinambur trifolati* (page 300). Broccoli also goes well with *Polpette alla pizzaiola* (page 208) and *Arrosto di agnello al ginepro* (page 236).

Broccoli al burro e formaggio
SAUTÉED BROCCOLI WITH BUTTER AND CHEESE

For four to six

680 g (1½ lb) fresh broccoli
60 g (2 oz) butter
Salt

50 g (1¾ oz) freshly grated Parmesan
cheese

1 Peel, wash, boil and drain the broccoli as directed on page 310.

2 In a frying pan large enough to hold all the broccoli without much over-lapping, melt the butter over medium heat. When the butter foam begins to subside, add the boiled, drained broccoli and salt, and sauté lightly for about 2 to 3 minutes, gently turning the broccoli two or three times. Add the grated cheese, turn the broccoli one more time, and serve.

Note On many distressing occasions I have seen people eat the florets and leave the stalks on the plate. They are evidently under the impression that they are choosing the more delectable part. Actually, it is just the other way around.

MENU SUGGESTIONS

Follow those for *Topinambur gratinati* (page 301).

Carote al burro e formaggio
CARROTS WITH PARMESAN CHEESE

For six

700 g (1 lb 9 oz) carrots
75 g (2½ oz) butter
Salt to taste

¼ teaspoon sugar
3 tablespoons freshly grated
Parmesan cheese

1 Peel the carrots and slice them into discs 9 mm ($\frac{3}{8}$ inch) thick. (The thin tapered ends can be cut a little thicker.) Put the carrots and butter in a frying pan large enough to contain the carrots in a single layer and add enough water to come 6 mm ($\frac{1}{4}$ inch) up the side of the pan. (If you have too many carrots for your largest pan, divide them equally between two frying pans, using 35 g ($1\frac{1}{4}$ oz) of butter per pan.) Cook over medium heat, uncovered.

2 When the liquid in the frying pan has evaporated, add the salt and sugar. Continue cooking, adding 2 or 3 tablespoons of warm water as required but not too much at one time. The object is to obtain carrots that are well browned, wrinkled, and concentrated in texture and taste, which will take about 1 to $1\frac{1}{2}$ hours of carefully watched cooking, depending on the carrots. When they begin to reach the well-browned, wrinkled stage do not add any more water, because there must be no liquid left at the end. (If you have been using two pans, the carrots reduce so much in volume that halfway through cooking they can be consolidated into a single pan.)

3 When cooked, add the grated Parmesan, stir once or twice over heat, and then transfer to a warm dish and serve immediately.

Note   This is a time-consuming dish, although not a complicated one. You can prepare it entirely ahead of time, however, stopping short of adding the Parmesan. Add the Parmesan only after reheating the carrots. Carrots cooked this way become very condensed in flavour, as they lose all their liquid, and very satisfying in texture.

MENU SUGGESTIONS

These carrots are a good accompaniment for all roasts, for grilled meats, for all sautéed veal dishes, for game – in short, for nearly all meats or poultry except those served with tomato sauce.

Cavolfiore

CAULIFLOWER

A head of cauliflower should be very hard, its leaves should be fresh, crisp and unmarked, and its florets should be compact and as white as possible.

If speckled or slightly discoloured, do not buy it. Fresh cauliflower keeps well in the refrigerator for several days.

HOW TO BOIL CAULIFLOWER

Remove all the leaves from a head of cauliflower and cut a cross at the root end. Bring 5 litres (8¾ pints) of water to the boil. (The greater the quantity of water you use, the faster the cauliflower cooks and the sweeter it tastes.) Add the cauliflower and cook at a moderate boil, uncovered, for about 30 minutes, or until it is tender when pricked with a fork. Drain immediately when cooked.

Boiled cauliflower can be served lukewarm or at room temperature as salad (page 356), or it can be gratinéed or fried.

Cavolfiore gratinato al burro e formaggio
CAULIFLOWER GRATINÉED WITH BUTTER AND CHEESE

For six to eight

1 head cauliflower [900 g to 1·15 kg (2 to 2½ lb)] 60 g (2 oz) butter	Salt 60 g (2 oz) freshly grated Parmesan cheese

1 Preheat the oven to 200°C/400°F/Mark 6.

2 Boil the cauliflower as directed above, and when it has cooled detach the florets from the head. If they are rather large, divide them into two or three parts.

3 Choose an oven dish large enough to hold the florets in a single layer. Smear the bottom with butter and arrange the florets so that they overlap slightly, like roof tiles. Sprinkle with salt and grated cheese and dot thickly with butter. Place on the uppermost rack of the preheated oven and bake for about 15 minutes, or until a light crust forms on top. Allow to stand a few moments before serving.

MENU SUGGESTIONS

Follow those for *Topinambur gratinati* (page 301).

Cavolfiore fritto
FRIED CAULIFLOWER

For six

1 head cauliflower [900 to 1·15 kg
    (2 to 2½ lb)]
2 eggs, lightly beaten with salt, in a
    bowl

120 g (4¼ oz) fine, dry plain
    breadcrumbs, spread on a dish
    or on waxed paper
Vegetable oil, enough to come 12 mm
    (½ inch) up the side of the pan

1 Boil the cauliflower as directed on the previous page. When it has cooled, detach the florets from the head and cut into wedges about 25 mm (1 inch) thick at the widest point.

2 Dip the florets in egg, letting the excess flow back into the bowl, then turn them in breadcrumbs. (They can be prepared up to and including this point a few hours ahead of time.)

3 Heat the oil in the frying pan over high heat. When it is very hot, slip in the floret wedges, no more at one time than will fit loosely in the pan. Fry to a nice golden crust on one side; then turn them. When both sides are done, transfer to kitchen paper to drain. Serve piping hot.

MENU SUGGESTIONS

Follow those for *Carciofini fritti* (page 294). Fried cauliflower is very nice also with *Fegatini di polli alla salvia* (page 256) and *Rollantini di petto di pollo e maiale* (page 266).

Coste di sedano alla parmigiana
GRATINÉED CELERY WITH PARMESAN CHEESE

In this recipe, celery undergoes a nearly complete range of cooking procedures. It is first blanched, then briefly sautéed, braised in broth and finished off in the oven. It is actually very much simpler than it sounds, and the result is a remarkably fine dish that is as elegant as it is delicious.

For six

2 large heads crisp, fresh celery	Freshly ground pepper, about 6
3 tablespoons finely chopped onion	twists of the mill
40 g (1½ oz) butter	450 ml (¾ pint) broth (page 8) **or** 1
25 g (1 oz) chopped *pancetta,* **or**	chicken stock cube dissolved
prosciutto, **or** green bacon	in the same quantity of water
Salt	1 cup freshly grated Parmesan cheese

1 Trim the tops of the celery and detach all the sticks from the bunches. Lightly peel the sticks to remove most of the strings. Cut the sticks into lengths of about 75 mm (3 inches). Drop into 2 to 3 litres (3½ to 4¾ pints) of rapidly boiling water, and 2 minutes after the water returns to the boil, drain and set aside.

2 Preheat the oven to 200°C/400°F/Mark 6.

3 Put the onion in a saucepan with the butter and sauté over medium heat until translucent but not browned.

4 Add the *pancetta,* stir, and sauté for about 1 minute.

5 Add the well-drained celery, a light sprinkling of salt, and the pepper and sauté for 5 minutes, turning the celery from time to time.

6 Add the broth, cover the pan, and cook at a gentle simmer until the celery is tender when pricked with a fork. (If, when the celery is nearly done, there is still much liquid in the pan, uncover, raise the heat, and finish cooking while the liquid evaporates.)

7 Arrange the cooked celery in an oven dish with the inner sides of the sticks facing up. Spoon the sautéed onion and *pancetta* from the pan over the celery, then add the grated cheese. Place the dish on the uppermost rack of the preheated oven and bake for 6 to 8 minutes, or until the cheese has melted and formed a slight crust. Allow to stand for a few moments, then serve directly from the baking dish.

MENU SUGGESTIONS

Follow those for *Topinambur gratinati* (page 301). This celery goes particularly well with *Stracotto al Barolo* (page 206), *Petto di vitello arrotolato* (page 215) and *Rollatini di petto di pollo e maiale* (page 266).

Sedano e patate all'olio

CELERY AND POTATOES BRAISED IN OLIVE OIL

For four to five

5 medium potatoes, about 560 g (1¼ lb)	6 tablespoons olive oil
	Salt
1 large head celery	2 tablespoons lemon juice

1 Peel the potatoes, wash them, and cut into halves.

2 Detach all the celery sticks. Since only the sticks are used in this recipe, remove the leafy end entirely, and set aside the white, inner heart for use in a salad. Snap off a small piece from the narrow end of each stick and pull down to remove as much of the celery strings as possible. Cut the sticks into 75 mm (3-inch) lengths and wash thoroughly in cold water.

3 Put the celery, olive oil and salt in a casserole and add enough water to cover. Cover the casserole and cook over medium heat for 10 minutes. Add the halved potatoes, more salt and the lemon juice. (If there is not enough liquid to cover the potatoes, add water.) Cover and cook for 25 minutes. Test both the celery and the potatoes for tenderness with a fork. (Sometimes the celery lags, while the potatoes are already tender. If this happens, transfer the potatoes to a warm, covered dish, cover the casserole and continue cooking the celery until tender.)

4 When the celery and potatoes are done the only liquid left in the pot should be oil. If there is still some water left, uncover the pot, raise the heat, and quickly evaporate it. If the potatoes were removed, return them to the casserole after boiling away the water. Cover, turn down the heat to medium, and warm up the potatoes for about 2 minutes. Check salt. Serve hot.

MENU SUGGESTIONS

This is a good vegetable to choose when making up a meal without pasta. It is excellent with *Frittate* (page 277–82), with *Rollatini di vitello al pomodoro* (page 224) and with *Fegato di vitello fritto* (page 252).

Coste di biete alla parmigiana
SWISS CHARD STALKS WITH PARMESAN CHEESE

For four

2 bunches mature Swiss chard, the ones with the broadest stalks Salt	60 g (2 oz) butter 60 g (2 oz freshly grated Parmesan cheese

1 Pull off all the leaves from the Swiss chard stalks. Do not discard the leaves; they make an excellent salad (page 356). Wash the stalks in cold water, trimming away any remaining leaves, and cut them in lengths of about 100 mm (4 inches).

2 Drop into abundant boiling salted water and cook for approximately 30 minutes. (They should be tender but firm because they will undergo additional cooking in the oven.)

3 Preheat the oven to 200°C/400°F/Mark 6.

4 Smear a rectangular oven dish with butter. Arrange a layer of stalks on the bottom of the dish, laying them end to end. Trim them to fit if necessary. Sprinkle lightly with salt and grated Parmesan cheese and dot with butter. Place another layer of stalks over this, season as above, and continue building up layers until you have used up all the stalks. The top layer should be generously sprinkled with Parmesan and well dotted with butter.

5 Place the dish in the upper third of the preheated oven. Bake for 15 minutes, or until the top layer acquires a light, golden crust. This dish is at its most agreeable in texture and flavour when warm, but not too hot, so allow it to stand and cool a little before bringing to the table.

MENU SUGGESTIONS

Follow those for *Topinambur gratinati* (page 301).

Melanzane
AUBERGINES

Italian aubergines are very small, often just slightly larger than zucchini, whose shape they resemble. The most consistently good aubergine is the medium-sized one, weighing about 700 g (1½ lb). The skin should be glossy, smooth and intact. Avoid aubergines with skin that is opaque, discoloured or even slightly wrinkled. Fresh aubergines are resistant to the touch and compact, never spongy. They will keep in the refrigerator for 5 to 6 days.

    The skin on many aubergines is sometimes quite tough, so it is best to peel it for any of the following recipes.

Melanzane fritte
FRIED AUBERGINES

Fried aubergines are the key ingredient in some very appealing Italian dishes, such as *Melanzane alla parmigiana* (page 319) or *Spaghettini con le melanzane* (page 84), and on its own it makes an excellent vegetable dish. There are two points to remember in order to fry aubergines successfully:

– Before they can be cooked, aubergines must be drained of their excess moisture. This is done by salting them and letting them stand for 30 minutes.
– Aubergines must fry in an abundant quantity of very hot oil. When properly fried, they absorb virtually none of the cooking fat. Never add oil to the pan while the aubergines are frying.

For six to eight

2 to 3 medium aubergines [1·35 kg to 2 kg (3 to 4½ lb)] Salt	Vegetable oil, enough to come 25 mm (1 inch) up the side of the pan

1 Peel the aubergines and cut them lengthways in slices about 9 mm (⅜ inch) thick. Set the slices upright in a pasta colander and sprinkle the first layer of slices generously with salt before setting another layer next to it.

Put a soup dish under the colander to collect the drippings and allow to stand at least 30 minutes.

2 Add enough oil to a large frying pan to come 25 mm (1 inch) up the side of the pan. Turn on the heat to high. Take as many slices of aubergine as you think will fit in one layer in the pan and dry them well with kitchen paper. When the oil is hot (test it with the end of one of the slices: it should sizzle), slide in the aubergines. Fry to a nice golden brown on all sides, then transfer to a dish lined with kitchen paper to drain. Dry some more slices and continue frying until they are all done. (If you see that the aubergines are browning too rapidly, lower the heat.)

Note   Fried aubergines can be served hot or at room temperature.

MENU SUGGESTIONS

Combined with *Pomodori al forno* (page 333), fried aubergines make a marvellous accompaniment to *Cotolette alla milanese* (page 228).

Melanzane alla parmigiana
AUBERGINES WITH CHEESE

For four

2 medium aubergines [about 1·3 kg (3 lb)], sliced, drained of their moisture, and fried as directed in previous recipe	1 Italian mozzarella cheese, coarsely grated on the largest holes of the grater
450 g (16 oz) tinned Italian tomatoes, drained, seeds removed, and coarsely chopped	25 g (1 oz) freshly grated Parmesan cheese
Salt	1½ teaspoons oregano 35 g (1¼ oz) butter

1 Preheat the oven to 200°C/400°F/Mark 6.

2 Line the bottom of a buttered oven dish (250 mm (10 inches) square, or its rectangular equivalent) with a single layer of fried aubergine slices. Top this layer with chopped tomatoes. Add a pinch of salt, a generous sprinkling of grated mozzarella, a tablespoon of grated Parmesan cheese and a pinch of oregano, and cover with another layer of sliced aubergine.

Continue building up layers of aubergine, tomatoes and cheese until you have used up all the aubergine. The top layer should be aubergine. Sprinkle the remaining Parmesan cheese over it and dot with butter. Place in the upper third of the preheated oven.

3 After 20 minutes pull out the pan and, pressing with the back of a spoon, check to see if there is an excess amount of liquid. If there is, tip the pan and draw it off with the spoon. Return to the oven for another 15 minutes. Allow it to stand and partly cool off before serving. It should not be piping hot.

Note It can be prepared entirely ahead of time, refrigerated when cool, and warmed up several days later. It will still be good, although not quite as fragrant as the day you prepared it.

MENU SUGGESTIONS

This dish is too hearty to be just a vegetable dish. It can be a light luncheon on its own followed by a mixed green salad or, in a fully organised meal, it can precede *Cotolette alla milanese* (page 228), *Fegato di vitello fritto* (page 252) or *Costolettine di agnello fritte* (page 239). It can also become a second course, preceded by *Gnocchi di patate* (page 167), with *Pesto* (page 118). Do not combine it with delicately flavoured dishes or ones with heavy sauces. In restaurants it is often served at room temperature as a summer antipasto.

Melanzane al funghetto
SAUTÉED DICED AUBERGINES

This aubergine dish is called *al funghetto*, 'mushroom style', because it is sautéed with olive oil, garlic and parsley. This is the same technique as that used in making *funghi trifolati*, or 'truffled' mushrooms (page 325), which are called 'truffled' for obscure reasons of their own. Some people also add anchovies and oregano. I do not.

For four to six

2 medium aubergines [about 1·35 kg (3 lb)]
Salt
1 clove garlic, peeled and finely chopped

5 tablespoons olive oil
2 tablespoons finely chopped parsley
Freshly ground pepper, about 6 twists of the mill

1 Peel the aubergines and cut them into 25-mm (1-inch) cubes. Put them in a colander and sprinkle liberally with salt. Toss and turn the cubes so that there is some salt on all of them. Allow to stand for at least 30 minutes, draining the aubergines of as much of their excess liquid as possible. Remove from the colander and blot with kitchen paper.

2 In a frying pan, over medium heat, sauté the garlic, with 4 tablespoons of the olive oil, until it colours lightly. Add the aubergine pieces, turning them frequently. At first they will absorb all the oil. Do not panic – turn the pieces rapidly and keep shaking the pan. Add 1 more tablespoon of oil after 5 minutes. (You will not need any more oil because as the aubergines cook the oil will reappear on the surface.) After 10 or 12 minutes, add the chopped parsley and stir it well. Add the pepper and continue cooking until the aubergines are tender but firm, about 30 minutes, give or take a few minutes, depending on the aubergines. Check salt; then spoon into a warm dish and serve.

Note   You can prepare the dish entirely ahead of time and when cool refrigerate in its cooking juices, under plastic film. When reheating, put it in a frying pan (no additional oil is required) and warm it slowly over medium-low heat.

MENU SUGGESTIONS

Follow those for *Topinambur trifolati* (page 300). Aubergines are also a tasty accompaniment to *Fettine di manzo alla sorrentina* (page 205) and *Scaloppine di vitello alla pizzaiola* (page 223).

Finocchio

FENNEL

Most people have seen fennel on vegetable stalls, many have had it raw in salads in Italian restaurants, but few know what a fine vegetable it is for cooking. It is sweeter cooked than raw, losing most of its slight taste of anise. It has an interesting flavour, gentle and forward at the same time, and its texture is quite similar to that of celery.

There are two basic types of fennel bulb. One is squat and bulbous, the other is flat and elongated. The squat, bulbous one is crisper, sweeter and less stringy and should be the only kind used for salads. For cooking, either variety will do, although the stocky one always gives better results. Fennel is generally available from late autumn to the middle of spring.

Finocchi al burro e formaggio

SAUTÉED FENNEL WITH BUTTER AND CHEESE

For four

3 large fennel bulbs **or** 4 to 5 small ones	Salt
75 g (2½ oz) butter	3 tablespoons freshly grated Parmesan cheese

1 Cut away any wilted or bruised parts of the fennel. Cut off and discard the tops and cut the bulbous lower parts into vertical slices no more than 12 mm (½ inch) thick. Wash thoroughly in cold water.

2 Put the sliced fennel and the butter in a fairly broad saucepan, and add enough water barely to cover. Cook, uncovered, over medium heat.

If there is too much fennel for your pan, put in as much as it will hold, cover the pan, and cook for 5 to 8 minutes, or until the fennel has softened and reduced in volume. Add the rest of the fennel, mix well, cover the pan, and cook for 3 or 4 more minutes. Uncover the pan and cook, turning the fennel from time to time, until it is tender when pricked with a fork, from 25 to 40 minutes altogether. You may add as much as 6 tablespoons of warm water if it is necessary, but at the end the fennel must have absorbed all the liquid and should have a glossy pale-gold colour. Before removing from the heat, add salt to taste and the grated cheese. Mix well and transfer to a warm dish. Serve while hot.

Note When cooked, the tender parts of fennel will be soft but the firm ones rather crunchy. Do not try to eliminate this natural and interesting contrast in texture by cooking until the fennel is all soft.

MENU SUGGESTIONS

Follow those for *Topinambur gratinati* (page 301). This dish is quite lovely with *Arrosto di maiale all' alloro* (page 241) and *Polpettone alla toscana* (page 211).

Finocchi all'olio
FENNEL BRAISED IN OLIVE OIL

For four

3 large fennel bulbs **or** 4 to 5 small ones

6 tablespoons olive oil
Salt

Follow the instructions for the previous recipe. The procedure is identical, step for step, except that olive oil is substituted for butter and the grated cheese is completely omitted. While the procedure is the same, the taste and texture are quite different when fennel is braised in olive oil. It is perhaps somewhat less elegant than fennel done in butter, but it is sweeter, with a smoother texture.

This is a suitable accompaniment for tangy dishes, such as *Bistecca alla diavola* (page 203), *Fettine di manzo alla sorrentina* page 205) and *Scaloppine di vitello alla pizzaiola* (page 223).

Finocchi fritti

FRIED FENNEL

For four

3 fennel bulbs
Salt
2 eggs, beaten lightly with salt, in a
     bowl

180 g ($6\frac{1}{4}$ oz) fine, dry plain
     breadcrumbs, spread on a dish
     or on waxed paper
Vegetable oil, enough to come at least
     12 mm ($\frac{1}{2}$ inch) up the side of
     the pan

1 Cut off the tops of the fennel and trim away any bruised or dis-coloured parts. Cut the fennel lengthways into slices about 9 mm ($\frac{3}{8}$ inch) thick. Wash thoroughly in several changes of cold water and drain.

2 Bring 3 litres ($5\frac{1}{4}$ pints) of water to the boil, add salt, then drop in the fennel slices. First drop in the slices that are attached to part of the fleshy core, since these take a little longer to cook. After a minute or so drop in the others. Cook at a moderate boil until the core feels tender but firm when pricked with a fork, about 6 to 10 minutes, depending on the fennel. When done, drain and allow to cool.

3 Dip the cooled, parboiled fennel slices in beaten egg, then turn them in breadcrumbs.

4 Heat the oil in the frying pan over high heat. When the oil is quite hot, slip in as many fennel slices as will fit loosely. Fry to a golden brown on one side, then on the other. Transfer to kitchen paper to drain. Check salt.

MENU SUGGESTIONS

Follow those for *Carciofini fritti* (page 294). Fried fennel is also particularly good with *Arrosto di agnello pasquale col vino bianco* (page 235).

Funghi trifolati

SAUTÉED MUSHROOMS WITH GARLIC AND PARSLEY

Trifolare describes the classic Italian method of quickly sautéing sliced vegetables or meat in olive oil, garlic and parsley. To these basic elements other flavours, such as anchovies or wine, are sometimes added. The term is derived from the word *trifola*, which in Lombardy and Piedmont means truffle. It is not exactly clear what the connection with truffles is, because there are no truffles in this dish. One explanation is that the ingredients are sliced thin, as one would slice truffles. Another is that anything cooked in this manner becomes so delicious it could almost be truffles.

For six

680 g (1½ lb) crisp white mushrooms	Salt
1½ cloves garlic, peeled and finely chopped	Freshly ground pepper, 5 to 6 twists of the mill
8 tablespoons olive oil	3 tablespoons finely chopped parsley

1 Slice off the ends of the mushroom stems. Wipe the mushrooms clean with a damp cloth. If there are still traces of earth, wash very rapidly in cold running water and dry thoroughly with a towel. Cut into lengthways slices 6 mm (¼ inch) thick.

2 Choose a large, heavy frying pan that can later hold all the mushrooms without crowding, and sauté the garlic in the olive oil over medium heat until it colours lightly but does not brown. Turn the heat up to high and add the mushrooms. When the mushrooms have absorbed all the oil, turn the heat down to low, add salt and pepper, and shake the pan, stirring and tossing the mushrooms. As soon as the mushroom juices come to the surface, which happens very quickly, turn the heat up to high again and cook for 4 to 5 minutes, stirring frequently. (Do not overcook, because the texture and flavour of mushrooms are not improved by prolonged cooking.)

3 Check salt. Add the chopped parsley, stir rapidly once or twice, and transfer to a warm dish.

Note Serve immediately if intended as a vegetable. If prepared ahead of time and allowed to cool to room temperature, this makes an excellent antipasto.

Follow those for *Topinambur trifolati* (page 300).

Funghi alla panna
SAUTÉED MUSHROOMS WITH CREAM

For six

680 g (1½ lb) mushrooms	Salt
1½ tablespoons finely chopped shallots **or** onion	Freshly ground pepper, about 4 twists of the mill
35 g (1¼ oz) butter	110 ml (4 fl oz) double cream
1½ tablespoons vegetable oil	

1　Slice off the ends of the mushroom stems. Wipe the mushrooms clean with a damp cloth. If there are still traces of earth, wash very rapidly in cold, running water, and dry thoroughly with a towel.

2　Cut the mushrooms into wedges, each section of which should be about 12 mm (½ inch) thick at the thickest point of the cap. (If the mushrooms are very small, cut them into halves or leave them whole.)

3　Choose a frying pan large enough to hold all the mushrooms later without crowding them. Over medium heat, sauté the chopped shallots in the butter and oil until pale gold in colour. Raise the heat to high, and add the mushrooms. When the mushrooms have absorbed all the fat, turn the heat down to low. Add salt and pepper and cook the mushrooms, stirring constantly, until their juices begin to come to the surface, in a few seconds. Raise the heat to high and cook for 3 to 4 minutes, shaking the pan and stirring the mushrooms frequently.

4　Add the double cream and cook for just 2 or 3 minutes longer until part of the cream has been absorbed by the mushrooms and the rest has thickened slightly. Transfer the entire contents of the pan to a warm dish and serve immediately.

Possibly the most delicious way to serve these mushrooms is to mix them with *Spezzatino di vitello alla salvia* (page 230). Another lovely combination is with *Nodini di vitello alla salvia* (page 229). Actually, they will go beautifully with any veal dish, as long as they do not have to compete with a sharp or tomato-based sauce.

Cipolline agrodolci
SWEET AND SOUR ONIONS

The secret of these delectably sharp and sweet onions is not so much in the preparation, which is rapid and simple, as in the very long, slow cooking. It takes 2 to 3 hours of patient simmering to bring them to their peak, but it is well worth while because this is one of the most successful dishes of vegetables you can serve.

Since vinegar varies in strength and acidity, adjust the dose in this recipe according to the vinegar you are accustomed to using.

For six

1·35 kg (3 lb) small white onions of uniform size	2 teaspoons sugar
	Salt
60 g (2 oz) butter	Freshly ground pepper, 3 or 4 twists
2½ tablespoons vinegar	of the mill

1 In peeling the onions it can save you a great deal of time and tears if you first plunge them in boiling water for about 15 seconds. Remove just the outside skin and any dangling roots. Do not remove any of the onion layers, do not trim anything off the top, and leave the base of the root intact or the onions will come apart during the long cooking. Cut a cross into the root end.

2 Choose a frying pan or a shallow enamelled cast-iron pan large enough to contain the onions in a single layer. Put in the onions, the butter and enough water to come 25 mm (1 inch) up the side of the pan. Cook over medium heat, turning the onions frequently, adding a little warm water from time to time as the liquid evaporates. After about 20 minutes, when the onions begin to soften, add the vinegar, sugar, salt and pepper. Turn the onions again. Continue to cook slowly for 2 hours or more, turning the onions frequently. Add a tablespoon or two of warm water as it becomes necessary.

They are done when they have turned a rich, dark golden brown all over and are easily pierced by a fork. Serve while hot.

Note   If prepared ahead of time, they can be reheated slowly before serving.

MENU SUGGESTIONS

This dish is a perfect accompaniment to almost any meat and poultry and it is particularly splendid with roasts. Avoid pairing it with any dish that is sharp in flavour, such as a spicy *pizzaiola* tomato sauce.

Pisellini alla fiorentina

SAUTÉED PEAS WITH PROSCIUTTO

In Florence, the peas one uses for this recipe are very tiny, freshly picked, early peas. They cook quite rapidly and are very sweet and tender. No other kind of peas really works as well, but, if you cannot find very young, fresh peas in the market, frozen tiny peas are to be preferred to mature, mealy fresh peas.

For four

2 cloves garlic, peeled
3 tablespoons olive oil
25 g (1 oz) prosciutto **or** *pancetta*,
     diced into 6-mm ($\frac{1}{4}$-inch) cubes
Scant 1 kg (2 lb) fresh, early peas
     (unshelled weight) **or** 300 g
     ($10\frac{1}{2}$ oz) frozen *petit pois*,
     thawed

2 tablespoons finely chopped parsley
Salt
Freshly ground pepper, 4 or 5 twists
     of the mill

1   Over medium-high heat sauté the garlic cloves in the olive oil until they have coloured well.

2   Remove the garlic, add the diced prosciutto or *pancetta*, and sauté for less than a minute.

3   Add the peas, parsley, salt and pepper, turn the heat down to medium, and cover the pan, adding 2 to 3 tablespoons of water only if you are using

fresh peas. Cook until done, 5 minutes or less for frozen peas, 15 to 30 minutes for fresh, which vary enormously. The only way to tell is to taste. While tasting, check salt. Serve immediately.

MENU SUGGESTIONS

These peas go well with practically any meat or chicken course, which is fortunate because this is one of the tastiest of all Italian vegetable dishes. Try them with *Ossobuco alla milanese* (page 216), *Costolette alla milanese* (page 226), *Costolettine di agnello fritte* (page 239) or *Petti di pollo alla senese* (page 265).

Purè di patate

ITALIAN MASHED POTATOES WITH PARMESAN CHEESE

There is something about potatoes that rarely seems to have stimulated Italian cooks to a very high pitch of creativity. Rice has had a similar perplexing effect on the French, whose *risotti* are so unsatisfactory. There are, however, one or two nice things we do with potatoes. *Gnocchi* is the most famous of these. Another is this luscious purée of potatoes made with butter, milk and a substantial amount of fresh Parmesan cheese.

For four

450 g (1 lb) boiling potatoes	30 g (1 oz) freshly grated Parmesan
40 g (1½ oz) butter	cheese
8 tablespoons milk	Salt to taste

1 Put the potatoes, unpeeled, in a large pot with enough water to cover them well. Cover the pot, bring to a moderate boil, and cook until tender. (Do not test the potatoes too often with your fork, or they will become water-logged.) Drain, and peel while still hot.

2 Bring water in the lower portion of a double boiler to a very slow simmer. Cut up the butter and put it in the upper portion. Purée the potatoes through a mouli-légumes directly into the upper pan.

3 In a separate pan, bring the milk to the verge of boiling. Turn the heat off just as it is about to boil.

4 Start beating the potatoes with a whisk or a fork, adding 2 to 3 tablespoons of hot milk at a time. When you have added half the milk, beat in the grated cheese. When the cheese has been very well incorporated into the potatoes, resume adding the milk without ceasing to beat, except to rest your arm for an occasional few seconds. The potatoes should become a very soft, fluffy mass, a state that requires a great deal of beating and as much milk as the potatoes will absorb without becoming thin and runny. (Some potatoes absorb less milk than others, so you must judge the correct quantity of milk as you are beating, both by taste and thickness of the mass.) As you finish adding the milk, taste and check salt. Serve piping hot.

Note If necessary, you can prepare this up to 1 hour ahead of time. Just before serving, warm in the double boiler and beat in 2 or 3 tablespoons of very hot milk.

MENU SUGGESTIONS

The perfect marriage for this dish is with *Fegatini di pollo alla salvia* (page 256). Other congenial combinations are with *Stracotto al Barolo* (page 206). *Petto di vitello arrotolato* (page 215), *Lo 'schinco'* (page 219) and *Rognoncini trifolati al vino bianco* (page 254). You will, of course, omit pasta from the same menu. Choose a light soup for the first course.

Patate spinose
POTATO CROQUETTES WITH CRISP-FRIED NOODLES

These tiny balls of mashed potatoes are fried with a coating of thin, crumbled noodles, which makes them look like large thistles. Not only is it an attractive dish, but also the creamy potato core and the crackly noodle surface offer an interesting and enjoyable contrast in textures.

For four to six

450 g (1 lb) boiling potatoes, unpeeled
15 g ($\frac{1}{2}$ oz) butter
1 egg yolk
Salt
$\frac{1}{8}$ teaspoon nutmeg
100 g ($3\frac{1}{2}$ oz) *fedelini* or *vermicelli*
    (hair–thin noodles), hand–
    crushed into fragments about
    3 mm ($\frac{1}{8}$ inch) long

40 g ($1\frac{1}{2}$ oz) plain flour
Vegetable oil, enough to come
    6 mm ($\frac{1}{4}$ inch) up the side
    of the frying pan

1 Put the unpeeled potatoes in a saucepan with enough cold water to cover them. Cover the pan and cook at a moderate boil until tender. Drain. Peel while still hot and mash through a mouli-légumes into a bowl.

2 Mix the butter into the potatoes. Add the egg yolk, mixing it in with a fork very rapidly, lest the heat of the potatoes cook it. Add salt and nutmeg and mix thoroughly again.

3 Combine the crumbled noodles and flour in a dish.

4 Put the oil in a 250-mm (10-inch) frying pan and heat over medium-high heat. Shape the puréed potatoes into 25-mm (1-inch) balls, roll them in the noodles and flour, and slip them, a few at a time, depending on the size of the pan, into the hot oil. (Do not crowd them in the pan or they will not fry properly.) Fry, turning them on all sides, until a crisp, dark golden crust has formed all around. Transfer with a slotted spoon to kitchen paper to drain. Serve hot.

MENU SUGGESTIONS

Follow the general indications for *Purè di patate* (page 330). These croquettes are also very nice with *Bistecca alla diavola* (page 203).

Patate spinose

Dadini di patate arrosto
POT-ROASTED POTATOES

For four to six

680 g (1½ lb) white potatoes
5 tablespoons vegetable oil

25 g (1 oz) butter
Salt

1 Peel the potatoes, rinse in cold water, pat dry, and dice into 12-mm (½ -inch) cubes.

2 Heat the oil and butter in a 300-mm (12-inch) heavy-bottomed or cast-iron pot over medium-high heat. When the butter foam subsides, put in the potatoes and turn them until they are well coated with the cooking fat. Turn the heat down to medium and let the potatoes cook until a golden crust has formed on one side. Add salt, turn them, and continue cooking and turning until every side has a nice crust. After 20 to 25 minutes, test them with a fork to see if they are tender. If not, turn the heat to low and cook until tender.

Note These potatoes cannot be prepared ahead of time and reheated, but they stay crisp even when lukewarm. They are at their best, of course, piping hot.

MENU SUGGESTIONS

These are an ideal accompaniment to any roast. They are almost equally well matched with most sautéed dishes. Do avoid potato soups or *gnocchi* as a first course if you are going to have potatoes later.

Spinaci saltati
SAUTÉED SPINACH

For four to six

700 to 900 g (1½ to 2 lb) fresh spinach
    or 600 g (21 oz) frozen leaf
    spinach, thawed

Salt
2 cloves garlic, peeled
4 tablespoons olive oil

1 If you are using fresh spinach, discard any leaves that are not crisp and green. Snap off the hard, lower end of the stem on young spinach, remove the whole stem on more mature spinach. Soak it in a basin of cold water, dunking it with your hands several times. Lift out the spinach, being careful not to pick up any of the sand at the bottom of the basin. Change the water and repeat the operation. Continue washing in fresh changes of water until there is no more sand at the bottom of the basin.

Cook the spinach in a covered pan over medium heat with a pinch of salt and no more water than clings to the leaves after washing. It is done when tender, 10 minutes or more, depending on the spinach. Drain well but do not squeeze. (If you are using frozen spinach, simply cook the thawed spinach with a pinch of salt in a covered pan over medium heat for $1\frac{1}{2}$ minutes; then drain.)

2 In a frying pan, over medium heat, sauté the garlic cloves in the olive oil. When the garlic is well browned, remove it and add the drained, cooked spinach and salt. Sauté for 2 minutes, turning the spinach frequently. Taste and check salt. Serve hot.

MENU SUGGESTIONS

Follow those for *Topinambur gratinati* (page 301). This sautéed spinach is also very good with *Scaloppine di vitello alla pizzaiola* (page 223) and *Arrosto di agnello al ginepro* (page 236).

Pomodori al forno
BAKED TOMATOES

In this recipe all the wateriness of fresh tomatoes is drawn off through long, slow cooking. What remains is a savoury, concentrated essence of tomato.

Do not let the quantity of oil alarm you. Nearly all of it gets left behind in the pan.

For six

9 ripe, medium tomatoes **or** 6 large ones
3 tablespoons finely chopped parsley
2 large cloves garlic, peeled and finely chopped
Salt to taste

Freshly ground pepper, about 6 to 8 twists of the mill
6 tablespoons olive oil, or enough to come 6 mm ($\frac{1}{4}$ inch) up the side of the baking dish

1 Wash the tomatoes in cold water and slice them in half, across the width. If the variety of tomatoes you are using has a large amount of seeds, remove at least a part of them.

2 Preheat the oven to 170°C/325°F/Mark 3.

3 Choose a flameproof baking dish large enough to hold all the tomato halves in a single layer. (You can crowd them in tightly, because later they will shrink considerably.) Arrange the tomatoes cut side up and sprinkle them with the parsley, garlic, salt and pepper. Pour the olive oil over them until it comes 6 mm ($\frac{1}{4}$ inch) up the side of the dish. Cook on top of the stove over medium-high heat until the tomatoes are tender, about 15 minutes, depending on the tomatoes.

4 When the tomato pulp is soft, baste with a little oil, spooning it up from the bottom of the dish, and transfer the dish to the next-to-the-highest rack in the oven. From time to time baste the tomatoes with the oil in which they are cooking. Cook for about 1 hour, until the tomatoes have shrunk to a little more than half their original size. (The skins and the sides of the pan will be partly blackened, but no not worry – the tomatoes are not burned.) Transfer to a serving dish, using a slotted spatula, leaving all the cooking fat behind in the pan. Serve hot or at room temperature.

Note   These tomatoes can be prepared several days ahead of time. Since they must be reheated, they should be refrigerated with all or part of their cooking fat. When refrigerating, cover tightly with plastic film. To reheat, return to a 170°C/325°F/Mark 3 oven for 10 to 15 minutes, or until warm.

MENU SUGGESTIONS

This dish is a tasty accompaniment to roasts and to *Bollito misto* (page 273). You would never use it, of course, with any dish already cooked in a tomato sauce or flavoured with tomato. Nor does it go well with cream or milk sauces. Its perfect marriage is with *Melanzane fritte* (page 318), when both are at their peak, in midsummer, and the two make a sensational combination as a vegetable dish with *Cotolette alla milanese* (page 228).

Pomodori fritti
FRIED TOMATOES

I have not yet found a vegetable that does not take well to frying, and among all fried vegetables none can surpass tomatoes. They reach that perfect combination of outer crispness and inner juiciness that is always the goal when frying vegetables.

The best tomatoes for frying are those that are firm and meaty, with few seeds and as little water as possible.

For four

2 **or** 3 large tomatoes
120 g (4¼ oz) plain flour, spread on a dish or on waxed paper
1 egg, lightly beaten with salt, in a soup dish or small bowl

120 g (4¼ oz) fine, dry plain breadcrumbs, spread on a dish or on waxed paper
Vegetable oil, enough to come 25 mm (1 inch) up the sides of the pan
Salt, if necessary

1 Wash the tomatoes and cut them horizontally into slices 12 mm (½ inch) thick, discarding the tops. Remove the seeds, but handle the tomatoes gently, without squeezing them.

2 Turn the tomato slices lightly in the flour, dip them in egg, then dredge them well in breadcrumbs.

3 Heat the oil over high heat. When the oil is very hot, slip in the tomatoes. When a dark golden crust has formed on one side, turn them and do the other side. When both sides have a nice crust, transfer them to kitchen paper to drain. Taste a little piece and check salt. Serve piping hot.

MENU SUGGESTIONS

Follow those for *Carciofini fritti* (page 295).

Zucchine
ZUCCHINI

Zucchini are one of the great favourites among Italian vegetables, and their first appearance in the markets in early spring is an event eagerly looked forward to in Italy. Their very delicate taste is sometimes mistaken for blandness, which some try to cover up with seasonings. In Italian recipes, however, their fine, distinct flavour is carefully nurtured and emerges quite clearly, undisguised.

WHAT TO LOOK FOR WHEN BUYING ZUCCHINI

Recognising quality in raw zucchini can make all the difference between a successful dish and a tasteless one. Good zucchini are never very large. Do not buy any that are much broader than 37 mm ($1\frac{1}{2}$ inches) or longer than 150 mm (6 inches). Unless you are going to stuff them, small, skinny zucchini that are 25 mm (1 inch) or less in diameter are the most desirable. Look for bright colour and glossy skin, and avoid zucchini whose skin is mottled or discoloured. Zucchini should feel very firm in your hands. If they are flabby and bend easily they are not fresh. When cut, the flesh of good, young zucchini should be crisp and show very tiny seeds.

CLEANING ZUCCHINI

Soak zucchini in a basin of cold water for 10 minutes, then scrub thoroughly under cold running water until the skin feels clean and smooth. Sometimes no amount of washing and scrubbing will loosen embedded earth. If the skin feels gritty after scrubbing, peel it lightly with a potato peeler. Cut off and discard both ends of the zucchini. They are now ready for the preparation of any recipe.

Zucchine fritte con la pastella

ZUCCHINI FRIED IN FLOUR-AND-WATER BATTER

Zucchini fried in *pastella* are crisp and light and absolutely irresistible. *Pastella* is a flour-and-water batter that produces a thin, crackly coating that stays perfectly bonded to the zucchini and keeps them from absorbing any of the frying fat.

If you like fried onion rings, but loathe, as I do, the thick spongy wrappings in which restaurants usually present them, try them at home with *pastella*. It will be a revelation.

For four to six

450 g (1 lb) zucchini
80 g (2¾ oz) plain flour

Vegetable oil, enough to come 18 mm
(¾ inch) up the side of the pan
Salt

1 Clean the zucchini as directed on page 336. Cut them lengthways into slices about 3 mm (⅛ inch) thick.

2 Put 250 ml (scant ½ pint) of water in a soup plate and gradually add the flour, sifting it through a sieve and constantly beating the mixture with a fork until all the flour has been added. The batter should have the consistency of double cream.

3 Heat the oil in the frying pan over high heat. When the oil is very hot dip the zucchini slices in the batter and slip only as many as will fit loosely into the pan.

4 When a golden crust has formed on one side of the zucchini slices, turn them over. When both sides have a nice crust, transfer the zucchini to kitchen paper to drain and sprinkle with salt. Continue in the same way until all the slices are fried. Serve piping hot.

MENU SUGGESTIONS

Follow those for *Carciofini fritti* (page 295).

Zucchine fritte all'aceto
FRIED ZUCCHINI WITH VINEGAR

For four to six

450 g (1 lb) zucchini
Salt
Vegetable oil, enough to come 6 mm
    ($\frac{1}{4}$ inch) up the side of the pan
120 g ($4\frac{1}{4}$ oz) plain flour, spread on a
    dish or on waxed paper

2 to 3 tablespoons good-quality wine
    vinegar, preferably imported
    French vinegar
2 cloves garlic, lightly crushed with
    a heavy knife-handle and
    peeled
Freshly ground pepper, about 4
    twists of the mill

1 Clean the zucchini as directed on page 336. Cut them into sticks about 6 mm ($\frac{1}{4}$ inch) thick. Sprinkle with salt and set aside for 30 minutes.

2 When the 30 minutes have elapsed, the zucchini will have thrown off quite a bit of liquid. Drain them and pat them dry with a cloth or kitchen paper.

3 Heat the oil in a frying pan over high heat. When the oil is quite hot, lightly dip the zucchini in flour and slip into the pan. (Do not put too many in at one time. They should fit very loosely in the pan.) Turn them as they brown.

4. When the zucchini are a deep golden brown, transfer to a deep dish, using a slotted spoon. While they are still hot, sprinkle them with vinegar. You will hear them sizzle.

5 When all the zucchini are done, bury the garlic in their midst, and season with pepper. Serve at room temperature.

Note After you have done these once, you can regulate the quantity of vinegar and garlic to suit your taste. I dislike any more than an intriguing suggestion of garlic, so I remove the cloves after about 5 minutes.

MENU SUGGESTIONS

In addition to being a superb accompaniment to meat, especially pork or sausages, these zucchini make an enticing antipasto. They are also a tasty vegetable dish for a buffet.

Zucchine all'aglio e pomodoro
SLICED ZUCCHINI WITH GARLIC AND TOMATO

For four to six

450 g (1½ lb) zucchini
1 medium onion, thinly sliced
200 ml (¼ pint) olive oil
2 small cloves garlic, peeled and
    coarsely chopped
2 tablespoons chopped parsley

150 g (5¼ oz) tinned Italian tomatoes,
    coarsely chopped, with their
    juice
Salt
Freshly ground pepper, 4 to 6 twists
    of the mill
4 to 6 fresh basil leaves (optional)

1 Clean the zucchini as directed on page 336 and slice them into discs 9 mm (⅜ inch) thick.

2 Put the onion and oil in a flameproof oven dish and sauté over medium heat until pale gold. Add the garlic and sauté until it colours lightly. Add the parsley, stir once or twice, then add the tomatoes and their juice. Cook at a steady simmer for 15 minutes.

3 Preheat the oven to 180°C/350°F/Mark 4.

4 Add the sliced zucchini, salt, pepper and basil. Cook until tender when pricked with a fork, 20 minutes or more, depending on the age and freshness of the zucchini. (Do not overcook. The zucchini should be tender but firm.)

5 Transfer the dish to the uppermost level of the preheated oven for about 5 minutes, until the liquid the zucchini throws off while cooking has dried up. Serve immediately in the baking dish.

MENU SUGGESTIONS

Serve with any simple roast or with grilled meat. Avoid competition with a strong tomato or garlic presence.

Barchette di zucchine ripiene al forno
STUFFED ZUCCHINI

For four to six

8 to 10 young, very fresh, firm
　　zucchini
Salt
25 g (1 oz) butter
1 tablespoon vegetable oil
1 tablespoon finely chopped onion
3 or 4 slices unsmoked ham, chopped
Freshly ground pepper to taste

Béchamel sauce (page 23), made with
　　250 ml (scant ½ pint) milk, 20 g
　　(¾ oz) plain flour, 25 g (1 oz)
　　butter and salt
1 egg
3 to 4 tablespoons freshly grated
　　Parmesan cheese
A tiny pinch of nutmeg
　　(optional)
Fine, dry plain breadcrumbs

1　Clean the zucchini as directed on page 336. Slice off the ends and cut the zucchini into lengths of about 62 mm (2½ inches). With a vegetable corer or potato peeler scoop out the zucchini from end to end, being careful not to perforate the sides. The thinned-out wall of the zucchini should not be less than 6 mm (¼ inch). Set aside the pulp extracted from the inside of the zucchini.

2　Cook the hollowed-out zucchini in abundant boiling water, to which salt has been added. Cook only until half done, or until lightly resistant when pierced with a fork. Drain and set aside.

3　Heat half the butter and all the oil in a frying pan. Sauté the chopped onion and chopped ham, and then add half the zucchini pulp, roughly chopped. Add salt and pepper and cook over high heat until the pulp turns creamy and acquires a mellow golden colour. Lift away from the frying pan with a slotted spoon or spatula, leaving all the cooking fat behind, and set aside.

4　Preheat the oven to 200°C/400°F/Mark 6.

5　Prepare a thick béchamel sauce using the quantities indicated above, remembering that to make a béchamel thicker you simply cook it longer. As soon as the béchamel is ready, add the cooked zucchini pulp and quickly stir in the egg, the freshly grated Parmesan, and the optional pinch of nutmeg. Mix well, then set aside.

6　Smear the bottom of a rectangular oven dish with butter. Split the cooked zucchini in half lengthways and line them up in the dish, hollowed side facing up. Salt lightly, and fill each zucchini half with the béchamel and zucchini-core mixture. Sprinkle with breadcrumbs and dot lightly with butter. (If you wish, you can wait up to a few hours before baking, but you must finish cooking the zucchini the same day or they will lose freshness.)

7 Bake in the upper third of the preheated oven for about 20 minutes, or until a light golden crust forms. Do not serve immediately but allow to stand until no longer steaming hot.

MENU SUGGESTIONS

Although this has been suggested elsewhere in the book as an elegant vegetable dish, it also makes an excellent first course. Serve before *Stracotto al Barolo* (page 206), any of the three lamb roasts on pages 235–8, *Arrosto di maiale all'alloro* (page 241) or *Piccioncini in tegame* (page 270).

Zucchine con ripieno di carne e formaggio
ZUCCHINI STUFFED WITH MEAT AND CHEESE

For four to six

10 fresh, young zucchini about 30 to 37 mm (1¼ to 1½ inches) in diameter
6 medium onions, thinly sliced
3 tablespoons vegetable oil
2 tablespoons chopped parsley
2 tablespoons concentrated tomato purée diluted with 250 ml (scant ½ pint) of water
3 tablespoons milk
⅔ slice firm white bread, crust removed

220 g (½ lb) lean beef, chopped
1 egg
3 tablespoons freshly grated Parmesan cheese
15 g (½ oz) chopped prosciutto, *mortadella, pancetta* or green bacon
Salt
Freshly ground pepper, 3 or 4 twists of the mill

1 Clean the zucchini as directed on page 336. Slice off the ends and cut the zucchini into lengths of about 62 mm (2½ inches). Hollow them out completely, removing the pulp with a vegetable corer or potato peeler, being careful not to perforate the sides. The thinned-out wall of the zucchini should not be less than 6 mm (¼ inch) thick. (You will not need the pulp in this recipe, but it would be a pity to throw it away because it makes a lovely *frittata* or an excellent *risotto*.)

2 Choose a covered frying pan large enough to hold all the zucchini in a single layer. Slowly cook the sliced onions in the oil until tender and considerably softened.

3 Add the parsley, stirring it two or three times; then add the tomato purée diluted in water and cook slowly over low heat for about 15 minutes.

4 Warm the milk and mash the bread into it with a fork. Allow to cool.

5 In a mixing bowl put the chopped meat, the egg, the grated cheese, the bread mush and the chopped prosciutto or its substitute. Mix thoroughly with your hands. Add salt and the pepper.

6 Stuff the mixture into the hollowed-out zucchini sections, making sure they are well stuffed but not pushing too hard, to avoid splitting the zucchini. Put the zucchini into the frying pan, turn the heat to medium low, and cover. Cook until done, from 40 minutes to 1 hour, approximately, depending on the quality of the zucchini. (You can tell for sure only by testing the zucchini. When done they should be tender, but not too soft.) Check the zucchini from time to time and turn them.

7 If, when the zucchini are cooked, there is too much liquid in the frying pan, uncover, raise the heat to high, and boil away the excess liquid for a minute or two, turning the zucchini once or twice. Check salt, transfer to a serving dish, allow the zucchini to stand for a minute or two, and serve.

Note This is a dish that has nothing to gain from being served the moment it is cooked. On the contrary, it actually improves in texture and flavour upon being reheated a day or two later. Always serve it warm, but not steaming hot.

MENU SUGGESTIONS

This is always served as a second course. It can be preceded by such antipasti as *Bresaola* (page 42), *Bocconcini fritti* (page 43) or mixed Italian cold meats. For a first course serve *Spaghetti* with *Pesto* (page 118), *Risotto alla parmigiana* (page 155) or *Riso filante con la mozzarella* (page 166). This also makes an appetising and easy-to-handle hot buffet dish.

Fiori di zucchine fritti
FRIED ZUCCHINI BLOSSOMS

Zucchini blossoms are extremely perishable, and for that reason they are seldom found in shops or markets. But they do appear from time to time, and, if you should happen to come across these luscious orange flowers, do buy them or pick the blossoms from your own plants after pollination. They make an attractive and delectable dish that is extremely simple to prepare. The method for cooking zucchini blossoms is identical to that for *Zucchine fritte con la pastella* (page 337).

For four to six

12 to 14 zucchini blossoms	The flour-and-water batter from page
Vegetable oil, enough to come 18 mm	337
($\frac{3}{4}$ inch) up the sides of the	Salt
frying pan	

1 Wash the blossoms rapidly under cold running water and dry them gently on kitchen paper. If the stems are very long, cut them down to 25 mm (1 inch) in length. Cut the base of the blossom on one side, and open the flower out flat, without dividing it.

2 Heat the oil over high heat. When it is very hot, dip the blossoms quickly in and out of the batter and slip them into the frying pan. When they are golden brown on one side, turn them and cook them to golden brown on the other side. Transfer to kitchen paper to drain, sprinkle with salt, and serve promptly while still hot.

MENU SUGGESTIONS

Follow those for *Carciofini fritti* (page 295).

Verdura mista in graticola

AN ITALIAN BARBECUE:
CHARCOAL-GRILLED VEGETABLES

Americans and Australians have practically re-invented cooking over charcoal, but the uses to which all the marvellously practical barbecue equipment is put are incredibly few. Whenever my family goes barbecuing on a public camp-site or picnic area, our grill sizzling with tomatoes, aubergines, peppers, onions, mushrooms and zucchini is soon the object of ill-concealed wonderment as the only bright island in the midst of a brown atoll of hot dogs, hamburgers and steaks.

Barbecuing vegetables is one of the most effective ways of concentrating their flavour. Charcoal-grilled peppers are all that peppers should be, and never are when done any other way. Zucchini turn out fresher-tasting than the most skilfully fried zucchini and are just as crisp and juicy. Even indifferent tomatoes are returned by the fire to their ancestral tomato taste and become nearly as full flavoured as the vine-ripened tomatoes of San Marzano.

Doing vegetables need not interfere with the unquestioned pleasure of charcoal-grilled steak. Cook the vegetables in the first flush of the fire. When they are done, the fire is ready for grilling steak or whatever else you are having. With a full load of vegetables, calculate about 25 to 40 per cent more charcoal than you would normally use for steaks or hamburgers alone.

For four

1 large flat Spanish onion	Olive oil
2 sweet green **or** red peppers	Crushed peppercorns
2 large, firm, ripe tomatoes	1 teaspoon chopped parsley (optional)
1 medium aubergine	$\frac{1}{4}$ small clove garlic, peeled and
Salt	chopped (optional)
2 medium fresh, young, firm, glossy	$\frac{1}{2}$ teaspoon fine, dry plain
zucchini	breadcrumbs (optional)
110 g ($\frac{1}{4}$ lb) very fresh and crisp	
mushrooms	

1 Remove the outer, crackly skin of the onion, but do not cut off the point or the root. Divide it in half horizontally.

2 Wash the peppers in cold water and leave whole.

3 Wash the tomatoes in cold water and divide in two horizontally.

4 Wash the aubergine in cold water, then cut in half lengthways. Without piercing the skin, make shallow cross-hatched cuts, spaced about 25 mm

(1 inch) apart, in the aubergine flesh. Sprinkle liberally with salt and stand the halves on end in a colander for at least 15 minutes to let the bitter juices drain away.

5 Wash the zucchini thoroughly in cold water. Cut off the ends; then cut the zucchini lengthways into slices about 9 mm ($\frac{3}{8}$ inch) thick.

6 Wipe the mushrooms clean with a damp cloth. Unless they are very small, detach the caps from the stems. You are now ready to light the fire.

7 When the highest flames have died down, place the onion on the grill, cut side down. Place the peppers on the grill as well, laying them on one side. After 4 or 5 minutes check the peppers. The skin towards the fire should be charred. When it is, turn another side of the peppers towards the fire, at the same time drawing them closer together to make room for the tomatoes and aubergine (see Step 10 below). Continue turning the peppers, eventually standing them on end, until all the skin is charred. Remove them from the grill and peel them while they are as hot as you can handle. Cut them into 50-mm (2-inch) strips, discard the seeds, put the cut-up peppers in a bowl, and add at least 3 tablespoons of olive oil plus large pinches of salt and crushed peppercorns. Toss and set aside.

8 While the peppers are still cooking, check the onion. When the side facing the fire is charred, turn it over with a spatula, taking care not to separate the rings. Season each onion half with 1 tablespoon of olive oil and with salt. Move to the edge of the grill, making sure there is some burning charcoal underneath.

9 When the onion is done, in about 15 to 20 minutes, it should be well charred on both sides. Scrape away part of the blackened surface and cut each half in 4 parts. Add it to the bowl of peppers, tossing it with another pinch of salt and crushed peppercorns. (The onion will be quite crunchy, which makes a nice contrast with the peppers, but it will also be very sweet, with no trace of sharpness.)

10 When you first turn the peppers (see Step 7 above), make room for the tomatoes and aubergine. Place the tomatoes, cut side down, on the grill. Check them after a few minutes, and if the flesh is partly charred, turn them. Season each half with $\frac{1}{2}$ teaspoon of olive oil, a small pinch of salt and the optional parsley, garlic and breadcrumbs, and cook until they have shrunk by half and the skin is blackened.

11 Shake off any liquid from the aubergine. Pour 1 tablespoon of olive oil over each half and place it on the grill with the cut side facing the fire. Allow it to reach a deep brown colour, but do not let it char, which would make it bitter. Turn the aubergine over and season each half with another tablespoon of olive oil. From time to time as it cooks, pour $\frac{1}{2}$ teaspoon of oil in between the cuts. The aubergine is done when it is creamy and tender. Do not cook it beyond this point or it will become bitter.

12 When the aubergine is nearly done, put the zucchini slices on the grill. As soon as they have browned on one side turn them over and cook until done, 5 to 8 minutes. Remove to a shallow bowl and season with a large pinch of salt, pepper and about $\frac{1}{2}$ tablespoon of oil.

13 When you turn the zucchini over, put the mushrooms on the grill. These cook very quickly, about 1 minute to a side, including the stems. Add them to the bowl of zucchini and season in the same way.

Note   It is unfortunate that the length of this recipe makes it appear so forbidding. It is actually about as simple to execute as grilled hamburgers and hot dogs. The whole secret lies in mastering the sequence in which the vegetables are put on the grill. Apart from that, there is very little to do except watch them. The fire does nearly all the work. The entire process should take about 35 minutes.

SALADS

Le Insalate

THERE are two basically different dishes that appear in an Italian meal, both of which are called salads.

One contains cold cooked fish, meat or chicken, and occasionally rice, mixed with either raw or cooked vegetables. Although it is called a salad, it is usually served as an antipasto, a first course or even a second course, but rarely, if ever, as the salad course. A choice group of these salads appears later in this chapter.

The true salad course is something else entirely, with a special and fixed role. It is served invariably after the second course, signalling the approaching end of the meal. It releases the palate from the spell of the cook's inventions, and leads it to sensations of freshness and purity, to a rediscovery of food in its natural and artless state.

In this kind of salad, vegetables are used raw or boiled, alone or mixed. Its composition changes with the seasons. There are always some greens available throughout the year, but in autumn and winter salads, raw fennel and artichokes are frequently dominant. Boiled asparagus and green beans appear in the spring, followed by new potatoes. Then there are sharp and nutty wild salad plants, and in the warmer months zucchini, both raw and cooked, and tomatoes.

Italian dressing

There is absolutely nothing mysterious about the dressing for an Italian salad. The ingredients are salt, olive oil and wine vinegar. Pepper is optional, and lemon juice is occasionally substituted for vinegar.

Italians would find any discussion of something called 'salad dressing' very puzzling. Although the term could be translated, it would have little currency. For Italians, salad dressing is not an element separate from the salad; it is not added to the greens as you might add a sauce to pasta. Dressing is a process rather than an object, a verb rather than a noun. It is the act that transforms vegetables into salad.

There are many old folk sayings that illustrate this. According to one of them, to make a good salad you need four persons: a judicious one with the salt, a prodigal one with the oil, a stingy one with the vinegar and a patient one to mix it. You do not need to know very much more than that to make a proper Italian salad. There is no way to give precise proportions of salt, oil and vinegar. It takes less oil to dress green beans than an equivalent amount of lettuce. Asparagus and potatoes take more vinegar, tomatoes and cucumber more salt. Other factors that vary are the fruitiness and density of the oil, the acidity and bouquet of the vinegar, and even the character of the salt. The only foolproof method is to taste and correct the salad before serving it.

Do not begin to dress the salad until it is quite dry. Water dilutes the flavour of the dressing. You can use a special wire basket to shake the lettuce or other salad plants dry, if you like. My own method is to wrap them in a towel, gather the corners of the towel in one hand, and give it a few vigorous jerks over the sink.

Seasonings and oil and vinegar are never mixed in advance. They are poured directly on the salad in the following order:

First: Sprinkle the salt. Do not overdo it. You can add more salt later if necessary.

Second: Add the oil. There should be enough oil to coat the salad or vegetables and give them a surface gloss, but not so much as to form a pool at the bottom of the bowl, which would make the salad soggy.

Third: Add the vinegar. This is the hardest ingredient to judge. A few drops too much will ruin a salad. There must be just a hint of sharpness, enough to be noticed but not so much as to grab your attention.

Toss the salad thoroughly and repeatedly, taking care not to bruise and blacken delicate leaves such as lamb's lettuce. Taste and correct for oil, salt or vinegar. Serve immediately. Never allow salad to sit and steep in its seasonings.

From time to time you can add other seasonings to sharpen the flavour of the salad and to avoid monotony. Shredded fresh basil leaves or chopped parsley go very well into an Italian salad. They are particularly nice with tomatoes and cucumbers.

For tang you can add chopped shallots or thinly sliced onion. After the onion is sliced very thin it should be soaked in two or more changes of cold water for at least $\frac{1}{2}$ hour before putting it in the salad. This helps to sweeten it.

To add the heartiness of garlic to a salad, rub a small piece of bread with a lightly crushed garlic clove. Discard the garlic and add the bread to the salad. After the salad has been seasoned, dressed and thoroughly tossed, remove and discard the bread.

Note on oil and vinegar: To call any oil that is not pure olive oil salad oil is a contradiction in terms. Tasteless vegetable oils merely grease the salad. The flavour of the olive is absolutely indispensable to a good salad, and the denser and fruitier the olive oil, the better.

The choice of vinegar is also very important. It should be wine vinegar, preferably red, with all the characteristics of good wine: strength, flavour and a well-developed bouquet. A fine vinegar should not be spiked with tarragon or other herbs, any more than you would make a fruit-flavoured wine-cup out of good Burgundy. Many familiar brands of vinegar, unfortunately, do not measure up to these standards. However, most delicatessens and many of the better supermarkets do stock good French wine vinegar. It is certainly not cheap, but a little goes a long way, and it will make all the difference in the world to your salads. On no account should you use malt vinegar.

Insalata di spinaci e topinambur
JERUSALEM ARTICHOKE AND SPINACH SALAD

For four

220 g ($\frac{1}{2}$ lb) Jerusalem artichokes	Olive oil
220 g ($\frac{1}{2}$ lb) very young, crisp spinach	Red wine vinegar, preferably French
Salt and freshly ground pepper, a liberal quantity, to taste	

1 Soak the artichokes for a few minutes in cold water, then scrub them thoroughly under running water or peel them, if you object to the hard bite of the peel. Cut into the thinnest possible slices, and put into a salad bowl.

2 Detach the stems from the spinach, pulling them off, in one motion, together with the thin central stalk on the underside of the leaves. Wash the spinach in a basin of cold water, changing water frequently until it shows no more trace of earth. Drain, shaking off as much water as possible from the leaves. Wrap the spinach in a dry cloth and give it a few sharp, brusque

jerks to drive away any remaining moisture. Tear the leaves in two or three parts and add to the salad bowl.

3 When ready to serve, toss with salt, pepper, enough olive oil to coat, and just a dash of vinegar.

Insalata di carote
SHREDDED CARROT SALAD

No salad takes so little effort to prepare as this excellent carrot salad. Its sharp, gently bracing taste is particularly welcome after a hearty, robust meal.

For four

5 to 6 medium carrots	6 tablespoons olive oil
Salt	1 tablespoon lemon juice

1 Peel and wash the carrots, and grate them on the largest holes of the grater.

2 When ready to serve, add salt, olive oil and lemon juice. Toss thoroughly and serve immediately.

Finocchio in insalata
FENNEL SALAD

When fennel is eaten alone, as it is here, neither vinegar nor lemon is used in the dressing.

For three or four, depending on the size of the fennel

1 medium fennel bulb	Olive oil
Salt	Freshly ground pepper

1 Cut off the tops of the fennel and remove any bruised, discoloured or wilted outside stalk.

2 Cut off about 3 mm ($\frac{1}{8}$ inch) or less from the base; then cut the fennel horizontally into the thinnest possible slices. (The slices will be in the form of rings, some half, some whole.)

3 Wash the slices thoroughly in cold water, then dry them well in a towel. Toss in a salad bowl with salt, an abundant quantity of oil and a liberal grinding of pepper.

MENU SUGGESTIONS

A salad of fennel is ideal after any substantial meat dish and is especially appropriate after roast pork.

Insalata mista
MIXED SALAD

Everyone makes mixed salads, but the Italian ones seem to have an equilibrium and a freshness that many others lack. This is because even the most wildly assorted salad is never a catch-all. It is assembled with an intuitive but nonetheless precise feeling for the correct proportions of salad plants and other vegetables. There is never the monotony of too much green pepper, carrot, artichoke, celery. There is just enough, so that what is missing from one mouthful of salad is suddenly and delightfully present in the next.

The ingredients for the salad given below can be found, all at one time, at only certain moments of the year. When one or more is not available, substitute for it, in approximately equal proportions, whatever is currently in season.

Prepare all the vegetables in any order you like, and add them to the salad bowl as they are ready. Save the tomatoes for last, however, or they may get crushed and watery.

For six

2 small carrots **or** 1 large one
1 fennel bulb
$\frac{1}{2}$ medium green pepper
1 celery heart
$\frac{1}{2}$ head endive, batavia or escarole
$\frac{1}{2}$ small bunch lamb lettuce
$\frac{1}{2}$ small bunch rucola, if available
1 medium globe artichoke
$\frac{1}{2}$ lemon

3 or 4 spring onions, thinly sliced, **or**
$\frac{1}{2}$ red onion, sliced and
pre-soaked as directed on page 348
1 large **or** 2 small tomatoes
Salt
Olive oil
Red wine vinegar, preferably French vinegar

1 Wash and peel the carrots, and shred them on the largest holes of the grater.

2 Trim the fennel and slice it into thin rings, as directed on page 351. Wash thoroughly and dry well in a towel.

3 Remove the inner pulp and seeds from the pepper. Peel with a sharp potato peeler and cut into very thin strips.

4 Strip the celery heart of any leaves, then slice it crossways into narrow rings, about 6 mm ($\frac{1}{4}$ inch) thick.

5 If you are using endive or escarole, discard all the outer, dark green leaves. Detach all the leaves from the head and tear them by hand into small, bite-sized pieces. Let them soak in one or two changes of cold water in a basin for 15 to 20 minutes, or until the water shows no trace of earth. Drain and dry thoroughly in a towel or a salad basket.

6 Trim away the stems of the lamb lettuce and rucola, tear the larger leaves into two or more pieces, and soak, drain and dry as directed above for lettuce.

7 Discard the artichoke stem, and trim the artichoke as directed for *Carciofi alla romana* (page 286), trimming a little more off the top than you would normally do, to make sure only the tenderest part goes into the salad, and

remembering to rub the cut parts with juice from half a lemon. Cut the trimmed artichoke lengthways into the thinnest slices you can.

8 Add the pre-soaked onion slices.

9 Cut the tomatoes into small chunks or narrow wedges, removing some of the seeds if there is an excess.

10 When ready to serve, sprinkle liberally with salt and add enough oil to coat all the ingredients well and a dash of vinegar. Toss thoroughly but not roughly, and serve immediately.

Note Other raw vegetables you can use are red cabbage, Savoy cabbage or ordinary cabbage. It should be finely shredded. Add white or small red radishes, thinly sliced. Substitute cucumber for carrot. (Never have the two at one time; they do not seem to be compatible.) Also, raw young zucchini may be used. They should be thoroughly scrubbed and washed or even lightly peeled, and cut into matchsticks.

Panzanella

BREAD AND VEGETABLE SALAD WITH ANCHOVIES

This salad was originally the poor man's dinner in parts of Tuscany and Rome. In the traditional version, two- or three-day-old bread is soaked in water, squeezed, and added to the salad in amounts proportionate to one's hunger. This procedure is quite successful with good, solid Tuscan country bread. I do not find it very appealing, however, when made with supermarket bread. I much prefer this version, however decadent it may be, in which the waterlogged bread is replaced by crisp squares of bread fried in olive oil.

For four

$\frac{1}{2}$ clove garlic, peeled and chopped
4 flat anchovy fillets
1 tablespoon capers
Salt
5 tablespoons olive oil
1 tablespoon red wine vinegar

$\frac{1}{4}$ sweet green, yellow **or** red pepper, cored, seeded and diced
$\frac{1}{2}$ recipe *Crostini* (page 75), but fried in olive oil rather than vegetable oil

Freshly ground pepper, 5 to 6 twists
    of the mill
½ cucumber, peeled and diced into
    12-mm (½-inch) cubes

1 medium, firm, meaty tomato,
    preferably peeled, and cut into
    12-mm (½-inch) chunks
½ red onion, thinly sliced and soaked
    as directed on page 348

1 Mash the garlic, anchovies and capers to a pulp in a mortar or in a bowl. Put into a salad bowl.

2 Add salt, olive oil, vinegar and pepper, and blend thoroughly with a fork.

3 Add the fried bread squares, sweet pepper, cucumber, tomato and onion, and toss thoroughly. Taste and check seasoning and chill for 30 minutes before serving.

MENU SUGGESTIONS

Although this can be served on occasion after the second course, it is more suitable as an antipasto or a first course in a fresh and tasty summer meal.

Insalata di asparagi
ASPARAGUS SALAD

When asparagus is at the peak of its flavour, one of the favourite ways of eating it in Italy is as salad. No other way of preparing it brings one so close to the essential asparagus taste. The very finest asparagus should be chosen, because it will confront the palate thinly clothed in a light dressing of oil and vinegar. It is never mixed with any other salad vegetables.

For four to six

Scant 1 kg (2 lb) asparagus
Salt and freshly ground pepper to
    taste
5 tablespoons olive oil

3 tablespoons red wine vinegar
    (approximately), depending on
    taste and the vinegar

1 Peel and boil the asparagus as directed on page 302. When the asparagus is done it should be spread on a dish, leaving one end of the dish free. Prop

up the end under the asparagus. After about 30 minutes some liquid will have collected at the other end of the dish. Discard it and rearrange the asparagus on the dish.

2 Add salt and pepper to taste. Season liberally with olive oil, and add the vinegar, taking into account the fact that asparagus requires a great deal of vinegar. Tip the dish in several directions so that the seasoning is evenly distributed. Serve either lukewarm or at room temperature, but never chilled.

Note An alternative to seasoning the asparagus in the dish is to provide everyone with the seasonings mixed in individual shallow bowls, into which they will dip the asparagus.

Fagiolini verdi in insalata
FRENCH BEAN SALAD

For four

450 g (1 lb) French beans   Olive oil
Salt   Lemon juice

1 Trim, wash, and boil the beans as directed on page 307.

2 Put the beans in a salad bowl and add salt to taste. Add enough olive oil to give all the beans a thin glossy coating. Add lemon juice to tase. (The salad should be just slightly, not aggressively, sharp.) Toss well and serve immediately.

Note French beans may be served slightly lukewarm or at room temperature, but never chilled.

MENU SUGGESTIONS

This salad may be served after any second course of meat, poultry or fish.

Cavolfiore lesso in insalata
BOILED CAULIFLOWER SALAD

For six to eight

1 head cauliflower [about scant 1 kg (2 lb)]	Olive oil
Salt to taste	Red wine vinegar, preferably French vinegar

1 Boil the cauliflower as directed on page 313.

2 Before the cauliflower cools, detach the florets from the head, dividing all but the smallest ones into two or three parts.

3 Put the florets into a salad bowl and season very liberally with salt, oil and vinegar. Taste and check all three. (Cauliflower needs a great deal of seasoning.) Toss the florets carefully so as not to mash them and serve either lukewarm or at room temperature.

Note If you cannot use the whole head for salad, season only what you need and refrigerate the rest. It can be made into gratinéed cauliflower (page 313, or fried (page 314) a day or two later.

MENU SUGGESTIONS

Cauliflower salad can follow any meat dish, but preferably not those that include tomato.

Insalata di biete cotte
BOILED SWISS CHARD SALAD

Cooked Swiss chard leaves make a lovely, sweet salad that is particularly good after pork or lamb. If the chard is mature and has large, white stalks, these can be utilised in *Coste di biete alla parmigiana* (page 317).

For four to six

2 bunches young Swiss chard **or** the leaves of 3 large bunches of mature Swiss chard	Salt
	Olive oil
	1 or more tablespoons lemon juice

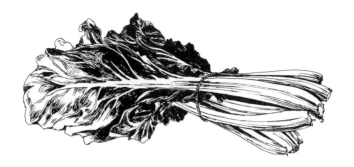

Biete (*Swiss Chard*)

1 If you are using young chard, detach the stems. If you are using mature chard, pull the leaves from the stalks, discarding any wilted or discoloured leaves. Wash in a basin of cold water, changing the water frequently until it shows no trace of earth.

2 Put the chard in a pan with whatever water clings to the leaves. Add salt, cover, and cook over medium heat until tender, about 15 to 18 minutes from the time the liquid starts to bubble.

3 Drain in a pasta colander and gently press some of the water out of the chard with the back of a fork. Place in a salad bowl.

4 Serve cool (not refrigerated) or lukewarm, seasoning with salt, oil and lemon only when ready to serve.

Insalata di zucchine

ZUCCHINI SALAD

An excellent demonstration that zucchini have a fine and distinctive flavour of their own is this salad of boiled zucchini. For a successful salad, it is absolutely essential that you choose young, fresh, firm zucchini. See the recommendations on buying zucchini on page 336.

For six

6 small to medium zucchini
3 large cloves garlic, lightly crushed
    with a heavy knife handle and
    peeled
8 tablespoons olive oil

2 to 3 tablespoons red wine vinegar,
    preferably French vinegar
2 tablespoons chopped parsley
Freshly ground pepper, about 8
    twists of the mill
Salt to taste

1 Clean the zucchini as directed on page 336.

2 Bring 4 to 5 litres (7 to 9 pints) of water to the boil, then drop in the zucchini. Cook at a moderate boil until tender but not soft and easily pierced by a fork – about 30 minutes, more or less, depending on the zucchini, from the time the water returns to the boil.

3 When done, drain, cut off the ends, and cut lengthways into halves.

4 While it is still hot, rub the zucchini flesh with the crushed garlic cloves. Arrange the zucchini, flesh side up, in a single layer on a dish. Prop up the dish at one end so that while the zucchini cool any excess liquid will gather at the other end. Do not refrigerate.

5 When the zucchini are cool, discard the liquid from the dish and season with oil, vinegar, parsley and pepper, adding salt only when just ready to serve, to prevent the zucchini from continuing to throw off liquid.

Insalatone

MIXED COOKED VEGETABLE SALAD

The sequence of steps indicated below is more or less arbitrary. Actually, all the ingredients can be prepared at the same time. This salad is at its most agreeable when its components are still slightly lukewarm. If you must prepare any part of it ahead of time, keep it at room temperature, do not refrigerate.

For four to six

3 medium white Desirée **or** new
    potatoes
5 medium onions
2 medium sweet green, yellow, **or** red
    peppers
175 g (6 oz) French beans

250 g ($8\frac{3}{4}$ oz) small beetroots, cooked
Salt
Olive oil
Red wine vinegar, preferably French
    vinegar
Freshly ground pepper

1 Preheat the oven to 200°C/400°F/Mark 6.

2 Boil the potatoes with their skins on, until tender. Cooking time varies greatly with size and type of potato. Peel while hot, and cut into 6-mm ($\frac{1}{4}$-inch) slices. Put into a salad bowl.

3 Put the onions, with their skins on, on a baking sheet, then into the upper third of the oven. Cook until they are tender all the way to the centre when pricked with a fork. Skin them, cut each one into three or four sections, and add to the salad bowl.

4 Grill and peel the peppers exactly as directed in *Peperoni e acciughe* (page 32). When peeled, cut the peppers into strips 25 mm (1 inch) wide, removing all the seeds and pulpy core. Add to the salad bowl.

5 Cook the beans until tender but firm, as directed on page 307. Drain and add to the salad bowl.

6 Cut the beetroots, into quarters if they are small, into 18-mm ($\frac{3}{4}$-inch) cubes if they are larger. Add to the bowl.

7 Add the seasonings, being liberal with the oil and pepper and stingy with the vinegar. Taste and check seasoning. Serve immediately.

MENU SUGGESTIONS

This salad is the ideal accompaniment to all grilled meats, and it can be served at the same time as the second course, in place of vegetables. It also goes well with fish, either grilled or poached. It can even stand on its own as a light summer meal, adding to it, if you wish, hard-boiled eggs, anchovy fillets or tuna.

Insalata di tonno e fagioli
TUNA AND BEAN SALAD

Although this famous salad has been given often enough before in Italian cookbooks, it is included here because no survey of Italian salads can fail to take notice of it. Moreover, while most of the English versions suggest spring onions, in this recipe we follow the traditional Tuscan use of purple onion. It is a small difference but a significant one, because the crunchiness of the onion is a delightful and essential relief from the creaminess of the beans and the tenderness of the tuna.

For four

170 g (6 oz) dried white kidney beans, cannellini, haricot **or** other white beans **or** 600 g (21 oz) tinned similar beans

½ onion, thinly sliced and soaked in water for 1 hour (see page 348)

Salt to taste

200 g (7 oz) tinned Italian or Spanish tuna **or** other tuna packed in olive oil, drained

5 tablespoons olive oil

2 teaspoons red wine vinegar, **or** more, according to taste and the strength of the vinegar

Freshly ground black pepper to taste (optional)

1 If using uncooked beans, cook them as directed on page 67. Drain.

2 Put them, or the drained tinned beans, into a salad bowl. Add the onion and season with salt to taste. Add the tuna, breaking it into large flakes with a fork. Add oil, vinegar and the optional pepper. Toss thoroughly and serve.

MENU SUGGESTIONS

This makes a very agreeable second course for a summer meal. It can be preceded by *Minestrone freddo alla milanese* (page 59), *Spaghetti* with Tomato Sauce with Marjoram and Cheese (page 81), *Spaghetti* with *Pesto* (page 118) or *Spaghettini alla carrettiera* (page 82). It can also be part of mixed antipasti for any meal with a rustic flavour, and is an excellent dish to add to a buffet.

Insalata russa con gamberoni
PRAWNS AND VEGETABLE SALAD

This salad is beautiful to look at, absolutely delicious, and very simple to execute. It does take time and patience to get the ingredients cleaned, boiled, and diced, but it can all be prepared and completed well in advance, whenever you are not pressed for time.

For six

450 g (1 lb) medium prawns, unpeeled
1 tablespoon red wine vinegar
110 g ($\frac{1}{4}$ lb) French beans
2 medium potatoes
2 medium carrots
35 g (1$\frac{1}{4}$ oz) frozen peas, thawed
3 small beetroots, cooked
2 tablespoons gherkins in vinegar,
     preferably French *cornichons*,
     cut up

2 tablespoons capers, the smaller the
     better
3 tablespoons olive oil
2 teaspoons red wine vinegar,
      preferably French
Salt
550 ml (1 pint) mayonnaise (page 22)

1 Wash the prawns. Put them, whole and unpeeled, in boiling salted water. Add the tablespoon of vinegar to the water and cook for 4 minutes. Allow the prawns to cool; then shell them and, if they are on the large side, remove the black intestinal tract, and set aside.

2 Snap the ends off the French beans, pulling away any possible strings. Rinse them and drop them into rapidly boiling salted water. Taste them early and drain them as soon as they are tender but still firm, in as little as 8 minutes if they are very young and fresh.

3 Rinse the potatoes and boil them with the peel on. When they are easily pierced with a sharp fork, drain them and peel them while they are still hot.

Insalata russa

4 Peel or scrape the carrots clean and drop them in boiling salted water. Do not overcook. Drain when tender and set aside.

5 Drop the frozen peas into boiling salted water and cook very briefly, not more than a minute or a minute and a half. Drain and set aside.

6 When the vegetables have cooled, set aside a very small quantity of each (potatoes excepted), which you will need later for decoration, and cut up the rest as follows: the green beans into pieces 9 mm ($\frac{3}{8}$ inch) long; the potatoes, carrots and beetroots diced into 9-mm ($\frac{3}{8}$-inch) cubes. The peas, of course, stay whole. Cut up the capers too, if they are not the very tiny ones. Put all the ingredients, including the cut-up gherkins or *cornichons*, in a mixing bowl.

7 Set aside half the prawns. Cut up the rest and mix with the vegetables. Season with the olive oil, wine vinegar and salt. Add 250 ml (scant $\frac{1}{2}$ pint) of the mayonnaise and mix thoroughly. Taste and check salt.

8 Turn the mixture over onto a serving dish. Shape it into a shallow, flat-topped, oval mound, pressing with a rubber spatula to make sure the surface is smooth and uniform. Now spread the remaining mayonnaise over the entire surface of the mound. Use the spatula to make it as smooth and even as possible. Indentations or deep pockets will spoil the effect.

9 Now decorate the mound. Here is one way of doing it. Place a thin carrot disc on the centre of the mound. Put a pea in the centre of the carrot. Make a rosette of prawns around the carrot, placing the prawns on their side, nestling one around the other. Over the rest of the flat surface scatter flowers made using carrots for the centre button, beetroots for the petals, French beans for the stems. Emboss the sides of the mound with the remaining prawns, heads and tails embedded in the salad, backs arching away. There are limitless ways in which you can use prawns and vegetables to decorate this salad. Use your imagination. Caution: if you are preparing this many hours or a day in advance, decorate with beetroots at the last moment before serving, as their colour has a tendency to run.

Note   This dish should be refrigerated at least 30 minutes before serving.

MENU SUGGESTIONS

This is a wonderfully cool dish for a summer day, splendid for a buffet, and a magnificent antipasto for an important meal. When it is used as antipasto, it can be followed by *Fettuccine al sugo di vongole bianco* (page 115), *Trenette col pesto* (page 121)(omitting the potatoes) or *Risotto con le vangole* (page 164). The second course should be a beautiful *Pesce ai ferri alla moda dell'Adriatico* (page 191) or *Branzino al cartoccio con frutti di mare* (page 181), substituting red snapper for the sea bass. It can also be handled as a second course, preceded by *Ostriche alla moda di Taranto* (page 28), *Cozze e vongole passate ai ferri* (page 30) and/or *Fettuccine al sugo di vongole bianco* (page 115). Alone, it is an exquisite midnight snack with champagne, followed by a bowl of *Macedonia di frutta* (page 389). It is worth staying up for.

Insalata di mare

SEAFOOD SALAD

This may well be the most popular cold seafood dish in Italy. Every region has its own version, each slightly differing in ingredients and seasonings. The one thing they all have in common, and the most notable characteristic of this dish, is the delectable juxtaposition of the varied textures of such crustaceans as shrimps, *scampi* and *cannocchie* and such molluscs as clams, mussels, scallops, squid and octopus. You can try making your own combinations, as long as they result in a variety of delicate tastes and interesting textures.

For six

220 g ($\frac{1}{2}$ lb) medium shrimps, **or** preferably very tiny shrimps

6 tablespoons vinegar

Salt

2 medium carrots, peeled and washed

2 sticks celery, washed

2 medium onions, peeled

220 g ($\frac{1}{2}$ lb) squid, cleaned as directed on page 196

450 g (1 lb) octopus tentacles, peeled like the squid

110 g ($\frac{1}{4}$ lb) scallops

1 dozen mussels, cleaned as directed on page 49

1 dozen clams, the tiniest you can find, washed and scrubbed as directed on pages 46–7

6 black Greek olives, pitted and quartered

6 green olives, pitted and quartered

$\frac{1}{2}$ sweet red pepper, grilled (page 32), cut into strips 12 mm ($\frac{1}{2}$ inch) wide

60 ml (2 oz) lemon juice

120 ml (4 oz) olive oil

Freshly ground pepper, about 6 twists of the mill

1 good-sized clove garlic, lightly crushed with a knife-handle and peeled

$\frac{1}{4}$ teaspoon dried marjoram or $\frac{1}{2}$ teaspoon fresh

1 Wash the shrimps in cold water, but do not shell them. Bring 2 litres (3½ pints) of water with 2 tablespoons of vinegar and 1 teaspoon of salt to the boil. Drop the shrimps into the boiling water and cook for 2 minutes after the water returns to the boil. (Very tiny shrimps may take 1½ minutes or less, depending on size.) Drain. When cool, peel the shrimps and cut into rounds 12 mm (½ inch) thick. If very, very tiny, leave whole. Set aside.

2 Using two separate pots, put 750 ml (1¼ pints) of water, 2 tablespoons of vinegar, salt, 1 carrot, 1 celery stick and 1 onion in each pot. Bring to the boil. Add the squid and their tentacles to one pot and the octopus tentacles to the other, and cover. Cook at a slow, steady boil, testing the squid with a knife or sharp-pronged fork after 20 minutes. Drain when tender, and when cool cut into strips 9 mm (⅜ inch) wide and 37 mm (1½ inches) long. Test the octopus tentacles after 40 minutes. Drain when tender, and when cool cut into discs 9 mm (⅜ inch) thick. Set aside.

3 Rinse the scallops in cold water. Bring 500 ml (scant pint) of water, with 1 tablespoon of vinegar and with salt, to the boil. Add the scallops and cook for 2 minutes after the water returns to the boil. Drain, and when cool cut into 12-mm (½-inch) cubes. Set aside.

4 In separate covered pans, heat the mussels and clams over high heat until their shells open. Detach the mussels from their shells and set aside. Detach the clams from their shells and rinse them one by one in their juice to remove any possible sand.

5 Combine all the seafood in a mixing bowl. Add the quartered olives, red pepper, lemon juice and olive oil, and mix thoroughly. Taste and check salt, and add pepper, the crushed garlic clove and the marjoram. Toss and mix all the ingredients thoroughly. Allow to stand for at least 2 hours, and retrieve the garlic before serving.

Note You can prepare this salad many hours ahead of time, if you like, but it is best if it is not refrigerated. If you absolutely must refrigerate it, cover it tightly with plastic film. Remove from the refrigerator well in advance of serving so that it has time to come to room tremperature.

MENU SUGGESTIONS

Its fragrance and cool, fresh taste make this an ideal summer dish. It can be served as antipasto for a multi-course fish dinner, or as a first course in a simpler dinner, followed by *Pesce ai ferri alla moda dell' Adriatico* (page 191), *Pagello con i funghi trifolati* (page 185) or *Sgombri in tegame con rosmarino e aglio* (page 184).

Insalata di riso con pollo
RICE AND CHICKEN SALAD

Cold boiled rice and cheese are the basic ingredients of a number of salads that are very popular in Italy, particularly in the summer. They can be varied with the addition of cold chicken, shrimps, lobster, finely diced cold boiled beef or veal, or cold, diced Frankfurters, which in Italy are called *wurstel*. These salads are never served after the second course, but are offered as an antipasto, a first course, or as the basis of a light lunch in hot weather.

For four to six

1 tablespoon salt
200 g (7 oz) raw rice

Dressing

1 teaspoon Dijon or German mustard   Salt
2 teaspoons red wine vinegar   6 tablespoons olive oil

75 g (2½ oz) finely diced Swiss cheese   3 tablespoons diced sour gherkins,
60 g (2 oz) black olives, pitted and   preferably French *cornichons*
   diced   1 whole breast of a young chicken,
2 tablespoons green olives, pitted and   boiled and diced into 12-mm
   diced   (½-inch) cubes
½ small sweet red, yellow **or** green
   pepper, seeded, cored and
   diced

1 Bring 2 litres (3½ pints) of water to the boil. Add 1 tablespoon salt; then drop in the rice. When the water returns to the boil, adjust the heat so that it simmers gently. Stir the rice, cover, and cook for 10 to 12 minutes or more, until *al dente*, firm to the bite.

2 Drain the rice, rinse in cold water and drain thoroughly once more.

3 Put the mustard, vinegar and salt into a salad bowl. Blend well with a fork, then add the oil, incorporating it into the mixture.

4 Add the drained rice and toss with the dressing.

5 Add the remaining ingredients, mix thoroughly, and serve cool, but not refrigerator cold.

THE CHEESE COURSE

Il Formaggio

SALAD, cheese and fruit, in that order, are the three courses that gradually cleanse the palate of the taste of cooking and bring an Italian meal to a natural close.

The simple, universal combination of cheese and good crusty bread is beyond discussion. But here are a few other ways in which cheese is served at an Italian table.

Parmesan

There is no more magnificent table cheese than a piece of aged, genuine *parmigiano-reggiano*, when it has not been allowed to dry out and it is a glistening, pale straw colour. It is frequently combined with the fruit course and eaten together with peeled ripe pears, or with grapes.

Gorgonzola

When it is soft, ripe and mild, gorgonzola is one of the world's loveliest blue cheeses. Italians sometimes mash it into a paste with some unsalted butter, or simply spread butter on the accompanying bread. (This is one of the rare occasions when Italians have bread and butter during a meal.) When gorgonzola is not over-ripe, it develops extraordinary flavour and texture if it is wrapped in aluminium foil and put into a 130°C/250°F/Mark $\frac{1}{2}$ oven for 2 to 3 minutes before serving.

Provola affumicata

This is smoked mozzarella, and looks exactly like any other mozzarella, except that it has a tanned skin. Remove the skin, slice the cheese into thin strips, and serve with good olive oil and a liberal amount of freshly ground pepper.

Cheese and olive oil

The combination of cheese and olive oil, as above, is a favourite one for both mild and pungent cheeses. A soft, white, full-flavoured cheese called Robiola is mashed through the largest holes of a mouli-légumes, and the resulting strands are soaked in olive oil for a day or more. It can be refrigerated, but must be served at room temperature. The same treatment is very effective with Taleggio or Fontina or with goat cheeses.

DESSERTS AND FRUIT

I Dolci e la Frutta

ITALIANS take their sweets and their apéritifs away from the dining table, at a pastry shop or café. Drinks, except for wine and liqueurs, do not belong in an Italian family meal, and desserts but rarely.

When the palate has travelled the peaks and valleys of an Italian meal with its first courses, second courses, vegetable dishes, salads and cheese, all it needs is the pause and refreshment of some fresh fruit. Of course there are circumstances in which a dessert does appear. These are almost always special occasions, either a religious holiday or a family celebration, such as a wedding. But these sweets, save those from Sicily, are, both in substance and appearance, modest, earthbound creations.

Italy does indeed produce some of the most luscious and beautiful desserts in Europe, as it has for centuries. But this is the work of pastry cooks. It is rarely done even in restaurant kitchens, and practically never at home.

Elaborate desserts do not have a significant part in Italian cooking or in the design of an Italian meal. For that reason there is no notice taken of them in this chapter. What you will find instead are some very plain but excellent traditional cakes and puddings, coffee and fruit ices, and a very good coffee ice cream. There is also a simple home version of that delicious Tuscan speciality *zuccotto*, and what is probably the most elegant dessert in the home repertoire, the chestnut-and-cream *Monte Bianco*.

In addition to desserts, there are two recipes for fresh fruit. In my opinion, these are the ones that take the cake, if that is the correct expression.

A RICE CAKE AND TWO PUDDINGS

Here are three traditional desserts based on such modest staples as rice, semolina and bread. The rice cake is the most famous one of the three. It is a speciality of Bologna, where it was customary to serve it only at Easter, with lively rivalry among those families that claimed to have the most delicious cake. The recipe given here is an authentically venerable one, belonging to Bolognese friends, who have had it in their family for generations.

None of the three desserts is a very glamorous creation. Their virtue is in their nostalgic, homespun flavour, their plain, straightforward goodness that seldom palls or cloys.

Torta di riso
RICE CAKE

For six to eight

1 litre (1¾ pints) milk
Salt
2 or 3 strips of lemon peel, yellow
    part only
220 g (8 oz) granulated sugar
70 g (2½ oz) raw rice, preferably
    Italian Arborio rice
4 eggs plus 1 yolk

60 g (2 oz) almonds, skinned, toasted
    and chopped as directed on
    page 386
35 g (1¼ oz) candied citron **or**, if not
    available, candied lemon peel,
    coarsely chopped
2 tablespoons rum
Butter
Fine, dry plain breadcrumbs

1 Put the milk, salt, lemon peel and sugar in a medium-sized saucepan and bring to the boil.

2 As the milk comes to the boil, add the rice and mix with a wooden spoon. Cook, uncovered, at the lowest possible simmer for 2¾ hours, stirring occasionally. The mixture should become a dense, pale brown mush, into which much of the lemon peel will have been absorbed, but remove any large, visible pieces. Set aside and allow to cool.

3 Preheat the oven to 180°C/350°F/Mark 4.

4 Beat the 4 whole eggs and the egg yolk in a large bowl until the yolks and whites are blended. Beat in the rice-and-milk mush a spoonful at a time. Add the chopped toasted almonds, the candied fruit and the rum. Mix all the ingredients thoroughly.

5 Smear butter generously on the bottom and sides of a rectangular 1½-litre (2½-pint) cake tin and then sprinkle with breadcrumbs, shaking off excess crumbs. Pour the mixture from the bowl into the tin and bake in the middle level of the preheated oven for 1 hour.

6 Remove the cake from the oven and let it cool to lukewarm. Put a dish

over the tin, turn the tin over onto the dish, give it a few vigorous taps, and lift it away. Serve the cake at least 24 hours after making it.

Note   This cake keeps improving for several days after it is made. Do not refrigerate if you are using it the next day.

Budino di semolino caramellato
GLAZED SEMOLINA PUDDING

For six to eight

100 g (3½ oz) plus 130 g (4½ oz) granulated sugar
65 g (2¼ oz) sultanas
450 ml (¾ pint) milk
Salt
100 g (3½ oz) semolina

15 g (½ oz) butter
1 tablespoon rum
25 g (1 oz) mixed candied peel
Grated peel of 1 orange
Plain flour
2 eggs

1   Choose a 1½-litre (2½-pint) metal mould. (A simple cylindrical shape is the easiest to work with.) Put the 100 g (3½ oz) sugar and 2 tablespoons water in the mould and bring to the boil over medium heat. Do not stir, but tilt the mould forward and backward from time to time until the syrup turns a light-brown colour. Remove from heat immediately and tip the mould in all directions to give it an even coating of caramel. Keep turning until the caramel congeals, then set aside.

2   Put the sultanas in a bowl with enough lukewarm water to cover and soak for at least 15 minutes.

3   Preheat the oven to 180°C/350°F/Mark 4.

4   While the sultanas are soaking, put the milk and salt in a saucepan over low heat. When the milk is just about to come to the boil, add all the semolina in a thin stream, stirring rapidly with a wooden spoon. Continue cooking, without ceasing to stir, until the semolina has thickened sufficiently to come away from the sides of the pan as you stir. Turn off the heat, but continue stirring for another 30 seconds to make sure the semolina will not stick.

5   Add the remaining sugar and stir, then add the butter and rum and stir. Add the candied peel and grated orange peel, stirring them evenly into the mixture.

6 Drain the sultanas and dry with a cloth. Put them in a sieve and sprinkle them with flour while shaking the sieve. When the sultanas are lightly floured, mix them with the other ingredients in the pan.

7 Add the eggs, beating them very rapidly into the semolina mixture. Pour the mixture into the caramelised mould and bake in the middle level of the preheated oven for 40 minutes. Remove from the oven and cool.

8 When the pudding is cold, refrigerate for 10 minutes to give it extra firmness. To unmould, first very briefly warm the bottom and sides of the mould over low heat to loosen the caramel, then place a dish over the mould, turn the two upside down, and give the mould a few sharp taps and downward jerks. It should lift away easily.

Budino di pane caramellato
GLAZED BREAD PUDDING

For six to eight

100 g (3½ oz) plus 65 g (2¼ oz)
    granulated sugar
120 g (4¼ oz) roughly cut-up stale,
    lightly toasted, crustless, good-
    quality white bread
60 g (2 oz) butter
450 ml (¾ pint) milk

60 g (2 oz) sultanas
Plain flour
25 g (1 oz) pine nuts
3 egg yolks
2 egg whites
4 tablespoons rum

1 Caramelise a 2-litre (3½-pint) rectangular cake tin as directed in Step 1 of the previous recipe, using the 100 g (3½ oz) granulated sugar.

2 Put the bread and the butter in a large mixing bowl.

3 Heat the milk, and as soon as it comes to the boil pour it over the bread and butter. Let the bread soak without mixing, and allow to cool.

4 Put the sultanas in a bowl with enough warm water to cover and soak for at least 15 minutes.

5 Preheat the oven to 190°C/375°F/Mark 5.

6 When the bread is cool, beat it with a whisk or a fork until it is an even, soft mass.

7 Drain the sultanas, and squeeze them dry in a cloth. Put them in a

sieve and dust them with flour while lightly shaking the sieve. Add them to the bowl with the bread mass.

8 Add the remaining sugar, pine nuts and egg yolks to the bowl and mix all the ingredients thoroughly.

9 Beat the egg whites until they form stiff peaks, then fold them gently into the mixture in the bowl.

10 Pour the contents of the bowl into the caramelised tin and place it in the middle level of the preheated oven. After 1 hour turn the heat down to 150°C/300°F/Mark 2 and bake for 15 more minutes.

11 While the pudding is still warm, pierce it in several places with a tooth-pick, and gradually pour 2 tablespoons of the rum over it. When the rum has been absorbed, place a dish on the pan, turn the tin over onto the dish, give it a few sharp downward jerks, and lift it away. Pierce the top of the pudding in several places with a toothpick and pour the rest of the rum over it.

Note Plan to serve the pudding the day after you make it. It improves in texture and flavour as it stands. You can refrigerate it for several days, but always take it out sufficiently ahead of time to serve it at room temperature.

Torta sbricciolona

CRUMBLY CAKE

For six

160 g (5¾ oz) plain flour
100 g (3½ oz) corn meal
120 g (4¼ oz) granulated sugar
Grated peel of 1 lemon
110 g (4 oz) almonds, skinned and
    dried as directed on page 386
    and ground to powder in a
    blender

2 egg yolks
110 g (¼ lb) unsalted butter, softened
    to room temperature
1 tablespoon icing sugar

1 Preheat the oven to 190°C/375°F/Mark 5.

2 In a bowl mix the flour, corn meal, granulated sugar, grated lemon peel

and powdered almonds. Add the two egg yolks and work the mixture with your hands until it breaks up into little crumbly pellets. Add the softened butter, working it in with your fingers until it is completely incorporated into the mixture. (At first it may seem improbable that all the ingredients can ever be combined, but after mixing for a few minutes, you will find that they do hang together, although forming a very crumbly dough.)

3 Smear the bottom of a 250-mm (10-inch) round baking tin with butter. Crumble the mixture through your fingers and into the tin until it is all uniformly distributed. Sprinkle the top with icing sugar and place in the upper third of the preheated oven for about 40 minutes.

Note This cake has a very crusty and crumbly consistency, which is part of its charm, but if you prefer to have it available in neat serving portions you can cut it into sections before it cools completely and hardens. It keeps beautifully for several days after baking.

This is an ideal cake to take with a glass of chilled dessert wine or in the afternoon with tea or coffee.

Chiacchiere della nonna

SWEET PASTRY FRITTERS

The dough for these fritters is cut into ribbons, then twisted into bows and fried in lard. For the sake of those who are put off by lard, I have tried frying them in every other fat, but they do not really come off as well. There is nothing terribly subtle about them, but they are very nice to have at the end of a hearty, homely meal or at any time of the afternoon or evening with friends over a glass of *vin santo* or other dessert wine.

For four to six

200 g (7 oz) plain flour	2 tablespoons white wine
Lard	Salt
1 tablespoon granulated sugar	Icing sugar
1 egg	

1 Combine the flour, 60 g (2 oz) lard, 1 tablespoon sugar, the egg, wine and salt, and knead into a smooth, soft dough. Put the dough in a bowl, cover, and allow to rest at least 15 minutes.

2 Roll out the dough with a rolling-pin to a thickness of 3 mm ($\frac{1}{8}$ inch), then cut into ribbons about 125 mm (5 inches) long and 12 mm ($\frac{1}{2}$ inch) wide. Twist into simple bowlike shapes.

3 In a frying pan, over high heat, melt enough lard to come 25 mm (1 inch) up the sides of the pan. When it is quite hot, add the pastry bows. (Do not put in any more at one time than will fit loosely in the pan.) When they are a nice, deep gold on one side, turn them over. When both sides are done, transfer to kitchen paper to drain, and sprinkle liberally with icing sugar. They may be served hot or cold.

Note   If kept in a dry place, they maintain their crispness for several days.

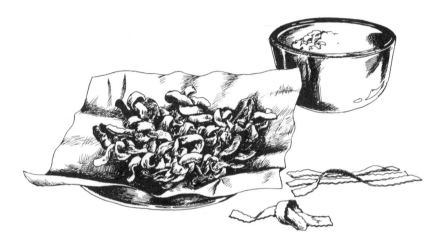

Chiacchiere della nonna

Frittelle di mele renette

APPLE FRITTERS

For four

3 apples, any firm, sweet eating
    variety
50 g (1$\frac{3}{4}$ oz) granulated sugar
2 tablespoons rum
1 lemon peel, grated

80 g (2$\frac{3}{4}$ oz) plain flour
Vegetable oil, enough to come
    12 mm ($\frac{1}{2}$ inch) up the side
    of the frying pan
Icing sugar

1 Peel the apples, core them, and cut them into slices 9 mm ($\frac{3}{8}$ inch) thick. (The slices should look like miniature cartwheels, each with a hole in the middle.)

2 Put the sugar, rum and lemon peel into a bowl and add the apple slices. Let the apples macerate for at least 1 hour.

3 Make a batter of the flour and 1 cup water, according to the directions in Step 2 of *Zucchine fritte con la pastella* (page 337).

4 Pour enough oil into a frying pan to come at least 12 mm ($\frac{1}{2}$ inch) up the side of the pan. Turn the heat on high.

5 Pat the apple slices dry with kitchen paper. Dip them in the batter, and when the oil is very hot slip them into the frying pan. (Do not put in any more at one time than will fit loosely in the pan.) When they are golden brown on one side, turn them. When both sides are nicely browned, transfer the fritters to kitchen paper to drain. Sprinkle with icing sugar. Serve hot.

Il Diplomatico

RUM-AND-COFFEE-FLAVOURED CHOCOLATE LAYER CAKE

The marvellous thing about this dessert is that it requires no baking, and you can put in a little less rum or a little more chocolate, add or subtract an egg, and you will still come up with a successful and delicious cake. It is practically foolproof. In its easygoing approach and its knack for transforming simple ingredients and procedures into a most enjoyable concoction, it is quintessentially Italian.

For six to eight

4 eggs	1 teaspoon granulated sugar

The rum mixture (to be repeated as often as necessary using the same proportions)

5 tablespoons rum	5 teaspoons granulated sugar
300 ml (generous $\frac{1}{2}$ pint) strong espresso coffee (see How to Make Italian Coffee, page 390)	5 tablespoons water
Two 220-g ($\frac{1}{2}$-lb) Madeira cakes	175 g (6 oz) cooking chocolate

The frosting
340 ml (12 fl oz) double cream   2 teaspoons granulated sugar

1 Preheat the oven to 130°C/250°F/Mark $\frac{1}{2}$.

2 Separate the eggs and beat the yolks together with 1 teaspoon of the sugar until the yolks turn pale yellow.

3 Line a 220-mm (9-inch) baking tin or any equivalent container with buttered waxed paper, extending it up the sides and above the rim. Combine the rum, coffee, 5 teaspoons sugar and 5 tablespoons water in a soup dish. Cut the Madeira cakes into slices 6 mm ($\frac{1}{4}$ inch) thick. Soak each slice in the rum-and-coffee mixture and place it on the bottom and along the sides of the baking tin, until it is completely lined with rum-soaked cake. (You have to be quick about dipping the slices in and out of the mixture before they get too soggy to handle.) If you run out of rum mixture, prepare more, following the same proportions.

4 In a small saucepan, melt the chocolate in the oven. (I have found this the easiest and least problem-fraught method of melting chocolate. If you have another method you are happy with, by all means use it.) Mix the melted chocolate into the beaten egg yolks. Whip the egg whites until they form stiff peaks. First combine 1 tablespoon of the beaten egg whites with the egg yolks and chocolate, mixing normally, then add the rest of the egg whites, folding them with care into the mixture.

5 Spoon the entire mixture over the rum-and-coffee-soaked cake in the tin. Cover the mixture with more slices of soaked cake. (Do not worry about how the cake looks at this point. What you are looking at is the bottom, and the rest will be completely covered by frosting.) Refrigerate overnight.

6 The following day turn the tin over onto a flat serving dish, holding your thumbs on the protruding waxed paper. The tin should lift away easily, leaving the waxed-paper-covered cake on the dish. Carefully peel off the waxed paper. The cake is now ready for the frosting.

7 The customary frosting for *il diplomatico* is chocolate, but for a lighter texture and more delicate taste you can substitute whipped cream. Whip very cold double cream together with 2 teaspoons of granulated sugar until it is stiff. Cover the entire exposed surface of the cake with cream. Decorate with candied fruit arranged in simple patterns. Cream is always best when freshly whipped, but, if necessary, it can be refrigerated for one or two days.

Zuccotto

Zuccotto is a dome-shaped Florentine speciality inspired, it is said, by the cupola of the Duomo of Florence. Whether that is true or not, I do not know, but it is a fact that almost anything hemispherical seems to remind Florentines of Brunelleschi's ever-present dome. Zuccotto used to be found only in Florentine cafés and pastry shops, but it is now mass-produced and distributed all over Italy. It requires no baking nor any special confectionery skills, yet it is an extremely presentable and successful dessert.

For six

60 g (2 oz) shelled, unskinned
    almonds
60 g (2 oz) shelled whole hazelnuts
One-and-a-half 220-g ($\frac{1}{2}$-lb) Madeira
    cakes
3 tablespoons Cognac **or** other grape
    brandy

2 tablespoons maraschino liqueur
2 tablespoons Cointreau
140 g (5 oz) cooking chocolate
450 ml (16 fl oz) very cold double
    whipping cream
110 g (4 oz) icing sugar

1 Preheat the oven to 200°C/400°F/Mark 6.

2 Drop the almonds into boiling water and boil for 20 seconds. Drain. With your fingertips, squeeze the almonds out of their skins. Place the peeled almonds on a baking sheet and put in the oven to dry for about 2 minutes. Remove from the oven and chop them roughly. Set aside.

3 Place the hazelnuts on a baking sheet and put in the oven for 5 minutes. Remove them from the oven and rub off as much of their skin as you can with a rough, dry towel. (Do not worry if it does not all rub off.) Chop roughly and set aside.

4 Reset the oven thermostat to 130°C/250°F/Mark $\frac{1}{2}$.

5 Choose a $1\frac{1}{2}$-litre ($2\frac{1}{2}$-pint), perfectly round-bottomed hemispherical bowl, and line it with a layer of damp muslin.

6 Cut the Madeira cake in slices 9 mm ($\frac{3}{8}$ inch) thick. Cut each slice on the diagonal, making of it two triangular sections. There will be crust on two sides of the triangle. Moisten each section with a sprinkling of the liqueurs and place it against the inside of the bowl, its narrowest end at the bottom, until the inside of the bowl is completely lined with moistened sections of cake. Where one side of the section has crust on it, make it meet the crustless side of the section next to it, because when the dessert is taken out of the mould the thin lines of crust running down the sides should form a sunburst pattern. Make sure that the entire inside surface of the bowl is lined with cake. If there are any gaps, fill them in with small pieces of moist-

ened cake. (Do not worry about the appearance of the dessert. A little irregularity is part of its charm.)

7 Coarsely chop 90 g (3 oz) of the chocolate. Then, in a chilled mixing bowl, whip the cold double cream together with the icing sugar until it is stiff. Mix into it the chopped almonds, hazelnuts and remaining chocolate. Divide the mixture into two equal parts. Set aside one half and spoon the other half into the cake-lined bowl, spreading it evenly over the entire cake surface. This should leave a still unfilled cavity in the centre of the bowl.

8 Melt the remaining chocolate in a small pan in the 130°C/250°F/Mark ½ oven. Fold the melted chocolate into the remaining half of the whipped-cream mixture. Spoon it into the bowl until the cavity is completely filled. Even off the top of the bowl, cutting off any protruding pieces of cake. Cut some more 9-mm (⅜-inch) slices of cake, moisten them with the remaining liqueurs, and use them to seal off the top of the bowl. Trim the edges until they are perfectly round. Cover the bowl with plastic film and refrigerate overnight, or for up to 1 or 2 days.

9 Cover the bowl with a flat serving dish and turn it upside down. Lift off the bowl and carefully remove the muslin. Serve cold.

Zuccotto

Monte Bianco

PURÉED CHESTNUT AND CHOCOLATE MOUND

This is an especially lovely winter dessert. The mound of puréed chestnuts and chocolate, topped with whipped cream, is supposed to recall Monte Bianco in the Italian Alps, whose upper slopes are always snow-clad. It should not be prepared too long in advance because the chestnuts turn sharp in taste. However, it can certainly be prepared in the morning for the evening.

For six

450 g (1 lb) fresh chestnuts	4 tablespoons rum
Milk, enough to cover	450 ml (16 fl oz) very cold whipping
Salt	cream
175 g (6 oz) cooking chocolate	2 teaspoons granulated sugar

1 Wash the chestnuts in cold water. Chestnuts have a flat side and a round side. Being careful not to cut into the chestnut meat itself, make a horizontal cut in each chestnut starting on one end of the flat side, coming across the entire width of the round side and terminating just past the other edge of the flat side; the cut should not go all the way around and meet. (This method loosens both the shell and the inside skin while the chestnuts boil and makes peeling them a fast and simple task.)

2 Place the chestnuts in a pot with abundant cold water, cover, bring to the boil, and cook for 25 minutes. Peel the chestnuts while still very warm, pulling them out of the hot water a few at a time, and making sure to remove both the outer shell and the wrinkled inner skin.

3 Preheat the oven to 130°C/250°F/Mark ½.

4 Put the peeled chestnuts in a saucepan with just enough milk to cover, and a pinch of salt. Boil slowly, uncovered, for 15 minutes more or less until the milk is entirely absorbed. The chestnuts should be tender but not mushy.

5 Put the chocolate in a small saucepan and place in the oven until melted.

6 Purée the chestnuts through a mouli-légumes into a bowl and mix with the melted chocolate and the rum. Pass this mixture through the mouli-légumes again, using the largest holes available, letting it drop directly onto a round serving dish. Start dropping it close to the dish with a circular movement, beginning at the edge of the dish, and as it piles up gradually move upward and towards the centre. You should end up with a cone-shaped mound. Do not pat it or attempt to shape it.

7 Whip the cream with the sugar. Use half the whipped cream to cover

the top of your mound, coming about two-thirds of the way down. It should have the natural look of a partially snow-covered mountain, so do not strive for smoothness and regularity, but let the cream come down the mound at random in peaks and hollows. When serving the dessert, bring the remaining half of the whipped cream to the table for anyone who would like to have a bit more 'snow' on his portion.

Monte Bianco

Spuma di cioccolata
COLD CHOCOLATE MOUSSE

For six

175 g (6 oz) cooking chocolate
2 teaspoons granulated sugar
4 eggs, separated

4 tablespoons strong espresso coffee
   (see How to Make Italian
   Coffee, page 390)
2 tablespoons rum
170 ml (6 fl oz) very cold whipping cream

1 In a 130°C/250°F/Mark ½ oven, melt the chocolate in a small saucepan.
2 Add 2 teaspoons of sugar to the egg yolks and beat with a whisk or

in the blender until they become pale yellow. By hand mix in the melted chocolate, the coffee and the rum.

3 Whip the cream in a cold bowl until it is stiff, then fold it into the choco-late-and-egg-yolk mixture.

4 Whip the egg whites until they form stiff peaks, then fold into the mixture. When all the ingredients have been gently but well combined by hand, spoon the mixture into glass or crystal goblets, custard cups or any other suitable and attractive serving container. Refrigerate overnight. (This dessert can be prepared even 3 or 4 days ahead of time, but after 24 hours it tends to wrinkle and lose some of its creaminess.)

Note   Do not exceed the recommended amounts of rum and coffee, or you may find a liquid deposit at the bottom of the dessert.

Zabaglione

ZABAIONE

Zabaglione must not cook over direct heat. It is necessary to have a double boiler. Since it is desirable for the upper part to have a heavy bottom, you might use an enamelled cast-iron saucepan or other heavy pot and hold it over water simmering in any other kind of pot. Be sure to choose a large enough pot – the mixture increases greatly in volume as you beat.

For six

4 egg yolks
50 g (1¾ oz) granulated sugar   8 tablespoons dry Marsala

1 Put the egg yolks and the sugar in your heavy-bottomed pot and whip them with a wire whisk (or an electric blender) until they are pale yellow and creamy.

2 In a slightly larger second pot, bring water to the brink of a simmer, not to the boil.

3 Place the pot with the whipped-up egg yolks over the second pot. Add the Marsala and continue beating. The mixture, which will begin to foam, and then swell into a light, soft mass, is ready when it forms soft mounds.

4 Spoon it into goblets, cups or champagne glasses, and serve imme-diately.

Crema fritta

FRIED SWEET CREAM

This cream requires substantially more flour than would a regular custard cream, otherwise it would not be firm enough for frying. In order for the flour to become evenly and smoothly blended, the cream must cook very slowly over very low heat, and you will have to stir virtually without interruption the entire time it is cooking. It takes patience, but it is not very hard work, and part of the time you can let your mind run on other thoughts while you are doing it. It is best to prepare it in the morning for the evening, or even a day ahead of time.

For six

3 eggs
100 g (3½ oz) granulated sugar
60 g (2 oz) plain flour
450 ml (¾ pint) milk
2 small strips lemon peel, yellow part
 only

130 g (4½ oz) fine, dry plain
 breadcrumbs, spread on a dish
 or on waxed paper
Vegetable oil, enough to come 25 mm
 (1 inch) up the side of the
 frying pan

1 Off the heat, in the upper part of a double boiler, beat 2 of the eggs together with the sugar until the eggs are well blended and the sugar almost completely dissolved.

2 Still off heat, add the flour to the eggs 1 tablespoon at a time, mixing thoroughly, until the eggs have absorbed all the flour.

3 While you are doing this, bring the milk to the edge of the boil in another pan. When the eggs and flour have been thoroughly mixed, add the hot milk very gradually, about 4 tablespoons at a time, beating it into the mixture. When all the milk has been well blended with the eggs and flour, add the lemon peel.

4 Unite the two parts of the double boiler and put it over very low heat. The water in the lower half must come to only the gentlest of simmers. Begin to stir, slowly but steadily. Fifteen minutes after the water in the lower pan has started to simmer, you may raise the heat slightly. Continue cooking and stirring for about 25 minutes more. When done, the cream should be thick and smooth and have no taste of flour.

5 Pour the cream onto a slightly moistened large dish, spreading it to a thickness of about 25 mm (1 inch), and let it cool completely. (If you are going to use it the following day, refrigerate it, when cool, under plastic film.)

6 When the cream is cold, cut it into diamond-shaped pieces about 50 mm

(2 inches) long. Beat the remaining egg lightly in a soup dish or small bowl. Dredge the pieces in breadcrumbs; then dip them in egg; then dredge them in breadcrumbs again.

7 Heat the oil in the frying pan over high heat. When the oil is very hot, slide in the pieces of cream. Fry them until a dark, golden crust forms on one side; then turn them and do the other side. When there is a nice crust all around, transfer them to kitchen paper to drain. Serve piping hot.

MENU SUGGESTIONS

Apart from its role in *Il grande fritto misto* (page 283), fried cream is an excellent accompaniment to many single meat courses. Serve it somewhat as you might a potato croquette. It goes beautifully with *Costolette alla milanese* (page 226) or *Cotolette alla milanese* (page 228), *Fegato di vitello fritto* (page 252) or *Costolettine di agnello fritte* (page 239). It is also, of course, a delectable hot dessert after any meal.

Gelato agli amaretti
VANILLA ICE-CREAM WITH MACAROONS

For this preparation you should use imported Italian macaroons. They are packed two to a wrapper, and that is why the quantities given below are for double macaroons. They keep crisp almost indefinitely.

For four

8 double macaroons, ground	450 ml ($\frac{3}{4}$ pint) vanilla ice-cream
$4\frac{1}{4}$ tablespoons strong espresso coffee (see page 390)	2 double macaroons soaked in 1 tablespoon rum for decoration
1 tablespoon ground dry espresso coffee, powdered in a blender	

1 Mix the ground macaroons with the brewed coffee until the macaroons are thoroughly moistened. Mix in the coffee powder.

2 Line a small dome-shaped bowl with lightly buttered waxed paper. Spread a little less than half the ice-cream along the sides and bottom of the bowl. Spread the macaroon mixture over the ice-cream, then cover with

the rest of the ice-cream. Place in the freezer for at least 4 hours before serving.

3 To serve, turn the bowl over on a plate, lift away the bowl, and gently remove the waxed paper. Decorate, pressing the four parts of the rum-soaked macaroons into the sides of the ice-cream. When cut into 4 portions, there should be a macaroon to each portion.

Gelato spazzacamino

VANILLA ICE-CREAM WITH POWDERED COFFEE AND SCOTCH

This is not just window dressing for plain ice-cream. It is a combination of unexpected textures and flavours that act upon each other with extraordinary success. Everyone must have a favourite way of serving ice-cream. This one is mine.

The doubly roasted taste of espresso coffee is essential here. Grind regular espresso coffee in the blender at high speed until it is a fine powder. You can make a substantial quantity at one time and keep it in a tightly closed jar.

For one

2 scoops vanilla ice-cream
2 teaspoons ground dry espresso
    coffee, powdered in a blender

1 tablespoon Scotch whisky

Spoon the ice-cream into individual shallow bowls, sprinkle 2 teaspoons of coffee powder over each serving, and over it pour the whisky.

Note The quantities of coffee and whisky given are suggestions. Regulate them according to taste.

Gelato di caffè con la cioccolata calda

ESPRESSO COFFEE ICE-CREAM WITH HOT CHOCOLATE SAUCE

For six

4 egg yolks
130 g (4½ oz) granulated sugar

325 ml (⅝ pint) espresso coffee, made using milk instead of water (see page 390)
240 ml (8 fl oz) double cream

The chocolate sauce
170 ml (6 fl oz) double cream
2 tablespoons cocoa

4 teaspoons granulated sugar

1 Beat the egg yolks and sugar until they become a pale yellow cream.

2 Combine the coffee and double cream and mix into the beaten egg yolks until uniformly blended. Warm the mixture in a saucepan over low heat, stirring constantly until it swells to nearly twice its original volume.

3 Pour into freezer trays. When cool, stir thoroughly and place in the freezer for at least 5 hours. Stir every 30 to 40 minutes.

4 Just before serving, prepare the sauce by combining the double cream, cocoa and sugar in a small saucepan and stirring it over low heat for about 6 minutes, or until it becomes a smooth, thick cream.

5 Spoon the ice-cream, which should be quite firm but not rock hard, from the freezer trays into individual bowls. Pour the hot sauce over each serving and serve immediately.

Granita di caffè con panna

COFFEE ICE WITH WHIPPED CREAM

A *granita* is a dessert ice made of very fine-grained frozen crystals of coffee or fruit syrup. By far the most popular *granita* in Italy is *granita di caffè*, coffee ice. It is usually taken at a café after lunch, and, as you sit outdoors on a steamy afternoon watching life flow by, you let the *granita* melt between tongue and palate, spoonful by spoonful, until the inside of your mouth feels like an ice cavern dense with coffee flavour.

It should go without saying that you use only Italian espresso coffee to make *granita di caffè*.

For six to eight

450 ml (¾ pint) espresso coffee (see page 390)

2 tablespoons sugar, or more to taste

Freshly whipped cream, made with 230 ml (8 fl oz) double cream and 2 teaspoons sugar (optional)

1 Put all the coffee in a jug and dissolve the sugar in it while it is still hot. Taste and adjust sugar. Do not make it very sweet because sugar weakens its flavour.

2 Remove the ice-cube grids from two freezer trays and pour the coffee into the trays. When the coffee is cold, put the trays in the freezer and set a timer at 15 minutes.

3 When the timer rings, remove the trays from the freezer and stir the contents to break up the ice crystals. (Ice forms first at the sides of the tray. It is important that you break this up thoroughly each time before it becomes solid.) Return to the freezer, and set the timer again for 15 minutes. When the timer rings repeat the operation and reset the timer for 10 minutes. The next time set the timer for 8 minutes, and continue to stir the coffee every 8 minutes for the next 3 hours. If you are not ready to serve the *granita* immediately, continue stirring every 8 minutes until just before serving. Serve in a glass goblet, or crystal bowl, topped with whipped cream, if desired.

Note By exactly the same procedure, you can make orange ice (*granita di arancia*), using 450 ml (¾ pint) freshly squeezed orange juice and 1 tablespoon granulated sugar, and lemon ice (*granita di limone*), using 8 tablespoons freshly squeezed lemon juice, 325 ml (⅜ pint) water and 50 g (1¼ oz) granulated sugar.

Croccante

CARAMELISED ALMOND BRITTLE

Croccante is the same thing as French praline, except that it is usually less sweet. Home-made, it is excellent and very much better than commercial imitations. Crushed or powdered it is marvellous in desserts or as topping for ice cream. In an airtight jar or tightly wrapped in aluminium foil it keeps almost indefinitely.

175 g (6 oz) shelled, unskinned
    almonds

200 g (7 oz) granulated sugar
A potato, peeled

1 Preheat the oven to 230°C/450°F/Mark 8.

2 Drop the almonds in boiling water. Twenty seconds after the water returns to the boil, drain the almonds. Squeeze the almonds out of their skins with your fingers and spread them on a baking sheet. Toast them in the preheated oven for 6 minutes, until they are a light brown. (Make sure they do not burn.) If you prefer to do them under the grill, watch them closely – it will take only a few seconds. Chop the toasted almonds until the slivers are half the size of a grain of rice.

3 Put the sugar and 4 tablespoons of water in a small, preferably thin-bottomed pan. Melt the sugar over medium-high heat, without stirring, but tilting the pan occasionally. When the melted sugar becomes a light golden colour, add the chopped almonds and stir constantly until the almonds turn a deep tawny gold. Pour out *immediately* onto a greased sheet of aluminium foil. Cut the potato in half and use the flat side to spread out the hot mixture to a thickness of 3 mm ($\frac{1}{8}$ inch).

4 If you want to use it for sweets, cut it into 50-mm (2-inch) diamond shapes before it cools. When cool, lift off and wrap each piece tightly in aluminium foil. Store in a dry cupboard, where it will keep indefinitely. (For use in desserts, it can be ground coarsely in a mortar or pulverised in a blender when it has cooled. Store in an airtight jar. Do not refrigerate.)

Frullati di frutta
FRESH FRUIT WHIPS

These are not served in Italy after meals, but they are a refreshing and nourishing accompaniment to a light summer snack. Italians, who, as a rule, eat nothing for breakfast, will sometimes have a *frullato* in the middle of the morning to tide them over until lunch. If you are travelling in Italy with the children and are enjoying an afternoon Campari at a café, this is a nice refreshment to order for them. If they are very young children, you can ask the waiter to omit the liqueur.

For two

150 ml ($\frac{1}{4}$ pint) milk
1 banana or a comparable quantity of
    fresh strawberries, peaches,
    apricots, etc. (see note below)

$1\frac{1}{2}$ teaspoons sugar
3 tablespoons crushed ice
2 tablespoons maraschino liqueur

Whip all the ingredients in the blender at high speed until the ice has completely dissolved. Serve immediately.

Note All the fruit except the banana must be washed in cold water, and all except berries must be peeled. Peaches and apricots, of course, must be pitted.

Arance tagliate
MACERATED ORANGE SLICES

Among all the ways in which a meal can be brought to a happy close, there is none, I think, that surpasses a dish of sliced oranges. Their bright, joyous colour is an instant promise of refreshment, which they maintain by loosening from our taste buds the thick traces of the preceding courses, leaving nothing but happy memories and a fragrantly clean palate.

For four

6 oranges
Grated peel of 1 medium lemon

4 tablespoons granulated sugar
Juice of $\frac{1}{2}$ medium lemon

1 Peel just four of the oranges, using a very sharp knife. Take care to remove all the white spongy pulp and also as much as possible of the thin skin beneath.

2 Cut the oranges horizontally into thin slices about 9 mm ($\frac{3}{8}$ inch) thick. Take out any pips. Put the slices into a shallow serving bowl or deep dish and then grate the lemon peel into the bowl. (Avoid grating the white pulp beneath the peel.) Add the sugar. Squeeze the other two oranges and add their juice to the bowl. Add the lemon juice. Turn the orange slices over a few times, being careful not to break them up. Cover the bowl with a dish and refrigerate for at least 4 hours, or even overnight. Serve chilled, turning the slices once or twice in the macerating liquid just before serving.

Note   You may add more sugar if you like the oranges much sweeter. Some people add 2 or 3 tablespoons of maraschino or Curaçao just before serving. I do not because I find it interferes with the fragrance of the lemon peel. Try it both ways, if you like, and decide for yourself.

Ananas al maraschino

PINEAPPLE SLICES WITH MARASCHINO

It is not without some embarrassment that I include this recipe for what is little more than pineapple slices out of a tin. Though it is quite popular with many Italian restaurants, pineapple is certainly not Italian. When I first started serving it, however, I discovered that people were startled by this version. It does not really have any pretensions, but if you like pineapple you might want to try this simple Italian approach.

For one

2 slices tinned pineapple, with 2 tablespoons of their syrup
1 maraschino cherry

1 tablespoon maraschino liqueur, or more to taste

Put 2 slices of pineapple in an individual dish or saucer. Place the cherry in the centre, in the hole. Add 2 tablespoons of the syrup from the tin, and 1 tablespoon of maraschino liqueur. Refrigerate for 2 hours or more. Serve chilled.

Macedonia di frutta

ITALIAN FRUIT SALAD

The name *macedonia* is borrowed from a region in southern Europe that includes parts of Yugoslavia, Bulgaria and Greece. It is an area known for the mixture of races that populates it, and its name is well taken for this dish, whose success depends upon the variety of its components.

The indispensable ingredients are apples, pears, bananas, and orange and lemon juice. To these you should add a generous selection of seasonal fruits, choosing them for the diversity of their colours, fragrances and textures. In Italy, when *macedonia* is made in summer, we always add peaches. Italian peaches are silken in texture and immensely fragrant. If you cannot obtain them, try using ripe mango, which is a thoroughly acceptable substitute. If it is locally available, I strongly recommend your using it.

For eight or more

325 ml ($\frac{5}{8}$ pint) freshly squeezed orange juice

Grated peel of 1 medium lemon, yellow part only

2 to 3 tablespoons freshly squeezed lemon juice, or to taste

2 apples

2 pears

2 bananas

680 g ($1\frac{1}{2}$ lb) of assorted other fruit, such as cherries, apricots, nectarines, plums, peaches, grapes, mango, cantaloupe, honeydew melon

40 to 50 g ($1\frac{1}{2}$ to $1\frac{3}{4}$ oz) granulated sugar, according to taste

8 tablespoons maraschino liqueur (optional)

1 In a large serving bowl (a tureen or punch bowl) put the orange juice, the grated lemon peel and the lemon juice.

2 If you are using grapes, wash them and detach them from the clusters. Add seedless grapes whole to the bowl. Cut the other varieties in half and remove the seeds before adding them to the bowl. The cherries, too, must be pitted before they are put in.

3 All the other fruit must also be washed, then peeled, cored or pitted, and cut into 12-mm ($\frac{1}{2}$-inch) cubes. Add each fruit to the bowl as you cut it, so that the juice in the bowl will keep it from discolouring. (Remember, do not put in any unpeeled fruit, except for grapes, cherries and berries.)

4 When all the fruit is in the bowl, add the sugar and the optional maraschino. Mix thoroughly. Cover the bowl with a dish and refrigerate for at least 4 hours or even overnight. Serve chilled, mixing three or four times before serving.

Note   For full flavour and fragrance, fruit should be ripe. Do not use any over-ripe fruit, however, or it will become mushy. It is better not to use strawberries for the same reason. If you really want strawberries in the dish, add them just 30 minutes before serving.

HOW TO MAKE ITALIAN COFFEE

Italian coffee has so many admirers throughout the world that it does not need additional appreciation from these pages. Apart from its merits as a drink, however, it is by far the best coffee to use in any dessert in which coffee is an ingredient, and for Italian desserts in particular it has absolutely no substitute.

Making Italian coffee at home is incredibly easy and quick. All you need is double-roasted espresso coffee and an Italian coffee-pot. All Italian coffee-pots, whatever their special design might be, share the same working principle. Water is heated to the boil in one chamber of the pot, then filtered through the ground coffee and collected in a second, serving chamber.

The traditional coffee-pot, which may or may not have been invented in Naples, is known in Italy nonetheless as *la napoletana*. Neapolitans, in fact, consider themselves supreme custodians of the secret of good coffee, and, without any doubt, no one in Italy makes better coffee.

HOW TO MAKE COFFEE WITH THE NAPOLETANA

1 Fill the bottom half of the pot, the one *without* the spout, with cold water up to the tiny escape hole near the top.

2 Insert the metal filter for the coffee. Fill with coffee until it forms a mound, but do not press the coffee down. Always fill the filter to capacity.

3 Tightly screw on the top of the filter.

4 Place the empty half of the pot, with the spout pointing *downwards*, over the filter, and snap the pot shut, pushing upper and lower halves together.

5 Place the pot over medium heat exactly as you assembled it, with the spout on top, pointing downwards.

The Napoletana

The Moka

6 When you see steam leaking out of the escape hole on the side, turn the pot over and turn off the heat. The spout should now be at the bottom, pointing upwards. It will take several minutes for all the water to filter through into the bottom chamber.

Note Some Neapolitans do not assemble the pot in advance. First they boil the water in the lower half of the pot, then they insert the coffee filter, attach the other half of the pot, and turn the pot over. Their explanation is that, by assembling the pot in advance, the heat of the water before it reaches the boil dissipates some of the coffee's flavour.

HOW TO MAKE COFFEE WITH THE MOKA

There is another, more modern type of pot that works faster and also makes first-rate coffee. In Italy it is known as *la moka*.

1 Fill the bottom chamber of the pot with cold water up to the small, round safety valve.

2 Put in the coffee filter and fill exactly as with the *napoletana*, up to capacity, forming a mound, but without pressing the coffee down.

3 Screw on the top of the filter.

4 Screw the upper half of the pot on tightly and place over medium heat. (In this system, hot water is drawn up through the filter and into the upper chamber, so that there is no turning over to do.) For best results, keep the lid open.

5 When the coffee begins to emerge, lower the heat to a minimum. (By reducing the speed at which the water seeps through the coffee, you concentrate the flavour.) When the chamber is nearly filled, close the lid. When you hear the coffee sputtering, it is all done. Turn off the heat.

Note Italian coffee should never be reheated.

Afterthoughts

What people do with food is an act that reveals how they construe the world. It is no coincidence that the country that produced the Confucian system of ethical conduct imposes on the ingredients of its cooking a rigid discipline of cut and shape. The work of art that is a Japanese meal is a natural legacy of the only society where aesthetics, at one time, entirely governed life. And the achievement of classic French cuisine, its logic, the marvellous subtlety of its discoveries, could have occurred only in the country of Descartes and Proust.

The world of the Italians is not a phenomenon that needs to be subdued, reshaped, arranged in logical patterns. It is not a challenge to be won. It is there simply to be enjoyed, mostly on its own terms. What we find in the cooking of Italy is a serene relationship between man and the sources of his existence, a long-established intimacy between the human and natural orders, a harmonious fusion of man's skills and nature's gifts. The Italian comes to his table with the same open heart with which a child falls into his mother's arms, with the same easy feeling of being in the right place.

The essential quality of Italian food can be defined as fidelity to its ingredients, to their taste, colour, shape and freshness. In the Italian kitchen, ingredients are not treated as promising but untutored elements that need to be corrected through long and intricate manipulation and refined by the ultimate polish of a sauce. The methods of Italian cooking are not intended to improve an ingredient's character, but rather to allow it as much free and natural development as the tasteful balance of a dish will permit. The taste of Italian cooking is discreetly measured but frank. Flavours are present and undisguised, but never overbearing. Pastas are never swamped by sauce. Portions are never so swollen in size as to tax our capacity for enjoyment.

Because Italian cooking simply does not work without raw materials of the freshest and choicest quality, it is sometimes the most costly of the world's cuisines to produce. But it is probably the one whose satisfactions are the most accessible to the home cook. Although a few of the recipes require a little practice and some manual dexterity, there is not a single dish in this book that is beyond the competence of any moderately alert person. Italian cooking techniques are disciplined by tradition, but they allow an individual approach to food that is spontaneous, immediate and uncomplicated. Italian cooking does not lend itself well to the regimentation of professional chefs. When Aristotle said that a work of art should imitate the motions of the mind and not an external arrangement of facts, he was anticipating a definition of the art of the Italian home cook. In Italy the source of the very best Italian food is the home kitchen. There is no reason why this should not be equally true elsewhere.

And so this book comes to a close. And with it, a long year's work, the exasperating and sometimes almost intolerable task of fixing the fluid intuitions of half a lifetime of cooking within the step-by-step framework of a recipe. Although frequently I felt like a gymnast forced to retrace his twists and somersaults in slow motion, I wrote, tested, rewrote each recipe until it was as clear and reliable as I was able to make it. I hope they will work as well in your kitchen as they have in mine. I cannot expect from anyone a total conversion to Italian cooking, but if even a few of these dishes together with their proper placement within an Italian meal become a natural part of your life at table, I shall feel handsomely rewarded for my efforts.

Index

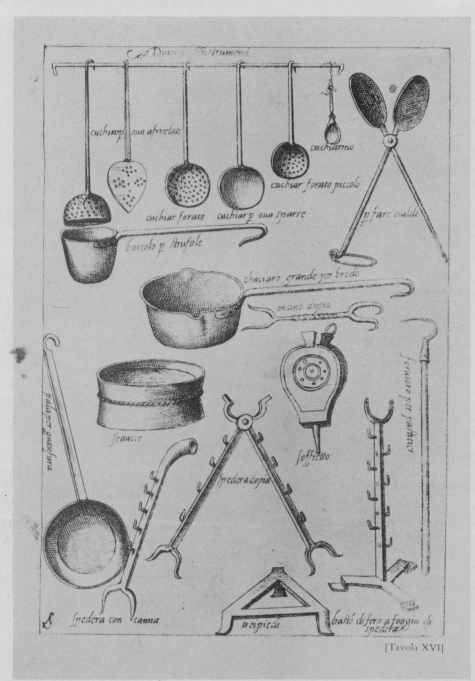

Diuersi Instrumenti

cuchiaro p oua. sbruclate

cuchiarino

cuchiar forato piccolo

cuchiar forato

cuchiar p oua sparse

p fare cialde

boccolo p strufole

cuchiaro grande per brodo

onano dopio

senacio

soffietto

sorauore per pasticci

spedera dopia

pala per guastara

spedera con canna

trespiedi

bastó di fero a foggia di spedcra

[Tavola XVI]